NELSON MANDELA
"We also honor the great Che Guevara, whose revolutionary feats in our continent were of such magnitude that no prison or censorship could hide them from us. Che's life is an inspiration for every human being who loves freedom. We will always honor his memory."

GABRIEL GARCÍA MÁRQUEZ
"Nothing illustrates the duration and intensity of the Cuban presence in Africa better than the fact that Che Guevara himself, at the prime of his life and the height of his fame, went off to fight in the guerrilla war in the Congo. In that fleeting, anonymous passage through Africa, Che Guevara was to sow a seed that no one will destroy."

Che
in Africa

Che Guevara's Congo Diary

by William Gálvez

Translated by Mary Todd

OCEAN PRESS
Melbourne • New York

B
Guevara, C

Cover design by David Spratt

ISBN 1-876175-08-7

First printed 1999

Printed in Australia

Published by Ocean Press
Australia: GPO Box 3279, Melbourne, Victoria 3001, Australia
   • Fax: (61-3) 9372 1765 • E-mail: ocean_press@msn.com.au
USA: PO Box 834, Hoboken, NJ 07030 • Fax: 201-617 0203

Library of Congress Catalog Card No: 98-65909

OCEAN PRESS DISTRIBUTORS
United States: LPC/InBook,
   1436 West Randolph St, Chicago, IL 60607, USA
Canada: Login Brothers
   324 Salteaux Cres, Winnipeg, Manitoba R3J, Canada
Britain and Europe: Global Book Marketing,
   38 King Street, London, WC2E 8JT, UK
Australia and New Zealand: Astam Books,
   57-61 John Street, Leichhardt, NSW 2040, Australia
Cuba and Latin America: Ocean Press,
   Calle 21 #406, Vedado, Havana, Cuba
Southern Africa: Phambili Agencies,
   PO Box 28680, Kensington 2101, Johannesburg, South Africa

19.95
3/28/00

Acknowledgments

Once again, I must express my thanks to many comrades who made it possible for me to finish this book.

To Nilda Rodríguez, who lent me a copy of the original, unpublished manuscript which Major Ernesto Che Guevara wrote on leaving that part of the Congo where the guerrilla war was fought, and to Pablo Rivalta, who had lent it to her and authorized her to lend it to me. To my beloved friend Jorge Enrique Mendoza, now deceased, who gave this project his full, fraternal support.

To Víctor Dreke and Ulises Estrada — who, in addition to providing important testimony, lent me photos and documents and helped locate other members of the internationalist column which Che commanded — whose cooperation was of key importance, as was that of Emilio Mena, Aldo Margolles and Rogelio Oliva. To Erasmo Videaux, who, with his prodigious memory, remembered the pseudonyms and real names of more than 90 percent of those who went to the Congo, and to my great friend Ramón César Cuenca, who was just as helpful.

To the organizations and institutions without whose help this book couldn't have been written: the Ministry of the Revolutionary Armed Forces (MINFAR), through Major General Ulises Rosales, Chief of the General Staff; the Combatants' Commission; the Information Center for Defense, of MINFAR; *Granma*, especially editor Jacinto Granda and journalist Delfín Xiqué; the Institute of the History of Cuba, through Manolo López, its president, and Maritza Dorta, in the photocopy department; and Offices of Historical Affairs and Publications, of the Council of State of the Republic of Cuba.

To Jorge Santamarina, my good friend and patient reader, who read over my rough drafts, always making helpful comments. To Jorge Risquet, Rodolfo Puente Ferro and Manuel Normando Agramonte, experts on Africa, whose help was worthy of respect, and to their secretaries, Ibis, Silva, Lucila Ramos and Conchita García. To my son William Sergio, for his constant, valuable help with the computer. Naturally, to all those who gave testimony, for, without them, this book would be incomplete. I ask those whom I didn't remember — and, therefore, left out — to forgive me for this oversight.

If this book helps Che to continue fighting for our revolution and for the cause of the oppressed all over the world — if it keeps him alive for those who seek a better world, especially the young people of all times, so that, when they have the opportunity to follow his example and retain their tenderness, they will do so — then it will have achieved its purpose.

Ernesto Che Guevara

Ernesto Guevara de la Serna was born in Rosario, Argentina on June 14, 1928. As a medical student in Buenos Aires and doctor he traveled throughout Latin America. Whilst in Guatemala during 1954 — then under the elected government of Jacobo Arbenz — he was an eyewitness to the overthrow of that government in a CIA-organized operation.

Forced to leave Guatemala, Guevara went to Mexico. There he linked up with exiled Cuban revolutionaries seeking to overthrow dictator Fulgencio Batista. In July 1955 he met Fidel Castro and immediately enlisted in the guerrilla expedition Castro was organizing. In November 1956, Guevara was part of the expedition that set out for Cuba to begin the armed struggle in the Sierra Maestra mountains. Originally the troop doctor, he became the first Rebel Army commander in July 1957.

In September 1958, Guevara and Camilo Cienfuegos each led guerrilla columns westward from the Sierra Maestra to the center of the island. In December 1958, Guevara led the Rebel Army forces to victory in the battle of Santa Clara, one of the decisive battles of the war.

Following the rebels' victory on January 1, 1959, Guevara became a key leader of the new revolutionary government. In November 1959 he became President of the National Bank; and in February 1961 he became Minister of Industry. He was also a central leader of the political organization that in 1965 became the Communist Party of Cuba.

Guevara heading numerous Cuban delegations and spoke at the United Nations and other international forums.

In April 1965 Guevara left Cuba and spent several months in the Congo in Africa, returning to Cuba secretly in February 1966. In November 1966 he arrived in Bolivia where he led a guerrilla detachment fighting that country's military dictatorship. Wounded and captured by U.S.-trained Bolivian troops on October 8, 1967, he was murdered the following day.

William Gálvez

William Gálvez Rodríguez (born Holguín, Cuba, 1933). As a young person, he took part in student struggles and joined the July 26 Revolutionary Movement (M-26-7) when it was created in 1955. He took part in anti-Batista actions and was subsequently imprisoned. On being released, he returned clandestinely to Holguín, where he reorganized the Movement and led it until he joined the Rebel Army in the Sierra Maestra mountains. He took part in the rebels' advance westward, serving under Camilo Cienfuegos and Ernesto Che Guevara with the rank of captain. Today he is a brigadier general in the Revolutionary Armed Forces of Cuba.

Introduction
by Jorge Risquet

I

In the second half of the 19th century, the territory of what is now the Republic of Zaire[1] was one of the areas least explored and known by Europeans. It was inhabited by more than 300 tribes (who spoke as many languages and dialects), who had settled on its 2,345,000 square kilometers in the course of 2,000 years of immigration, internal displacements, wars and integration.

The Europeans were well aware that this immense basin of the Congo River had been an endless source of slaves. Through Portugal's relations with the royal family of the Congo, who had been converted to Catholicism, and its introduction of Portuguese and other European slave traders in northern Angola, where that kingdom had its capital, several million African men and women were sent across the Atlantic Ocean to Brazil and other parts of the New World starting in the 16th century and continuing up to the middle of the 19th century. In addition, Arab slave traders sent millions of slaves from what is now Zaire to other parts of the world.

Naturally, the Africans didn't surrender meekly to their captors, but provided resistance with their primitive weapons: lances and arrows. It is estimated that for every slave who reached the end of the journey, at least another died on the way and a third was killed fighting against the slave hunters.

In the era when slavery proved uneconomical and was cast aside by a European bourgeoisie in full development and enrichment, fewer inhabitants were left in this martyred region of Central Africa than there had been when the slave trade to the Americas — whose indigenous population was also ruthlessly exploited and exterminated by the *conquistadores* — had begun, centuries before.

---

[1] Since this introduction was written, the country's name has been changed to the Democratic Republic of the Congo.

The Western powers began the exploration and conquest of what is now Zaire between 1870 and 1890. Henry Morton Stanley, an audacious English journalist, made the most important journey, starting from the western bank of Lake Tanganyika.

Stanley's reports, together with earlier ones, awakened the greed of Leopold II, King of the Belgians, who recruited the adventurous explorer for the "peaceful" conquest of that fabulously rich territory. With tremendous skill (and resorting to the use of arms when they believed it necessary), Stanley and his contingent, acting as the private representatives of Leopold II, managed to get the chiefs of local tribes to sign several hundred agreements on trade and concessions.

At the Berlin Conference (1884-85), in which the European colonial powers carved up Africa, the Belgian sovereign managed, with the support of the United States, to get the territory which Stanley had "contracted" to be recognized in the Minutes as the Congo Free State, the personal property of Leopold II.

The Conference also recognized the territory running from the Atlantic to the western bank of the Congo River, which French military expeditions had explored, as belonging to France. In its final course, to its mouth, the great river marked the border between the new possession of the Belgian King and the Portuguese colony of Angola. The former Kingdom of the Congo was divided into three parts, assigned to three separate colonial powers. The Lunda Empire and other large ethnic groups were also split up.

Leopold II went down in history as one of the cruelest, most rapacious colonialists ever known. In 1888, he created the Force Publique (FP), commanded by Belgian officers, whose soldiers were Africans whose induction was compulsory and who were turned into the executioners of their brothers. Later, the FP obtained its agents from among young people who had left the elementary schools created by the religious missions and who were forcibly enrolled for at least seven years. The soldiers of the FP didn't work in their regions of origin. Thus, their carrying out the draconian orders of their officers exacerbated intertribal rivalries.

Rubber and ivory were the main products exploited. Hamlets which didn't meet their quotas were razed, their inhabitants whipped and the more rebellious murdered. As macabre proof of their efficiency in repression, soldiers of the FP were required to present the right hand of each person killed.

Mining wealth soon became the most sought booty. The reserves of the area's minerals constituted a veritable "geological lavishness": copper; cobalt (three fifths of the world's production); industrial diamonds; zinc; iron; gold; silver; tungsten; manganese; bauxite; and such rare metals as beryllium, cadmium, germanium, niobium, tantalum and lithium, whose strategic importance is well known.

Companies from Belgium and other capitalist countries started exploiting the mineral wealth intensively. By 1906, there were 85 mining companies. Thumbing his nose at the Berlin Agreement, Leopold II imposed conditions on the foreign corporations that were disadvantageous to them but favorable to the Belgian corporations — in which he was the largest stockholder. The United States, Great Britain and other powers bewailed the Belgians' excesses in the Congo, but, in fact, what upset them wasn't the abuses of the population but rather the monarch's maneuvers which hindered the free trade and navigation stipulated in the Berlin accord.

II

On November 15, 1908, one year before the death of Leopold II, under his will and by resolution of the Brussels Legislature, the Congo Free State became a colony of Belgium. This was in payment of the king's debt of 25 million francs to the national treasury.

The "new" administration established a Colonial Charter. It reformed the rudimentary administration which had existed under Leopold. The Chieftainships, the basic divisions of the country, remained as the colonial bodies of power. An African from the tribal hierarchy or one of the hired assassins of the FP who was submissive to the Belgians was appointed to head each of them and was paid by the Belgians. Several Chieftainships made up a Sector. Several Sectors formed a District, Region or Province, the name changing from one period to another.

The Governor General's decrees had the force of law. He was assisted by a Council of Government. Up until 1947, there were no Africans on the Council.

Although the Colonial Charter ordered the abolition of the forced labor which had reigned in the Free State, the authorities and the mining companies managed to maintain it through several formulas. It was especially brutal in periods of crisis in the colonial powers, such as World War I and the Great Depression which hit the capitalist world in the 1930s. Great uprisings took place in several regions during those years and were crushed by military forces sent from Belgium — the same method employed since in the previous century.

The great need for strategic materials in World War II triggered a boom in production, and the number of miners rose to around 700,000. The Africans who worked in the mines and in the construction of railroads were subjected to bestial exploitation.

The Belgian Government in Exile in London recruited thousands of

Congolese for the regular Army, and they joined the Allied troops fighting in northern Africa and Ethiopia.

The only religions permitted by the colonialists were Christian, which had been the age-old spiritual accomplices of the slave trade and the savage oppression by Belgium. When, in 1921, a local sect — Kimbanguism — appeared and spread quickly through the population, its prophet, Simon Kimbangu, was given a death sentence, later commuted to life imprisonment. He died in prison after serving 30 years. Even so, this and other syncretic sects spread and constituted an element of resistance to the sway of colonialist ideology. Thousands of preachers became "political prisoners."

In 1955, Van Bilsen, an eminent Belgian professor, submitted a plan to his government for having the Congolese advance to independence. The plan included several stages which, in 30 years, would lead to an independent Congo — which, of course, would be a Belgian neocolony. The business sectors linked to the exploitation of the country rejected the plan. The recalcitrant Belgian colonialists claimed that "their Negroes" didn't want independence. Meanwhile, Great Britain, France and Holland took cautious steps forward in the inevitable process of decolonization.

III

In 1956, the year when the first Congolese obtained a university degree, while 90 percent of the population was illiterate, the word "independence" was spoken in public for the first time by a Congolese, Joseph Kasavubu — head of the Bakongo tribe and a frustrated student of theology — while addressing a huge crowd. However, Kasavubu was referring to only a part of his country, the Lower Congo, with the illusory project of joining it to the French Congo and to northern Angola and Cabinda. All of this was with the intention of rebuilding the former Kingdom of the Congo.

In June 1957, an amazing event took place: serious disorders broke out in Leopoldville [now Kinshasa] for the first time in over 70 years. It was set off by a Belgian ruling considered anything but impartial in a soccer game between Belgian and Congolese teams. The Force Publique controlled the situation, using its usual ruthless methods.

In 1957 and 1958, the first municipal elections were held. Another reformist measure was the authorization of labor unions (after the permission of the colonial authorities had been obtained) and of the right to strike.

In 1958, Charles de Gaulle, President of France, traveled to Africa, publicizing his country's plan for granting independence to its colonies, which was done in 1960. He made the announcement in a meeting held in August that was broadcast over Radio Brazzaville, a city within sight of Leopoldville, on the other side of the Congo River. Many families belonging to the Bakongo and Laris tribes lived in both cities. To some extent, the cities were but two halves of a single unit, where French and the African languages were spoken. Obviously, the announcement of French decolonization had a tremendous impact on the local population of Leopoldville and all of what is now Zaire [Democratic Republic of the Congo].

In December 1958, representing the recently-created Congo National Movement (MNC), Patrice Lumumba took part in the Pan-African Conference of Accra, which had been called by Kwame Nkrumah. The MNC was influential throughout the country, but its main strength was in the northeastern province and Stanleyville [now Kisangani], its capital. On his return, Lumumba gave a fiery pro-independence speech before a large crowd in Leopoldville.

There was a new and larger outbreak of violence in Leopoldville on January 4, 1959, this time anticolonial in nature, protesting the banning of a meeting of Kasavubu's Bakongo Abako Party. The violence lasted for three days, in the course of which entire blocks were burned and turned to ashes. The FP bloodily repressed the uprisings, with official figures stating that 42 people were killed and 250 wounded.

In view of that explosive situation, young King Baudouin quickly announced in Brussels that he would "lead the Congolese to independence in prosperity and peace." The Belgian businesses and settlers, the Force Publique and the most reactionary circles managed to halt the King's precipitate announcement in Brussels and turn it into a deferred and imprecise plan to be carried out in stages of at least four years.

In a fiery speech responding to this affront, Lumumba announced that, "The divorce between Belgium and the Congo is definitive. The Belgians don't even want to study our proposals. Therefore, today, I am launching a decisive plan of action for the liberation of the Congo. It is better to die than to put up with the regime of servitude any longer. We must win our independence."

Uprisings broke out again, this time in several parts of the country. The repression was brutal, with thousands of dead and wounded. In the midst of the Belgian-Congolese confrontation, bloody clashes broke out between tribes, and secessionist initiatives were proposed.

Kasavubu and Kanza sought the independence and separation of the Lower Congo, most of whose population were of the Bakongo ethnic group. It included Leopoldville. In Katanga, Moise Tshombe, a wealthy merchant, and Godefroid Munongo sought the secession of the great southeastern mining center. Jean Bolikango, in the northern region of Equateur, and Albert Kalonji, in Sud Kasai, were other separatist leaders.

Lumumba and his MNC party spoke out for immediate and full independence and the unity of the Congo. From his bastion in Stanleyville, Lumumba led the people's protest against the colonialist delays. As a result, he was captured and imprisoned.

The African Solidarity Party (PSA), led by Antoine Gizenga, Pierre Mulele, Thomas Mukuidi, Leonard Mitudidi, Cleophas Kamitatu (who later created a second PSA, which submitted to the regime) and others also sought an independent and united Congo. Their main influence was in Kuilo and Kuango.

In January 1960, Belgium was forced to call a meeting of the most prominent Congolese leaders. Kasavubu, Tshombe and 40 other representatives of diverse political currents and regions of the country participated. The delegation demanded that Lumumba be freed so he could take part in the Brussels conclave. Because of his talent, tact and firm adherence to principles, he had become the guiding force of the Congolese nationalists.

The date of independence was set for June 30, 1960, preceded by an election in May to elect the members of six provincial assemblies and of the bicameral national parliament, to serve for three-year terms. The members of parliament were to appoint the head of state and the prime minister, who would be in charge of forming the government of the Republic of the Congo, according to the provisional constitution decreed by the Belgian Parliament.

Dozens of political parties took part in the election. The MNC obtained the most deputies in both chambers and Lumumba set about creating a government representing all the parties, ethnic groups and regions, which would work for the required unity of a country obtaining its independence. It was an immense task, but he achieved it. Lumumba, as the leader of the MNC, became head of government and Minister of National Defense. Gizenga, President of the PSA, was Deputy Prime Minister. Kasavubu, the leader of Abako, was Head of State.

The first clash with the colonialists, seeking to play a neocolonial role, took place during the ceremony proclaiming the country's independence. King Baudouin gave a speech praising Belgium's civilizing work in the Congo, its generous concession of independence and the ties of friendship that united the two peoples. He eulogized Leopold II, his father's great-uncle. Lumumba's response was not diplomatic, but an angry expression of the Congolese people's feelings. Among other things, Lumumba said:

While it is true that we are now proclaiming our independence in agreement with Belgium — a friendly country with which we are now equals — it is also true that no Congolese worthy of the name can forget that independence has been won through daily struggle. It has been an impassioned struggle, in which we have spared no forces, sufferings, sacrifices or blood....

Who can forget the bullets that have killed so many of our brothers or the cells into which those who didn't want to submit to a regime of oppression, exploitation and injustice — the tool of colonialist rule — were cast?

In short, I ask that the lives and property of our fellow citizens and foreigners residing in our country be respected unconditionally. If the conduct of any of them leaves something to be desired, our justice will result in their expulsion from the territory of the Republic; if their conduct is good, they will be left in peace, because they, too, will work for the country's prosperity.

Lumumba wound up his reply by saying, "Thus, both inside the country and abroad, the new and independent Congo will, with my government, advance toward wealth, freedom and prosperity."

If the Belgian colonialists and their NATO allies had harbored any hopes of breaking the will of the leader of full independence for the Congo, Lumumba's history-making speech put paid to all that.

Under the Belgian Crown's absurd plan, the ruthless Force Publique would assume the function of the National Army, on the same old racist basis of white officers and black soldiers, with promotion of the latter limited to sergeant major. During the first week of the Congo's independence, a mutiny broke out within the FP. The African troops called for the abolition of those discriminatory limitations. The rebellion began in the capital. Lumumba intervened, to direct the justified demands through organized channels, but he didn't manage to convince the insurgents. The confrontation spread to the main garrisons in the country.

General Janssens, the racist chief of the Force Publique, fled to Brazzaville. On July 10, Belgian paratroopers intervened in Elisabethville, Leopoldville and Luluabourg, and Belgian forces landed at Matadi under the pretext of rescuing and evacuating the white officers. Belgian Marines massacred Africans in that port city.

Lumumba appointed Víctor Lundula — his uncle, who was President of the Congolese veterans of World War II — General in Chief of what from then on would be the Congolese National Army. He named Joseph-Desiré Mobutu as colonel and Chief of Staff. Having dropped out of junior high school, Mobutu had served in the Force Publique for seven years and had risen to the rank of sergeant-assistant bookkeeper before returning to civilian life and becoming a journalist and supposed supporter of the MNC. The appointment of Mobutu was a fatal mistake. In fact, Mobutu was an undercover agent of the Belgian special services and, in 1960, began to collaborate also with the CIA.

On July 11, Tshombe, with the support of the powerful Mining Union of Upper Katanga and Belgium, declared the secession of the south-eastern province.

On July 12, Kasavubu and Lumumba asked the United Nations to intervene to protect the Congo from foreign aggression and secession. On July 14, the UN Security Council responded to the petition, calling for the Belgian troops to withdraw and authorizing Secretary General Dag Hammarskjold to send in troops. The advance force of the UN contingent of troops reached Leopoldville the next day. All of the Belgian military except for those in Katanga withdrew, taking with them most of the Belgian technicians and former officials, whom it was impossible to replace immediately.

The UN peace-keeping forces did not halt the secession of Katanga. For long months, they negotiated with Tshombe, made threats and engaged in military actions, but Tshombe's government, supported by the Katangan gendarmery commanded by Belgian officers and white mercenaries, maintained its separatism from the central government.

Lumumba went to New York in an effort to get the United Nations to fulfill its mandate in favor of the territorial integrity of the Congo and to expel the mercenaries. He did not achieve anything, however. The UN Secretary General supported the interests of the United States and the other Western powers. Lumumba had a meeting in Washington with representatives of the U.S. State Department, headed by Christian Herter. Those talks with U.S. officials led Allen Dulles, Director of the CIA, to conclude that Lumumba was "another Castro."

Towards the end of August 1960, Lumumba declared martial law for a period of six months, arrested some secessionist politicians and ordered the troops of the National Army who were loyal to advance toward the separatist provinces of Katanga and South Kasai. Lumumba was willing to receive assistance from the Soviet Union and to confront the foreign aggression. For the imperialists and their Congolese followers, the time had come to get rid of Lumumba.

On September 5, Kasavubu made a surprise appearance over Radio Leopoldville, announcing that Lumumba had been removed from office as prime minister and that Gizenga and some other members of the Cabinet had also been removed. He named Joseph Ileo, a deserter from the MNC, to form a new government. He also removed General Lundula from command and personally assumed supreme command of the Army.

Using the same radio station, Lumumba immediately denounced that illegal action, accusing Kasavubu of high treason and declaring his removal as Head of State.

That was the last time Lumumba was able to use the radio in the capital, because the UN troops — carrying out the instructions of Andrew Cordier of the United States, who represented the UN Secretary General in Leopoldville — took over the broadcasting station. Lumumba was denied access to the main means of communication with the rest of the country. Meanwhile, Kasavubu was able to use Radio Brazzaville, which Fulbert Youlou, a Francophone puppet who was president of the other Congo, made available to him. And Tshombe had control of the powerful Radio Elisabethville.

Cordier also ordered all the airports closed except for use by the United Nations. This kept Lumumba and his forces from using planes or to receive help from abroad. Even so, Mobutu on several occasions used planes to hunt Patrice Lumumba.

Parliament accepted neither of the removal announcements and called for reconciliation. There was a power vacuum, which Mobutu occupied on September 29, 1960. He named a "technical cabinet," which he called the Council of Chiefs of Ordinance, under Justin Bomboko, and he suspended the functions of parliament "until December 31." In the same address, he stated, "The communist ambassadors have 48 hours to get out of the Congo."

Gizenga, General Lundula and other patriots managed to reach Stanleyville, the MNC's stronghold, set up the government there and organized the resistance. But Lumumba couldn't get there. He was being held under house arrest, protected by friendly Ghanaian troops from the UN forces but also watched by a second cordon of Mobutu's forces. Even so, he managed to make a daring escape on November 27 and set out on a long and intricate route toward Stanleyville. On the way, he was recognized by his supporters, cheered and forced to address them. From then on, his approximate whereabouts became public knowledge, which made it easier for Mobutu to capture him.

The CIA and other special foreign services collaborated in tracking down the great leader: a plane with a European pilot flew low over the area in the direction where the crowds had, unfortunately, gathered spontaneously. This made it relatively easy to locate the convoy in which Lumumba, his wife, a young son and several comrades traveled.

Lumumba was taken prisoner near Port Franqui early in the morning on December 2. He was first flown to the capital and then taken to the military camp of Thysville. Then, on January 17, 1961, he and his ministers Joseph Okito and Maurice M'Polo, who had also been taken prisoner and tortured, were sent with their hands tied behind their backs to Elisabethville [now Lubumbashi], the capital of Katanga. The CIA, which had been given the green light by the outgoing Eisenhower Administration, wanted to settle the matter before the new U.S. president was inaugurated. A previous attempt that two CIA agents had made to poison Lumumba had failed.

On the same day they arrived in Elisabethville, Lumumba and his comrades were assassinated near the airport. Munongo, Minister of the Interior in Tshombe's secessionist government, took part in the vile deed.

Through Lawrence Devlin, its station chief in Leopoldville, the CIA masterminded — and Tshombe, Mobutu and Kasavubu carried out — Lumumba's assassination. It was a blow to honest people the world over when it was officially announced four weeks later, on February 13.

A few days earlier, a new government team had been formed in Leopoldville, with Ileo as Prime Minister and including Cyrille Adoula, Bomboko and Bolikango. Kasavubu remained Head of State.

Meanwhile, in Stanleyville, Gizenga exercised power in the province. He extended his control toward Luluabourg, Manono and Port Franqui and proclaimed himself Lumumba's legitimate successor. Several African and Asian governments, the Soviet Union, the rest of the European socialist countries, China and Cuba recognized the Gizenga government. Some of those countries sent it military matériel.

The United Nations, which was controlled by the Western powers and where the Soviet Union's protests were barely heard, continued acting in favor of the imperialists' interests. The UN Secretary General died in a strange plane accident in September of that tragic year, 1961, while flying to Northern Rhodesia (now Zambia) to negotiate once more with the dissident Tshombe, who had obtained provisional refuge in that British colony bordering on Katanga.

In January 1962, caught in a clever "reconciliation" maneuver that had been cooked up in Leopoldville, Gizenga was imprisoned, and the Stanleyville government collapsed.

The new Kennedy Administration in the United States corrected Eisenhower's tendency to go to the aid of his country's European allies. Defending its own interests, which were different economically from those of Belgium, Great Britain and France, Washington began to exert pressure against the secession of Katanga, where the three European powers — unlike the United States — were well entrenched. Ever since the end of the previous century, when it was the first country in the world to recognize Leopold II's Congo Free State, the United States had wanted a substantial part of the Katangan and Congolese resources.

Moreover, this position enabled the United States to appear to be in agreement with both the group of Afro-Asian nations and the socialist camp, whose UN representatives had called for a united Congo. Circumstantially, this made Washington's policy on the Congo look better, both internationally and in the United States itself, where Kennedy had beaten Nixon by only 100,000 votes — votes given him by African Americans.

At the same time, the United States sent five warships to the Gulf of Guinea. Violating the Security Council resolution which prohibited any military aid apart from the UN's peace-keeping force, the Pentagon began to collaborate with Mobutu's army in October 1962. Israel did the same. And, in mid-1963, Belgian military assistance was renewed.

The results of the U.S. economic penetration weren't long in coming. In 1962, the United States tripled its 1961 exports to the Congo and became the Congo's main trading partner.

Tshombe declared his willingness to negotiate with the United States, the United Nations and the central government. Their maneuvers, which are too lengthy to describe here, continued throughout 1962.

In January 1963, the UN forces forced the Katangan secessionists to renounce separatism. Tshombe left Kolwezi, though he maneuvered for several months, trying to act as President of the Provincial Government. Finally, he went into temporary exile in Spain.

After the Katanga issue had been solved, the Soviet Union once more called for the UN contingent to be withdrawn. Prime Minister Adoula's government asked it to stay. U Thant, the new Secretary General of the United Nations, drastically reduced the UN peace-keeping force and set a limit to its mandate.

The situation was aggravated by inaction of the central government, corruption of public officials, economic bankruptcy and total chaos that had prevailed since September 1960. The population's living conditions became untenable. Workers' strikes and political and tribal disturbances grew throughout the country, while, for months, Adoula pretended to comply with the UN request for national reconciliation in a parliament where the people's real representatives were dead, imprisoned or outlawed. At the end of August 1963, Adoula announced the discovery of "a Lumumba plot" and ended the "reconciliation" maneuver. Political and union leaders who didn't support the regime were persecuted.

In late September 1963, the crisis led to a virtual coup d'état: President Kasavubu suspended Parliament permanently and decreed a state of emergency throughout the country and a new wave of terror engulfed the capital. The prisons were filled.

Lumumba's followers — comprising several parties and splinter groups running a wide political gamut — were persecuted and went underground and into exile in the neighboring former French Congo. They immediately met in Brazzaville, where, six weeks before, the people had overthrown Fulbert Youlou's puppet pro-Tshombe regime, which had been placed in power by France, and installed a progressive government headed by Massemba Debat.

On October 3, the National Liberation Committee (CNL) was created. Gizenga, who was still in prison, was named Honorary Chairman.

The CNL was a coordinating body for the parties which were opposed to the Leopoldville regime. It declared its support for Patrice Lumumba's ideas, and its avowed purpose was "to overthrow the Adoula government and totally and effectively decolonize the Congo, now ruled by a coalition of foreign powers."

Christophe Gbenye, President of the MNC (Lumumbist), and Thomas Mukuidi, Secretary of the PSA (Gizenguist), signed the CNL's declaration of principles, as did the leaders of three other small opposition parties. Mulele had sent Mukuidi from the guerrilla front to try to unite with the Lumumba forces and get them to join in armed action.

The split between the political forces was one of the main weaknesses of the Congolese people's movement. It reflected class, ideological and tribal contradictions; personal ambitions; and great political immaturity. In the same city of Brazzaville, some months later, Davinson Bochelay, Vice-President of the MNC (L), formed his own CNL. From then on, there were two organizations bearing the same name: one led by Gbenye and the other by Bochelay.

Gbenye had been Minister of the Interior in Lumumba's Cabinet and had held the same post in Gizenga's rebel government, but in 1962 he was not loath to holding the same position under Prime Minister Adoula, going along with his "reconciliation" farce. The CNL arose as a very heterogeneous grouping, encompassing everything from Lumumbists with deeply patriotic and revolutionary convictions, such as Mukuidi — who, while marching toward Mulele's front, was killed in battle against the regime in 1967 — to vacillating elements who were ready to accept any kind of "reconciliation" or worse, such as Gbenye himself.

Pierre Mulele, Minister of Education in Lumumba's Cabinet and Minister of Foreign Relations in Gizenga's, had started preparing the political and organizational conditions for armed struggle in his bastion of Kuilo before the CNL was created. After the first Stanleyville government was destroyed, Mulele had traveled to several progressive countries and studied guerrilla warfare in China. He returned to Kuilo in the summer of 1963 and worked carefully, laying the bases for armed struggle.

In September 1963, the Provincial Government responded to the first signs of life of Mulele's guerrillas and offered a high price (half a million

Belgian francs) for his head. In January 1964, the state of emergency was declared and Mobutu was asked to send forces to contain the growing rebellion.

Mulele extended the insurrection, won the people's support and engaged in military actions. Lieutenant Colonel Ebeya, Mulele's Chief of Staff and right-hand man, was killed in a guerrilla action.

Months later, in April 1964, armed insurrection broke out in the east. Massengo and Laurent Kabila headed the Lumumba forces in northern Katanga; Gastón Soumialot, in central Kivu; and Olenga, in Maniema.

The United Nations withdrew its small contingent on June 30, 1964.

The failures of Mobutu's Army against the expanding insurgents and the manifest incompetence of Adoula and his government were cause for serious concern by the Western powers.

The U.S. Ambassador to the Congo informed the Secretary of State in Washington that they were all agreed to giving Tshombe an important post in the government. Mobutu and Adoula, with the reticent approval of Kasavubu, allowed Tshombe to return from Spain and he was named head of the "transition government" on July 6.

The evil trio tried to halt the rebellion, but it was spreading quickly. Rather than an insurrection that was structured nationally, it was a series of explosions by the desperate masses in different parts of the country, a large proportion of whom were adolescents who often advanced with their rudimentary weapons against the rifles of the demoralized forces of Mobutu's Army. They were tired of bloodshed and oppression and eager to have freedom. Patrice Lumumba was their God, and they had blind faith in the idol of *dawa*. (It is necessary to assess the full extent of the mystic strength of idols in the Congo in order to understand their effect, both in supporting the combativity of the *simbas* (lions in Swahili) and in opposing the government's soldiers — who were also believers and among whom they caused real panic.)

In May 1964, the Lumumbist forces seized Uvira and Fizi, in the eastern part of the country. In June and July, they took Albertville, the capital of northern Katanga, and Kindu, the provincial capital of Maniema. Soumialot announced "the creation of a government in charge of administering the liberated territories."

Tshombe made unsuccessful attempts to come to an agreement with the rebels, including carrying out an act of incredible cynicism — laying a wreath at the monument to Lumumba in Stanleyville at the beginning of August. A week after that act of profanity, that city, capital of the northeastern province and the third largest city in the country, was seized by the *simbas*, an achievement considered the crowning point of the rebel offensive in the eastern Congo. More than half of the huge country was in the hands of the Lumumbist forces.

On September 1964, in Stanleyville, the CNL proclaimed the People's Republic of the Congo. Gbenye named himself Head of State, conferred eight "Ministries" on himself and named Olenga commanding general of a new "People's Liberation Army."

The U.S. Government understood the seriousness of the situation and cast all political scruples aside, taking a series of loathsome measures after the universally hated Tshombe had been reinstated.

Nearly a month earlier, on August 11, CIA chief John McCone reported to the U.S. National Security Council that Leopoldville was in danger of falling into the hands of the insurgents and said that Brussels refused to use its troops. The United States contacted its European and African allies, trying to get them to send troops, but those efforts also failed.

In view of that situation, U.S. President Johnson decided to use white mercenaries. They were euphemistically called "special volunteers." The U.S. solution was accepted as a lifesaver by Tshombe (who had always been an enthusiastic employer of "dogs of war"), Mobutu and Kasavubu.

The United States provided the money, and accelerated the recruitment of "soldiers of fortune" in Belgium, France, Great Britain, South Africa and Rhodesia, including the notorious Mike Hoare, Bob Denard and John Peters. There was only one restriction, which showed the characteristic hypocrisy of White House policy: no U.S. citizens could be recruited as mercenaries.

With its C-130s piloted by U.S. citizens, Washington guaranteed the transportation of men, weapons and other supplies for the mercenaries, the Katangan gendarmery and Mobutu's Army. It also provided them with B-26 and T-28 planes piloted by Cuban counterrevolutionaries recruited in Miami.

In short, the CIA and the Pentagon set about crushing the Congolese rebellion. Colonel Dudds was the U.S. "logistics officer" on Mobutu's Staff.

In the new stage of the fighting, with all-out U.S. support and leadership, Operation Ommegang was initiated in late August. The government troops led by the "dogs of war" recaptured Kivu and, a week later, Albertville. In September 1964, they seized Boende and Lisala and, in October, Uvira and Kindu. By that time, over 1,000 white mercenaries were directly commanding the Katangan gendarmery and other Mobuto troops and were flying the warplanes.

A great many whites lived in Stanleyville and Paulis. The U.S. and Belgian governments decided to use their own forces. The United States provided planes piloted by U.S. and anti-Castro Cuban mercenary pilots, and Belgium provided its elite paratroopers. The pretext was the usual one: that of saving white hostages.

Operation Red Dragon was carried out November 24-27. Around 200 of the foreign hostages died in that brutal "humanitarian" action; the rest, a somewhat larger group, were evacuated. The paratroopers and Hoare's Marines and their gendarmes killed more than 10,000 Congolese the first day alone. On the following days, the death toll rose to 30,000. The same forces were used in Paulis, with equal cruelty.

From then on, the rebel forces beat a retreat, and the divisions among the ruling groups were exacerbated. The dispute between Gbenye and Soumialot ended with the creation of the Supreme Council of the Revolution, headed by the latter. Gbenye, who was secretly making contact with the Belgian Government and the CIA, sought refuge in a neighboring country.

Mulele, who didn't have any foreign help, kept on fighting in Kuilo. The mercenaries used their weapons and the bombings and strafing by their planes to wipe out the concentrations of fighters. Meanwhile, Mobutu's infantry occupied and razed the hamlets and fields, depriving the guerrillas of support from the people. In 1965, a counter-offensive of the pro-U.S. and mercenary-backed Leopoldville government was successful.

Two African leaders who were pillars of support for the Congolese patriots — Algeria's Ben Bella and Ghana's Nkrumah — were deposed by military insurrections. In Southern Rhodesia (now Zimbabwe), the racist Ian Smith took power, ignoring London and declaring his unilateral independence with a white-minority government aligned with South Africa. Imperialist supremacy spread in Africa.

Meanwhile, Tshombe had been gaining ground in his political ambitions, gathering 49 parties — all of the existing groups except Kasavubu's Abako Party and, of course, the Lumumbist revolutionaries — into a coalition (CONACO). With that force, he won a landslide victory in both chambers in the 1965 electoral farce.

For his part, Kasavubu remained Head of State, because the constitution — which the Belgian jurists had thrown together in 36 hours — didn't set any limits to that term of office, as if it were for life, like that of a king.

Using that power, Kasavubu declared the end of the "transitional mandate of Tshombe's government" on October 13. He ordered Evaristo Kimba, also of Katanga, to form a new government. However, on November 14, Parliament refused to recognize Kimba's government and Kimba had to name other cabinet members and present the list to the legislature.

This new governmental crisis lasted for 10 days. On November 25, 1965, Mobutu ordered his troops to the streets, removed Kasavubu and proclaimed himself President of the Congo, with General Mulamba as Head of Government, both for five-year terms. Mobutu did not forgive Kasavubu for having pledged in Accra, without consulting him, that the mercenaries would be sent home.

Tshombe went into exile in Franco's Spain and finally died in captivity in Algeria. Kasavubu was confined near Matadi, where he died some years later. *Rome pays traitors but despises them.* The CIA is as generous in rewarding its servants as it is expeditious in eliminating them when it no longer needs them and they get in the way.

Strong man Mobutu Sese Seko climbed to the top through genocidal dictatorship for 30 years. His cruelty, rapaciousness and deceitfulness are comparable only to those of Leopold II. In addition, Mobutu betrayed his own people. That abominable exponent of "Western values" and a "market economy" (he is one of the richest men in the world) is still in power, supported on an immense lake of blood and the suffering of the Zairian people, thanks to the continuous, unlimited assistance given him by the United States and its NATO allies.

On November 21, 1965, four days before Mobutu assumed absolute power in Leopoldville, the Internationalist Column [Column One] — consisting of more than 100 fighters headed by Che Guevara — left the Congo, crossing Lake Tanganyika to Tanzania, at the request of the Dar Es Salaam government and the Congolese leaders of the Eastern Front.

Seven months earlier, Major Guevara (using the pseudonym Tatu) and the vanguard of Column One had entered the Congo along that same route, beginning the tremendous, heroic effort of revitalizing the Lumumbist forces to make them the nucleus of a new liberation army which would halt the enemy offensive and begin to recover the positions that had been lost. It was too late, for the Congolese people's rebellion was being wiped out by enormously superior enemy forces.

As General of the Cuban Army Raúl Castro said on the 20th anniversary of the founding of Columns One and Two:

> The Lumumba patriots took the path of armed resistance, but they lacked experience, unity and a high degree of conscientiousness… It wasn't possible to turn the Lumumbist forces into a cohesive whole. A time came when the Internationalist Column was fighting alone on unknown terrain. In view of those adverse circumstances, the Column had to leave that country. It wasn't defeated by the enemy, but the lack of a structured patriotic movement with which it could cooperate made it impossible for it to carry out its mission.[2]

---

[2] Raúl Castro, November 7, 1985.

The bodies of six Cuban veterans who were killed in combat will remain forever in the Congo. Their sacrifice was not in vain. Their example inspired hundreds of thousands of Cubans, who joined new columns and learned from the valuable, bitter experiences of that first internationalist mission in sub-Saharan Africa to win history-making victories together with the peoples of the Congo (Brazzaville), Guinea-Bissau, Angola, Namibia, Zimbabwe and South Africa against colonialism, mercenary armies and racism.

Mobutu's troops were dissuaded from their plan to attack the Congo (Brazzaville) in 1965-66: a Cuban battalion and the people's militias which it organized were in that African country, providing unlimited political support to the Lumumbist combatants. Radio Brazzaville was firmly at the service of the Lumumbist cause. Our Column Two, the Patrice Lumumba Battalion, was deservedly a reserve of Che's Column One, ready to fight if the course of struggle in the other Congo made it necessary.

Ten years later, detachments of the Zairian Army were defeated by Angolan and Cuban forces at Kinfangondo, in Cabinda and at Negage-Uige and were forced to leave Angola. Dozens of white mercenaries left their bones in Angola, and others were taken prisoner and placed on trial in Luanda. The rest fled in haste to save their lives. The myth of their invincibility was destroyed.

The troops of the apartheid regime of South Africa were dealt an annihilating defeat in Angola. In 1975-76, FAPLA and the Cuban troops halted the racist troops' sweeping advance toward Luanda on the banks of the Queve River. In just five months, the racist forces were pushed back beyond the Cunene River, to behind the borders of occupied Namibia. In 1987-88, a new attempt to subjugate Angola was halted in Cuito Cuanavale, and the Cuban, Angolan and South West Africa People's Organization (SWAPO) troops made the invaders retreat to the Cunene. In view of that dangerous military situation with unforeseeable consequences, Pretoria was forced to begin peace negotiations, which led to its definitive withdrawal from Angola and to Namibia's independence. The apartheid regime of South Africa never recovered from that military and political defeat. Besieged by the growing struggle waged by the movement of Nelson Mandela, it was abolished and buried by the crushing majority the African National Congress won in the first multiracial election held in South Africa after three centuries of Boer rule.

Most of the combatants in Che's Column turned their grief in the eastern Congo in 1965 into a spur for taking part in those new, victorious efforts in other African countries for a quarter of a century. Some lost their lives while fighting for African freedom or for freedom in Bolivia and other countries of Our America.

Che Guevara, the Heroic Guerrilla, described and analyzed the seven months in which Column One was in action (April 24–November 21, 1965) and their immediate antecedents in his unpublished manuscript *Pasajes de la guerra revolucionaria: Congo* (*Episodes of the Revolutionary War: The Congo*), which he wrote in Dar es Salaam in the 10 weeks immediately following the period described, based on the diary in which he kept detailed records of the events of his 215 days of struggle in the Congo.

In his recent investigation,[3] Brigadier General William Gálvez — the distinguished author of several books on the Cuban Revolution, including biographies of Camilo Cienfuegos and Frank País — gathered together Major Ernesto Guevara's impassioned document, his tender letters to his children and other relatives, the notes in the Column's *Campaign Diary*, other documents, photos and the testimony of several of Che's closest comrades in arms. The author doesn't claim to have exhausted the subject; rather, he offers us a vivid picture which is rich in details of that unparalleled struggle.

Gálvez not only compiled that documentation — of such great historical and human worth — which had been known only in parts prior. He has also contributed his own opinions, using the objectivity given him by his own experience as a guerrilla in Cuba and internationalist combatant in Africa and the lessons of happenings in Africa and the rest of the world in the last three decades.

This combination of elements gives the book a singular character and makes it indispensable as a reference work for understanding the full stature of Che Guevara, the courage of those shaped by the Cuban Revolution and Cuba's contribution to the cause of the independence of its brothers and sisters in Africa. Patrice Lumumba and Ernesto Che Guevara's dream of freedom is now a reality in the Southern Cone of Africa. Someday it will also be a reality in Zaire.

Havana, January 17, 1996
Jorge Risquet Valdés[4]

---

[3] Published in Cuba as *El sueño africano de Che* [Che's African Dream].
[4] Jorge Risquet was the head of Column Two, which arrived in Africa shortly after Column One, headed by Che Guevara. He is a member of the Central Committee of the Communist Party of Cuba.

Noms de Guerre

Abdala — Luciano Paul
Abdalla — Aliopio del Sol
Adabu — Dioscórides Romero
Afendi — Roberto Rodríguez
Aga — Virgilio Jiménez Rojas
Agano — Arquímides Martínez
Agile — Dioscórides Meriño Castillo
Aguie — Esmérido Parada Zamora
Ahili — Eduardo Castillo Lora
Ahiri — José Antonio Aguiar
Aja — Andrés A. Arteaga
Akiki — Roger Pimentel
Alakre — Sinecio Prado
Alau — Lorenzo Espinosa García
Ali — Santiago Terry Rodríguez
Amba — Luis Díaz Primero
Ami — Ezequiel Toledo Delgado
Amia — José L. Torres
Anchali — Sandalio Lemus
Andika — Vicente Yant
Anene — Mario Thompson Vegas
Anga — Juan F. Aguilera
Angari — Arquimedes Martínez
Ansa — Moisés Delisle
Ansalia — Luis Monteagudo
Anzala — Octavio Rojas
Anzama — Arnaldo Domínguez
Anzurune — Capt. Crisógenes Vinajera
Arobaine — Salvador José Escudero
Arobo — Mariano García
Asmari — Argelio Zamora Torriente
Au — Andrés J. Jardínes
Aurino (Zuleimán) — Francisco C. Torriente A.
Awirino — Francisco Semanat (lost in the Congo)
Azi — Lt. Israel Reyes Zayas
Azima — Lt. Ramón Armas

Badala — Bernardo Amelo
Bahasa — Orlando Puente Mayeta
Bahati — Melanio Miranda (turned traitor)
Barufu — Ismael Monteagudo

Carlos — Florentino Nogas
Changa — Roberto Sánchez
Chembeu — Eddy Espinosa
Cheni — Raumide Despaigne
Chepua — Roberto Pérez Calzado
Chesue — Tomás Rodríguez
Chumi — Dr. José Raúl Candevat
Chunga — Luis Hechavarría

Danhisi — Nicolás Savón
David — Rogelio Oliva (at the Cuban Embassy in Dar es Salaam)
Dogna — Arcadio Hernández Betancourt
Doma — Arcardio Hernando
Dufu — Armando Martínez
Dukuduko — Santos Duquesne
Dwala — Dionisio Madera

Fada — Antonio Pérez Sánchez
Falka — Fernando Aldama
Fara — Dr. Gregorio Herrera
Fizi — Dr. Diego Lagomozino

Hanesa — Osvaldo Izquierdo
Hansini — Constantino Pérez Méndez
Hatari — Adalberto Fernández (deceased)
Hindi — Dr. Héctor Vera
Hukumu — Rodobaldo Gundín

Inne — Lt. Norberto Pío Pichardo
Ishirini — Martín Chibás

Kadatasi — Arcadio Puentes
Kahama — Alberto Man Sieleman (deceased)
Karín — José Palacio
Kasambala — Roberto Chaveco
Kasulo — Dr. Adrián Zanzaligc (Haitian, died in 1966)
Kawawa — Corp. Wagner Moro Pérez
Kigulo — Noelio Revé

Kimbi — Domingo Oliva
Kisua — Erasmo Videaux
Kulula — Augusto Ramírez
Kumi — Dr. Rafael Zerquera

Mafu — Lt. Catalino Olachea
Maganga — Ramón Muñoz
Marembo — Isidro Peralta
Masihisano — Casiano Pons
Mauro — Justo Rumbaut
Mbili — José María Martínez Tamayo (killed in Bolivia)
Milton — Jesús Alvarez Morejón
Moja — Víctor Dreke C.
Mongueso — Germán Ramírez
Morogoro — Dr. Octavio de la Concepción de la Pedraja
Mustafá — Conrado Morejón

Nanne — Sgt. Eduardo Torres Ferrer (Coqui in Cuba)
Natutu — Giraldo Padilla
Njenje — Marcos A. Herrera
Nyeñeña — Luis Calzado Hernández

Okika — Herminio Betancourt
Ottu — Santiago Parada

Paulu — Emilio Mena
Pilau — Daniel Cruz
Pombo — Harry Villegas

Rabanini — Lucio Sánchez
Rafael (with guerrillas and internal contacts) — Oscar Fernández Padilla
    (head of G-2 liaison with Che office in Dar es Salaam)
Raimundo (in communication with Havana) — Oscar Fernández Padilla
    (head of G-2 liaison with Che office in Dar es Salaam)
Rebocate — Mario Armas

Saba — Pedro O. Ortiz
Safi — Vladimir Rubio
Sakumu — Florentino Limindu Zulueta
Samani — Wilfredo de Armas
Samuel — Fidencio Semanat
Sheik — Virgilio Montoya Muñoz
Siki — Oscar Fernández Mell

Singida — Manuel Savigne Medina
Sita — Pablo B. Ortiz (deceased)
Sitaini — Angel Fernández Angulo
Siwa — Víctor Chué Colá (deceased)
Sultán — Rafael Vaillant

Tamusini — Domingo Pie Fiz
Tano — Aldo García González
Tatu — Ernesto Che Guevara
Telathini — Víctor M. Ballester
Tembo — Capt. Emilio Aragonés
Tiza — Julián Morejón Gilbert
Tom — Rafael Hernández (deceased)
Tremendo Punto — Godefrei Tchamlesso (Che called him Chamaleso)
    (Congolese)
Tulio — Tomás Escadón Carvajal
Tumaini (Tuma) — Carlos Coello (killed in Bolivia)

Uta — Capt. Aldo Margolles

Víctor — Víctor Cañas

Wasiri — Golván Marín

Zilay — Elio H. Portuondo
Ziwa — Víctor Schueg
Zuleimán (Aurino) — Francisco C. Torriente

1

December 1964–
April 1965

An unexpected journey

The whine of the turbines indicated that the engines of the huge plane had been switched on. Later, the control tower told the pilot, "Taxiway B," and the plane trundled toward the end of the runway.

Every time he flew, the traveler felt the same confidence as soon as the crew members started their routine, for he knew every step of it. He was reassured. He remembered how, when he was quite young, an uncle had taught him how to fly gliders. Years later, he became a pilot.

He observed the other maneuvers until the plane reached its cruising altitude. A few minutes later, he listened to the voice of one of the flight attendants giving details on the flight and the necessary instructions. He leaned back in his seat and began to read. He would spend his travel time in reading and writing. Speaking was difficult because of the prosthetic device he wore to make his lips thicker as a disguise. It also caused problems at mealtimes. It was bothersome, and he went to the toilet several times to get relief by removing it for a while.

VICTOR DREKE: When we were in the plane, sitting in the second
    compartment close to one of the emergency doors in a row of three
    — Papi in the aisle seat, Che in the middle and me by the window —
    we noticed that the journalist Luis Gómez Wangüemert, who had

interviewed and spoken with Che countless times, was sitting in the row next to us, but he didn't recognize him. I don't think Wangüemert ever found out that he had traveled with Che on the day Che left Cuba for Africa.

Why was Che Guevara afraid of being recognized? Why did he have to travel so heavily disguised? Why was he leaving Cuba for another country? Those who have read about his life may know part of the reason; those who haven't done so can't know why. But, in both cases, they couldn't know the real reasons and how he managed to reach his destination without being detected by the enemy. To know this, we have to go some years back.

It was April 1965. It had taken him six years and four months — from the time of the 1959 Cuban Revolution — to do what he had written to his mother from Mexico, July 15, 1956: "After righting wrongs in Cuba, I will go somewhere else..." Thus, when enough time had passed so he felt that other comrades could carry out his assignments for the Cuban Revolution, that idea returned and remained constantly with him.

South America was the goal

The idea grew stronger after his experience in the 1956-59 war of liberation which overthrew the Batista dictatorship, in which he played a leading role. It grew with his contact with many revolutionaries from Latin America and other countries ruled by dictatorships, as in his beloved homeland, Argentina. He never lost sight of that goal even with his great responsibilities as a commander in the new Armed Forces and one of the central leaders of the Cuban Revolution. Among other positions he held, he was head of the Department of Industries of the National Institute of the Agrarian Reform (INRA), President of the National Bank and finally Minister of Industry.

FIDEL CASTRO: Che very much wanted to go to South America. This was an old idea of his, because when he joined us in Mexico — although it is not that he made it a condition — he did ask: "The only thing I want after the victory of the revolution is to go fight in Argentina" — his country — "that you don't keep me from doing so, that no reasons of state will stand in the way." And I promised him that. It was a long way off, after all. Firstly, no one knew if we would win the war or who was going to be alive at the end — and he surely, because of his impetuousness, had little chance of coming out alive — but this is what he asked. Once in a while, in the Sierra and afterward, he would remind me of this plan and promise. He was certainly farsighted.

After gaining experience in the Sierra Maestra, he grew more enthusiastic about the idea of making a revolution in South America, in his own country. Che knew first hand our exceptional experience, beginning with the difficult conditions in which we rebuilt our army and carried through the struggle, and he developed a great faith in the possibilities of the revolutionary movement in South America. When I speak of South America, I am actually speaking of the southern part of South America. The promise had been given and I always told him, "Don't worry, we will keep our word." He raised it perhaps two or three times.

With the triumph of the revolution there were many tasks to carry out and problems of all kinds to be solved. We had political problems, problems with the unification of our forces, state problems, economic problems, and so on...

He had several responsibilities. Every time a serious comrade was needed for an important post, Che would volunteer... Che always had great authority... He participated in almost every activity. He was very consistent in everything he did; he set an example in everything he did.

That is how he spent the first years of the revolution. Evidently, he later began to feel impatient about carrying out his old plans and ideas. I believe he was influenced in part by the fact that time was passing. He knew that special physical conditions were required for this. He felt he was capable of doing it and, in reality, he was at the peak of his mental and physical capacities. He had many ideas, based on the experience he had gained in Cuba, of what could be done in his native country. He was thinking of his country, but not only of his own country. He thought of all the Americas.

He was impatient. From our own experience, I knew the difficulty of the initial phase of a process like the one he wanted to carry out. I thought better conditions could be created for what he was thinking of doing. We attempted to persuade him not to be impatient, to convince him that more time was needed. He wanted to start out from the very first day and do it all, while we wanted other, less well-known cadres to carry out the initial steps.[5]

ULISES ESTRADA: I worked for the Deputy Minister of the Interior in charge of intelligence, Major Manuel Piñeiro Lozada. As Cuba's support for other countries' national liberation struggles grew, a section called MOE (the special operations section of Department M) was created. Orlando Pantojo (Olo) was its chief, and I was second in command. That department began to create training schools and do operative work. Che often directed our work. Everything related to

---

[5] Gianni Miná, *An Encounter with Fidel*, 220-3.

the guerrilla and underground movements had to be submitted to him and discussed with him, even though Fidel was the highest ranking chief.

The first operation that I remember we worked on was Operation Sombra, which Jorge Ricardo Masseti, José María Martínez Tamayo (Papi) and another comrade carried out. The three went to Algeria; the government of that country supported the operation. Later, using Algerian documents, they went to Brazil as a National Liberation Front delegation, and the Algerian officials got them into Bolivia. There, they bought a farm and prepared underground caches for weapons and other supplies they would obtain. They also explored the terrain where guerrilla operations would be begun.

A small group of Argentines joined them. They included Dr. Leonardo Wertein and the painter Ciro Busto. Later, the [Cuban] Revolutionary Government decided that Papi and the other comrade should return. Still later, it was decided that Wertein and Busto should return, the doctor because of illness and Busto because he said he had problems — I can't remember the details. As had been planned, the rest of the comrades who would constitute the rebel detachment started arriving. They included Captain Hermes Peña and First Lieutenant Alberto Castellanos. Both had fought under Che's command. It was Che's idea that a mother guerrilla group would be created there, which Che would join.

While that organizational work was being carried out, Che called Oscar Fernández Mell, who was Chief of Staff of the Western Army and a doctor by profession — although he had set that aside — to the 9th floor of the Ministry of Industry where Che told him to go and see Manuel Piñeiro.

After explaining that Che was going on a mission outside the country and that he had to change his appearance, Piñeiro told him that, because he was a doctor and had close relations with Che, he should make some plaster casts of Che's teeth, because the dentist who would make the prosthetic devices shouldn't know who his patient was.

Shortly afterwards, in Dr Montoto's office at L and 17th Streets, Oscar learned how to make the paste for the casts. Later, he was given the materials and instruments and told how to use them. That same day, in Che's office as Minister of Industry, the first step was taken in making upper and lower plates for Che.

ULISES ESTRADA: The Argentine guerrilla center in Bolivia was wiped out in April 1964 as a result of enemy infiltration. A series of events then took place which led to the capture of several rebels and to the death in combat of others, including Captain Hermes. Masseti managed to escape by going deep into the Argentine jungle in the Salta region and disappeared.

Lieutenant Alberto Castellanos, a member of that guerrilla group, told me that Masseti was captured alive in bad physical condition and murdered. His murderers kept the thousands of dollars he had on him, which is why they hid his body. What happened with the Argentine group was very traumatic for Che. He made a big effort trying to locate Masseti and his comrades, to revive the guerrilla center. Later, he began preparations for the operation that would make it possible to establish the mother guerrilla group in Bolivia. That's when Tamara Bunke (Tania) began to be trained so she could be sent to Bolivia to prepare the conditions for a future mission which Che explained to her, though neither she nor I knew what was really planned... Along with Operation Sombra, Operation Matraca was prepared with a group of Peruvian guerrillas headed by the poet Héctor Béjar.

At the same time, work was done with other Peruvians, headed by Luis de la Puente Uceda. They were being trained in the Southern Cone of South America at that time. Che directed both operations to create the mother guerrilla group; they were to begin with combatants from those countries and then incorporate personnel from other countries. As soon as they were trained as guerrillas, they were sent to their own countries to fight...

Che worked with those comrades in the early morning hours in his office in the Ministry of Industry. Fidel also met with the groups, but Che was the one who discussed operational matters with them. Naturally, Fidel decided what plans to follow. That was the strategy.

Che's interest in Africa

FIDEL CASTRO: Che was also very interested in international questions, in the problems faced by Africa. At the time, mercenaries had intervened in the former Belgian Congo, now Zaire. Patrice Lumumba had been killed, a neocolonial regime was established, and an armed struggle movement emerged in Zaire.[6]

Che's interest grew greater when he visited several African countries after his December 11, 1964, address to the 19th General Assembly of the United Nations.

His historic speech denounced imperialism and expressed Cuba's solidarity with the oppressed peoples of the world. He referred to "the painful case of the Congo, unique in modern history, that shows how the

---

[6] Gianni Miná, *An Encounter with Fidel*, 223.

rights of the peoples can be thwarted with the utmost impunity and the most insolent cynicism. The Congo's immense wealth, which the imperialist nations want to keep under their control, is the direct motive for all this."

He went on to ask, "How can we forget the way the hope that Patrice Lumumba placed in the United Nations was betrayed? How can we forget the trickery and maneuvers that took place when that country was occupied by troops sent by the United Nations, under whose auspices the murderers of the great African patriot acted with impunity?"

Still later, he noted the criminal actions of Moise Tshombe, carried out with the consent of the United Nations. Citing the mercenaries' massacre of the Congolese, Che said, "As an extreme insult, they now say we were responsible for those last actions, which have angered everybody all over the world. Who committed those crimes? Belgian paratroopers, brought in by U.S. planes, which left from English bases… All free men in the world should prepare to avenge the crime in the Congo."

Those who "discovered" in Che's UN speech a clear allusion to his decision to go and fight in Africa were mistaken, for he made similar references to other countries in different continents. However, his contacts with African leaders in that period helped him to acquire information about the next meeting of representatives of the African and Asian peoples, which would be held in Algiers. Three days after his UN address, Che appeared on the CBS's *Face the Nation* program and, the next day, accepted the invitation of an old friend from Córdoba, Spain, to have dinner at the home of one of the Rockefellers. On both occasions, in spite of provocative questions, his replies were both conclusive and well put. Major Guevara left for Gander, Newfoundland, on December 17, 1964, accompanied by Héctor García and José R. Manresa.

Che visits several African countries

Everything indicates that the mission in Africa had a double purpose: Che was both promoting trade relations as Cuban Minister of Industry, in charge of the most important branches of the Cuban economy, and strengthening Cuba's ties with the revolutionary movements and countries in that continent. The testimony of Jorge Serguera (Papito), Cuban Ambassador to Algeria in those years, confirms this: "The main aim was to create an alliance between Cuba and Algeria to support the liberation movements and independent nations against colonialism and imperialism in the economic, political and military spheres in Africa."

Che's plane stopped over in Dublin and Berlin. From Dublin, he wrote his father jokingly:

Dear Dad:
Here I am in this green Ireland of your ancestors with anchor down and all sails set. When the television people learned about my ancestry, they asked me about the genealogy of the Lynches, but I didn't speculate whether they had been horse thieves or anything like that. Happy holidays. Hoping to hear from you.
Ernesto[7]

Che reached Algiers on December 18, 1964, and was met at the airport by representatives of the Council of Ministers and the Cuban Ambassador. It was his third visit to that country. The next afternoon, he met with Ben Bella, leader of the Algerian Government, who had done everything possible to help the liberation movements in sister nations. Relations between the Algerian and Cuban governments were strong, and Ben Bella was receptive to doing his utmost to further the cause of these liberation movements.

The second African country Che visited was Mali, where he met with President Modibo Keita on December 26. He also gave a press conference in which he said:

The revolutionary struggle against U.S. intervention is acquiring more and more of a continental nature in the hemisphere. In Latin America, revolutionary action is now in the stage of armed struggle. The more time passes, the more risks there are of a brutal confrontation between the Latin American peoples and the U.S. Government.[8]

From that distant nation, he sent a short note to his oldest daughter, Hildita (who has since died):

My Darling,
Since I haven't heard any news of the family and am continuing my journey, I can only send you a hug and say that everything is fine. The trip is very interesting because I'm learning about countries and the people of those countries who are struggling just like us for a better future. Here's a kiss from your dad. Happy New Year.[9]

He spent the New Year in Bamako, the capital of Mali, and on January 2, 1965, flew to the Congo (Brazzaville), a former French colony which had

---

[7] "Cartas a su padre," in Adys Cupull and Froilán González, *Un hombre bravo*, 274.
[8] *Granma*, October 22, 1967. Translator's note: Some of Che's writings weren't published until after his death.
[9] Hilda Gadea, *Che Guevara, años decisivos*, 212.

gained its independence in 1963. There, he met with President Alphonse Massemba-Debat and Prime Minister Pascal Lissouba, both of whom were very willing to increase their cooperation with the liberation movements. Che was shocked by their lack of concern with the defense of the country, which was only five kilometers (the width of the Congo River) away from the Congo (Leopoldville) — a very dangerous neighbor. He told them so jokingly: "Well, look, I won't sleep here. It isn't that I won't sleep; I just won't be here."[10]

During his meeting with the leaders of the Congo (Brazzaville), they asked for military aid, for instructors to train the militia and for troops with which to counter any attack that the government of the Congo (Leopoldville) might make.

As quickly as possible, Che began to make contact with the leaders of the liberation movements, most of them from the Portuguese colonies. They included Samora Michel and Marcelino Dos Santos from Mozambique and Agostinho Neto and Lucio Lara from Angola. An article about those early contacts was published in the *Buletim do Militante MPLA* (People's Movement for the Liberation of Angola), printing part of Che's speech during his 1965 visit:

> "It is a great pleasure for me to be here with you and to see in practice how you are structuring and developing your armed struggle against Portuguese colonialism. I am simply going to tell you something that I have already repeated many times: Cuba is with you, with all the Angolan people, as it is also with the people of Mozambique and the people of Portuguese Guinea.
>
> "Our principle is that of supporting all peoples who are struggling to free themselves of colonialism, and, naturally, I would like to tell you a few things related to our experience which was not extensive, but was very valuable.
>
> "Cuba is a country barely 114,000 square kilometers in size, just a tiny bit of Angola. It is flat. The Spanish colonizers destroyed nearly all the woods long ago, so there was practically nowhere to fight except in the Sierra Maestra; it is a large, unpopulated mountain range, around 80 kilometers long but only 20 kilometers wide. That was where the struggle was waged. Sometimes, they threw 10,000 soldiers against us and we could depend on only those who had weapons, because a soldier without weapons isn't worth anything in organizing your defense.
>
> "Even so, we inflicted many losses on the enemy, because we had a lot of experience. We knew how to make the best use of the terrain,

---

[10] *El Che en la Revolución Cubana*, 386.

and the main factor on our side was the moral superiority our guerrillas had over the army of Batista, the oppressing army. That's something basic you have to achieve.

"If you will let me tell you this — without any pretensions and based on the experience that I have placed at the service of such a noble cause as yours — the most difficult problem is to get a man in the mountains to become a guerrilla. I think that's a basic problem.

"Somebody who isn't in the mountains — or in any other area of operations — isn't a guerrilla. A guerrilla is someone who has already learned to adapt to their environment and use whatever it offers them and who has lost their fear of the enemy army. This is something that isn't achieved overnight, and nobody is born a hero. Heroism isn't something that is planted.

"Heroism is a part of ideological work, of the work of constant teaching, of the example set by your leaders. This way, you can create an army that can overthrow the oppressing army.

"At first, we used to run away. When the planes came, we would run; when the tanks came, we would run; and we even ran away from the soldiers. We weren't an army of heroes; we were far from that. But, in the end, our relatively small group overthrew the army of the dictatorship. The Rebel Army destroyed it in pitched battles; we seized the cities and forced Batista's army to surrender.

"That process took two years of fighting, failures, new starts and privations, holding firm to our faith in victory, to make those who were in the mountains the backbone of the entire movement. They were the ones who determined the success of the struggle, and they were the ones who had to be given our full attention, not forgetting that later they would be the cadres who were required to handle whatever situations arose in spheres such as public health. In short, those who would have to handle everything you can prepare for. The guerrilla force was the key to victory. If you don't give them attention, if you don't send them the best cadres, if there isn't a clear awareness of what the strategy should be and what guerrilla tactics should be followed, and if you don't have fighting as your main school for guerrillas, victory will be at least slower. This is the experience we have. I have already told you it wasn't very extensive — only two years — but it was very valuable. Now, we have enriched it more with contacts in other countries who have waged revolutions of their own. And all of us agree on the main things.

"It may be useful to you."

The Angolans also asked for instructors for the guerrillas, weapons and money. On behalf of the Cuban Government, Che promised to grant their request.

On January 8, 1965, Che was in Guinea, which had won its independence from France in 1958. He met with President Sékou Touré, who had a leftist position and was in favor of helping the African liberation movements. During his stay, Che went with Touré to a meeting with Senghor a Labe, President of Senegal, on the border between Senegal and Guinea.

President Kwame Nkrumah of Ghana also met with Che and his companions. As in the earlier talks, the results were positive. They had arrived in Ghana on January 14. During his stay, which lasted until January 24, Che was interviewed by a journalist from the Ghanian daily *L'Etancel* and by the representative of Prensa Latina news agency. In that interview, he said:

> On several occasions, we have ratified our identification with the progressive African countries, but we don't know much about Africa. Now, we will learn more, to give the Cuban Party a clear idea of the needs and possibilities of the African countries that are advancing together and have economic ties with us.[11]

In addition, Che spoke at a Press Club gathering, where he stated clearly, "We should meet more often and exchange experiences so we can be better prepared in order to fight against our common enemy."[12]

On January 24, the Cuban delegation went to the capital of Dahomey. In press interviews, Che referred to the strong African influence — mainly from this country — on Cuban culture, because Cuba had many descendants of slaves who had come from what is now Dahomey. From there, he wrote to his daughter Hildita:

> My Darling,
> Here's a photo of a friend of yours from school. I don't know if you'll recognize him. I'm in Dahomey. Look for it on the map. Hugs for everybody, and a big kiss for you from your Daddy[13]

On January 27, 1965, he was back in Algeria. Two days later, he told the daily *Alger Ce-Soir*, "The greatest danger of neocolonialism isn't its most visible aspect. To the contrary, it is the false veneer of development which pretends to be brilliant and rapid."[14]

---

[11] *Revolución*, January 19, 1965.
[12] *Revolución*, January 20, 1965.
[13] Hilda Gadea, *Che Guevara, años decisivos*, 211.
[14] *Política Internacional*, no. 9, January-March 1965, 197.

ANTONIO CARRILLO (Cuban Ambassador to France when Che visited Paris in February 1965): I went from Paris to Algeria with Osmany Cienfuegos and Aragonés, and they met with Che there. That was at the beginning of February. Then I returned to France, and Major Guevara returned to Paris with Osmany, Aragonés, Papito and, I think, Manresa, on the 6th of that month. That was when they visited the Louvre.

The Chinese Ambassador gave a dinner for Che and the members of his delegation. The next day, they went to Pakistan, where the Chinese had a plane waiting to take them to China. They returned to Algeria through Cairo. I don't think Che ever visited Paris again.

On February 6, 1965, Che arrived in China. He later wrote: "The trip to China was a very brief one, to discuss a series of views with the Chinese Party. The discussions were with Liu Chao Chi and practically all of the Party Secretariat. I was there for four or five days. We presented our mutual points of view. There was nothing special. From the economic point of view, we entered into a long-term agreement for exchanging opinions to see if, finally, we could develop some specific aspects of mutual assistance. Then [illegible in original] they already know. There is nothing new about it."[15]

Che doesn't waste time

Thanks to modern communications, it took only a few minutes to span the thousands of miles between Algiers and Havana. Che reported on the need to start choosing personnel for the assistance that some of the African liberation movements had requested. The Cuban revolutionary leadership immediately gave instructions to locate members of the Cuban Armed Forces who were willing to go on such a mission.

Thus, following orders, Major Víctor Dreke went to the office of the head of the Army one afternoon in late January. Dreke was a pleasant, thin 27-year-old black Cuban of medium height who had been second in command of the Fight against Bands of Counterrevolutionaries (LCB) in the Central Army — in the old provinces of Camagüey and Las Villas and part of what is now Matanzas Province. During the struggle against the Batista dictatorship he had been a student in his home town of Sagua la Grande, in Las Villas Province, where he had joined the July 26 Movement. In line with the unity pact between the July 26 Movement and the March 13 Revolutionary Directorate, he joined the guerrillas in the Escambray mountains and served under the Directorate from the time Che arrived in Las Villas heading the Ciro Redondo Column until

---

[15] *El Che en la Revolución Cubana*, 392.

the end of the war.

Dreke was given a brief explanation. If he accepted, he would be in charge of choosing around 50 of the men who had fought in the LCB, but all had to be black Cubans who were willing to carry out an internationalist mission. Similar selections were also being made from among members of the Eastern and Western Armies and units of the High Command. A few days later, Dreke and the men he had chosen were taken to the mountains in Pinar del Río Province.

Some days earlier, another group of black soldiers, chosen from the units of the Western Army, had traveled to the same place from Las Mercedes, in Santiago de las Vegas, under the command of Lieutenant Normando Agramonte.

Dreke was driven to Pinar del Río by Ulises Estrada, who gave him additional, secret details about the mission and told him that Fidel Castro had decided that he, Dreke, should be in charge. According to Dreke, they reached the Piti 1 Camp on February 2.

A few days later, a large number of black soldiers from Oriente Province, headed by Captain Santiago Terry Rodríguez, were taken to Pinar del Río from the Ministry of the Revolutionary Armed Forces in Havana. Emilio Mena, from a Havana unit, went with them. He was amazed to see so many blacks from Oriente.

ERASMO VIDEAUX: We left Santiago de Cuba and went to Havana, where we were taken to the La Tropical Stadium. There, we got into closed trucks, which took us to the Candelaria Hills, in Pinar del Río. When I got up in the morning, I found a lot of people I knew.

DREKE: The next day, after breakfast, I ordered the men to form ranks, and I organized the column. [Santiago] Terry was named second in command, and Catalino Olachea, Normando Agramonte and Erasmo Videaux, chiefs of the platoons from the Central Army, the Western Army and High Command, and the Eastern Army. After that, I talked to the men explaining that we would be going on an internationalist mission, so their documents would have to be prepared. Nobody had been told what the mission was and I couldn't tell them where we were going. I told them it was important for them to create close ties, even though they had come from different commands. When I ordered them to break ranks, they began to hug one another.

Corporal Wagner Moro Pérez jubilantly told others, "Damn, but there are a lot of blacks! Somebody picked up all the blacks in Cuba and brought them here." Wagner would lose his life while carrying out the mission.

In Algiers, Che spent a few more days gathering information about Africa and preparing to go to Tanzania. A few days before February 15, his daughter Hildita's birthday, he wrote her:

My Darling,
When you get this letter, I'll be in an African country and you will be 9 years old. I send you this little present as a keepsake. I don't know if it's the right size or too big, but it ought to fit on one of your fingers.

I very much want to see you. I have been away for two months, and everything will be a little changed.

Let's see if you're an exemplary student this year, too, to impress me and your mom.

Here's a big kiss and a bear hug from your dad, who loves you. Greetings to everybody.[16]

From his February 18, 1965, statement in Dar es Salaam, where he had arrived the week before, we know that Che must have gone to another country besides Algeria, Mali, Dahomey, the Congo (Brazzaville), Guinea and Ghana before visiting Tanzania. Serguera says it was Zanzibar, which hadn't yet joined with Tanganyika.

In his talks with the leaders of several of the countries he visited, Che noted that some of them were motivated by personal ambitions and tribal rivalries, as a result of ancestral divisions which the colonialists had stirred up.

PABLO RIVALTA: When I was named Cuban Ambassador to Tanzania, Fidel and Che told me to establish very close relations with the government of that country and to contact the representatives of African liberation movements who lived in Dar es Salaam, and that is what I did. Kabila, Mukjumba and Tchamlesso were the first with whom I established contact. Later, I got to know Soumialot. I didn't know the other Congolese leaders.

I remember that Serguera accompanied Che. I obtained an interview for Che with President Julius Nyerere during a reception at the Palace. He also talked with Oscar Salathiel Cambona, Minister of Foreign Relations; Minister of the Interior Lucinde; Vice-President Kawawa; and Babu, the head of Zanzibar. He made a great impression on them. Later, he met with all who said they represented the liberation movements of the various African countries.

---

[16] Hilda Gadea, *Che Guevara, años decisivos*, 209.

Beginning of the dream

Pasajes de la guerra revolucionaria. Congo [Episodes of the Revolutionary War: Congo – cited throughout this book as *Congo]*, Che Guevara's previously unpublished manuscript, contains the following about his participation in the Congolese guerrilla war:

CHE: In this kind of analysis, it's difficult to pinpoint where it all began. In my account, I considered it to have been a journey I took to Africa, in the course of which I had an opportunity to rub shoulders with many of the liberation movement leaders. My visit to Dar es Salaam, where many freedom fighters lived, most of them comfortably installed in hotels, was particularly instructive. They had turned their situation into a veritable profession – a job that was nearly always comfortable and sometimes lucrative. The meetings were held in that atmosphere. In general, they asked for military training in Cuba and financial assistance. That was the recurring theme of nearly all of them.

I also met the group of Congolese combatants. Right from the first meeting, I noted the tremendous number of different opinions and trends which characterized the group of leaders of the Congolese revolution. First, I made contact with Kabila and his Staff; he made an excellent impression on me. He said he didn't come from the capital; it seems that he was from Kigoma, a Tanzanian town on Lake Tanganyika, one of the main scenes of this account. It served as a bridge for crossing to the Congo and also as a comfortable home and refuge for the revolutionaries, who were tired of the more or less difficult life in the mountains on the other side of the strip of water.

Kabila made a clear, specific, firm presentation of his views. He hinted at his opposition to Gbenye and Kanza and at how little he agreed with Soumialot. Kabila's theme was that it wasn't possible to speak of a Congolese Government, because Mulele – who had begun the struggle – hadn't been consulted, and that, therefore, the President could only hold the title of Head of Government of the northeastern part of the Congo. With that statement, he also left his own area – which was in the southeastern part of the country and which he led as Vice-President of the Party – outside Gbenye's influence.

Kabila was well aware that the main enemy was U.S. imperialism and said that he would struggle against it to the end. As I have already noted, his statements and serious tone made a very good impression on me.

Another day, we spoke with Soumialot. He was a different man, much less politically developed and much older. He barely had the primary instinct of remaining silent or speaking little, with vague phrases, with which he seemed to express a great subtlety of thinking, but, the harder he tried, he couldn't impress anyone as a real leader. He explained what he stated publicly later on: his participation as Minister of Defense in the Gbenye Administration, how the eastern action took them by surprise, etc. He also clearly stated his opposition to Gbenye and, above all, to Kanza. Apart from a brief handshake with Kanza when we met in an airport, I didn't meet these figures.

We spoke with Kabila for a long time about what our government considered a strategic mistake by some African friends — their use of the slogan "The problem of the Congo is an African problem" when faced with manifest aggression by the imperialist powers. We thought that the problem of the Congo was a problem of the world, and Kabila agreed. In the name of the [Cuban] Government, I offered him around 30 instructors and whatever weapons we had, and he was very happy to accept. He urged speed in sending both, as Soumialot did also, in another discussion; the latter recommending that the instructors should be black. [*Pasajes de la guerra revolucionaria. Congo*, 4-5.] ·

GODEFREI TCHAMLESSO (of the Congolese Liberation Movement, now living in Cuba): We sat down and talked. After that conversation, Kabila explained the characteristics of the Movement to Che, its origins and the state it was in at that time. Then the sending of a group of trainers and weapons was suggested.

When asked who was helping us with weapons, we said that they were sent from China and that our combatants were being trained there, too. Bulgaria was also training some of our people, especially in light artillery.

During his talk with Kabila, Che proposed the following: to train a group of combatants from the liberation movement of the Portuguese colonies starting with the Eastern Front and including Mondelane's Mozambican Liberation Front (FRELIMO) and some people who might come from the MPLA in Brazzaville, groups with which he had already made contact.

Kabila expressed some reservations about incorporating groups of combatants from other countries who didn't have support in the United Nations — such as those who were fighting against Portuguese colonialism, which still existed at that time — in a movement that was fighting against neocolonialism. He said that could lead to a powerful attack on our guerrilla forces, because we would be accused of raising the level of subversion throughout Africa. Many peoples, especially the Portuguese colonies, still had colonial relations. He was very reluctant about that, I can tell you. But he said that if that was the price we had to pay to get international assistance for fighting against the mercenaries paid by Tshombe, then we would accept that assistance. He told me that privately.

That is, Che suggested three things: assistance in weapons, training and organizing the front with maximum security for receiving international combatants and eventually including or incorporating the people of FRELIMO and the MPLA and training them there. As I have told you, there were some reservations to this, especially from Kabila.

JUAN CARRETERO (head of the Latin America Section of the Intelligence Department of the Cuban Ministry of the Interior): I was sent to see Major Che Guevara while he was visiting Africa; because of the position he held, he had to be informed about the situation of the movements in Latin America. I was to do this because my section was in charge of intelligence and operations helping the national liberation movements in Latin America. Our relations began when I was to go to Bolivia in 1963 to take charge of the Center there, which was handling two important assistance operations.

I went to Brazil with Olo Pantoja. We went to the Butantan Institute in São Paulo, which was doing research on snakes, trying to produce vaccines and other medicines against various jungle diseases. There, I made contact with a liaison of [Ricardo] Masseti's, who took me to see the future guerrillas who had come from Algeria, and we checked the plan for entering Bolivia. Later, I went to La Paz, to contact two comrades and create the conditions for bringing revolutionaries into Argentina.

From then on, I stayed in La Paz as head of the Center and liaison between the movement and the Cubans. The members of the Bolivian Communist Party, the brothers Inti and Coco Peredo and Rodolfo Saldaña supported this work. Later, Jorge Vázquez Viaña, known as Bigote (moustache) or Loro (parrot), and some others joined me. At about that time, the Peruvians who had gathered in Bolivia went back to their country up the Madre de Dios River. After several days of hard marching through the jungle, the guerrilla group ran short of food, which caused generalized exhaustion, and the Army caught them off guard. The poet Javier Heraud was killed and the others were pursued and had to fall back to the Bolivian jungle.

Even though that wasn't part of the plan, I had to gather together those scattered combatants and weapons. The Communists I mentioned helped in that task. The police arrested most of the

Peruvian combatants, but a mass demonstration and efforts by the Paz Estenssoro Administration resulted in their being released and granted political asylum, after which they once again established themselves in a revolutionary organization. Luckily, there were good relations between the Bolivian and Cuban governments.

My ties with Major Guevara continued, because he was the one who had the most direct links with Operation Segundo Sombra, which was aimed at getting Che into Argentina. That never happened, because of the difficulties that movement had and its final liquidation. Later, I came back to Cuba and continued in my activities as head of the Latin America Section. I also continued my contacts with Che related to providing assistance to the revolutionary movements. That's why I took part in many meetings with him and many leaders of those organizations.

Those were our work relations, and that's why I was sent to Africa to inform him about what was going on in Latin America. I remember that I went to Algeria and didn't find him; when I learned that he was in Tanzania, I went to that country.

When I arrived in Dar es Salaam, I found Che at Ambassador Rivalta's home, playing dominoes with him, Papito Serguera and another comrade. He was very pleased when he learned of the progress of the various Latin American revolutionary movements.

During the several days of my visit, Che held a meeting in the Embassy with several leaders of the African liberation movements, and I participated in it. After that meeting, I lost contact with him, because he went to the Congo. That operation was carried out in a continent I didn't have any relations with.

CHE: I decided to size up how the other freedom fighters felt, planning to hold separate meetings and friendly chats with them. Somebody in the Embassy made a mistake and called them all together in one, disorderly meeting attended by 50 or more people representing the movements of 10 or more countries, each one divided into two or more splinter groups. I exhorted them, analyzing the requests which, almost without exception, they had made for financial assistance and training. I explained how much it cost to train one man in Cuba, the amount of money and time that would have to be invested and the limited guarantee there was that the people trained would prove to be useful fighters for the movement.

I told them about our experience in the Sierra Maestra mountains [in Cuba], where we got an average of one soldier out of every five recruits we trained, and one good one out of every five soldiers. I was vehement, telling the exasperated freedom fighters that the money invested in training was going to be largely wasted; soldiers can't be created in a military academy — especially not revolutionary soldiers. They are created in war. Someone can get a degree from a military academy, but their real graduation, like that of any other professional, comes in the exercise of their profession, through their reaction to enemy fire, suffering, defeat, continuous attacks and adverse situations. Neither someone's statements nor their prior history can tell you how they will react to all those accidents of struggle in a people's war. Therefore, I suggested that they be trained not in distant Cuba but in the nearby Congo, where they were fighting not against that two-bit puppet Tshombe but against U.S. imperialism, whose neocolonialism was threatening the recently acquired independence of nearly all the peoples of Africa as well as subjugating those colonies which remained. I told them that we considered the liberation struggle of the Congo to be of basic importance. Victory would have a continent-wide effect and repercussions — as, too, would defeat.

Their reaction was extremely chilly. Even though most of them didn't make any comments, some asked for the floor to reproach me violently for that advice. They said that their people, mistreated and debased by imperialism, would protest if anybody was killed in a war to free another country, rather than by the oppressors in their own country. I tried to make them see that in Africa it was a matter not of fighting within national boundaries but of waging war against our common enemy, which was omnipresent both in Mozambique and in Malawi, Rhodesia, South Africa, the Congo and Angola. However, nobody understood it that way.

They gave us a cold but courteous good-bye, leaving a clear impression on us that [illegible]. Africa had a long way to go before it achieved real revolutionary maturity, but I was always glad to have met people who were willing to keep on fighting to the end. Our next task was to choose a group of black Cubans and send them — voluntarily, of course — to buttress the Congo's struggle. [*Congo*, 5-6.]

PABLO RIVALTA: Later, we met with President Nyerere about the assistance that Cuba would give to the Congolese Liberation Movement and the Tanzanian Government's agreement to that — to allow and protect the passage of what the Cubans sent to the Congo. Kawawa, Lucinde and Cambona were present at that meeting.

We said that, to ensure what had been agreed on, we would rent a house to serve as an embassy office and residence. Nyerere said I could visit him whenever necessary, but extraofficially. We discussed relations with the Israelis who were living in Dar es Salaam; they were friendly to the President, but Che didn't want anything to do with them. Che asked me to obtain information on the eastern part of the Congo and Lake Tanganyika and to establish relations with the authorities in Kigoma, a port in northwestern Tanzania across the Lake from the Congo. I was to also work to promote closer relations with the ministers and other government officials who knew about our plans and make contact with Army officers and others who might be useful at a given moment..

Create a common front of struggle

In spite of everything, on February 18, 1965, Che told Prensa Latina in the Tanzanian capital, "I am convinced that it is possible to create a common front of struggle against colonialism, imperialism and neo-colonialism."

He sent his daughter Hildita a postcard from Tanzania:

My Darling,
Here's another small reminder of your dad, who's now getting closer to Havana. This is the religious dance of a tribe of very proud people who have always fought for their freedom.
Here's a big kiss from your father. Greetings to your mom.[17]

ROGELIO OLIVA: I went to Tanzania with [Pablo] Rivalta in November 1963. Before that, along with other comrades who were to go there, I received some elementary instructions in security from [Manuel] Piñeiro's people. There was a comrade in our embassy in Dar es Salaam who was in charge of relations with the parties and liberation movements represented in that country. On Rivalta's instructions, he began to give me some tasks related to the representatives of those organizations, which is how I met Soumialot, Mojumba, Tchamlesso and Kabila.

My work made it necessary for me to study English and Swahili, the national language of Tanzania and Kenya and the language spoken by the Congolese living in the areas bordering on the Lake, especially in the area where Che was located. They also spoke Kigongo and Kibembe. Later, I also learned French, because the Belgians speak it.

Che's visit was the first such official one. I was his driver, but I can't say that I took part in what was discussed. I also served as Swahili translator in some of the places he visited. Later, I learned something about the assistance that Cuba was going to give the Congolese, because Rivalta got us busy on that as soon as Che left.

---

[17] Hilda Gadea, *Che Guevara, años decisivos*, 212.

He explained it to the comrades who were working with the liberation movements. That's when they began to give me things to do, even though I wasn't told in detail what the purpose was. I found out that my pseudonym would be David. My mission was to go to Kigoma and enter the Congo together with Tchamlesso to make a study of that area. I had a camera and took several photos. A jeep was purchased for the trip.

The first thing we had to investigate was the state of the roads. We arrived at Kigoma at dawn and contacted the Governor, since he knew about the assistance Cuba was giving the Congolese guerrillas. Then Tchamlesso spoke with the boatmen he knew and hired one to take us across the Lake. We left that same day, at around 9 in the morning. The pseudonym I used for the Congolese was Seremano, which is a religious greeting.

We informed the Ambassador and those in charge of working with the liberation movements about our mission. The other task was to buy knapsacks, boots, coats and other things for the guerrillas. We couldn't buy everything all at once but had to have different comrades make small purchases so as not to arouse suspicion. We also bought a van with a removable canvas top.

Che returned to Algiers, where he participated in the 2nd Economic Seminar of Afro-Asian Solidarity. Osmany Cienfuegos and Ambassador Rivalta were also there. On February 24, Che addressed the meeting, setting forth his views on how to wage the struggle to build socialism in the countries that wanted to do so.

The socialist countries should help pay for the development of the underdeveloped countries, we agree. But the underdeveloped countries should be mobilized and set out firmly along the path to the construction of a new society — it doesn't matter what name you give it — in which machines, the tools of labor, won't be the tools for any man's exploitation of another. Moreover, you can't expect the socialist countries to trust you when you swing back and forth between capitalism and socialism, pitting those forces against each other so as to benefit from their rivalry. A new policy of absolute seriousness should govern the relations between the two groups of societies.[18]

Che also visited Cairo. In order to get there they flew to Paris, and when they were on the plane and the flight attendant saw Che, she said, "Look at that crazy guy pretending he's Che Guevara." They heard similar

---

[18] *El Che en la Revolución Cubana*, vol. 7, 365.

comments on the streets of Paris.

Che met with Nasser for the second time during that visit to Cairo. The Egyptian President invited Che to tour the country with him, since he was in the midst of campaigning. They took advantage of that trip to discuss plans for helping liberate the African countries. Nasser felt the same way as the other heads of state with whom Che had talked. The only thing was that, even though he agreed with everything, Nasser thought that it was a very difficult undertaking. Those leaders weren't told that Cuba was willing to supply soldiers, weapons and other kinds of assistance.

The next day, on returning to Cairo, Che began a series of meetings with various Egyptian government officials. There were good relations between the Egyptian rulers and Che — especially Nasser's supporters. Colman Ferrer was another of the diplomats who went with Che and his companions. Later, Ferrer was one of those chosen to protect the rear guard of the Cuban internationalists who went to the Congo.

ARNOLD RODRIGUEZ: From Cairo, Che went back to Havana via Prague. Engine trouble kept us in the Shannon airport for two days. At his initiative, we went to the city one night to try to see a cowboy movie, but we couldn't find one. Osmany Cienfuegos and Roberto Fernández Retamar, who had boarded the plane in Prague, went with us. To kill time, we went into a bar and asked for beer. When my mug was still nearly full, somebody bumped me, and the beer slopped all over Che. He smiled, made a dry comment, and, after he and Osmany had wisecracked some more about the incident, ordered another beer for me.

Return to Cuba

Che returned to Cuba on the evening of Sunday, March 14. He was wearing his black beret and olive green jacket and had an olive green coat over his arm and a black suitcase in his hand. Osmany followed him down the plane's ramp. Aleida March, Che's wife; Hildita, his daughter from his previous marriage; Fidel Castro; President Osvaldo Dorticós; Carlos Rafael Rodríguez; Emilio Aragonés; Orlando Borrego; and other officials from the Ministry of Industry were at the airport to welcome him home.

The U.S. Department of State, Director of Intelligence and Research, on April 19, 1965, issued a 12-page report on "Che Guevara's African Venture," discussing "Cuba's growing interest in the dark continent." In closing, it described the trip as a modest success, pointing out that Che carried Cuba's message to meetings with high-ranking officials and reiterated it in speeches and interviews. The report concluded that his visit helped Cuba to forge closer relations with Algeria and that Che received several invitations to attend future African conferences, including the Afro-Asian Peoples' Solidarity Organization (AAPSO) conference programmed for May 1965 in Ghana.

The report wound up by saying that the Cubans must have been very pleased with the AAPSO communiqué, which seemed to reflect a considerable Cuban influence in its call on the Afro-Asian nations to "strengthen their ties in all fields with the revolutionary countries of Latin America, especially Cuba."

It was followed by an appendix with the chronology of Che's trip. However, there was no mention of the fact that Che was personally willing to fight in Africa. It can only be assumed that the authors of the report couldn't imagine that someone who had risen to such a high position would be willing to leave everything and go fight for an oppressed people.

A CIA document, dated January 31, 1964, reported on Cuba's supposed training of and support for African nationalists, saying that Cuba was involved in the coup in Zanzibar. This was not true. The only truth in the report concerned the scholarships that Cuba was giving to African students.

The background to events — Act One

In his manuscript — on which I have drawn heavily in this book, supplementing it with testimony, documents and photos — Che called everything related to his contacts with the "revolutionary" Congolese leaders "Act One." That manuscript is dedicated "To Bahasa and his fallen comrades, trying to find meaning for their sacrifice."

Those who have wondered why nothing had been written before now about Che's participation in the Congolese guerrilla struggle will find the answer in the second paragraph of the preface to his manuscript.

CHE: This is the account of a failure. It goes into anecdotal detail, as is done with war episodes, but it is colored by observations and a critical spirit, since I believe that if this account has any importance, it is to provide a series of experiences that may be useful to other revolutionary movements. Victory is a great source of positive experiences, but so is defeat. This is especially so, in my opinion, when, as in this case, the participants and others providing information are foreigners who go to risk their lives in an unknown land where a different language is spoken and to which they are joined only by bonds of proletarian internationalism, inaugurating a method not practiced in modern wars of liberation. The account closes with an epilogue which raises the questions of struggle in Africa and, in general, of national liberation struggles against the neocolonial form of imperialism. This new form of imperialism constitutes its most fearful manifestation, because of its camouflages and subtleties and the long experience the imperialist powers have in this kind of exploitation.

These notes will be published long after they are written, and, perhaps, the author won't be able to take responsibility for what is stated here. Time will have smoothed the edges, and, if their appearance has any importance, the editors may make whatever corrections are deemed necessary, making the pertinent footnotes to clarify events or opinions, in view of the time that has passed.

More correctly, this is the account of a collapse. When we arrived in Congolese territory, the revolution was taking a breather. Later, episodes occurred that led to its definitive regression.... What may be of interest here isn't the account of the collapse of the Congolese revolution, whose causes and characteristics go too deep to be described from my observation point. Rather, it is the process of the collpase of our fighting spirit... [Emphasis by W.G.] [*Congo*, 1.]

With the authority thus given to make "whatever corrections are deemed necessary," I have made some clarifications in brackets throughout this book. This is not to justify Che and his companions, but to situate the facts as they were and thus show Guevara's modesty, honesty and the significance of his account — qualities which he, as such, wouldn't mention.

The first of these is related to the sentence beginning the preface: "This is the account of a failure." He went on to qualify this, saying, "More correctly, this is the account of a collapse," and then added that it referred to the "Congolese revolution," which can be taken to cast aside failure. But he wound up the paragraph by equating himself and his companions in what he described as "the process of collapse of our fighting spirit." Che was aware that experiences — whether positive or negative — could and should provide useful lessons for the cause of the peoples' liberation. Here, self-criticism predominated in his analysis. An assessment of the human dimension of his own action wasn't important to him, for his own and his comrades' modesty prevented him from doing that.

CHE: Our idea was to have veterans of the struggle for Cuba's liberation — and, of course, against the counterrevolution — fight alongside men who didn't have experience and, by so doing, promote what we called the "Cubanization" of the Congolese. You will see here that the effect was precisely the opposite — how, in time, the Cubans were "Congolized." By this, I mean that they acquired a series of habits and attitudes toward the revolution that characterized Congolese soldiers in that period of the struggle. This doesn't imply any derogatory opinion of the Congolese people, but it does imply this view of the soldiers at that time. In the course of this account, I will also try to explain why those combatants had such negative characteristics. [*Congo*, 2.]

The idea didn't work out, not so much because of the "Congolization" of the Cubans, but because of failure of the Congolese to be "Cubanized," because most of them were totally ignorant of what a real revolution meant. The explanation will follow "in the course of this account."

CHE: As a general rule — a rule I have always followed — this will contain nothing but the truth, or, at least, my interpretation of what happened, although it may be challenged by other subjective views or corrections if errors slip into this account.

In some parts in which the truth may be indiscreet or inconvenient, the reference has been omitted, since there are things that the enemy shouldn't know. Here, I am setting forth problems which may help friends to eventually reorganize the struggle in the Congo (or in any other country in Africa or another continent with similar problems). The references that have been omitted include how we reached Tanzania, which was the jumping-off point for our entering the scene of this account. [*Congo*, 2.]

Those of us who have had the honor of having known Ernesto Che Guevara cannot doubt that everything he wrote was the truth. But, as he himself pointed out, some of his interpretations are challenged by "subjective views," and "errors slip into this account" in others. Now, years later, those indiscreet truths can be revealed.

I feel that the last paragraph of the preface should conclude Che's writing, so it has been included in the closing section of this book.

Other clarifications will be seen in the course of this work.

Hasty preparations — Act Two

CHE: Act Two began in Cuba and included some important episodes that cannot be clarified at the moment, such as why I was designated to head the Cuban group even though I was white, how the future combatants were chosen (the process was already under way), what preparations were made for my clandestine exit, the few farewells I could make and what explanatory letters were written — a whole series of hidden maneuvers which it is still dangerous to set down on paper and which, in any case, can be explained later on. [*Congo*, 7.]

What he couldn't set down on paper at the time was the following:

FIDEL: We never made this public. But the revolutionary movement [of the Congo] asked us for help, so we sent instructors and combatants on an internationalist mission... I myself suggested the idea to Che. He had time on his hands, he had to wait. At the same time, he wanted to train cadres, to develop their experience. So we put him in charge of the group that was going to help the revolutionaries in what is today Zaire.[19]

After putting his work in order, as a means of bidding farewell he went to the auditorium in the Ministry of Industry and gave a talk about the trip he had made to Africa. He was rested, happy and jocular. However, he couldn't hide his indignation over what was going on in Africa, especially the Congo. With the help of a map, he went into details. It was clear that he was very familiar with that region and with what was happening there, but he didn't let slip any hints that he wouldn't be back cutting sugarcane in a few days. He was about to leave to offer his "modest efforts" to that long-suffering land. It was his last public appearance in Cuba.

In the last week in March 1965, Che began to live in a residence in the La Coronela part of Havana. There, skilled hands cut his hair and shaved off his beard. He began to practice using the prosthetic devices which had been created to make his lips thicker as a disguise for his departure and for joining the guerrilla group in Argentina. Osmany Cienfuegos took several photos of him, including one for the passport that was being prepared for his new identity and appearance. Che also had to try on the civilian clothes that he would be using for several days.

Close to 500 black Cubans were chosen more for their willingness to carry out an internationalist mission anywhere in the world than for their military knowledge (their ranks ranged from major, which was the highest in Cuba's Armed Forces at that time, to private). They began to gather in camps in the mountains in Pinar del Río Province on February 2, 1965. Most of them had had some combat experience in the Rebel Army, armed conflict against bands of counterrevolutionaries in the early years of the Cuban Revolution, the battle against the mercenaries during the 1961 Bay of Pigs invasion and in other actions as members of State Security units. The members of the internationalist contingent who would fight in Africa would be selected from that group.

[19] Gianni Miná, *An Encounter with Fidel*, 223.

NORMANDO AGRAMONTE: During the training, which was tough, I was in the Piti 1, 2 and 3 camps. The preparation was very hard, including going on long marches with knapsacks, weapons, cartridge belts and canteens and going over obstacles and through dangling tree trunks. We also had a lot of rifle practice with different kinds of rifles, worked with light artillery, planted and deactivated mines, made Molotov cocktails, engaged in guerrilla warfare and had political classes.

Fidel and Raúl visited us. On one of those visits, Fidel had us shoot with rifles and demonstrated his proverbial skill.

Honorable substitution

DREKE: Most of the comrades went to Pinar del Río without saying good-bye to their families. After several days, during one of Fidel's visits, he called us together and gave us permission to go home for a visit. He asked all of us to be absolutely discreet. Some of the people didn't want to give us permission, but Fidel said, "We have to trust them; let them go." Around 100 comrades went to see their families, all of them returned in time and there wasn't any indiscretion.

By the end of March, those who were to go to the various African countries had been selected, though none of them knew for sure where they were going. Many of them realized that it would be one of the two Congos because, as Agramonte pointed out, they were given materials on those countries and on Lumumba's assassination. One hundred and thirteen internationalists were to go to the Congo (Leopoldville): 11 officers, 19 sergeants, 11 corporals and 72 privates. A column with a general staff, three infantry platoons and one of artillery was formed with the idea of training them.

A few days before the end of March, Osmany Cienfuegos, who was Minister of Public Works, visited the camp, took Dreke aside and told him, "Fidel has decided to appoint another comrade as head of the mission in the Congo." As he said this, he took a photo out of an envelope and showed it to him. "Look, this is the comrade. Do you know him?" Dreke looked at the photo, which showed a 40-year-old, close-shaven white man with a round face and glasses. He had straight black hair that was parted on one side and was plastered down, and he had a huge cigar in his mouth.

"Do you know him?" Osmany asked again.

Without taking his eyes from the photo, Dreke scratched his head and replied, "No, I don't know this man. I've never seen him in my life."

"But he knows you. Another thing, Fidel decided that you should go as second in command of the column. What do you think of that?"

"Tell Fidel that all I want is to go. I don't care if it's as head of the column, second in command or private. I don't want to be left behind."

Osmany came looking for Dreke on March 30. Under the plan, he was supposed to leave in the first few days of April, without knowing the exact date or who would go with him. They drove out of the camp and went to a large, comfortable country house — which had been owned by a member of the wealthy elite who had left Cuba — in the La Coronela part of Havana, several kilometers from the heart of the city. It was surrounded by a high wire fence covered with vines, which hid it from passers-by. On the way, they spoke about the training and details of the mission. Once inside the house, they walked to a small inner patio and sat down. Then Osmany told him, "I brought you to see the man in the photo. Remember? The one I showed you at the camp. Do you know him?"

"No, I really don't know who he is."

At that moment, a white man of medium height, wearing glasses, came into the patio from the living room and extended his hand to Dreke, who stood up to take it. Then the three sat down.

"Do you know him?" Osmany repeated.

"I already told you, I don't know him. By no means. I haven't even seen pictures of this man in the newspaper."

"Well, he's the comrade who's been appointed as head of the column."

The young black Cuban immediately asked the stranger who had just come in, "Do you need me to explain everything about the column?"

"No, we'll go into that later. We're going to tell you the truth. Osmany, don't tease Dreke any more!"

"Don't you know Che?" Osmany asked with a big smile.

Dreke leaped to his feet, and Che and Osmany burst out laughing.

"Well, we've run one more test with an old comrade, and he didn't recognize me," Che said.

"Really, if you hadn't told me, I wouldn't have known it was you," Dreke said, not yet recovered from his surprise.

They spoke some more about the disguise, and Dreke asked for permission to give Che details about the training of the column.

DREKE: As I spoke, I realized that he knew even the smallest details of the men's training, even though he wasn't with us — which he regretted. He told me that we would have long, hard sessions in tricky mountain terrain. He knew about the problems that had arisen, about the people who had to be weeded out and why, and about the work of the Party commission. He knew some of the comrades. Then Che set forth his ideas about the Congo with great enthusiasm: how we had to help them, how difficult the situation was, the country's history and what he had seen during his recent trip to Africa. He also gave me a Makarov pistol. I remember that Chino, his aide, was there. Che also asked about my daughter, who was sick. That concern showed his great humanity.

The next day, I saw Che doing exercises. Later, he spent a long time writing letters, occasionally tearing up and burning the pages. As he said in his letter to Fidel, "I've thrown away enough rough drafts." He spent a long time writing letters — there were a lot of them. I wrote one myself, in case anything happened.

He also left several books to some of his dearest friends as mementos. For example, he left *El ingenio* by Manuel Moreno Fraginals, to Alberto Granado, writing in it: "I don't know what to leave you as a memento, so I'm forcing you to learn about sugarcane. My mobile home will have two feet once again, and my dreams will have no bounds, at least until bullets put them there. I'll be waiting for you, sedentary gypsy, when the smell of gunpowder lessens. Hugs for all of you and for Tomás. Che"

He gave several volumes on economics to Orlando Borrego, including *Capital*. All have commentaries written in the margins. In one of the volumes of *Capital*, Che wrote: "Borrego, this is the source. Here, we learned everything together by fits and starts, seeking what is still barely an intuition. Now that I am going to do my duty and what I long to do, and you remain doing your duty but not what you long to do, I leave you this as proof of my friendship, which hasn't been put into words very often. Thank you for your staunchness and loyalty. May nothing separate you from the way. A hug. Che."

He left *Vuelo nocturno*, by Antoine de Saint-Exupery, to his pilot, Eliseo de la Campa, with this inscription: "For Eliseo, friend and comrade on my first adventure in night flying. In memory of always. Che, Havana, 1965."

DREKE: The night before we left Cuba, Fidel came to say good-bye to Che and the rest of us. They had a long talk, and Osmany took a picture of them together. Then Fidel spoke with José María Martínez Tamayo (Papi), who had arrived a little after the rest of us, and me, stressing, "You have to see to it that Che reaches the Congo without any trouble... Remember that you have to go through several countries. You must protect him and ensure that nothing happens to him."

Three R's heading for the Congo

The morning of Thursday, April 1, 1965, was cool, the tail end of Cuba's mild winter, so the future travelers didn't find their suits too hot when they got into the car. Dreke and Papi sat in back, and Che, wearing a hat, in front. Osmany was in the driver's seat. When they left the camp, they turned right onto the Mediodía Highway and, after driving several kilometers, turned left toward the town of Wajay, heading for Rancho Boyeros Avenue and José Martí International Airport. Osmany parked in front of a house in front of the airport. Enio Leiva, who was in charge of handling the travelers' departure, came out immediately. He spoke with Che and Osmany and then withdrew.

DREKE: When we got to the airport, we were given copies of a newspaper whose front-page, banner headline was "Unrationed Eggs in Cuba." You know how we Cubans are; we joked about it.[20]

There, we were given our passports. Che's new name was Ramón Benítez. Papi's was Ricardo something — I don't remember his last name — and mine was Roberto Suárez Milián. In previous interviews, I said it was Roberto Salceiro Tapia, but that was a mistake; it was the name on the other passport I had, to be used in case of need. I think that each of the others also had a passport in reserve. Since all of our names began with the same letter, we were called "the three R's."

They stayed at the house for around 30 minutes, until they were told they could go to the plane. The three walked to the plane. Each carried a piece of hand luggage in one hand and had a winter overcoat over his other arm.

CHE: I left behind almost 11 years of work for the Cuban Revolution at Fidel's side, a happy home — if you can call the house of a revolutionary who is dedicated to his work a "home" — and a lot of kids [three girls and two boys] who were barely aware of my love. The cycle was renewed. [*Congo*, 7.]

He also set aside, though only for a short time, his olive green uniform, belt and pistol, black beret and lace-up boots.

The plane made an hour-long mechanical stopover in Gander. When the landing was announced, Che quietly went to the bathroom. There, he took out the troublesome prosthetic devices and waited until he was the last one to leave the plane; his comrades were waiting for him. A cold wind caught them as they left its shelter. To avoid meeting a journalist on board the same flight, they sat in a corner of the large waiting room filled with display cases. Che kept reading a book in French on the Congo. Time passed, and the loudspeakers announced the

---

[20] Translator's note: "Eggs" in Spanish also means "balls."

continuation of the Cubana flight to Prague, where the plane landed several hours later. Che and his companions were again the last to leave the plane. A Cuban intelligence officer was waiting for them in the airport.

Unrationed eggs

Dreke said that Papi was the one who made the contacts and knew the man who would be waiting for them. He also had photos of the people to contact in each country. The person waiting wanted to have them go to the room for incoming passengers, but Papi said he should put them somewhere apart from the others and get them out of there as quickly as possible. When the official didn't do as requested, Papi insisted, and the other man, who didn't know who they really were, asked jokingly, "What's the matter? Are you afraid?"

Dreke smiled at him and, showing him the Cuban newspaper that he was carrying, replied, "Look what it says here: 'Unrationed Eggs in Cuba.' We've got what it takes."

That made their host think a bit, and he took them to a small protocol room. Then he left and came back quickly. Since they had nothing but hand luggage, the delay was a short one. The official then drove them to a house on the outskirts of Prague and stayed with them during the two days they remained there — without leaving the house — while waiting for the next twice-weekly flight to Egypt. Che spent all the time in his room reading, especially a French dictionary, and writing. He also asked that certain books be purchased. Staying cooped up, he could remove the prosthetic devices and have some respite. He left his room only for meals.

They left Prague the same way they had come, but with the advantage that they didn't meet any Cubans who might recognize them. Several hours later, they arrived in Milan. The cold weather continued. They stayed in the waiting room for an hour, until the plane resumed its flight to Cairo, which they reached the next day. They had gone from a cold climate to a hot one. There was also a change in clothing, for robes, turbans and veils now prevailed. It was Che's fourth visit to the Egyptian capital; the others had been of an official nature, in June 1959 and in February and March 1965.

Nobody recognized him

JOSE A. ARBEZU: I was an adviser in the Cairo embassy, but I worked in intelligence. One morning when the Ambassador was in Cuba I received a cable instructing me to meet some agricultural technicians who were on their way to Tanzania. The three "technicians" arrived that evening. I put them up in a hotel; I don't remember its name, but it was a good one, which our embassy used a lot. It wasn't very centrally located. They had to wait there until the middle of the night to catch the plane for Dar es Salaam. I knew Dreke and Papi, and I supposed that something special had been or was going on. Naturally, they didn't tell me anything, and I didn't ask.

I had never seen the other man. He was very quiet; he didn't say anything. I asked who the weird guy was, and they told me he was a Russian, an agricultural technician. That is, they spun me a yarn, and I swallowed it whole. They asked me to get them some cigarettes, and I bought some in the hotel. When it was time to eat, he didn't come down, but ate in his room. The others told me he didn't feel well, he had a headache, and they'd take him some food. I said good-bye and left. I went back to get them at around 2:00 a.m., and we went to the airport. We were there for a while, and then they left. They were in Cairo for less than a day. When Che had visited Cairo before, I'd spoken with him a few times, but, honestly, that time I didn't recognize him.

According to Colman Ferrer, they left on April 5, for he was one of the passengers on that same flight to Dar es Salaam. Without knowing why, Colman Ferrer had been transferred to the Cuban Embassy in Tanzania, to be secretary there. He thought it was because Pablo Rivalta, the Cuban Ambassador in Dar es Salaam, who had been in Cairo, had requested his services, but he was far off the mark. He didn't recognize the "agricultural technicians," but the one called Ramón Benítez remembered the thin diplomat, whom he had met during his earlier visits to Cairo.

The plane made a stopover in Nairobi, Kenya. Since the sun was well up, Colman Ferrer took some footage of his three unknown traveling companions with his 8-mm movie camera. A few days later, he learned that one of them was Che. Colman told me that he kept the film for many years but that it was lost in one of his many moves.

Shortly before landing, the passengers were impressed by seeing 5,895-meter-high Mount Kilimanjaro (also called *Uhuru*, or Freedom), which very few people have climbed. Before lining up with the landing strip, the plane made a sweep over the Indian Ocean, making it easy to see the beautiful beach, the narrow-mouthed sack-like bay and Dar es Salaam, a medium-sized city that melted into its surroundings.

RIVALTA: I had informed Nyerere that Cubans were being sent to the Congo as instructors, and he was in agreement with that. The United Arab Republic also approved, after I went to that country to arrange for our people to go through there without any problems.

A few meters from the plane's ramp, Ambassador Rivalta — a tall, robust black Cuban with a big smile, wearing a dark blue safari suit, in the latest African fashion — and Juan Rodríguez, the adviser, were waiting, as requested in the cable from Havana, to meet three fellow countrymen. The embassy in Cairo had also informed them of Colman's arrival. Both knew of the mission they were to carry out and had been anxiously awaiting their arrival for some days. However, they didn't know who had been selected for the job — much less, who had been appointed as the chief.

CHE: One fine day, I appeared in Dar es Salaam. Nobody recognized me — not even the Ambassador, an old comrade in the struggle who had been a captain of the Rebel Army with me when we marched westward and should have been able to see through my disguise. [*Congo*, 7.]

RIVALTA: I received a cable saying that three comrades would be arriving. I didn't know who they were, but I did know why they had come.

I told the Tanzanians, because the airport was operated by Indians. To facilitate airport procedures, I spoke with the Ministers of Foreign Relations and the Interior, who knew what it was about and who went there themselves, though they didn't see the comrades. I knew Dreke, but not Martínez Tamayo. When I looked at the other one, I thought, "I've seen that face before." I kept staring at him until Che came over and told me under his breath, "Stop being a fool, and take it easy."

Just imagine! When I was no longer doubtful but sure, it was worse. I almost peed in my pants. There wasn't any real cover, and we weren't prepared to receive such an important person. We got in my car and went to a hotel. They spent the first night there. That was because I had instructions not to take anybody to the Embassy. Che's biggest worry at that moment was if a launch had been purchased for crossing the Lake, and I had to take him to the port early in the morning to try out the one we were thinking of buying. When he gave it his OK, we closed the deal. A small boat technician had been sent from Cuba to choose one. The next day, we went to a house in the country that we had bought. It was about four or five kilometers from the city, and Oliva was in charge of it.

CHE: We settled in at a small farm that had been rented to house us while we waited for the group of 30 men who were supposed to come. Up until then, there were three of us: Moja [Dreke], a black major, who was officially the head of the troops; Mbili [José María Martínez Tamayo], a white comrade with a lot of experience in this kind of fighting; and Tatu (that was me), who served as doctor. I explained my color by speaking French and having guerrilla experience. Our names meant one, two and three, in that order. To save ourselves headaches, we decided to number ourselves in the order we arrived and use the corresponding Swahili numbers as our names. [*Congo*, 7.]

At that time in Havana, Fidel Castro, Manuel Piñeiro and Osmany Cienfuegos went to a house in Nuevo Vedado and bade farewell to the comrades in the second group. Fidel saw them off in small groups, not all together, and he filled them with his tremendous optimism. "When you get to the Congo, you'll find a leader who's like me," he said.

DREKE: The others began to arrive in Tanzania three or four days later. They left Cuba in twos and threes, taking different air routes and going through different countries. People said there was a flood of blacks through those places, all with the same suitcases and wearing identical suits. They looked like a bunch of musicians. Che had thought of entering with the largest possible number of Cubans, foreseeing that, if the enemy learned of the crossing, it would close the Lake border. But, since it took so long for the people to arrive, he said that 10 or 15 were enough to start with.

The first problems

CHE (TATU): I hadn't told any Congolese about my decision to fight here or of my presence. I couldn't do so in my first talk with Kabila, because nothing had been decided, and then, after the plan was approved, it would have been dangerous if he had known of my plan before I had arrived there; there was a lot of hostile territory to be crossed. Therefore, I decided to present a fait accompli and to act in accord with how they reacted to my presence. I didn't lose sight of the fact that a refusal would place me in a difficult position, since I couldn't return, but I also figured that it would be difficult for them to refuse. I was blackmailing them with my presence.

However, there was one problem we hadn't thought of. Kabila, like all the other members of the Revolutionary Government, was in Cairo, discussing aspects of the unity of struggle and the new constitution of the revolutionary organization. Masengo and Mitudidi, his seconds, were with him. The only one left here was a representative named Chamaleso [Tchamlesso], who later took the Cuban *nom de guerre* of Tremendo Punto (What a Guy). On his responsibility, Chamaleso accepted the 30 instructors whom we offered at first, and, when we told him we had around 130 men, all black Cubans, ready to begin fighting, he accepted them, too, on his responsibility. This somewhat changed the first aspect of our strategy, since we thought they would limit the number to the 30 we had already spoken about. [*Congo*, 7.]

GODEFREI TCHAMLESSO (TREMENDO PUNTO): After the first meeting with Che, I went to China to get military training. When I returned, we were told that the Cuban comrades would soon arrive, but we weren't given an exact date. They were coming from Dar es Salaam. We were called to the Embassy and Che explained it to us. He was in disguise, however, and we didn't know who he was.

CHE: The most pressing task was to find a fast boat with a good motor that would enable us to cross the 70-kilometer width of Lake Tanganyika with relative safety. One of our experts had arrived earlier to both buy the launches and make an exploratory crossing of the Lake...

Right from the start, we came up against something that was to haunt us throughout the struggle: lack of organization. This worried me, because I thought that the imperialists, who controlled all the airlines and airports in the area, must have already detected our movements. In addition, the purchase of unusual quantities of knapsacks, sheets of plastic, knives, blankets and other articles in Dar es Salaam must have caught their attention. Not only were the Congolese badly organized; we were, too. [In fact, the CIA didn't detect the Cuban presence in the Congo until the battle of Fort Bendera, and it couldn't verify Che's presence, even though it suspected it. — W.G.] We hadn't prepared in enough detail for undertaking the task of equipping a company; we had only guaranteed the soldiers' weapons and ammunition. (All were armed with Belgian FALs.)

Kabila hadn't arrived, and it was announced that he would stay in Cairo for at least two more weeks; so, without having been able to discuss my participation with him, I had to continue my trip incognito and, therefore, couldn't let the Tanzanian Government know who I was and ask for its acquiescence. To be honest, these difficulties didn't upset me much, because I was interested in the struggle of the Congo and feared that my offer would cause too sharp a reaction and some of the Congolese or the friendly government would ask me not to get into the fray. [*Congo*, 8.]

During that meeting in Cairo, Soumialot was named President of the National Liberation Council (CNL). He had been Minister of Defense prior to this.

DREKE (MOJA): It was said that all the equipment for the combatants had been purchased, but, when we got there, it wasn't so. Things were missing; the boots didn't appear. Then Tatu [Che] decided to go without them and not go on buying that way, because those purchases could make people suspicious. Oliva had been in charge of that, and Che really bawled him out.

During the days we were there, Che spoke with Pablo Rivalta, Oliva and another official from the Embassy about the mission. The last two had traveled to Kigoma to arrange the crossing into the Congo; moreover, Oliva served as our translator in Swahili, and the other one, in English. We began a plan of physical exercises and studied the history of the Congo. Pablo visited often and one night we went out with him to see the city, to amuse ourselves a little.

RIVALTA: Buying the knapsacks and all the rest of the things was quite a mess, because we had to use an Indian merchant in Dar es Salaam; I asked him to send for the things from England and other distant places. I think he knew what it was for, but he was a businessman and wanted to keep his business. That's why he didn't talk, and he helped us a great deal.

In spite of the setbacks, Che used the delay in the departure for Kigoma to increase his knowledge of the country to which he was going, even though he was already well up on happenings in Africa. He was familiar with most aspects of the struggle that the African countries were waging — either to become independent or to free themselves of neocolonialism. The "Belgian" Congo was in this second group.

Where is Che?
Since the absence of Cuba's Minister of Industry began to be noted in Cuba, the foreign press began a malicious campaign. Therefore, on April 20, 1965, during an informal chat with reporters, Fidel answered a question concerning his whereabouts: "The only thing I can tell you about Major Guevara is that he will always be where he is most useful to the revolution. I think that his visit to Africa was very beneficial."[21]

Later, Hilda Gadea wrote, "That day, we received the first letter since his departure or 'disappearance' from the local scene; it was addressed to our daughter."

Beloved Daughter,
I am writing some lines so you will know that your old man is thinking of you. I saw some recent photos of you and feel that you

are becoming a woman. Soon, we will need to have a guard in the house to fend off your suitors.

I am quite far away, doing some work that was entrusted to me, and it will be some time before I return. Don't forget to go by the house every so often to check on your brothers and sisters, who are a little undisciplined and don't always study.

Well, darling, that's it for now, until I find another moment to drop you some lines. I'm always very glad to get letters from you.

Give my love to your mom and your cousin. A big hug and kiss and many fond memories from your Dad.

The first group leaves

CHE: After some days' wait in Dar es Salaam — which, even though short, was no less distressing for me, because I wanted to get into the Congo as soon as possible — the first group of Cubans left on the night of April 20. There were 14 of us, plus two drivers, the Congolese representative [Tchamlesso] and a representative of the Tanzanian Police, to avoid problems on the way. We left four behind who had just arrived and whose equipment hadn't yet been purchased. [*Congo*, 8.]

All of them wore civilian clothes but were armed with FAL rifles and UZI submachine guns.

DR. RAFAEL ZERQUERA (KUMI): I went to Kigoma with Che, Dreke, Oliva and Tchamlesso in one of the two cars. There was also a van with a tarpaulin. Che drove part of the way. It took two days of traveling on extremely bad roads with a lot of dust. We had to cross a river on a barge, which delayed us considerably. Che and Mbili [José María Martínez Tamayo] took some photos.

DREKE: We took food that didn't have to be cooked. I remember an anecdote about bread. There was a single loaf of bread and Che told me, "Hey, see if you can distribute the bread so everybody gets some." Each one of us got a little piece, and he got the last one. I knew what he was doing, because I had gotten to know him in the Escambray mountains: he would get the smallest piece. I left his and mine for last.

He told us not to throw the cans away, but we threw a lot of them out along the road, when we passed vehicles with people on safari and we pretended we were partying, too; the people who saw us thought we were just another group on safari. There were a lot of little shops owned by Lebanese in the tiny villages or hamlets along our route.

During the trip, I saw Che reading every chance he got. When I asked him what he was reading, he said he was looking for information about the area in which we would be operating.

"The setting in which we lived"

CHE: I will emphasize the area which constituted the Eastern Front, because it was the one I knew and so as not to generalize an experience in a country with such diverse characteristics as the Congo.

The geographic setting in which we lived is characterized by the great depression filled by Lake Tanganyika, which covers an area of around 35,000 square kilometers and an average width of around 50 kilometers. It separates Tanzania and Burundi from the Congo. On each side of the depression, there is a mountain chain; one is in Tanzania and Burundi, and the other is in the Congo. This last has an average height of around 1,500 meters above sea level (the Lake is at a height of 700 meters) and extends from near Albertville, to the south, to beyond Bukavu, to the north, dropping into hills that blend with tropical forests. Those mountains were the scene of all the fighting. The width of the system varies, but it was an average of around 20 or 30 kilometers wide in the zone of the fighting. There are two taller mountain chains, tree-covered and sloping, one to the east and the other to the west, framing a rolling plateau whose valleys are good for agriculture and for cattle raising, an occupation mainly carried out by herdsmen of the Rwandan tribes, who have traditionally dedicated themselves to it. To the west, the mountain drops off to a plain 700 meters high which belongs to the Congo River basin. It is a kind of savanna, with tropical trees and grass and some natural meadows that break the continuity of the bush. The underbrush isn't homogeneous near the mountains; to the west, in the Kabambare region, it is dense and tropical.

The mountains emerge from the Lake and make the terrain very rough; there are small plains good for landing, but they are very hard to defend if you don't hold the heights. The southern end of land communication was at Kabimba, where we had one of our positions. The mountains shape the westward route between Albertville and Lulimba-Fizi and, from the latter, go on toward Bukavu, with one branch heading toward Kuenga and another running through Baraka and Uvira, along the coast, to reach that point. From Lulimba, the road goes into the mountains, a good area for ambushes — as, to a lesser degree, is also the part that goes through the plain of the Congo River.

It rains every day from October through May, and there is almost no rainfall from June through September, although isolated showers begin in September. It always rains in the mountains, but with less frequency in the dry months. On the plain, there are plenty of animals of the deer family to hunt; in the mountains, there are buffalo, though not very abundant, as well as elephants and large numbers of monkeys. The flesh of monkeys is edible and doesn't taste too bad; the flesh of elephants is gummy and tough but quite edible when seasoned by hunger. The main vegetables are yucca and corn, which constituted the vegetable base of our diet; oil is extracted from the palm trees. With some difficulty, guerrilla troops that don't have a base of operations can live off the area. There are a lot of goats, and fowl are raised; in a few places, there are pigs.

North of Baraka-Fizi, there is a greater variety of crops. A little north of Uvira, there is a sugar mill. A lot of rice and peanuts are grown in the Kabambare-Kasengo area. Cotton used to be raised there, too, but it had been practically suppressed as a crop by the time we were there. I don't how cotton is exploited in the agricultural phase, but it was capitalist production, with modern cotton gins in strategic centers, owned by foreign companies.

The Lake is rich in fish, but, in the recent period, there was almost no fishing, because of plane flights during the day and incursions by the dictatorship's launches at night. [*Congo*, 149-50.]

Of the more than 1,700 kilometers of road between the capital and Kigoma, west of Dar es Salaam, only a little more than 100 kilometers, toward Borogoro, the second most important town, are asphalted. From there on, it is a dirt road with large sandy stretches, most of it in bad condition. There are many towns and hamlets. The most important towns are Manyoni, Encega and Zinguida. After this last comes the longest unpopulated stretch, through a semi-desert, very sandy area, to Cajama, where more leafy, jungle-like vegetation begins to appear and where you can sometimes see wild animals, some of which are dangerous. You also have to cross several rivers, one by ferry because it is so wide and deep.

Kigoma finally appears

CHE: On the evening of [Thursday] April 22, after a tiring journey, we reached Kigoma, but the launches weren't ready and we had to stay there waiting until the next day to cross. The Commissioner of the region, who welcomed us and put us up, immediately passed on the complaints of the Congolese. Unfortunately, everything seemed to indicate that many of their views were justified; the military officers in charge of troops in the area, who had welcomed our first, exploratory delegation, were now in Kigoma, and we could confirm that they issued passes from the front to go there. This town was a backwater to which the more fortunate could come to escape the hazards of the struggle. The revolutionary leadership never sufficiently assessed the nefarious influence of Kigoma — with its brothels; its liquor; and, above all, the certain refuge it offered. [*Congo*, 9.]

DREKE: We entered the little town of Kigoma at around 8:00 at night and went straight to a large house on the outskirts. There, we put on our uniforms and ate supper in a lean-to.

TCHAMLESSO: We reached Kigoma and began to prepare for crossing the Lake. Here, the Cubans were put with the men in Security, because Sinfua, the Governor of Kigoma, was a very good friend of Kabila's. Kabila had won him over and had him under control. Kabila slept in his residence — it had to be that way to have him on our side. Sinfua was a very heavy drinker but was very loyal to Nyerere.

ZERQUERA: We stayed in two places in Kigoma, because there wasn't enough room for all of us in the Governor's house. Tatu [Che], Moja [Dreke], Mbili [José María Martínez Tamayo] and some other comrades were put up there. I stayed with Tatu because I was a doctor. The others spent the night in a place the police found for them.

The Governor's house was quite large, and the Cubans were assigned a part of it. Kigoma, which had a good view of the bay, had around 60,000 or 70,000 inhabitants, many of whom had come from India. Only two or three of its streets were asphalted, and they, like the port, were filled with shops, most of which were owned by Indians.

The docks, small piers made of wood, were in a small, horseshoe-like indentation in the Lake shore. The port was linked to the railroad infrastructure by a train that ran from Dar es Salaam to that point, mainly to carry minerals from the Congo, plus other goods and passengers.

A dangerous crossing

They made the crossing shortly before midnight on Friday, April 23, 1965, nearly nine and a half years after the young Ernesto Guevara had boarded another boat on the Tuxpan River in Mexico to make a similar journey on November 25, 1956. That earlier journey had been longer, but both involved the same dangers and were made for the same purpose. The 1956 journey was made after Che had agreed to be the doctor on the expedition headed by Fidel Castro in which 82 men crowded onto the cabin cruiser *Granma* to fight against the dictatorship in Cuba. That departure was as clandestine as possible, to evade the Mexican authorities, and, for the first few miles down the river, they had sailed without any lights. This time, too, they had to navigate without any lights, going around 70 kilometers across an immense lake and facing the same risks of being captured or sunk.

Before midnight, the 14 men drove in two cars to a small pier far from the main dock. There, they got into two launches with outboard motors. They carried FAL automatic rifles and wore uniforms with olive green berets. When all were on board, the order was given to set out.

The first Cuban internationalist expeditionaries who crossed the Lake had the following names, corresponding to the ordinal numbers in Swahili: Major Víctor Dreke, Moja (1); Ministry of the Interior officer José María Martínez Tamayo, Mbili (2); Major Ernesto Che Guevara, Tatu (3); Lieutenant Norberto Pío Pichardo, Inne (4); Private Aldo García González, Tano (5); Corporal Pablo Osvaldo Ortíz, Sita (6); Corporal Pedro Ortíz, Saba (7); Sergeant Eduardo Torres Ferrer (Coqui), Nanne (8); Sergeant Julián Morejón Gilbert, Tiza (9); Dr. Rafael Zerquera Palacios, Kumi (10); Private Martín Chivás, Ishirini (11); Sergeant Víctor Manuel Ballester, Telathini (12); Private Salvador José Escudero, Arobaini (13); and Private Constantino Pérez Méndez, Hansini (14).

The four who stayed in the capital were Private Angel Fernández Angulo, Sitaini (15); Private Lucio Sánchez Rivero, Rabanini (16); Private Noelio Revé Robles, Kigolo (17); and Sergeant Ramón Muñoz Caballero, Maganga (18).

DREKE: According to the information given to Che, the crossing should be made in a straight line, but the boat went crooked, changing its route, when we had gone some distance from the pier. A short time later, it repeated the maneuver, going from one side to the other, which of course lengthened the time of the journey. When Che, who was a little angry, asked about this, they told him that the lights that could be seen in the Lake might be enemy vessels. He accepted the reason, and we kept on zigzagging.

Later, we heard the sound of motors, apparently of several launches. The Congolese became scared, creating tension among us all. Then Che ordered us to take combat positions, since we couldn't allow ourselves to be caught. The launches passed by close to us without anything happening.

OLIVA: We made the crossing in three wooden boats that were quite bad and we had a scare during the trip. Sometimes there are strong gusts of wind and the trees that have been blown down are carried by the current in the Lake. You have to be very careful at night, because if a tree crashes into a boat it can cause it to sink. Moreover, there are several military posts along the Congo side of the Lake and the whole area is patrolled.

We also saw fishing boats with lights, and some of the people thought they might be enemy launches. The worst danger, however, was that the current might carry us toward one of the Congolese Navy posts.

DREKE: When we were over halfway there, a gale blew up and began to lash us; it wasn't a hurricane, but one of the storms that are so frequent in Africa. Often, they send boats to the bottom, especially small ones, like ours. We were worried. The wind whipped up huge waves and we had to keep bailing.

ZERQUERA: The storm that caught us really scared me. If I fell into the water, I would drown because I didn't know how to swim. I was worrying about this when Che asked me, "Doctor, do you know how to swim?" When I replied that I didn't, he smiled and said, "Who would ever have thought you would die in this way?"

DREKE: The boat leaped around like an eggshell in the middle of the terrible darkness. It was impossible to see anything, even if we could have put the lights on. The Congolese started arguing. They were ordered to be quiet, and then they started singing to drive away the evil spirits of the Lake.

The wind grew stronger, and the Lake became ever more threatening. A new wave broke over the vessel Che was in and it keeled over. The boatmen were ordered to head blindly for any shore, to take shelter. If they hadn't done that, the Lake would have swallowed them. Che and the Cubans thought of how fruitless such a death would be. Time passed, and no shore could be seen. They scrutinized the horizon anxiously, and finally a Congolese pointed with his arm and exclaimed, "The shore!"

DREKE: Two comrades and I threw ourselves into the water. We didn't let Che be the first to land. After walking several meters, we reached the shore. Once on land and seeing that there wasn't any danger, we signaled the others to land, too.

ZERQUERA: It was nearly dawn when we reached the Congo. We had to wade quite a distance to get ashore. There weren't any docks on the shores of Kibamba in Bukavu Province.

Landing in the Congo

From what Che wrote, they first set foot on Congolese soil at dawn on Saturday, April 24, 1965.

DREKE: We began to look for the camp, because we had been told that it was there, but it wasn't. Then Che ordered a scouting party to go out, and three or four of us set out to do reconnaissance. We took Tchamlesso with us. He said the camp was there, but we still couldn't find it. After walking one and a half kilometers, we found a thatched-roof hut where there were guerrillas sleeping on the floor with their women and rifles. Tchamlesso told them who we were, and they got up. Other men came out of other huts. It didn't look like it, but that was the General Staff of the Northern Front of the Congolese guerrillas. Later, he and I went back and told Tatu [Che] and two other Cubans who were waiting. Tatu was surprised to hear what we had seen, especially because the rebels were allowed to have their women there, but he ordered us to go there.

When they reached the camp, a platoon of soldiers formed a small guard of honor for them with some solemnity, and one of them gave a message to Dreke, who seemed to be the head of the Cuban contingent. Then they demonstrated marching, at which they were quite good.

The arms they had were 10-shot SKS rifles, Soviet PPCH submachine guns and 12.7 AA machine guns, and Chinese 75-mm recoilless cannon. Later, the Cubans found out that the weapons were mainly used for fishing in the Lake, where a large part of their ammunition was wasted. The weapons depots were small huts made of straw, which lacked the required conditions.

TCHAMLESSO: That day — that is, that morning — I introduced the Cuban comrades to the African guerrillas. Then I sent for the commander of the camp. Moja [Dreke] appeared as the chief, Mbili [José María Martínez Tamayo] as second in command and Tatu [Che] as doctor and French translator. The doctor was the *muganga*, or witch doctor... Well, everybody formed ranks and presented arms, the cannon was shot off once and Tatu said they shouldn't be wasting ammunition. It was as a salute, because the guys were happy. When they saw the whites, they said, "We have mercenaries, too." That is, the Africans thought that we, too, had hired mercenaries. In some words of introduction, I told them that the combatants who had arrived were comrades from far away, from Cuba — I had to tell them the truth — who had come to help us, that they were volunteers and nobody was paying them. We didn't have the money to pay them and they were there out of solidarity.

A cool welcome

Page one of the *Campaign Diary* which Dreke ordered Comrade Emilio Mena (Paulu) to keep contained the following:

> Right from the first moment when we arrived, we noticed something that seemed like coldness among the Congolese and we wondered if it was because there were whites among us or because we were foreigners.

They spent the night there. The first home of the recent arrivals was a tiny abandoned hut and their first bed was the hard, cold ground. There, with their knapsacks piled around them, they had their first dreams on Congolese soil. They didn't get a very long rest, because they were so anxious to make contact with Congolese reality that resting longer would have been too much of a luxury. However, their "first impressions" were annoying, both to Che and to his comrades in arms.

CHE: The cause of the division that could be sensed in the first moments was hard for us to understand. Some of the people — perhaps farmers — had very little education, and there were others with a higher level of culture, who wore different clothing and knew more French. There was a coldness between the two groups of men. [*Congo*, 10.]

For Che, that first impression of a division which he found in the troop continued to be a surprise, inasmuch as he had thought that it existed only at the highest level of the African liberation movements. It took some time for him to understand the real reasons for that problem and how much work would have to be done before the African peoples could overcome it, since the colonialists were familiar with and had always applied the axiom of divide and conquer.

This was the beginning of something which Che hadn't foreseen and it would become the most difficult and disagreeable problem of all: that of making many of his comrades understand that, in spite of everything, it was necessary to remain in the Congo to carry out the mission for which they had been sent. That same morning, he talked with two representatives of the General Staff, Enmanuel Kasabudacha, in charge of supplies and weapons, and Kiwe, the information chief. As Che put it, they were the first with whom he established relations at the base, and both held nothing back, offering more information about the substantial division there was in the country.

Later, Tchamlesso called a meeting of Che; Dreke; the commander of the base; Colonel Bidalila, of the Uvira Front, who commanded the 1st

Brigade; Lieutenant Colonel Lambert, of the 2nd Brigade, who represented General Moulane; and Ngojo Andre, who came from the Kabamba area and would head another brigade. One of the points Tchamlesso raised was that Dreke, who appeared to be the Cubans' leader, should take part in the meetings and decisions of the General Staff and that another Cuban whom he would designate could also attend. Che noted that the expression on their faces showed that the Congolese weren't happy about this. Che came to the conclusion that the representative from the supreme command wasn't very popular among the leaders.

CHE: The cause of the hostility toward the other group [the Congolese Staff] lay in the fact that these men spent some time at their fronts, whereas the most the others did was move between the base in the Congo [Kimbamba] and Kigoma, always looking for something that wasn't available. The case of Tremendo Punto [Tchamlesso] was more serious in the eyes of the fighters, because, as the representative in Dar es Salaam, he came only occasionally. [*Congo*, 10.]

Dawa

Another point raised was the *dawa*.

CHE: Lieutenant Colonel Lambert, a likable man with a festive air, explained to me that, since they possessed *dawa*, a medicine that made them impervious to bullets, they considered planes to be of no account.

"They've hit me several times, but the bullets fall to the ground without any force."

He smiled broadly while telling me this, and I felt obliged to enjoy the joke, which I considered a way of showing the little importance given to the enemy's weapons, but I soon realized that he was serious and that the magic protection was one of the great weapons in the triumph of the Congolese Army. [*Congo*, 10-11.]

Dawa is a liquid made from the sap of several "magic" vines and herbs. It is made by the *muganga*, or witch doctor of the tribe or hamlet, who pours it over the warrior before they go into combat and then draws a mythical symbol on their forehead with a piece of charcoal. This provides "total protection" against all weapons. To make it really effective, the one who has been given *dawa* must abstain from eating, having sexual relations and feeling afraid at the time of the action — which is very natural in everyone who is going to fight. If they incur any of these three faults, the "magic protection" disappears. Therefore, if the soldier is wounded or dies, they must have committed one of those offenses. No matter what happened, the Congolese didn't take part in the fighting if they weren't protected by *dawa*.

This practice dates back to the beginnings of humanity itself.

CHE: I was always afraid that that superstition would be turned against us and that they would blame us for the failure of some battle in which many men were killed. Several times, I tried to talk with various leaders to convince them not to trust in it. That was impossible; it was recognized as an article of faith. The most politically advanced said it was a natural, material force and that, as dialectical materialists, they recognized the power of *dawa*, whose secrets were understood [only] by the jungle witch doctors. [*Congo*, 11.]

Lightning on a calm day

CHE: After the talk with the chiefs, I took Tremendo Punto aside and explained who I was. He was completely floored. He kept repeating "international scandal" and "nobody must find out; please, nobody must find out." It had come like lightning on a calm day and I feared for the consequences, but my identity couldn't remain hidden any longer if we wanted to use the influence that my activity could have here.

Tremendo Punto left that same night to tell Kabila that I was here in the Congo. The Cuban officials who had accompanied us in the crossing and the naval technician returned with him. The technician was to send back two mechanics — by the next mail, as it were — since one of the first things we had observed was the total lack of maintenance for the various motors and vessels used in crossing the Lake. [*Congo*, 11.]

TCHAMLESSO: Then Tatu [Che] took me by the shoulders and we went over to a rock. I'll never forget this. Look, I still get goose bumps. He told me, "I'm Che... When you go back to Dar es Salaam, tell Kabila when you're alone with him."

When he told me that, I was frightened. Che was there! Although I didn't have the knowledge I have now, I did have some training and I could figure out the responsibility that had fallen on top of us by having that man with us — who was not only an expert guerrilla, a veritable strategist, but also the number-three figure of the Cuban Revolution.

It was too much. I tell you, I broke out in a cold sweat. He saw that I was disconcerted and said, "Don't worry, I'm not going to take over the command. Major Moja [Dreke] will command; he's in charge of the troops... What worries me is that there should be somebody with some rank with whom I can talk about our plans... The first thing we're going to do is train them." He explained that to me. Then he called over Moja and Mbili [José María Martínez Tamayo], so there were four of us. We sat on the rock, and the river flowed by. I remember it very clearly. It was in the early evening.

We were in Kibamba. Then Che said to me, "Please, you have a double mission: to be discreet and to convince Kabila to send me someone or to come here himself to organize this." I told him, "Major" — that's when I started calling him "Major" — "don't worry about discretion. Everything that goes into me goes out into the toilet, and anybody who wants it will have to look for it there."

The Lake base

The next day, the recent arrivals got a second surprise — the first had been the welcome they had been given. To reach the camp, they had to climb what to Che was "a fatiguing hill that was harder for us because of our total lack of training." It wasn't more than 150 meters high. They had been told that there was a 10 kilometer-wide plain between the shore and the heights, but, in fact, the ground rose straight from the edge of the Lake. This showed that the person who had told them about the terrain had never been there. The General Staff of the Northern Front of the Congolese guerrillas was at that camp, but none of the three main leaders were there. That place was known as the Lake base, and the area was called Kibamba.

Since they had arrived in the Congo, Che had demanded that they eat the same food as the Congolese. They hadn't brought many canned goods with them and what they had was always shared with the Congolese rebels, so it was quickly consumed.

CHE: The basic food of the revolutionary soldiers was *bucali*, which is made as follows. Peel some yucca and let it dry in the sun for a few days. Then pound it with a mortar... Put that flour through a sieve and drop it in boiling water until it becomes a paste and that's how it's eaten. With willingness, *bucali* replaces carbohydrates, but what we were eating was nearly raw yucca flour without salt. This was sometimes complemented with *zombe* — crushed and boiled yucca leaves seasoned with a little palm oil and with the meat of some animal that had been killed. There was good hunting in that area, but it wasn't customary to eat meat. It couldn't be said that the combatants were well fed; very little was received from the Lake. Their bad habits also included that of not going to the base to get food. Each man carried only a rifle, cartridge belt and his personal effects — which, generally, consisted only of a blanket — on his shoulders. [*Congo*, 20.]

The delays began

On April 25, Che asked to be sent where they thought of establishing the Cubans' training camp, around five kilometers away, but they claimed that since the commander was in Kigoma they would have to wait until he returned. Che noted, "That's when the delays began." Since he had to wait, he decided to begin the Cubans' work there, so he analyzed the Congolese military training program — which he didn't approve of — with the members of the Staff. He proposed that they have a four- or five-week training program, depending on the men's knowledge; take 100 men and form a company; and take groups of no more than 20 and begin to teach them the rudiments of infantry fighting, engineering — mainly digging trenches, with the double purpose of learning and defending the place — weapons (including some of the kinds they had), communications and scouting. As part of the training, the groups should carry out military actions directed by Mbili [José María Martínez Tamayo].

While that company went out on operations, another would remain in camp, getting instruction. Che explained to the Congolese that, of every 100 men, some of them might become future soldiers and, of them, two or three might become command cadres. But, again, the response was evasion — which became a constant. The reply was that he should make the proposal in writing. There was no problem in doing this, but, as Che noted, he never knew where the paper on which he set this down ended up.

Those of us who knew Che realized that it must have been a very unpleasant time for him and that he must have had to grit his teeth to bear such lack of seriousness. However, as the training plan wasn't carried out, Che again asked for authorization to go to what would be their base and get it ready. He thought the work would take a week.

CHE: So the days passed. Whenever the subject was raised again (and I did so with truly irritating persistence), they always came up with a new pretext. Even today, I don't know what to attribute it to. Perhaps they really didn't want to begin the preparatory work so as not to bypass the corresponding authority — in that case, the commander who was away in Kigoma. [*Congo*, 12.]

Kabila didn't want Tanzanian Government to be informed

TCHAMLESSO: I went to Dar es Salaam and convinced Kabila. He, too, was frightened. Everybody was. First of all, they had told us they were trainers, and then we could see that it was a small detachment.

His reaction was, "OK, that's very important. It will offset the attacks by Tshombe's mercenaries. From now on, we must be more serious, more consistent, more disciplined and organized." That's what Kabila said.

I've never questioned that Kabila was a revolutionary. This isn't just to defend him now; I'm going to stay in Cuba for the remainder of my life. I've never questioned his capacity as a leader, but what I have always thought is that he was looking for a soft billet, and he didn't have enough — any, in fact — military experience. He was an agitator with the makings of a political leader, but he lacked the seriousness, the self-assurance, the knowledge and the innate talent you can see in a Fidel and that you could see in other leaders, who headed the guerrilla force. He was a political-military leader — nominally military — but he was more of a politician who knew about urban insurrections and how to conspire in the streets. Heading an urban conspiracy isn't the same as leading a guerrilla force. That's when I began to disagree with him and to understand him.

He was frightened when he knew of Che's presence, but he took up the challenge and instructed that nothing be said to the Tanzanians, who should find out for themselves. Then he asked me, "Tcham, will they take measures so there won't be any leaks?" I said, "Look, we have to deal with cultural backwardness, the low level of all the members, including us and all the combatants, from the rank and file up to and including the rank of major, who don't know where Cuba is or who Che is. They have never heard anything about this." We were the only ones who did know, because we had gone to high school and knew and understood the value of the Cuban Revolution, though with some limitations at that time.

Then I told myself, there can't be any leaks, can there? There's discretion. Yes, we who are in the city must be discreet. Even Mojumba, who knew about the Cubans, didn't know Che was there. He couldn't be told, to prevent leaks.

Kabila, Masengo and Mitudidi were informed. We were in a hotel, and we went outside, to the patio, in case there were any microphones. Then, about two weeks later, Mitudidi was instructed to be Kabila's permanent representative at the front.

Several days later, as Dreke recalled, without having done anything militarily, Che and Zerquera, his medical colleague, set about providing medical care for the farmers who lived in the area. Paulu (who was a counterintelligence officer), Julián Morejón and Martín Chibás were assigned for Che's protection, and he accepted them, although reluctantly. The doctors were freed from the guard duty the other

Cubans carried out; Dreke recalled that they told him the doctors couldn't do guard duty.

ZERQUERA: As soon as we were organized, Che ordered me to provide medical care for the population. I told him the only things I had were aspirin and malaria tablets. "During the first few days in the Sierra Maestra, I didn't even have that much, and I took care of everybody," he replied jokingly. He, too, worked as a doctor.

Seeking to know about the conditions at the future upper base, Che told Dreke to choose some men and, on the pretext of doing training marches, reconnoiter the terrain. When they returned that night, they were wet, exhausted and numb with cold. Dreke told Che that the upper base had very dense vegetation, tall trees, and a very cold, damp climate with permanent fog and frequent rainfall. A house was being built there which he was told was for the Cubans, but it would take some days to complete it.

Che used that information to suggest that he be allowed to go up and help finish the house, since all of them were ready to do whatever work was necessary so as not to be a burden. But he always got the same reply: "Wait for the commander to come."

The characteristics of some personalities

As Che spoke French, he spent a large part of that time chatting with Kiwe, the head of information for the Congolese. Kiwe talked nonstop, speaking French at almost supersonic speed, and also liked to talk a blue streak about many of the revolutionary leaders of the Congo. From Kiwe, Che learned that General Olenga had achieved that rank because, when he was some kind of lieutenant, his chief, Bidalila, had ordered him to advance toward Stanleyville. Olenga was promoted one rank for every town he reported taken. Since the people were giving the guerrillas a lot of support, Olenga "took" the towns without firing a shot. Luckily, he didn't go to Stanleyville, because he had already become a general, and they would have had to invent a new rank if he'd "taken" it, too.

Kiwe considered Colonel Pascasa, Mulele's representative, to be a genuine revolutionary and military chief, but Pascasa had been killed in a dispute among the Congolese in Cairo.

Another day, he criticized Gbenye, to such an extent that he said Gbenye was better suited to head a pack of thieves than a revolutionary movement. He couldn't imagine Gbenye as President, because he had acted dishonestly at the beginning. He spoke of the part Gbenye had taken in Gizenga's imprisonment, but added that Gizenga was a leftist opportunist who, when he had been given money to organize the revolutionary forces in Leopoldville, had used it to create a political party. He accused him of trying to assassinate Mitudidi and of having contacts with the U.S. Embassy.

CHE: My talks with Kiwe gave me some idea of the characteristics of some personalities and, above all, clearly showed the shifting alliances among the groups of revolutionaries, or discontents, who formed the General Staff of the Congolese Revolution. [*Congo*, 13-14.]

Ever since their arrival at the Lake camp, the Cubans had been making furniture for an open-air classroom and a series of benches around the huts where the Cubans spent the night, so they would have somewhere to sit and rest or talk. This work was done quickly, which left the men with nothing to do. The days passed, and nothing changed. The news — whether factual or invented — which came from Kigoma over the Lake helped to break their boredom a little.

Che returns to his profession
Che managed to fill his time better than the others because, in addition to knowing French, which helped him talk with some of the Congolese and to read whatever appeared in that language, he also read the books he had brought and began to exercise his profession. Although he described himself as "an epidemiologist, that illustrious branch of fauna of Aesculapius gave me the right to know nothing of medicine," he kept working as a doctor in the rustic consulting room they set up for Rafael Zerquera.

Without intending to, he did something that he had wanted to do a long time before, when, in Mexico, he had asked to go to Africa as a doctor. While treating the sick Congolese, he became very aware of the countless venereal diseases caught in Kigoma when the members of the Congolese Liberation Army went there on passes. That port town was full of brothels and Che was worried about what appeared to be an epidemic — and, even more, about where the money came from which gave those "vacationers" access to them.

Another problem was the drunkenness caused by *pombe*, a liquor made from fermented corn meal and ground yucca; even though its alcohol content was low, it was harmful because of the rudimentary, unhygienic way it was distilled. Whenever *pombe* was brought into the camp, there were fights and all kinds of other problems.

Although there was little combat activity, both in the General Staff and on the other fronts, some wounded were brought in. They had been shot accidentally, since most of the soldiers didn't know anything about handling weapons, and the guns went off frequently.

The civilians who lived in the area started coming to the improvised "hospital," because news that there was a doctor in the area spread like wildfire, by word of mouth. There were few medicines. Although a large shipment of Soviet medicines had arrived by then, most were reserved for the military. Che's health work taught him about the disorganization of supplies. When it was time to distribute medicines and medical equipment, the people requesting them on each front claimed to have more men than they really did.

CHE: I had quarrels on several occasions, trying to keep them from taking specialized equipment and medicines that would be lost to no effect on the fronts, but all of them wanted to have everything. [*Congo*, 15.]

There was worse chaos with the weapons. Those that came from Kigoma were incomplete, and a large quantity remained in the hands of the Tanzanian military. Most of the cannon and mortars had parts missing; there were mines without fuses and rifles with the wrong ammunition. A lot of the food was taken. In addition, the supplies were indiscriminately stacked along the edge of the Lake, in no kind of order and with very little protection, because the people assigned to that task weren't capable.

CHE: Several times, I tried to get them to let us organize the depot and suggested that some kinds of munitions, such as the bazooka or mortar grenades, be taken away from there. Nothing was achieved, however, until much later. [*Congo*, 15.]

The barrage of news from Kigoma reported that a group of Cubans had arrived there and that they were waiting for some kind of vessel in which to cross the Lake. Mitudidi, the long-awaited commander of the base, announced that he would come the next day or the day after, but, when that time had passed, the same predictions were made.

Information also came in about the Cairo conference, which, according to Enmanuel, who spent most of his time crossing the Lake from one side to the other, was a success for the revolutionary forces. The news about Kabila, the top-ranking leader of the Eastern Front, for whom Che was waiting anxiously, was that he would be delayed in coming because it was necessary to ensure the fulfillment of the agreements, and it was also said that he had to have a cyst removed.

More internationalists leave Cuba

At around that same time, in April 1965, Raúl Castro, Minister of the

Revolutionary Armed Forces of Cuba, bade farewell to another group. All were black Cubans, headed by Captain Santiago Terry, and, like the others, they left by air, taking different routes and meeting again in Dar es Salaam so as to go on together to their goal: Kigoma and the Congo. That group was part of the extra 100 men whom Che had offered to Tchamlesso.

At night, the port workers in the Cuban port of Matanzas began to load the ship *Uvero* with crates bearing labels saying they contained agricultural machinery. At the same time, more black Cubans, commanded by Lieutenant Normando Agramonte, began to go on board. Everything seemed normal, but one of the wooden crates fell off a pallet and broke, and the stevedores saw that it contained weapons. As a result, they had to be detained until the ship weighed anchor. Some of the "agricultural machinery" was for Che, and some, for Guinea-Bissau. Some of it had to be left in Algeria and in the Republic of Guinea. The combatants disembarked in Guinea and then flew to the Congo (Brazzaville). Ulises Estrada was in charge of that operation.

A considerable limitation on that trip was the lack of nautical charts for African waters, but it was finally solved in the port of Santiago de Cuba, where the captain of a Greek ship gave a set to his Cuban colleague. Then several U.S. warships appeared in international Caribbean waters — on their way to invade Santo Domingo. One of them tried to intercept the Cuban vessel, but the Cuban captain detoured from his route and evaded it. Though successful, the maneuver lengthened the journey. That was on the night of April 27, 1965. The U.S. 82nd Airborne Division landed in the Dominican Republic on April 28 and 29.

When the Cuban ship was off Santo Domingo, some speedboats approached and began to circle the ship, illuminating it with searchlights. One of the officers said that that was the tactic used when U.S. vessels had attacked a Spanish ship that was taking cargo to Cuba. Ulises Estrada immediately ordered the crates opened and armed everyone in order to repulse any possible attack. The speedboats kept on circling the ship, illuminating it for a while and then withdrew.

When the foreign press confirmed that Che Guevara was no longer in Cuba, it began to speculate and spread countless lies, including that Che had been murdered and his body hidden; that he had been imprisoned and was being held incommunicado; and that he had been put away in a psychiatric hospital, where he was being held incommunicado and various drugs were being given to him. Naturally, Fidel Castro was the main villain in all these stories. All kinds of disagreements between them were alleged.

When the conflict arose in Santo Domingo, the foreign press claimed that Che was fighting there. Rumors also had it that Cuban intelligence had circulated a report that Che had died in one of the battles against the U.S. troops invading the Dominican Republic. According to a CIA think tank, that would free Fidel Castro of blame for what had supposedly happened to Che.

2

May 1965

The Congo — late April, early May
Irritation was widespread among the Cubans and Che began to worry about the generalized idleness. He was aware that it would lead only to indiscipline and lack of support for the operation. In his own case, he managed to occupy his time. He was up before dawn, drank some tea — there wasn't any coffee in the area, nor was it customary to drink it. That was breakfast, though sometimes it included a little *bucali*. Then he would light a cigar or, later on, when those he had brought had run out, smoke a pipe. He then called the comrades who would do some scouting or other tasks, which usually was to look for wood, help with KP or repair some of the buildings.

For exercise, he walked two or three kilometers every day, climbing up and down in the surrounding area, while working as a doctor. Lunch was at midday. After it, Che studied political literature and read other works or, if the newspaper had arrived — always terribly late — he usually sat on one of the benches to read it. Supper was in the late afternoon.

Before going to sleep — which the others thought he did quite early — Che read and wrote in his campaign diary. He did that inside the hut, by the light of a pressure lamp. Dreke said that he used a pocket notebook with a black cover for jotting down notes.

Early in the morning, he listened to the news in French over the radio. He had drawn up a schedule of those programs. It included some in English, but, as he hadn't mastered that language completely, he didn't tune in to them very often. It was his custom to pass on interesting information to the other comrades, even though none of it mentioned Cuba.

Classes in Swahili, French and other subjects

He solved the problem of idleness by having the political officer give Swahili classes to the Cuban contingent. In addition, Che taught French, Spanish and mathematics, and other Cubans taught other subjects. The classes were from 2:00 to 4:00 in the afternoon; at about that time, fog generally appeared that reduced visibility to zero, plus the temperature dropped so much that fires had to be lit immediately.

DREKE: It's important to see Tatu [Che] as a teacher, as an educator. He also set up political study circles, in which he talked to us about *Capital* and African history.

CHE: Because of their nature and the teachers, the classes couldn't add much to the comrades' cultural knowledge, but at least they took up time, and that was an important function. Our morale was still high, but there was some murmuring among the comrades, who saw the days passing unfruitfully. [*Congo*, 15.]

In addition, after the first week, some of them caught malaria, the fever of the Congo, which is endemic in that country. Dreke, Nanne and Tano were the first victims. Sometimes they got light cases of short duration, but, even so, the men had no appetite and were weak for several days. This, of course, contributed to the nascent discontent of some of the Cubans.

Kabila sends Mitudidi as Chief of Staff

The 18 Cubans who had been waiting in Kigoma to cross the Lake arrived at the camp on Saturday, May 8, 1965. Rebel Army Captain Santiago Terry — a humorous, pop-eyed tall black Cuban with a stutter and a long history of revolutionary struggle and proved valor in battle — headed them. His name in the Congo was Ali (19).

Mitudidi, the long-awaited Chief of Staff — and, therefore, the highest-ranking officer among the Congolese guerrillas — arrived with them. After all the men had greeted one another, Che spoke with the Congolese officer.

CHE: I had a friendly talk with him, and was pleased to note his confidence, seriousness and organizing spirit. Kabila sent a message that I shouldn't let people know who I really was, so I continued incognito, carrying out my apparent tasks as doctor and translator. [*Congo*, 16.]

Che's camp

As a result of the talk with Mitudidi, the Cubans were authorized to move to what would be the upper base, in the Luluabourg area, where the mountains were more than 1,500 meters high and five kilometers from Kibamba. Che set up his camp at that place on Sunday, May 9. The men who were sick remained under Rafael Zerquera's care. Mitudidi didn't accompany them, for he said he had to immediately return to Kigoma to collect weapons, ammunition and other provisions; he left as soon as the conversation was over. Che set a fast pace to the base, even with his enormous knapsack filled with books, medicines and bullets. When they arrived there, they confirmed what Dreke had told them some days earlier about the climate and the score of men who were building the house for the Cubans; in spite of the biting cold, the Congolese showed little or no desire to work. Since they had to seek shelter, they immediately set about building dormitories with fireplaces, both to cook on and to offset the low temperatures at night. The classes continued, and benches and other furniture for another classroom were made. They had to go to a clearing to get any sun, because the trees shaded the camp.

Two weeks had passed since their arrival on Congolese soil on April 24, and they hadn't been able to attain any of the goals that had led them there.

On May 10, the day after going to the upper camp, they visited a group of small hamlets around four hours' hike from the camp to find sources of food. The people who lived there were Rwandan and, although they had lived in the Congo for years, retained their own customs, including herding, though they weren't nomads. During the Cubans' stay in the area, they sometimes managed to get some "precious beef, which is almost a cure even for nostalgia," Che noted.

When he visited those neighbors, Che learned of another serious problem, which was a tremendous obstacle to unity: the bad relations between the Rwandans and the Congolese, who had always been viewed as enemies. The colonialists had fomented ethnic pride and differences, not only in that region but throughout the country.

Meanwhile, the *Uvero* reached Guinea after two weeks at sea. Before tying up at the dock, it had to wait four days for Ambassador Serguera, who was in charge of coordinating matters with the Guinean Government. They offloaded an important load of weapons, medicines, food and other supplies for the African Party for the Independence of

Guinea and Cape Verde (PAIGC). Nine Cubans commanded by Captain Normando Agramonte also went ashore, to fly to the Congo (Brazzaville).

Che seriously ill

A few days after moving to the upper base, Che woke up with a very high fever, "thus rendering tribute to the Congo's climate," as he put it. The men sent for Rafael Zerquera, but Che sent him back, thinking that he would quickly recover and that his colleague was in greater need at the little hospital. Sure enough, he didn't have a fever on the second or third day. However, when Che had to go out in a cold rain to take care of a man who had a bullet wound, he suffered a relapse, with a very high fever and delirium.

Once again, Rafael Zerquera had to make the hard climb, "which was like climbing Everest" — the young doctor was somewhat overweight. When he reached the summit, he was in worse shape than the unconscious Che.

ZERQUERA: When Che had his relapse, Catalino Olachea came to get me. Everybody was worried because he was also bleeding from the nose. He was very sick, with a high fever, high blood pressure, vomiting and delirium. Relapses are very serious and it really worried me. I wanted to give him penicillin, but he refused, saying, "Dammit, man, don't give me that; I'm allergic to penicillin! Give me kanamicin."

I also gave him some chlorophenicol and chloroquinine and this began to bring his fever down on the fourth day. It's very good against malaria. I insisted on staying a few days more, but he ordered me to go down. He told me he felt well and I should take care of my patients. He ordered a sheep to be killed and gave me the meat to take with me.

CHE: My relapse didn't last long, either — five days at most — but I could see the results: extraordinary weakness that overcame me, taking away even my desire to eat. During the first month, at least a dozen comrades paid for being new to a hostile land with those violent fevers which had such troublesome aftermaths. [*Congo*, 17.]

DREKE: When Tatu [Che] got so sick, one comrade — who, of course, was worried — said, "If the Major doesn't get better, he will have to leave." Tatu heard this and got furious, saying, "I'm not leaving. I will die here first! This is nothing but a shitty disease that'll soon be over."

Since he couldn't go on his usual hikes, he had more time for reading and for playing chess with Ali or sometimes Arcadio Hernando. He played the most with Ali, and also argued the most with him, too, because, since Che had less scientific mastery of the game, Ali laid traps for him. Spectators found the "fights" between the two very funny, because of Ali's stuttering. Che, who was always trying to get his comrades to do something in their free time, followed up their interest by giving them classes in chess.

On May 20, 1965, Captain Agramonte and eight other combatants reached the capital of the Congo (Brazzaville) to make contact with the Congolese Government and coordinate the reception of Column Two, which had traveled to Conakry on board the *Uvero* and had then flown to Accra and Brazzaville. Captain Rafael Moracén Limonta, heading five other comrades, established contact with the MPLA leadership and joined its guerrillas in Cabinda. Thus, the requests that Massemba Debat and Agostinho Neto had forwarded to Cuba through Che the previous January were beginning to be met.

Heated tempers

In spite of all those measures, tempers sometimes got heated and, as always, although some people like joking, others don't. Dreke reported that this is what happened one afternoon with Ngenge — a fun-loving guy who liked to sing — and Zuleimán. Those two liked to sing and dance the rumba, and everybody else liked to watch them. But, that day, Ngenge got into an argument with Ali — Dreke thought it was over who had written the words to a rumba — and Ali was in a bad mood and got mad over one of Ngenge's replies, and the argument got acrimonious. If the others hadn't intervened, they would have gotten into a fight.

Che reprimanded them violently, since that was one of the most serious things a guerrilla could do. He even threatened to send them back to Cuba in disgrace if it ever happened again. They admitted they were wrong and everything was truly forgotten; they got along together fine after that. And, Dreke reported, there were no more arguments like that ever again.

Mitudidi returned right about then and sent Che what he considered "the first formal order" he had received. It was to get ready to take part in the attack on Albertville. Che considered the order to be absurd, because no preparations had been made for that action. Moreover, he was worried because 10 of the 30 Cubans were sick. Nevertheless, he gave them their instructions and said they should be ready to go into combat, adding that not much thought had gone into how that was to be done. He said he would speak with Mitudidi to change the plan or postpone the date it was to be put into effect.

The next day, May 22, Che had just finished teaching when another crazy rumor — they spread like wildfire every day — reached him.

CHE: "A Cuban Minister is climbing up the hill. A lot more Cubans have come." That was so absurd that nobody could believe it, but, to get a little exercise, I walked down the mountain a way and, to my great surprise, met Osmany Cienfuegos there. [*Congo*, 18.]

Seventeen other Cuban came with him and 17 more were waiting to cross the Lake. The encounter pleased Che. I think Che always saw Osmany as someone who was continuing the revolutionary work of his brother, Camilo, who had been Che's comrade in struggle in the Sierra Maestra mountains and one of his closest friends. The news Osmany brought about the prospects of the struggle was good. Moreover, Che learned that the Tanzanian Government still didn't know he was there.

The saddest news
CHE: However, [Osmany] also brought me the saddest personal news of the war: a telephone call had come from Buenos Aires reporting that my mother was very ill. The news was given in a tone that indicated it was an announcement to prepare me for the worst. Osmany hadn't succeeded in getting any other news. I had to spend a month in that sad uncertainty, waiting for the results of something at which I guessed but with the hope that the news was mistaken, until confirmation of my mother's death was received. Presumably feeling ill, she had wanted to see me shortly before my departure, but it hadn't been possible for me to go, as preparations for my trip were already far advanced. She didn't get the farewell letter I had left in Havana for my parents; it wasn't sent on until October, when news of my departure was made public. [*Congo*, 18.]

His mother, Celia de la Serna de la Llosa, died on May 19, 1965. She was 59 and had lung cancer. The Cuban press published the news three days later. Dreke told me that Che learned of her death from the Cuban Embassy in Tanzania. I believe that, for him, it was the saddest news not only of the war but also of his life. On saying that he hoped it was mistaken, he reacted in the same way she had when newspaper accounts reported him killed in the battle of Alegría de Pío on December 5, 1956, after the landing of the *Granma*. That time the news had been false. Che had prepared the following farewell letter, which she never saw:

Dear Mom and Dad,
Once again I feel beneath my heels the ribs of Rocinante. Once more,

I'm on the road with my shield on my arm. Almost 10 years ago, I wrote you another farewell letter. As I recall, I lamented not being a better soldier and a better doctor. The latter no longer interests me; I am not such a bad soldier.

Nothing has changed in essence, except that I am much more conscious. My Marxism has taken root and become purified. I believe in armed struggle as the only solution for those peoples who fight to free themselves, and I am consistent with my beliefs. Many will call me an adventurer, and that I am — only one of a different sort: one who risks his skin to prove his truths.

It is possible that this may be the end. I don't seek it, but it's within the logical realm of probabilities. If it should be so, I send you a final embrace. I have loved you very much, only I have not known how to express my affection. I am extremely rigid in my actions, and I think that sometimes you did not understand me. It was not easy to understand me. Nevertheless, please believe me today.

Now a willpower that I have polished with an artist's delight will sustain some shaky legs and some weary lungs. I will do it.

Give a thought once in a while to this little soldier of fortune of the 20th century.

A kiss to Celia, to Roberto, Juan Martín and Patotín, to Beatriz, to everybody. For you, a big hug from your obstinate and prodigal son,
Ernesto[22]

The letter has no date, but, based on what Dreke said, it was written on March 31, the day Dreke saw him writing his farewell letters. Che didn't mention Ana María, one of his sisters, which may have been a mistake, since Juan Martín and Patotín are the same person.

Some authors refer to a letter that Che is supposed to have sent to his mother via a friend. The question arises why Che didn't mention that letter in his book about the Congo, referring only to the one he wrote bidding his parents farewell. Ricardo Rojo — the most dishonest author of all and the one with the most evil intentions — who is cited by the others in this instance, says he read it with her. In his book, Rojo included Celia's supposed reply to her son. I asked Che's sister Ana María (who has since died in Cuba) and Roberto (whom I visited in Buenos Aires) about that "letter" supposedly sent by Che, but they neither saw nor heard of it and the "reply." However, Roberto told me that he thought their mother had written to Che and that when Che's father asked Rojo for the letter, Rojo refused to give it to him. "It's another of his despicable actions," he concluded.

---

[22] Ernesto Che Guevara, *Che Guevara Reader*, 350.

Exploratory delegations
Chief of Staff Mitudidi visited Che to discuss the various aspects of the military situation on the Northern Front.

CHE: He insisted on drawing up a big strategic plan for the taking of Albertville, but I managed to convince him it was too ambitious — and therefore too risky — to have anything to do with Albertville right then. It was more important to get real knowledge of the entire zone of operations and of the means we had. The Staff wasn't clear about what was happening on each of the isolated fronts. Everything depended on the information sent in by the chiefs, who inflated quantities when demanding things and claimed lack of ammunition or weapons to explain failures. We resolved to send four teams to different points to determine both our own the situation and that of the enemy's troops and the exact correlation of forces. [*Congo*, 18-19.]

Ali headed the first of those teams, which consisted of three other combatants. They went to the Kabimba zone. In the second, Inne and two others went to Front de Force; in the third, Dreke, Paulu and Waziri went to Baraka, Fizi and Lulimba; and, in the fourth, Che and Mitudidi would study the Uvira region.

CHE: The last trip was never made. First, there were the usual delays: lack of boots, lack of gasoline and unforeseen problems that came up. Then Kabila announced that he was about to arrive, and we had to wait for him — three days, with no results. [*Congo*, 19.]

The Cuban scouts were well received by the people living in the areas visited, but they became aware of the immense generalized poverty. However, they found that there were armed men in Kabimba and Front de Force who seemed ready to fight but lacked training. There was also poor organization of weapons and political work. Discipline was very poor. In Front de Force, they once again noted the bad relations between the Rwandans and Congolese. A battalion of Rwandans was concentrated in that place.

First Lieutenant Inne added that when Kasambal, Lawawa, two Rwandans and the Cubans went to do some reconnaissance around Front de Force, they observed several rubblework barracks painted white, and the others told them that was the enemy camp. They crept in a ditch to within 500 meters, and Inne let off a few shots to see how good their defenses were. The response was many bursts of 50-caliber machine-gun fire and they withdrew under a heavy hail of bullets. Even after they were back in their camp that night, the shots continued.

Dreke's group of scouts came back last. The information it brought of its tour through Baraka, Fizi and Lulimba was very bad, for, in spite of the welcome given them by the inhabitants and rebel chiefs in the area, the chiefs didn't hesitate to express the bad opinions that were prevalent about Kabila, Masengo and Mitudidi. Instead of staying at the front together with the people, they went through there like tourists in transit. Dreke's group found a lot of armed men, but they were totally disorganized and hadn't engaged in any fighting. For example, the only thing the men on the Lulimba Front did was fire on the town with a 75-mm recoilless cannon from a hill seven kilometers away — to be effective, the range should be less than one kilometer. The worst thing was that the chiefs at all levels were drunk most of the time — publicly, since they considered drunkenness a sign of manliness.

Dreke also said that, in Lulimba, he met with the king of the region — a tall, muscular African with a big hat that symbolized his crown, who gave him an effusive welcome sitting on his throne. He ordered the flag of the liberation of the Congo raised in honor of his visitors and gave a militant speech to which Dreke replied with another in the same tone. Then a banquet was served, in which the special dish consisted of butterflies — which it took courage and determination to eat. Each butterfly was cooked whole in grease, and Dreke said that the worst thing was that the wings stuck to the roof of your mouth, tongue and lips, causing a very unpleasant sensation.

The King had all the fringe benefits connected with his position: the best house; lots of food and drink; and, naturally, all the women he wanted. He also had a modern launch for going to Kigoma, where he spent most of his time. Months later, he went over to the enemy. In that place, the so-called rebels lived in houses with their women and with notable lack of concern about an enemy attack. The reports had said there were thousands of rebels, but Dreke and his group counted around 80. Dreke also reported that they did reconnaissance in the area, found an abandoned barracks and made a sketch of the terrain.

DREKE: We were present when a woman was giving birth. When her pains began, an old man came and helped deliver a fat little girl. The next day, they baptized the baby and had a party. They called her Mavita. I gave one of my own daughters the same name.

Later, they went to Fizi in a slow *motumbo* (canoe), paddling close to the shore. A large part of the town had been destroyed in air attacks. However, many houses were still standing. The chiefs with the highest ranks lived in those in good condition, and the soldiers — who also bivouacked with their women — lived in the worst ones. There, they met "General" Shaubani Moulane, who said he was a comrade of and had fought alongside Lumumba. He lived in one of the best houses, surrounded by a large General Staff. On that occasion, in honor of their visitor, they presented arms and carried out a demonstration exercise, simulating a battle between rebels and enemy soldiers.

After dinner, the General invited the Cubans to visit the defense area, seven kilometers away, on a treeless hill. It consisted of a group of little straw huts next to the road to Lubondja. As a result, just like Lulimba, it was exposed to enemy attacks by air and land.

They told Mitudidi all this, and he replied that it was all true, adding that the self-styled "General" Moulane, chief of the Lulimba Front, was an anarchist without any revolutionary integrity who would have to be replaced, but, every time he called him in, he refused to go, for he imagined they were going to imprison him.

Since they couldn't do anything else, Che sent out new exploring parties headed by Inne and Nanne, with several Congolese, and they returned to the Front de Force and Katenga areas. Ali returned to Kabimba with another Cuban and some Congolese.

The May 22-23 edition of the enemy daily *L'Etoile du Congo* reported some incidents of the internal struggles of the so-called Congolese revolutionary movement which took place in the Cairo conference: "Gbenye and Olenga, who are vying for influence, have taken asylum in Khartoum." And, on May 28, it published the following:

Soumialot has removed Kanza from his post as Foreign Minister... He has said that the Congo is divided into three military zones: 1) Leopoldville and Kasai, 2) Kivu and Katanga and 3) the Eastern Province and Equateur. Mulele, Kabila and Olenga head the political-military leaderships in these three zones.

At the conference, far from being resolved, the splits in the organization grew larger, for the latent contradictions among the Congolese leaders appeared to be insuperable. Gbenye and Soumialot constantly attacked each other, reflecting great tension between them. Therefore, Gbenye thought that the dissolution of the National Liberation Council (CNL) would help his faction to grow. For his part, Soumialot considered that this implied his separation from the organization and that it was vital for carrying out the Revolution. However, he created the Higher Council of the Revolution (CSR), for the clear purpose of eliminating Gbenye's group.

Optimism intact

While all that was going on, back in the Congo, unaware of the full dimensions of the internal struggles, Che was making other plans, as shown in his diary at the end of May:

CHE: Before Mitudidi came, we wasted time. Since then, we have been able to carry out reconnaissance missions, and there has been good receptivity to our suggestions. Perhaps his promise of the serious training of a group of men will begin tomorrow. It's almost certain that, in June, we'll be able to show something, going into battle. [*Congo*, 19.]

Unquestionably, Che's optimism was still intact at that time and he conveyed it to the other Cubans. He was confident and hoped that all problems would be worked out and that, at last, he would be able to begin to make his dream of organizing the Congolese Liberation Army a reality.

3

June 1965

The month began with a new spirit. Che considered that discipline on the fronts was improved, but the disorganization remained the same everywhere. The groups which formed those fronts were of a tribal nature, with a mistaken concept of the war. Instead of being mobile, they held positions, forming what they called barriers. The only acceptable thing about them from the tactical point of view was the terrain that was chosen: high positions that were hard to get to. However, the disadvantage was that there wasn't any training or actions against the enemy, which also remained inactive.

The farmers supported the Congolese guerrillas, even though most of the time the guerrillas seized their crops and animals by force. Che observed, "The People's Liberation Army was parasitic; its members didn't work, train or fight." [*Congo*, 20.] Moreover, an enormous amount of ammunition was used in every skirmish, no matter how insignificant. Knowing that the reason for that waste was ignorance of the rules of guerrilla warfare, Che gave instructions for their training, adding some military and organizational norms, especially as regards ambushes.

"Mini hapana cuban"

While the Cubans were somewhat separated from the rest of the people living in the area when they were at General Staff headquarters, this changed when they went to the upper base. There, they began to have closer relations with the farmers in the area and therefore increased their knowledge of Swahili. Naturally, the phrases which were used most frequently in the course of hard work — for which the Congolese were anything but eager — were more easily understood than others. For example, when materials had to be carried from one place to another, they would respond, "*Mini hapana motocari*" (I'm not a truck) or "*Mini hapana cuban*" (I'm not Cuban), because the Cubans didn't protest about carrying materials needed in making fortifications.

CHE: The farmers had to transport the food, weapons and ammunition for the front. Obviously, an army of that kind could be justified only if, like its enemy counterpart, it fought once in a while. As will be seen, it didn't meet that requisite, either. If that order of things didn't change, the Congolese Revolution was doomed to failure, because of its own inner weaknesses. [*Congo*, 20.]

It seems that the enemy wasn't entirely aware of what Che described, although it did have information about the use of particular weapons, as might be deduced from the following, which appeared in the June 1, 1965, edition of *Le Soir*: "The rebels are well armed. They have Chinese and Russian weapons."

The worst problem continued to be that time kept passing, whilst the purpose of the internationalist mission was not being fulfilled.

When Ali got back from scouting, he said that he had wanted to fire on the enemy position in the Kabimba zone, but the rebel chief there refused to let him. Moreover, Kabila's practically daily announcements that he was about to arrive never proved true, even though boats frequently crossed the Lake, bringing weapons.

Mitudidi

CHE: In spite of his goodwill, Mitudidi didn't find the formula for letting us work. He was probably held back by some specific order of Kabila's and was waiting anxiously for his arrival. All of us waited just as anxiously, while the days kept passing without any change for the expeditionary force...

Mitudidi was young, around 30. He had been an official in Lulimba and had fought alongside Mulele. According to Mitudidi, Mulele had sent him to that zone before there was any revolutionary organization acting there. In the frequent conversations we had, he told me about Mulele's methods, which were diametrically opposed to Kabila's, and the entirely different characteristics that the struggle in the other part of the Congo had assumed. He never even hinted at a criticism of Kabila or Masengo and attributed all the confusion to the specific characteristics of the region.

I don't know why — perhaps for racial reasons or because of earlier prestige — but, when Kabila arrived in the zone he was the Chief, and Mitudidi was his Chief of Staff. [*Congo*, 21 and 24.]

His full name was Leonard Mitudidi. He had studied at the Sorbonne in Paris. He visited Algeria and China as a member of the African Solidarity Party (PSA) and envoy of the National Liberation Council (CNL) of the Congo. Later, he visited Moscow and then met with Gizenga in Stanleyville. Mulele, who was already operating in the Kwilu region, instructed him to tour several African capitals. In 1964, he was sent to northern Katanga as political commissar of the CNL, to make contact with Soumialot.

During those days of waiting, Mitudidi spent his time well, organizing the base camp. He demanded more discipline and prohibited the drinking of hard liquor — which, as Che said, was "not a very easy task, because it meant fighting with 90 or 95 percent of the men." He also stopped handing out artillery pieces and ammunition to just anybody. To get them, you had to show you knew how to handle them. Lack of control had resulted in the loss of many weapons sent from China and the Soviet Union. The Chief of Staff was making a start on the many things that had to be done, but it was too much for just one person and the other officers didn't give him much cooperation.

Che told Mitudidi that lack of knowledge of Swahili prevented his having contact with the personnel at the base who didn't speak French, so Mitudidi appointed Ernest Ilunga, a young combatant whom the Cubans called Freddy, to give him classes (the other teacher had left).

ZERQUERA: Freddy Ilunga continued teaching Swahili to Che — both of them knew French — and Che taught Spanish to Freddy. For example, Freddy would write a phrase in Swahili and its meaning in French, and then Tatu [Che] would translate it into Spanish. In addition, Freddy was Che's interpreter; he went many places with him and sometimes slept in his hut. Che gave that young man a lot of confidence.

Che's diplomacy
Mundandi, an outstanding Rwandan commander in the Front de Force area, visited and was introduced to Che, impressing him with his seriousness and firmness. It was an impression that was not to last long, after he reported a "violent battle" in which 35 enemy soldiers were put out of action. Che asked, "How many weapons did you get from those 35?" and the reply was, "Weapons? None, because we attacked with bazookas, and all their weapons were shot to bits."

CHE: I've never been much of a diplomat and I simply said that it was a lie. He made excuses, saying that he hadn't been present during the battle, that his subordinates had told him about it, etc., and that's where the incident ended. Since exaggeration is customary in this area, stating frankly that a lie is a lie isn't the best method for establishing fraternal relations with anybody. [*Congo*, 23.]

Secretly, Mitudidi told Che that Kabila wouldn't be coming, especially since Chou En-lai was about to visit Dar es Salaam. Che and the other Cubans returned to the upper base on Monday, June 7, and, as soon as they arrived there, Che was given disturbing news: Mitudidi had drowned in the Lake. It took three days for his body to be found.

CHE: Thanks to the presence of two Cubans who were in the boat at the time of the accident, plus a series of conversations and inquiries I made, I came to the following conclusions:

Mitudidi was going to Rwandasi, a place to which he was thinking of moving the Staff headquarters. It was around four kilometers from the Kabimba base, but, because the path was a hard one, he went by water. A strong wind blew up, creating huge waves in the Lake. It seems that his fall into the water was an accident; everything indicates that. From then on, a series of strange happenings occurred. I don't know whether to attribute them to imbecility — to the extraordinary superstition that the Lake is inhabited by all kinds of spirits — or to something more serious. The fact is that Mitudidi, who could swim a little, managed to take off his boots and was calling for help for around 10 or 15 minutes. Several witnesses have testified to this. Several men jumped into the water to save him; one of them, his orderly, drowned, too. Major François, who was with him, also disappeared; they never found out if he fell out of the boat at the same time or jumped overboard in an attempt to save him. The first thing they did when the accident happened was turn off the motor. As a result, the boat lost all its maneuverability. Later, they again started the motor, and it seemed that some magic power didn't allow them to get close to where Mitudidi was. Finally, while he continued to call for help, the boat went to the shore, and his comrades saw him disappear shortly afterward.

The human relations among the Congolese chiefs are so complicated that you don't know what to say about them. The fact is that the commander of the boat at that time, who was also an Army major, was sent to another front later on, and I think this was done because of a series of incidents involving that comrade at the base. [*Congo*, 23-24.]

The two Cubans in the boat were Arcadio Hernández Betancourt (Dogna) and José Antonio Aguiar (Ahiri). They had gone with Mitudidi because Che had ordered them to look for a good place to build an emplacement for an antiaircraft gun.

CHE: Thus, in a stupid accident, the man who had established the beginning of organization in that terrible chaos that was the Kabimba base lost his life. The fact is that the only person with authority had now disappeared in the Lake. [*Congo*, 24.]

For the Cubans, that loss was more serious. As Che noted, it meant "the death of a hope."

CHE: The news was already known in the surrounding area the next day, and Kabila showed signs of life with a small note in which he told me the following:

"I have just learned of the fate of Brother Mitu and other brothers. You can see, it wounds me deeply.

"I am concerned about your safety. I want to arrive immediately, because, for us, this sad story is our destiny. All of the comrades you came with should stay there until my return, unless they want to go to Kabimba or to Bendera, to Mundandi.

"I trust in your firmness. We will do everything possible to move the base on a precise date.

"I have discussed some matters with Comrade Muteba and with Mulongai and Kasabi during my absence.

"Friendship,

"Kabila" [*Congo*, 24.]

Another report

Muteba visited Che to find out what he thought of the accident. Muteba noted that Che was greatly saddened by the death of his comrade but, considering this a very delicate matter, made no comment. Che took the opportunity to remind Muteba that soon they would have been there for two months and still hadn't done anything. He mentioned the reports that he had made for Mitudidi, but, since they had disappeared along with the drowned man, the new chief asked Che to repeat them and send them to Kabila. Che immediately set about writing them.

CHE: *General considerations*

In view of only a month and a half of Congolese experience, I can't hazard many opinions. I think that we will be faced with one main danger: U.S. imperialism.

It isn't necessary to make an analysis of why the United States is a specific danger. The Congolese revolution is in a period of regrouping its forces after the last defeats dealt it. If the United States has learned from other revolutions, this is the moment it will choose to hit hard, first taking measures such as neutralizing the Lake — that is, it will do everything required to close off our main means of obtaining supplies of all kinds. However, world events — such as the struggle in Vietnam and the recent intervention in Santo Domingo — somewhat tie its hands. Therefore, the time factor is of key importance for consolidating and developing the revolution, which cannot be done except by hitting the enemy hard. Passivity is the beginning of defeat.

Our own lack of organization works against the mobilization of all our forces and our ability to attack the enemy forces. This may be seen in various related aspects:

1. The lack of a single central command with real power over all the fronts, to bring what in military terms is called the unity of doctrine (I refer specifically to this zone, not to the Congo as a whole).

2. The general lack of cadres with a high enough cultural level and absolute fidelity to the revolutionary cause. The consequence of this is the proliferation of local chiefs with authority of their own and tactical and strategic freedom of action.

3. The dispersion of our heavy arms by means of equal distribution, which leaves the headquarters without reserves. This is apart from the misuse of those weapons.

4. The lack of discipline in the units, which are infected with the prevailing localism and have had no prior training.

5. The commands' inability to move large units in a coordinated way.

6. The general lack of even the minimum training needed for handling firearms, which is aggravated in the case of weapons that require special combat training.

All this results in an inability to carry out major tactical actions and, therefore, strategic paralysis. They are problems which every revolution must face. There is no reason for us to panic, but systematic measures must be taken to correct them.

The Cubans' participation
Blacks were the most exploited and discriminated against of all Cubans. Black farmers from the eastern part of the country, the vast majority of whom were illiterate, played a very important part in our struggle.

As a result, very few of our main military figures or middle-level cadres who had received serious training were blacks. When we were asked to send Cubans — preferably black Cubans — we looked among the best members of the Army who had some combat experience, and the result is, we feel, that our group has very good fighting spirit and precise knowledge of tactics in the field, but little academic training.

The foregoing is an introduction to our proposal for action: in view of the characteristics of the troop, our participation should be mainly in combat tasks or other tasks directly related to fighting.

We could do this in either of two ways:

1. Break up our group and spread its members among the various units of the front as instructors for the Congolese forces in arms handling and fighting, or

2. Fight in mixed units (because our forces are so small, there shouldn't be more than two of these units) commanded at first by Cubans. They will carry out well-defined tactical actions and extend their radius of action by developing and training Congolese command cadres. A central training base would be maintained with Cuban instructors as long as they were needed.

We tend to favor this second proposal, for military and political reasons: militarily, because we would guarantee direction of the fighting in line with our concept of guerrilla warfare (which we think is correct), and, politically, because, with our political successes, we would be able to dissipate the environment that surrounds foreign troops with different religious, cultural and other concepts, and it would give us better control of our forces. If they were dispersed, conflicts might arise through lack of understanding of Congolese reality, which we believe our leaders are acquiring.

We could carry out some complementary (and necessary) work, such as training the units, helping to train a General Staff (mastery of duties and especially armaments is weak), organizing public or military health care and doing any other tasks assigned to us.

Our view of the military situation

There is a lot of talk now about seizing Albertville. We think that, at the present time, it is too great a task for our forces, for the following reasons:

1. We haven't managed to dislodge the enemy from positions in our natural defense system (these mountains).

2. We don't have enough experience for such a long-range attempt which supposes the mobilization of units up through at least the battalion level and their synchronization with an operations high command.

3. We don't have enough war matériel for an action of that size.

Albertville should fall as the result of a slow and tenacious action. It might be more correct to say that the enemy will abandon it. First, we have to demoralize the enemy, whose morale is quite good now, by systematically attacking its communications and reinforcements and by wiping out the forces from Kabimba, Front de Force, Lulimba, etc. or forcing them to withdraw by means of these tactics, combined with frontal attacks wherever the correlation of forces is most favorable to us; penetration along all the roads that lead to Albertville, with frequent ambushes and acts of sabotage; and the paralysis of its economy. Then we can seize Albertville.

For reasons that I will go into in more detail in another report, after learning the results of the reconnaissance, it seems to me that Katenga is the best place from which to begin the operations.

The reasons which I can give now are the following:

1. Its garrison is relatively small.

2. We think that we can ambush the reinforcements, since their supply line runs parallel to the mountains.

3. If it falls and remains in our hands, this will isolate Lulimba, the port for Kasongo.

After this letter, I sent the report on the reconnaissance of Katenga, the analysis of the situation and an attack recommendation. At that time, it was relatively easy to attack Katenga, because total lack of activity by our forces had led the enemy to lower its vigilance throughout most of the area. [*Congo*, 25-28.]

Che's considerations were very carefully written. Whenever referring to the possibilities of the Congolese, he used the first person plural, assuming them jointly. His precise proposals were ignored. Muteba took that document with him when he left with Mulongai and Kasabi, all of them very cheerful. Immediately, disorder was more pronounced than ever. An order came to place antiaircraft guns at various points on the Lake, to be manned by Cubans, but there was no logical plan.

CHE: In view of the prevailing conditions of indiscipline, it was impossible to aspire to defend the base against air attacks with Congolese machine gunners, who (with a few honorable exceptions) didn't know how to handle the weapon and didn't want to learn. [*Congo*, 29.]

The above has a tone of disgust about a situation which really existed, but it isn't fair to include the Congolese rebel soldiers in this evaluation, because the main leaders, with their long or total absences, were the cause of the generalized apathy and lack of combativity — "with a few honorable exceptions." Moreover, no matter how much the Cubans wanted to do, they were viewed as foreigners who didn't have to be obeyed. It should be recalled that if the guerrilla leaders at all levels didn't set a good example, nothing could be achieved. Innumerable cases bear this out.

DREKE: On Terry's instructions, Falka, another Cuban whose name I don't remember and two Congolese set an ambush near the shore of the Lake. We had received reports that many of the traders were spies and that their boats drew close to the shore there.

When they saw that a not very big launch was coming inshore, they shot at it with mortars, letting loose a curtain of fire which kept it from withdrawing. The men on board hoisted a white flag. Around seven enemy guards were captured. They were wearing civilian clothes, but their weapons were found in the little boat. One of the prisoners was a French mercenary, and they put him in a hole.

We don't know what they did with the others. But instead of interrogating the prisoners, they either killed them or held them captive without doing anything with them.

A note on page 4 of the *Campaign Diary* which Emilio Mena kept for Dreke's group, stated that this action took place on June 9.

Although the enemy planes were repulsed every time they attacked, Che felt that the dispersal of the Cubans was a useless waste of forces and resulted in their inactivity, because when the mercenary pilots of the four T-28s ("Tataguas") and two B-26s — which were quite old — were shot at, they looked for targets that didn't have any antiaircraft defenses.

For the Cubans at the upper base, the days passed by in almost total idleness, except for their classes, guard duty, looking for firewood, doing KP, finishing some buildings and doing other minor tasks around the camp. No military actions were carried out, because the students Mitudidi had said he would send didn't appear and Muteba, who took the report to Kabila, never put in another appearance.

To complete that discouraging situation, around 10 of the internationalists came down with the Congo fever. Arms and ammunition continued to be delivered, but Che and his comrades realized that they would surely be wasted, since they would be given little or no use.

Kabila writes to Che

In an encouraging sign that things would change and that Kabila would deign to visit them, Mundandi appeared in the latter half of June, bringing several letters from Kabila. Che cited one dated June 16:

> "Comrade,
> I have read and reread the report you wrote to Brother Muteba for my knowledge. I already told you, Comrade, that I want to begin setting ambushes. Comrade Mundandi will talk to you. Let around 50 Cuban comrades participate in the June 25 attack with the rank of combatants under Mundandi.
> "You are a revolutionary and should put up with all of the difficulties there are there. I will arrive at any moment. You can also send around 10 men to Kabimba.
> "With fondest greetings,
> "Kabila
> "P.S. I have studied the plan on Bendera that Nando showed me. It is almost the same as the one we have drawn up. Courage and patience. I also know that you are suffering from the disorganization, but we will do everything to alleviate the situation. It is a defect stemming from the absence of leaders. Good-bye,
> "Kabila" [*Congo*, 29.]

Che Guevara demonstrated admirable patience and discipline for the sake of his ideas and internationalism. The most absurd aspect of this letter was that Kabila accepted as the most natural thing in the world that the lack of leaders was causing their problems yet continued living very comfortably in his mobile command post in Kigoma or Dar es Salaam, protected from the fighting by a strip of water 70 kilometers wide.

Even so, Che and Mundandi analyzed the plan for attacking the selected spot — which was very different from the one he had proposed. It is possible that Kabila thought that a surprise attack on Front de Force — instead of Katenga, which was what had been proposed — would mean an important victory over the military. During that discussion, Che noted that Mundandi was "evasive" and that "he acted like an unfortunate wretch who has been assigned a task beyond his powers; there was something of that, but also a large dose of pretense."

Che became worried about the safety of his men and the Rwandan combatants, because they weren't familiar with the position they were to attack. It had fortifications, artillery and a good number of soldiers with military training. They didn't even know how many defenders there were, because they had no reports about the enemy. This led him to do everything possible to participate in the action:

CHE: Kabila had specified that the men should place themselves under
   Mundandi's orders. By doing so, he subtly rejected one of my

proposals, that the Cubans should direct the tactical actions in which mixed troops took part. [*Congo*, 30.]

As a result, Che wrote the following:

"Dear Comrade,

"Thank you for your letter. I can assure you that my impatience is that of a man of action; it doesn't imply any criticism. I can understand, because I myself have lived in similar conditions.

"I also await your arrival with impatience because I consider you an old friend and owe you an explanation. At the same time, I should place myself at your orders unconditionally.

"According to your orders, the Cubans will go toward Front de Force tomorrow. Unfortunately, many of them are sick, and there will be slightly fewer than 40 of them. There are four comrades in Kabimba. As the others arrive, we will send them on.

"I would like to ask a favor of you. Give me permission to go to Front de Force as my comrades' political commissar, completely under the orders of Comrade Mundandi. I have just spoken with him, and he is willing to have me. I think that this could be useful. I would be returning three or four days after you send me word.

"Greetings,

"Tatu [Che]" [*Congo*, 30.]

Kabila's reply "was evasive," Che noted, adding, "I still had time to write one more letter, asking him to give me a clear yes or no — a letter which didn't allow for a tangential reply — but he simply didn't reply, so I didn't go to Front de Force." [*Congo*, 30.]

Even though Che wasn't authorized to go to battle, that day he sent 36 of the 40 men requested, including a surgeon, an orthopedist and a specialist in internal medicine. Later on, he sent seven more men, and, still later, when they asked for another doctor, he sent one. A total of 44 Cubans participated in the attack on Front de Force.

It is strange that Che didn't realize that the Rwandan and Cuban internationalists were the largest forces that went into battle. The Congolese leaders didn't risk many of their own men.

ERASMO VIDEAUX (KISUA): After a long training hike in the Sierra Maestra mountains, groups of us were sent to various houses in the Miramar and Siboney districts of Havana. Fidel bade us farewell. We left in small groups. When I got to Tanzania, I met Osmany [Cienfuegos], who had been with Fidel when he said good-bye to us in Havana. He appointed me chief of the men who were there and those who were arriving. There were 39 of us in all. I think we were the fourth group.

Oliva from the Embassy told me that the Cubans' chief, who was already in the Congo, had ordered that, as we arrived, we should take Swahili names and that we should give him the money we had left.

Each of us had been given $100 for personal expenses during the trip. I collected around $700. Nobody objected to handing over the money, which was voluntary.

I used a Swahili-French-Spanish dictionary to assign names to the men and I gave each one two: a first and a last name. Since I was the chief, I thought that I would have to think, and I chose Kisua Kitambo, "thinking head." I did the same with the others. We didn't use numbers.

The first Cuban shots

The first shots the Cubans fired — on Saturday, June 19, 1965, against two planes that had strafed and bombed the hamlet of Kisoso, near Lake Tanganyika, causing some casualties among the inhabitants — were with 12.7-mm antiaircraft guns, emplaced on the heights of Kibamba. The air attacks were repeated on an irregular basis, making it dangerous to cross the Lake in daylight.

At 1730 hours on that same day, Che called all the Cubans at the Luluabourg base together and explained the discipline to be maintained in the Front de Force action, stressing that they should be good instructors and even better combatants.

After that meeting, there was another, of the Cuban Communist Party members, in which he told them to continue their French and other classes and to keep on reading José Martí and other authors that he would assign. He told the Party members that they would be leaving for Front de Force the next day and that Moja — Víctor Dreke — would be the head of the troops. The *Campaign Diary* noted that, "This pleased all the comrades — who had been waiting for nearly two months for a chance to fight."

Early on the morning of June 19, a coup d'état in Algeria overthrew the government of Ben Bella. Che didn't mention the coup in his manuscript, but Dreke told me that when he went down to where they had gathered, they talked about it. Che was very worried about what had occurred in Algeria; he didn't know the reasons for the coup. There was reason for his concern, because Ben Bella had upheld a position that was very important for the African liberation movements and Che could not be sure that the new ruler would maintain it.

Ulises Estrada told me that the coup in Algeria caught his group on board the *Uvero*, in the port of Kirga, where they stayed for two or three days, until the Cuban Ambassador gave them new instructions to weigh anchor for Tanzania. They left without unloading anything. When the ship drew away from the Algerian coast, the crew relaxed a little, even though they were all upset about the delay in getting where they were going.

DREKE: Before we left on Sunday, June 20, Che told us we should take prisoners, to get information about the enemy. He was pleased because there would be some action, but didn't like not being able to participate. Since we didn't have any radios, we chose the men who walked most quickly to be liaisons.

That day, a fire broke out in Che's hut, but, since there were plenty of men, we put it out immediately. When it was time to leave, we sang the [Cuban] National Anthem and the July 26 Hymn. I remember that he shook hands with all the combatants who were in formation. He also gave us a box of cigars so we could smoke them after the battle — naturally, we thought we would be victorious. We began the march before dawn, at 0540 hours. I headed the vanguard; Nanne, the center; and Azi, the rear guard.

We had to go through tangled forests and over high mountains and cross five rivers. Yanga was the first hamlet we reached and we camped there. It was in a barren region. Its inhabitants gave us a warm welcome. After posting guards, we cooked dinner and went to sleep. In the early morning, it got so cold that we had to get up and huddle by the fires.

We were beset not only by the cold but also by fear of snakes, so we put our hammocks away and made beds of grass and sticks on the ground. The Congolese said that if you beat on the ground with a stick, the snakes would go away. They said that we should wear wide-brimmed hats and long-sleeved shirts and turn our collars up to protect ourselves against those in the trees. To keep them out of our pants, we should to tie our pants to our legs and tuck the cuffs in our boots.

We could do almost all of this, but where were we going to find so many hats? After a while, we stopped being afraid of snakes. I don't remember any cases of either Congolese or Cubans being bitten by cobras, which is what the Congolese called them. We learned that they don't attack you if you don't annoy them.

They stayed in the same place on Monday, June 21, because they knew that Major Mundandi, the chief of the Rwandans, wasn't at the camp to which they were heading. Early the next day, they heard over the radio about the coup in Algeria. They left at 0620 hours. The path was easy, but there wasn't any vegetation. At midday, they arrived at the hamlet of Kañaña, where they were warmly welcomed.

Looking after Che's safety

VIDEAUX: I think we encountered Che one or two days before Dreke and the others left for Front de Force. Because of Villegas's and Coello's presence in our group, I was already quite sure that "the man" Oliva had mentioned was Che. I knew that they were members of his guard. When I saw him, my hunch was confirmed. I came to attention in front of him, but he told me that kind of discipline wasn't necessary there. He praised the men's gesture of turning in the money that was left over [from the journey to Africa] and told me to give my men a one-name pseudonym.

The next day, he assigned the group, sending around seven combatants to Dreke, including one of the doctors. Some others were sent to man the pieces of artillery, and the rest of us stayed at the base, covering defense positions. As in the army, we went up and down mountains every day as training. Later, I became a part of Che's guard, along with Pombo and Tuma, whom Fidel had sent for his protection. Chino, Mena and Julián had protected him before.

When we realized that it would be a very hard job for just three of us to guard him — from dusk to dawn — we got together and decided to ask Che to include one more man. Since none of us wanted to be the messenger, all three went.

We explained that it was necessary to reinforce the guard to look after his safety. "It sounds like you're ass-licking," he replied. "Don't you realize there aren't enough of us here to have any more comrades spending their time looking after me? Having three of you is a privilege I don't like very much."

In spite of that, we decided to include Savón (Danhse) and then Twenty-Four, who was a cook.

At 0915 hours on Wednesday, June 23, they arrived at Front de Force. Mundandi hadn't yet arrived. There they found the first battalion of Rwandans, who formed ranks and presented arms, and then the men of the two forces greeted one another. They spent June 24, 25 and 26 cleaning the Rwandans' weapons. Many of them still had the grease put in them at the factory. They also trained the Rwandans and carried out ambush and reconnaissance actions for the attack on the Front de Force garrison, where the former colonialists had concentrated a large force. Mundandi appeared on June 25. They kept Che informed about how those actions were going to be carried out, and Inne went on several reconnaissance missions.

On June 27, according to the *Campaign Diary*, six Cubans whom Che had sent arrived. The additional weapons and personnel were assigned for attacking the enemy positions. At dusk, the groups went out to their positions.

Study of the plan of attack

DREKE: On June 28, I took part in reconnaissance, in which we went right up to the walls of the garrison. I wanted to check some of the things that Inne had told me, because we were at a great disadvantage: we weren't familiar with the terrain, and, even though the Rwandans said they knew every inch of it, we wanted to prepare for the action.

Mbili and I met with Major Mundandi to study the plan of action.

CHE: Front de Force, or Front Bendera, is built around a hydroelectric power plant on the banks of the Kimbi [Kimvit] River. The water intake is practically in the mountains controlled by the Rwandans. The power lines go along the plain (the mountains fall straight down to the high plateau of the Congo River Basin). The town is divided in two parts: an old section, which was there before the power plant, and a newer one, near the building housing the turbines, where there is a military residential area with more than 30 houses. The Kimbi [Kimvit] River is one of its natural defenses and was reinforced by trenches that had been explored only very superficially prior to the attack. The town has an airfield for small planes. It was estimated that an enemy battalion of from 500 to 700 men might be there, and there was another group composed of special troops four kilometers away, at the junction with the road to Albertville. It was said that the Cadets' Academy or military training school was there. [*Congo*, 31.]

As Che later wrote, the two Cuban officers tried to convince Mundandi that it would be crazy to carry out the attack as planned. Mundandi claimed that he couldn't change the plan, because it was an order from Kabila. Later, Kabila would deny that. The only thing they achieved was that Mundandi agreed to having the Cubans direct the main points of attack. Filled with confusion but aware that they had to carry out Che's orders, they left for the Front de Force garrison along different routes shortly before 1800 hours on June 28.

Cuban blood on African soil

DREKE: We agreed on beginning the attack at 0500 hours and the officers of all the groups synchronized watches. We opened fire with a direct hit. We placed our command post around 800 or 1,000 meters back, beside the river. Mbili, Paulito, Saba, and Anga, the military health officer, were with me. Mundandi and around five of his men were there for the Rwandans. Bahasa and Ananane, who had malaria, remained at the camp.

CHE: The first battle report read as follows:

"Tatu [Che] or Kumi,

"The attack began at 0500 hours today, June 29, 1965. We are doing well. It seems that Katenga is being attacked. Five of our comrades; Nanne, as head of the group; and two Rwandan comrades are there.

"Homeland or death,

"Moja [Dreke]"

And then:

"It's 1930 hours. Everything is going well. The men are very happy and behaving well. Everything began at the time stipulated. We opened fire with a cannon and mortar.

"I'll send you more information later." [*Congo*, 31.]

In another short note, they informed Che, "We did the thing in Force on June 29. It isn't possible to convince the man. We'll report on this later."

The foregoing seems to be the reason why, from another source, Che received alarming reports of 20 Cuban dead and many wounded. If such were the case, things weren't going so well. Later on, Che reconstructed the attack plan and its development with the principal leaders of the action and wrote of this in his manuscript.

CHE: A small group headed by Ishirini [also consisting of Nahalla and Amba] would attack what is called the *charriot*, the intake that supplies water to the turbine of the hydroelectric power plant; below, crossing the Kimbi [Kimvit] River, a group of men headed by Lt. Azi, would attack the fortified positions closer to the mountains; in the center, Lt. Azima, with a group of Rwandans, would seize the airport and advance to join Azi; Lt. Mafu, with another group [Afendi, Maganga, Alau, Kukula and Wasiri], would prevent any advance from Lulimba; and Lt. Inne would hold the strongest position, with a 75-mm cannon and other heavy weapons, in an ambush on the road from Albertville. The command post would be on the other side of the Kimbi [Kimvit] River, in the first foothills of the mountains, and Moja [with Mbili, Paulu, Saba and the medical health officer Angari] and Mundandi would stay there. At first, Mundandi had said there should be two command posts, but he was convinced it would be better to unify them.

This plan had some serious drawbacks: Inne was to go [with nine other Cubans, including Ansurune, Kawawa, Sultán, Arobaine,

Kasambal, Selasine, Aga and Ajili, and a group of Rwandans] to an area they knew nothing about, since it hadn't been reconnoitered. Mafu knew something of the terrain, as did Azi [who was with nine other Cubans: Azima, Asmari, Angalia, Abdala, Sita, Ansali, Anchali, Tano and Arobo]. Azima had given the ground a superficial once-over, using binoculars, from the mountain. Although we should have laid a very good ambush for the reinforcements that were bound to be sent from Albertville, we had to go about it blindly. The Cubans argued a lot with Mundandi, trying to get him to direct the main effort to Katenga and they finally got him to agree to sending an attack order to Captain Salumi, but, as was proved later, he gave the order for June 30, while Mundandi attacked on June 29.

In Front de Force, events turned out far from as well as the first dispatches had indicated.

Ishirini had to go with two other Cubans and seven Rwandans with rocket launchers and rifles to silence the nest of machine guns at the *charriot* and try to damage the plant; they put the lights out for a few minutes, but that was all. The Rwandan combatants stayed around two kilometers from the place, and only the Cubans took part in the action. To give an idea of the reigning disorder, I am including the full report of Lt. Azi, who was in charge of attacking from the Kimbi [Kimvit] River:

"On going to carry out the mission, I placed the mortar, cannon and antiaircraft and other machine guns for shooting directly at the enemy at a range of around 300 meters, except for the mortar, which was at a range of 500 meters. Some 49 Rwandans and five Cubans then crossed the river, which was 150 to 200 meters from the enemy mortars. While we were crossing the river, around 100 meters from the enemy position, a Rwandan's gun went off, the troop dispersed, and five of them disappeared, leaving a unit of 44. I organized the personnel in three groups, with two Cubans in my group and one in each of the other two groups.

"By 0300 hours on June 29, we had occupied our positions, some of them 25 meters from the enemy and others a little farther away. We heard some enemy machine-gun shots. At 0500 hours, as planned, we opened up with the cannon, mortars and antiaircraft and other machine guns and then immediately started shooting at the infantry. All of the weapons hit their targets; the firing continued steadily until 0600 hours. By that time, three men had been wounded on my front. By 0700 hours, no shots could be heard from our troops on the left flank. I shifted a little and noted that many of the Rwandans weren't there. I armed three Cubans — Anchali, Angali and myself — and a Rwandan captain with machine guns instead of

FALs. At 0845 hours, two Rwandans were killed. I shifted to the left to look for Tano, to send a message to Moja [Dreke] that the personnel in the center and the group on the left, including their Rwandan officers, had withdrawn on their own, leaving me with 14 Rwandans. One Cuban — Tano, who was in the group in the center — had disappeared. I sent the first message to Moja with Angali. By 1000 hours, there were four Rwandans left, including one officer. I held out until 1200 hours and then withdrew around 25 meters. There were two more dead and three wounded.

"I sent another message to Moja, held out there until 1230 hours and then withdrew to the mortar and cannon position, crossing the river. Before withdrawing, I looked for Tano and Sita at their position but couldn't find them. Later on, Sita appeared. At the mortar's position, I received Moja's orders to withdraw the mortar, the machine guns and the cannon and leave an ambush for the guards if they crossed the river. I held that position until 0600 hours on June 30, when I was ordered to pull everyone out.

"Only Cubans — Anzali, Anchali, Aziri, Abdala, Asmari and Azi — remained in the ambush, since there were no Rwandans left. The Rwandans received orders from the command post to occupy the positions, but they went back to their camp. The Rwandan personnel dropped their weapons and ammunition and didn't bring in their dead. Comrade Azima was under my orders, carrying out the mission to occupy the other position (the right bank of the river, around 500 meters from our positions) with Alakre, Arobo and 40 Rwandans. On the night when they moved to occupy that position, the Rwandans heard a noise which they said was a *tembo* (an elephant) and fled, leaving him alone with the two other Cubans, so they had to return to the command post at 0700 hours on June 29."

That was about typical of the operation. It began well, even though men had been lost from many positions even before the fighting began, and then there was a rout.

Comrade Tano, who showed up seven days later, had been wounded, and his [Rwandan] comrades had abandoned him. He dragged himself into the woods, where some Rwandans who were on patrol found him. After recovering from his wounds, he joined the fighting again.

To complete the picture, here is another dispatch from that same day:

"We can inform you that the Rwandan comrades fled, leaving weapons, equipment, wounded and dead, all along the front. Our [Cuban] comrades brought them in, as Comrade Major Mundandi witnessed…

"Comrade Inne had the main mission, that of occupying the road from Albertville to Force to prevent enemy reinforcements from coming up. According to the information we have so far, he didn't reach the place indicated, because the guide said he was lost. Inne then made the erroneous decision to attack the Military Academy. According to the reports we have from our comrades and from the Rwandans who took part in the attack, our men and some of the Rwandans were the only ones there when the fighting began. Two were wounded, and the rest were killed. Comrade Inne had even asked them to place the cannon at the beginning of the fighting, but the Rwandans who carried the cannon withdrew, taking it back toward the camp and abandoning the missiles and other pieces of artillery, which some of our comrades picked up.

"On hearing of the death of Comrade Inne, we sent Mbili there with 20 men to reinforce that position and also see the reality of the situation. They met Comrade Mafu near the ambush, and, in it, Kasambala, Sultán, Ajili and others who belonged to Inne's group. On seeing the situation, Comrade Mbili informed me about it, at the same time asking for more men so that, if I thought it a good idea, he could move to the highway with them. That was at 1800 hours on June 29.

"When I spoke to Major Mundandi about that problem, he told me that the Rwandan comrades refused to fight. He didn't have any more men to send with whom to lay the ambush, since the Rwandans in Inne's group who had survived had gone to the base, while the 20 Rwandans whom Mbili had taken also refused to fight, and the personnel Mafu had were in the same situation. Therefore, we considered telling Mbili to leave four or five of our comrades to look for bodies and have the rest withdraw, planning the withdrawal for the night of June 30, 1965. But, at 0400 hours on June 30, Comrade Azi and the other Cubans were the only ones left in his position. Mundandi was informed of that situation, and it was decided to withdraw to a nearby woods in that area.

"Comrade Mbili will give you the details about the other problems that arose in the course of the operation.

[This was followed by a paragraph that was crossed out.]

"Moja [Dreke]"

Comrade Inne had nothing but difficulties. He had argued with Mafu before, because he had thought of acting in the ambush and then going back to attack the enemy post. This had been proposed to the command, but it hadn't agreed. He nevertheless kept insisting on his idea. When the fighting began in other places, there was little possibility of reaching the point assigned to him, because the guide, who was in the grip of mortal terror, refused to take another step and nobody else knew the way. Inne decided to attack the position in front of him when the fighting broke out. This was the Military Academy and he was met with heavy fire by well-combined heavy weapons. Witnesses said that Inne himself was hit very early in the action. He left his post at the machine gun to Kawawa, who was killed by a mortar, and two other comrades were less seriously wounded and withdrew. A scout who was sent out shortly afterwards found the body of Telathini; Anzurune had disappeared and was presumed dead. The fighting got bogged down around 200 meters from the enemy, apparently in an area it had in its sights. In addition to the four Cuban comrades, at least 14 Rwandans were killed. One was Major Mundandi's brother. It isn't possible to know the exact number, because the Rwandans' figures were very deficient.

The Cuban command was largely to blame for that unfortunate action; Comrade Inne underestimated the enemy. In an action undeniably daring, to carry out what he considered his moral duty even though it wasn't his specific task, Comrade Inne threw himself into a frontal attack in which he and other combatants were killed. In doing so, he left open the road to Albertville, along which the enemy's reinforcements could come.

As a security measure, before initiating the battle, the comrades had been ordered to leave behind all documents and papers which might make it possible to identify them. They had done that, but Inne's group had kept some documents in their knapsacks, since it was thought that they would leave their belongings before entering into combat at the ambush site. Since they started fighting earlier than planned, they still had their knapsacks with them. The enemy found a diary in the knapsack of one of the dead men which showed that Cubans were participating in the attack. What they didn't know is that four Cubans had been killed there; the newspapers always spoke of just two.

Quite a large amount of weapons and equipment was abandoned in their flight, but, since there were no prior figures, it isn't possible to calculate exactly how much; the wounded were left to their fate — as, of course, were the dead. [*Congo*, 32-35.]

The Katenga disaster

CHE: Meanwhile, what was happening at Katenga?

One hundred and sixty Congolese with weapons that were very inferior to those of the Rwandans — the most effective weapons they had were rifle-machine guns and short-range missile launchers —

went to the attack. The surprise factor was lost, because, for reasons which he never explained, Mundandi had ordered the attack for a day later, June 30, when enemy planes were flying over the entire region and the men defending the post were, logically, on alert.

Sixty of the 160 men deserted before the fighting began, and many more never used their weapons. At the time agreed upon, the Congolese opened fire against the garrison, almost always shooting into the air, because most of the combatants closed their eyes and simply held the triggers of their automatic weapons down until their ammunition ran out. The enemy replied with accurate fire from a 60-mm mortar, killing several men and causing the rest to flee.

The losses were four dead and 14 wounded, these last in the retreat, since they fled in terror, in total confusion. At first, they claimed they had been defeated because the witch doctor was inefficient and had given them a bad *dawa*. He tried to defend himself by blaming the women and fear, but there weren't any women there, and some of the men (the more sincere ones) were ready to confess their own weaknesses. The witch doctor was in a tight spot and was replaced; the biggest job that Major Calixte, the head of that group, had was to find a new *muganga* with the correct characteristics. He went all over the region for that purpose.

The result of that double attack was enormous demoralization among the Congolese and Rwandans, and the Cubans were very dejected, too. Each of our combatants had the sad experience of seeing how the troops that went to the attack dissolved in the moment of fighting and how precious weapons were thrown away in order to make it easier to flee. They had also observed the lack of comradeship among them, leaving the wounded to their fate, the terror that had taken possession of the soldiers and the ease with which they had been routed, not following orders of any kind. In their flight, those who set the example were often the officers, including the political commissars (a defect of the Liberation Army, whose members I will assess later on). The heavy arms had generally been manned by Cubans, and nearly all were saved; some of the FM and DT machine guns, which were manned by Rwandans, were lost, and so were the rifles of all kinds and other equipment.

During the days following the attack, a large number of soldiers deserted or asked to be released. Mundandi wrote me a long letter, filled as always with heroic tales, in which he lamented the loss of his brother but announced that he had been killed after having wiped out a truckload of soldiers (a complete fabrication, since there had never been any truck there). He was saddened by the loss of several of the staunchest cadres of his group and protested because the

General Staff was at Kigoma, while the men were fighting and making sacrifices in the Congo. In passing, he announced that two thirds of the enemy troops had been wiped out — a figure that couldn't have come from any reliable source, since, of course, it was false. Because of his fanciful spirit, he had to make those statements while excusing himself from his own weaknesses.

In short, Mundandi made a complete confession of dismay. I had to send him a reply filled with advice and analysis of the situation, trying to encourage him. Those letters simply presaged the confusion in which the entire Liberation Army — and the Cuban troops — would later be enveloped.

On June 30, when the fighting at Front de Force had already begun but, because of the distance, we hadn't yet received any news of it, I summed up the month as follows in my diary:

"This is the poorest showing so far. When everything seemed to indicate that we were beginning a new era, Mitudidi was killed, and the haziness is thicker. The exodus to Kigoma continues, Kabila has repeatedly announced that he would come but hasn't yet arrived, and there is total chaos.

"On the positive side, the men have gone to the front; on the negative side, there is the announcement of an attack that may be crazy or totally ineffective and alert Tshombe's forces.

"Several questions remain to be answered. What attitude will Kabila have toward us — and, particularly, toward me? In short, will he be man enough for this situation? Will he be able to judge the situation and see how chaotic everything is here? Until we see each other on the spot, there is no way of knowing, but, at least with regard to the first question, there are serious indications that he isn't at all pleased by my presence. I have yet to find out if this is caused by fear, jealousy or because his feelings have been hurt by my methods."

During the last few days, I had written a letter to Pablo Rivalta, Cuban Ambassador to Tanzania, in which I instructed him to tell the Government that I was here, to apologize for the method used and to explain the obstacles that had arisen because Kabila wasn't in the territory at that time, making it very clear that it had been a decision of mine, and not of the Cuban Government. The man bearing the letter was to talk with Kabila in Kigoma first, asking for his opinion. When Kabila learned of my intentions, he flatly refused to allow anything to be said, explaining that he would talk with me when he reached the Congo. [*Congo*, 35-37.]

Naturally, the Front de Force fighting was followed by a storm of publicity against the presence of Cubans in the Congo. However, there was no mention that the legendary Che Guevara was commanding the Cuban troops. Those in charge of supplying the information also "forgot" to mention that anti-Castro Cuban mercenary pilots from the United States were working for Tshombe.

The CIA continues to be confused

An "R"-classified CIA memorandum which was circulated in June 1965 stated that Che was hospitalized and in terrible physical and mental condition. The memo went on to say that he had written countless letters, most of them to Fidel Castro, referring to grandiose plans for an ongoing revolution and the exporting of his guerrilla strategy. It continued by claiming that there were well-founded reasons for Guevara having disappeared from public life, because there had been and still was a serious threat that his appearance in public would unleash great unrest and confusion, and not even Aleida March, his wife, could see him.

4

July 1965

The Rwandans blame the Congolese

During the first few days of the new month, Kabila made several new announcements of his long-awaited visit. Che and his comrades didn't believe those messages and spent the time on matters which concerned them, such as further reconnaissance at Front de Force. This reconnaissance had the dual purpose of looking for any wounded who might have been left abandoned — because Mundandi, the chief of the front, wasn't aware of the loss of the Rwandans who had disappeared — and obtaining more knowledge about the enemy.

The Rwandan commander sent many letters to Che complaining that he wouldn't have any combatants left for making the revolution in his own country, because many men had been killed in the last actions, including his best cadres. He also said that he had been planning that, once Albertville had been taken, he would return to his own country to begin the struggle, but, with so many losses in his ranks, it would be impossible. He blamed the Congolese for everything, ignoring his own mistakes, including that of keeping his troop separated from the Congolese. However, they refused to undertake reconnaisance with the Cubans and, when Che insisted, Mundandi said that it was "a political matter," claiming that his men were "dispirited by the limited Congolese cooperation, which is why they refused to act."

If it hadn't been for the farmers who brought the wounded men whom they found after the Front de Force and Katenga battles into the base, many of them would have died. The soldiers not only didn't go out to look for them, but also refused to go through the hardship of carrying them on their shoulders on the steep mountain paths. But how could you expect the soldiers to do it, if their officers didn't tell them to? The officers didn't give them any such orders, because they didn't have the moral authority to do so.

There was a new officer in charge at the Staff base: Major Kasali, who refused to see Che when he went to see him. Kasali claimed he had a headache. Kasali delegated Kiwe, the information chief who had met Che when he arrived in the Congo, to listen to him and pass on what was said and then send on his proposals to Kigoma.

In another demonstration of selflessness, Che accepted this and presented the following ideas to Kiwe:

CHE: A) What should I do with the 40 men who had just arrived? Where should I send them?

B) I expressed my disagreement with the way everything related to the attack on Bendera had been handled.

At the same time, I gave him a short letter for Kabila, explaining that there was an ever greater need for me to be at the front. [*Congo*, 38.]

Che's concern had increased after the last battle, since several Cubans said that they wouldn't fight any more with people such as that and that they preferred to abandon the mission. He trusted that his presence and personal example would reverse the discouragement that could be seen in some comrades. But the reply which he urgently requested from Kabila didn't come, so he sent another, longer letter, once again insisting on the need to be at the front. He also advocated the creation of a single command, incorporating Cubans. Moreover, Che went more deeply into the defeat at Front de Force.

CHE: The situation of the Rwandans was very strange. On the one hand, they were given more demonstrations of trust and esteem than the Congolese; on the other, they were blamed for the defeat. Both factions stopped being self-critical and competed in an incredible war of abuse against each other. It is a shame that they didn't save that energy and use it against the enemy. Mundandi told me that Calixte had on one occasion gone so far as to shoot at him — an extreme measure of which I have no proof. But it is true that the two were equally inefficient.

My analysis of our mistakes:

First, we underestimated the enemy. Thinking that they had the same characteristics as the rebel soldiers who opposed them; attacking without protection and with a spirit of victors; counting on making a clean sweep, not remembering that they had received military training, that they were protected by parapets and that they were, seemingly, on alert.

Second, lack of discipline. I placed emphasis on the need to maintain strict discipline. No matter how painful, it was necessary to criticize what Inne did, which was heroic but harmful, for it led not only to the deaths of three more Cuban comrades but also to those of more than a dozen Rwandans.

Third, a decline in fighting spirit. It was necessary to keep morale high; I insisted on that a great deal.

I publicly criticized Comrade Azima, who had made some defeatist remarks and was very explicit about what awaited us: not only hunger, bullets and suffering of all kinds, but also, on some occasions, to be killed by our own comrades, who didn't have any idea about shooting. The struggle would be very long and hard. I made that warning because I was ready at that moment to let the men who had just arrived express their doubts and go back, if they wanted to. Later, it wouldn't be possible.

My tone was tough, and the admonition clear. None of those who had just arrived showed any weakness. However, to my surprise, three of the combatants who had taken part in the attack on Front Bendera and who were back at base bringing some messages, said that they wanted to leave. The worst thing was that one of them was a Party member...

I reproached them for their attitude and warned them that I was going to ask for the strongest sanctions against them. I hadn't made any promises to them, because I had been speaking to the new soldiers, but I promised I would let them go in the future — I didn't say just when. [*Congo*, 39-40.]

One combatant, who had been one of his comrades in the anti-Batista struggle in the Sierra Maestra mountains, also asked to return to Cuba. His arguments hurt Che greatly, although it was true that he was ill.

Che's disappointment is understandable, but I think he should have foreseen those weaknesses. The history of humanity is filled with that kind of sentimental reaction. It is a far cry from desertion, which is secretive flight and unjustifiable. Desertion is nothing but cowardice. This wasn't the case with those comrades, who expressed their feelings because of what Che had said. There had been many cases of that kind in the Sierra Maestra, and some of those men had continued fighting in the urban underground and even lost their lives.

Others had deserted, but, in both situations, this hadn't held back the progress of the war. For every one who asked to leave or deserted during the guerrilla war in Cuba, there were 10 or more who wanted to join and often they had to be turned down, either for lack of weapons or for other reasons. In Cuba, in those early years immediately following the 1959 revolution, there were hundreds of comrades who wanted to carry out internationalist missions as combatants. Years later in Angola, hundreds of thousands of them would do so. Slightly over 2,000 Cubans were killed during those internationalist missions to Africa in the 1970s and 1980s.

No war has been lost because of deserters and the attitude of those who asked to leave the struggle had no weight in what happened in the Congo. Unfortunately, Che couldn't know that most of those who asked to leave the Congo would later carry out internationalist missions of the same kind in an exemplary manner.

Kabila's short stay

The days were more bitter because of what had happened and Che admitted that he felt quite pessimistic. This was offset by Kabila's arrival on July 7. He was accompanied by Masengo, who was named the new Chief of Staff.

Che immediately went to meet Kabila, observing that, "He was cordial but aloof." Che reiterated what he had already stated several times by letter, saying that the Tanzanian Government should be informed of his presence, but "[Kabila] replied evasively, leaving it for another time."

CHE: [Kabila] seemed enthusiastic and asked me what I wanted to do. Naturally, I repeated my old refrain: I wanted to go to the front. My most important mission, in which I could be most useful, was to train cadres, and they were trained in the course of war, on the battlefront, not in the rear guard. He expressed his reservations, saying that a person such as myself, who was useful for the world revolution, should take care of their safety. I argued that I didn't think of fighting on the front line, but wanted to be in the front line with the soldiers; that I had enough experience to take care of myself; that I wasn't going to seek any laurels in the fighting, but wanted to carry out a specific task, which I felt would be the most useful thing I could do for him, because it might produce efficient, loyal cadres.

He didn't reply, but he maintained a cordial tone and told me that we were to go on a series of trips. We would go to the interior to visit all the fronts. As a kind of preview, we would go to Kabimba that very night to visit the area. That night something came up that prevented our going, and we didn't go the following night, either. On the third night, he had to have a meeting with the farmers to tell them about the results of the Cairo conference and answer their questions. Provisionally, Ali and 10 other men were sent to carry out some minor action in the Kabimba area; Lieutenant Kiswa went to Uvira to do reconnaissance. [*Congo*, 41.]

Kabila impressed Che when he talked with the farmers. "He showed that he was very familiar with the way the people thought; he was quick and charming." He provided details about the Cairo conference and gave convincing replies to questions from the audience. Che described the end of the meeting as "a small party at which the participants danced to a chorus that went 'Oh, Kabila; yes, Kabila.'"

Unquestionably, Kabila had some authority, which he showed when he said that a defense plan had been drawn up for the small bay where the base was. He ordered that 60 men be found who, with three Cuban instructors, would build the trenches and also be given classes in shooting. Che and his comrades felt that Kabila was trying to make up for lost time, but all that "intensive activity" didn't last long. On July 11, the Congolese leader told his Cuban counterpart that he would be leaving for Kigoma immediately. Soumialot was there and Kabila "severely criticized that leader for his organizational mistakes, demagogy and weakness." [*Congo*, 41.] Later, Kabila told Che that Soumialot had freed a group of enemy agents whom he had sent to be imprisoned in Kigoma.

CHE: [Kabila] had to clarify the division of labor with Soumialot once and for all. Soumialot had been named President so he could travel and explain the revolution and not upset things very much — he had no organizational ability at all — but their spheres had to be clearly defined. He analyzed Soumialot's influence in that area, where he had been born, and said that they had to have a final explanation, because his action could be fatal for the future of the revolution. He said he would be away for just one day and would return the next one.

In the course of our conversation, he let it slip that Soumialot had already gone back to Dar es Salaam. I asked him a little sarcastically how he was going to cross the Lake, have a meeting with Soumialot in Dar es Salaam and return the next day, but he replied that Soumialot's departure hadn't been confirmed and that, if the report were true, he would have to go to Dar es Salaam but would be right back. [*Congo*, 42.]

The enthusiasm disappeared in those who learned of the imminent "urgent return," and exclamations of all kinds could be heard in all of the languages spoken there.

CHE: Changa, our hard-working "admiral" of the Lake, broke off his cursing to ask, "Why did that man bring so many bottles of whiskey, if he was only going to stay five days?"

Kabila was discredited, and it was impossible to reverse that situation if he didn't come back immediately. We had one last conversation, in which I hinted at that problem with all the diplomacy of which I was capable. We also talked about some other topics and he referred — in passing, as was his style — to what my position would be if there were a break. I told him that I hadn't come to the Congo to intervene in matters of domestic politics, that this would be fatal. The [Cuban] Government had sent me to that area and that, over and above everything else, we would try to be loyal to him and to the Congo. I said that if I had any doubts about his political position I would express them frankly to him before talking to anybody else, but I insisted that wars were won on the field of battle, not in clandestine meetings in the rear guard.

We spoke of future plans, and he told me that he was making arrangements to move the base farther south, to Kabimba, and that measures had to be taken to keep the arms from being distributed in the areas of his political enemies. I explained that, in our view, the wealth of Katanga made it the key area of the Congo and that it was the place where the hardest battles should be fought. I said that we agreed with what he said, but that we couldn't consider that the Congo's problem should be solved in a tribal or regional way. It was a national problem and should be understood as such. Moreover, I insisted, it wasn't as important to have the loyalty of a given tribe as to have the loyalty of revolutionary cadres, and, to have that, it was necessary to create and develop them. And, once more, I insisted that it was necessary for me to go to the front (my old refrain)...

We said good-bye, Kabila left and the next day the rhythm of activity at the base, which had begun to accelerate in response to his presence and dynamism, declined. The soldiers in charge of digging the trenches said that they weren't going to work that day because their chief had left; others who were building the hospital downed tools, and everything went back to the tranquil, bucolic rhythm of a provincial hamlet far from the hazards not only of war but even of everyday life. [*Congo*, 42-43.]

That situation seems to have led five more Cubans to say that they wanted to leave the Congo, which made Che much more bitter. He was "much more wounding" to those of the highest ranks.

CHE: Simple [Cuban] soldiers reacted to events in a more or less primitive way. The selection that was made in Cuba wasn't good enough, that is evident. It is difficult, however, to manage to make a good selection in the present conditions of the Cuban Revolution. You don't have to base yourself just on the man's military record; that is a great precedent, but subsequent years of comfortable living can change individuals. Then there is the vast majority, whom the Revolution made revolutionaries. I still don't know how to make a selection of this kind. [*Congo*, 44.]

I consider Che's view to have been correct, but it should be added that the comprehensively negative behavior by the members of the Congolese Liberation Army created a culture. It was this culture that produced the attitude of those who wanted to leave the struggle. Che wanted to apply to the others the moral demands which he himself practiced in all his actions, forgetting that these standards were higher than that of the average revolutionary anywhere in the world.

It isn't possible to solve the problem of selection of cadre; whenever a selection of that kind is made among volunteers who haven't been thoroughly toughened in armed struggle, you always run the risk that some of them will change their minds while on the mission — as may also happen with veterans. Che saw that again in Bolivia. The first deserters from that mission had never fought before and others deserted later on, even though they had taken part in several battles. We shouldn't forget that the hardest trial of being a guerrilla is your immediate environment. The majority of the Cubans never said they wanted to go home.

A strange execution

Among the Rwandans, the situation bordered on rebellion, to such an extent that three Rwandans were executed. Among those executed was Major Mitchell, Mundandi's second-in-command. This happened on July 13. It was claimed that the *dawa* he gave his soldiers was bad. Others suspected that, when he went in search of the witch doctor, he told the enemy an attack was coming. It was also claimed that it was over a problem of women.

CHE: The execution was connected with other recent events that it would have been good to get to the bottom of. It came about after a serious defeat. Mundandi was the one mainly responsible for the defeat, but somebody else was shot for it. Everything happened at a time when there was practically a rebellion against Kabila and the high command of the Liberation Army, since the Rwandans categorically refused to take part in any more war actions. Many of them deserted and those who remained in the camp said that they would only go to fight when they saw the Congolese fighting. If Kabila came to see them, they would give him food without salt and tea without sugar — as they had it — so he would understand the scope of the sacrifices (of course, this didn't involve a real threat, for Kabila had no intention of going anywhere near there). [*Congo*, 44-45.]

At 1600 hours on July 14, after having received a letter from Kabila, Mundandi informed Dreke and Mbili that he was going to Kigoma to talk with his chief and would arrive at the base on July 15 with many armed men.

CHE: He looked threatening, but, in fact, he was afraid and wanted to ensure that he would get to Kigoma safely to talk with Kabila... He visited me, treating me with solicitude, almost humility. First, we talked about the general problems of the attack, and then we went on to the specific topic of the murder. [*Congo*, 46.]

Mundandi claimed that Major Mitchell's indiscretion had alerted the enemy to the attack. Che argued that, even if that were true, the attack had failed because of his incorrect planning and leadership of the actions. Mundandi said that the case had been discussed in assembly and the majority voted for the execution — so, even though he didn't agree with it, he had to accept it. Che explained that that kind of democracy wasn't valid in any army anywhere in the world, and told him about a similar case in the Sierra Maestra mountains. Executing an officer without the participation of the higher Staff was one more example of disregard of a central command. When Masengo heard of Mundandi's claim, he simply said that what had happened was due to superstition and it didn't go beyond that.

One more of them...
Up until then, the only place where the Cubans functioned as so-called instructors — even though they couldn't do anything as such — was in the Rwandan camps. Che tried to convince Masengo that they should all be together arguing that, "To be successful in the struggle, we had to become an ever more integral part of the liberation movement, so the Congolese soldiers would consider us just one more of them..." [*Congo*, 45.] Masengo agreed to having the Cubans work with Major Calixte, chief of the Kazolo-Makungo Front. Che sent Dreke and 12 other Cubans to that front.

With the idea of establishing coordination with the various fronts, the Congolese chief called a meeting with the Rwandan commander; Captain Salumu, Calixte's second-in-command; Lambert, chief of operations on the Fizi Front; and their aides. There was a lot of talking, but everything remained unchanged: "To maintain the fronts' independence of action." In fact, Masengo, with his utter lack of authority, couldn't have achieved anything else. This ended Che's hope of creating a united front under a firm command.

On July 16, Dreke described the situation at that time and gave instructions for the future ambush. The next day, he sent a report to Che.

Captain Zakarías took command in the Front de Force area. Considering that, with the change in command, they might carry out new actions, Che told Mbili to go to that front. Before he went, they discussed how to teach the Rwandans how to lay ambushes, so they would learn gradually, beginning with small objectives — that is, not attacking more than one military transport at a time. The same number of Cubans as Rwandans should take part in the action and they should be volunteers. Mbili took those instructions to Dreke, so he could put them in practice.

For the first ambush, Azi reconnoitered the road between Front de Force and Albertville, and a good spot was selected.

On the Kabimba Front, Ali reported a clash with four policemen. Only one of them was armed and he was killed; the others were taken prisoner. The job of the police was to burn the nearby woods so enemy troops would be seen more easily. However, 16 of the 20 Congolese under his command fled as soon as the first shot was fired. In his report, Ali noted the low morale and insignificant combat training of the friendly troops.

Another problem which was getting steadily more acute was the loss of weapons. None of the fronts reported that they had the amount that had been turned over to them, because they didn't know about those that the combatants threw away in their precipitous retreats or those that deserters took with them. Since the vast majority of the men came from the region, a commission was created to go and recover those rifles or, if they couldn't, to imprison the family members and force them to return the weapons.

CHE: The measures were presented with a lot of tough talking, but they were put into practice with great weakness. In fact, no deserters were seized; no weapons were recovered; and, as far as I know, no long-suffering farmer families were imprisoned. [*Congo*, 47.]

At last, Che can tour the fronts

It wasn't easy for Che to get permission to tour the fronts. When Masengo refused to allow him to go, claiming that he had to look to his safety, Che got mad and asked him point-blank, "Do you distrust me or have some specific reservation? If so, I demand that you tell me what it is."

Clearly, "the blow was too direct," and Masengo, surprised, replied, "No, don't think that. Look, let's wait four or five days, until the inspectors I sent to the fronts come back, and we'll tour the fronts together." But Che knew that he had reservations, because the fact that Che was to visit the fronts and be with the combatants would further discredit the representatives of the higher command, who hadn't put in an appearance at the fronts for a long time.

CHE: I was aware of that aspect, but, apart from my interest in being able to analyze the situation directly, I also thought that they might be forced to make a tour of the fronts, to get to know the real problems that existed — food, clothing and medicine — and find solutions for them. [*Congo*, 48.]

When the four or five days had passed, Che and Masengo at last began the long-awaited tour. The first place they visited was Kazi, 27 kilometers north of Kibamba, where they noted the same disorder as in the other places. Masengo made a show of authority by replacing the head of the camp — who was afraid of planes and, therefore, stayed in the mountains all the time. Four of the Cubans there had to be sent to Kibamba because they had high fevers from malaria.

Sacred weapons

Che noted that they were in the political domain of General Moulane. In this region the settlers and combatants weren't eager to welcome the representative of the central power and clearly had reservations about Masengo. They went on to Katamba, where the Rwandans weren't under Mundandi because of differences of an ideological nature. Che didn't find out what those differences were based on. The visitors went to see "some of the most original barriers": a 75-mm recoilless cannon placed on a height, whose only possible use was to shoot at boats as they passed near the shore. They had already done this, but without any results, because the boats stayed away from the coast and the gun crew didn't know how to handle their weapon effectively. Che's suggestion that it be sent to Kibamba, where it might be more useful, and that several men be instructed in how to handle it went unheeded, for the weapons which the fronts received were sacred; only the enemy could take them away — which wasn't very hard to do.

Wanting to change the existing passivity, with the greatest naïveté or irresponsibility, Masengo suggest that an attack be made on Uvira. Che opposed this, since the information from those who went to inspect that front showed the same situation as the others: indiscipline, disorder, lack of knowledge of even the most elementary methods of combat, total lack of fighting spirit and lack of authority among the officers. The Cubans wanted to lay ambushes on the other side of Uvira, which required crossing the enemy lines, but the chiefs didn't provide any men for the action and refused to authorize them to go to that area, saying that they were planning an attack and that any action would put the enemy on the alert.

Word came from Dar es Salaam that the newspapers had carried reports of two Cubans killed in the attack on Fort de Force and that the Cuban Embassy had convinced the Congolese leaders to publicly deny their presence. Word also came that a ship had come from Cuba, arriving in the capital with weapons and 17,000 rounds for FAL rifles.

CHE: That didn't seem to me to have been an intelligent thing to do, since those truths can't be hidden, and the only correct thing was silence. I let Pablo Rivalta know what I thought. [*Congo*, 49.]

The reply was taken by two Cubans who were sick and the Swahili teacher, Ernesto Ilunga. Che already treated Ilunga as a younger brother. He showed signs of epilepsy, though the doctors suspected he had a brain tumor. They wanted him to consult specialists in the Tanzanian capital, but Masengo said that it was a problem of his spirit and that he would be cured in Kigoma.

The ship was the *Uvero*, which also brought around nine men who were to have joined the guerrilla groups in Mozambique. When they arrived, however, the Mozambicans said that they had asked for weapons and food, not men, and refused to accept them, so they were sent to the Congo. Manuel Piñeiro had given Ulises Estrada instructions to talk with Che to find out about the situation, and he had traveled with them. Moreover, José Ramón Machado Ventura, Minister of Public Health of Cuba, had arrived in Dar es Salaam by air. In addition to several tasks related to his job, Fidel had given him one similar to that of Ulises. The two entered the Congo with the other comrades.

The Kazolo-Makungo Front

Che ordered Dreke to go to the Calixte Front, from where Dreke sent him the following note:

"Tatu [Che],

"I am writing you from the Kazolo-Makungo Front, where the group of 10 men was sent. I arrived here yesterday, when I learned that a Congolese patrol going through a hamlet on the plains had captured a civilian whose ID states that his name is Tshombe.

"Today, the 19th [of July], I met with Major Calixte, who had interrogated the prisoner. He is holding the prisoner in a hamlet far from the front, and none of the Cubans can see him.

"According to Calixte, the prisoner told him that he had been in prison at Force when the attack was made, and four officers had been killed there, and two in Katenga, in addition to the soldiers. He didn't know the dead officers by name, but he saw their ranks. The prisoner's ID isn't that of a soldier, but one of the kind they give to everybody who goes to Albertville. The prisoner said that there were 25 guards at Nyangi, with a mortar and a cannon — these last situated on the road to Makungo. He said that the prison was a kilometer from Force, going toward Albertville, where the attacking revolutionaries were picked up... and that the guards took the watches and shoes off some of them, and the bodies were buried by civilians.

"Major Calixte agrees to having some men trained to use mortars, cannon and antiaircraft guns. He doesn't have any of those weapons, however, so we are waiting for Captain Zakarías (Mundandi's substitute) to bring those men to Front de Force.[1]* The comrades who are at the Makungo Front began giving classes to the rest of Major Calixte's personnel today. I can't tell you anything about Faunne[2] yet. We will send you more details about the situation in a few days; naturally, we will send them with a Cuban, in a sealed envelope.

"Moja [Dreke]"

[1] Captain Zakarías refused to accept the Congolese at his front, claiming that they had come to his camp to steal.
[2] We had heard that Major Faunne had split with Calixte, seemingly because of disagreements between them, and was on the plains with a lot of weapons. At that time, we were feeling our way, trying to find a man among the Congolese leaders. [The notes are Che's.] [*Congo*, 50-52.]

Ambush and primitivism

The ambush was laid on the Front de Force road on July 23, because,

---

* In the original document, Che's notes aren't placed at the foot of the page or separated from the text, but are found within it. The editor decided to respect not only the spelling but also the formal aspects of the checked work.

during his reconnaissance, Azi had observed that the military trucks transporting supplies went by one by one, without any extra guards. Twenty-five Cubans and the same number of Rwandans, under the command of Mbili and Zakarías, attacked one of those vehicles, which had five soldiers on board. Sultán opened fire with a bazooka and this was immediately followed by rifle fire at the truck, which was loaded with food, cigarettes, cases of beer and bottles of whiskey. The five soldiers were riddled with bullets; only one of them was armed.

CHE: The capture couldn't have been better from the point of view of gradual training for larger-scale actions, but several accidents clouded the action.

As soon as the shooting began, the Rwandans began to run to the rear, shooting off their weapons. This endangered all our men. Specifically, Comrade Arobaini was wounded in the hand, a bullet passing through the metacarpus and tearing off a finger.

Two examples give an idea of the primitivism that still reigns in the Congo: When Captain Zakarías found out about the wound caused by the FM's burst, he examined the injury and declared that two fingers had been lost. Deciding to apply the law of an eye for an eye, a tooth for a tooth, he pulled out a knife and would have cut the fingers off the poor wretch if Mbili hadn't intervened and, with great tact, managed to get him to forgive the man. The other example is that of a Rwandan soldier who ran off as soon as the first shots (which we ourselves fired; there wasn't any fighting) were heard. One of our men, acting as custodian — each Cuban accompanied a Rwandan — grabbed him by the arm to stop him, and the terrified boy gave him a terrible bite in the hand in his effort to free himself.

These are just samples showing how far we would have to go to turn this amorphous mass of men into an army. Unfortunately, the tragicomedy of this ambush didn't end here. After the first few moments of stupor, the brand-new victors found themselves with the most highly prized contents of the truck: bottles of beer and whiskey. Mbili tried to take charge of the food and destroy the liquor, but it was impossible. Within a few hours, our men — who didn't allow themselves to drink — were astonished and horrified to see that all of the others were drunk. Later, they held a meeting and resolved not to stay on the plains, as had been planned, to carry out another action, but to return to the base; they had done enough. Out of diplomacy and so as not to force the issue, since the Cubans were alone, Mbili agreed. On the way back in the truck, Captain Zakarías, who was drunk, met a farmer and, saying he was a spy, shot him dead.

The most curious aspect of all those incidents is that, when I explained the danger of such an attitude toward the farmers, he tried to justify Zakarías somewhat by saying that the tribe that lived in that area was hostile to the revolution. It should be noted that men aren't judged by their personal characteristics; rather, they are lumped together within the tribal framework, and it is very difficult to get them out of it. When a tribe is friendly, all of its members are; when it is unfriendly, the same is true. Of course, aside from not allowing the revolution to develop, those schema were dangerous. As was shown later, some of the members of the "friendly" tribes were informers for the enemy army, and, in the end, nearly all of them turned into our enemies.

We had had our first victory, reversing the trend of the earlier battle, but there were so many problems that I began to change my calculations of the time it would take. Five years was a very optimistic forecast for carrying the Congolese revolution to a successful outcome, if everything was to depend on the development of those armed groups until they became a real liberation army, unless something changed in how the war was directed — an ever more distant possibility. [*Congo*, 51-52.]

July 26

Che received the report on the Front de Force ambush on July 24 or 25. On July 26, Mbili and Tamusine went to the base to give Che more details about what had happened on the front. They also celebrated the 12th anniversary of the attack on the Moncada Garrison in Cuba. Three days later, there were new expressions of disenchantment; three more men, sent by Dreke, asked to go back to Cuba.

CHE: I was very hard on them, flatly refusing to consider their transfer. I ordered them to stay at the base and work in supplies. [*Congo*, 54.]

The most important thing that happened in what remained of that month was that, at the end of July, news arrived that the Cubans in the Katenga area had laid an ambush; had waited for four days while nothing appeared; and, in their withdrawal, had burned a bridge. The panorama was the same on that front: indiscipline and lack of fighting spirit. During that period, the Cubans in the various camps discussed Fidel's speech on what had taken place in Algeria. As Che later told Dreke, he considered that its content increased concern about the future of assistance for the African liberation movements.

5

August 1965

Slight improvement

CHE: As usual, I made an analysis of the last month (July) in my campaign diary: "Slight improvement over last month; Kabila came, stayed for five days and left, increasing the rumors about him. He doesn't like my being here, but he seems to have accepted the fact for the moment. So far, nothing makes me think that he is the man for the situation; he lets the days go by without concerning himself about anything except political disagreements, and everything indicates that he is too addicted to liquor and women.

"In the military sphere, following the Front de Force disaster and the near disaster of Katenga, there are small triumphs to note: two small actions in Kabimba, the ambush at Front de Force and the one in Katenga with the burning of the bridge. In addition, some training is beginning, and it has been said that better-quality men will be sought on other fronts. The terrible method continues of haphazardly distributing weapons. I think that it is possible to advance, though very slowly, and that there is a chance that Kabila will let me do something. For now, I continue to sit around." [*Congo*, 53.]

Che noted modest progress in the implementation of the military recommendations which he had been making ever since his arrival in the Congo some 97 days earlier.

The Cubans at Front de Force planned another ambush with more important targets. Azi went to the base to get food, since it was difficult to obtain yucca and sometimes meat in that area. To do so, they had to make long, dangerous incursions, which only the Cubans would carry out, because the Rwandans claimed that the higher command had to provide their food. When food was scarce, they didn't go to the weapons classes or dig trenches and they also refused to do any other kind of work.

CHE: Another of the hackneyed phrases from which we suffered while in the Congo was "Hapana chakula, hapana travaillé" — something like "No food, no work." [*Congo*, 54.]

At around that time, something else happened that once more demonstrated the apparent lack of combativity. When a combat alarm was given because a small enemy plane appeared nearby, the men who had been assigned to cover the defenses couldn't be found. Only by asking for volunteers could one of the two lines of the half-built, half-destroyed trenches be covered.

Two hundred combatants of Column Two left Mariel, Cuba, on board the Soviet ship *Félix Zdherzinski*, which Cuba had chartered, on August 6, 1965. They were headed for Punta Negra, in the Congo (Brazzaville). Fidel saw them off. Jorge Risquet Valdés was placed in charge of the contingent. Oscar Fernández Padilla, Deputy Minister of the Interior, was that force's liaison with Che's Column One. Fernández Padilla went straight to Dar es Salaam, where he was to stay. From then on, Ambassador Rivalta would concentrate on diplomatic tasks and relations with the Tanzanian Government.

Struggle at the top — *Hapanas* continue

Changes took place in the top-level Congolese leadership of the Council of the Revolution. On August 6, news arrived that Soumialot had removed Gbenye. Masengo said that Kabila had sent for him, so he would have to go to Kigoma but would be back the next day. Che noted that, in Masengo's opinion, "Soumialot didn't have the power to take a measure of that kind, but he would discuss all of those things with Kabila and then be better able to tell me what had happened." For Che and his comrades, Masengo's absence meant that all activities at the base would be paralyzed, as had happened when Kabila left. When the Cubans asked the soldiers why they had stopped coming for military instruction and stopped working on the fortifications, the only reply they got was "Hapana comandan, hapana travaillé" — "No Major, no work." Since they also said that they didn't study on Saturdays and

Sundays, it is easy to see that it would take a long time and plenty of patience to achieve anything with those "soldiers of the Congolese revolution."

Consumption of *pombe* increased and, as a result, fights once again broke out among the soldiers — and, sometimes, between soldiers and officers. Che reported that, in many cases, some of them saved themselves by seeking shelter "in the Cubans' temple, which, fortunately, was respected." The worst thing was that, most of the time, no sanctions of any kind were applied. Foreseeing possible contamination, the "useful Cubans" were ordered to move to the upper base. Che stayed with the sick, several instructors, the antiaircraft crews and those waiting to return to Cuba. He decided that he would wait a few days more for the Congolese leaders to visit the fronts but that, if authorization didn't come, he would go without it.

L'Etoile du Congo reported on the discrepancies among the leaders in its August 7 issue: "In Cairo, Soumialot has officially declared a split between himself and Gbenye." The next day it continued: "The hostility between Soumialot's guerrillas and those of Gbenye reached its peak in June in Juba, the Sudan. It has been learned that the encounter ended in violence, with deaths in both groups."

On August 10, the same newspaper denounced the fact that Africans had been in Cuba since 1961 — where, it claimed, they were given courses in guerrilla warfare and a Center of African Studies was created.

During the next few days, life at the Cubans' upper base remained more or less the same. Where Dreke and the other comrades were, some advances could be noted in the military training of the Rwandans. They went together on several reconnaissance missions and planned an ambush in the Makungo area. On the night of August 10, Dreke and Tom, the Cuban political commissar, wrote a report to Che on the latest events. It reached Che the next day, leading him to make the following reflections in his diary.

CHE: From the tone of some notes and talks with several comrades, I began to fear the significance of certain phrases: in the short dispatches in which they announced guerrilla or reconnaissance actions, the time came that, whenever the main point of the operation had failed, the following explanations would appear: "The Congolese refused to go," "The Congolese refused to fight," "The Congolese..." Analyzing that and the tension that existed between those who had said they wanted to leave the struggle and those who remained, I drew up a "Message to Combatants," to be read at the fronts where the troops were situated. The whirlpool of the following months and the instability of my situation, moving from one place to another, kept me from repeating the messages, though I don't know if it had any influence. I include the only one that was read, which gives an idea of the situation up to that time and my opinion of the problems with which we were faced:

"Message to combatants
"Comrades:
"In just a few days, some of us will have been here for four months. It is necessary to make a brief analysis of the situation.

"I can't say that the situation is good. The leaders of the movement spend most of their time outside the territory, which may be understandable in the case of political leaders, whose work has many facets, but never in that of the middle-level cadres. However, those middle-level cadres travel just as frequently and remain outside the country for weeks at a time, setting a terrible example. There is almost no organizational work, precisely because the middle-level cadres don't work. They don't know how. In addition, nobody trusts them.

"The local chiefs blackmail those middle-level cadres, who are in charge of tasks similar to those of the Staff. They obtain weapons and equipment without showing that they will use them correctly. More weapons are given to an increasing number of people who have had no training and lack fighting spirit, while no progress is made in organization. This means that the guerrilla troops lack discipline and a self-sacrificing spirit. Naturally, you can't win a war with such troops.

"It is worth asking if our presence has had any positive effect. I think that it has. Many of the difficulties we have — including my near-imprisonment here — stem from the difference that can be noted between one troop and the other and the fear of confrontations between one kind of leader and the other. Our mission is to help win the war; we should make use of that negative reaction and turn it into something positive. To do that, we must place more emphasis on our political work. We must show the differences by means of our example, but without making ourselves hateful to the cadres, who may see in us the reverse image of all their faults.

"To do this, it is first necessary to strive to have true revolutionary comradeship among the combatants at the base. The middle-level leaders of the future will come from there. In general, we have more clothes and more food than the comrades from here. We must share to the maximum, doing it selectively with those comrades who show their revolutionary spirit, while, at the same time, teaching them as much as possible. Our experience should be conveyed to the combatants in one way or another. We should be ruled by an eagerness to teach, but not in a pedantic way (looking down on those who don't know). Rather, we should teach with human warmth. Our political work should be governed by a revolutionary lack of pretension, complemented with a spirit of sacrifice that sets an example, not only for the Congolese comrades but also for the weaker ones among us. We should never look to see if our position is more dangerous than another or if more is demanded of us. More demands should be made of real revolutionaries, because they have more to give. Lastly, we shouldn't forget that we know only a very small part of what we should know. We must learn the way things are done in the Congo so we can unite more closely with the Congolese comrades. We must learn what we lack in culture and warfare without believing ourselves to be experts in warfare or thinking that it is the only thing we should know.

"To wind up this message, I would like to warn you of two things:

"1) Relations between comrades: Everybody knows that a group of comrades didn't honor their word as revolutionaries and the trust placed in them and have said they want to leave the struggle. That fact cannot be justified, and I will ask for the severest moral sanctions against those comrades. But we shouldn't lose sight of another fact: they are not traitors, and they shouldn't be treated with open scorn. Get this straight: what they did can only be repudiated by a revolutionary, but a person has to be a revolutionary for such a thing to deserve repudiation. If a person who isn't a revolutionary does such a thing, it is simply running away, as so many people have done. Now, those comrades have been marginalized and have grouped together as a means to defend themselves and justify their action — which has no justification. They still have to spend some more months here; if the shame which they surely feel, even though they hide it, is approached in a spirit of comradeship, we may save some of them and convince them to stay to share our fate. Come what may, that is a thousand times preferable to their moral desertion. Without forgetting their faults, we should offer them a little support, not force them to erect barriers of self-justification in defense against our coldness.

"2) The scorn that is felt toward the Congolese comrades' attitude to fighting has been observed in some dispatches and especially in comments by comrades. There are two problems that arise. The first is that the Congolese are aware of it; watch two people speaking in any of the languages you don't understand, and you will see that you know if they're talking about you, and whether they're saying good or bad things. Moreover, the Congolese can be turned into scapegoats. I note symptoms that the attitude of the Congolese is being exaggerated, and that this may be used as a good reason for not doing a given task. Our main function is to train men for combat, and, if we aren't close to them, we can't teach them. Our instruction should be not only in how to kill an individual but also, and especially, the attitude to have toward the sufferings of a long struggle; this is achieved when the teacher can also be taken as a model for his students to follow. Don't forget this, comrades, just as you should also remember that if a veteran of our war of liberation says that he's never run from battle, you can tell him to his face that he's a liar. Everybody runs, and we all go through terrible periods when we are scared by shadows; it's a stage that we should help people to overcome, because, naturally, the level of consciousness and the level of development are much lower than ours was in that period.

"This message should be discussed among the Party members; send me any suggestions you have. It should then be read to the other comrades and then immediately burned. It shouldn't remain at the front. Don't read it among the comrades who are leaving the struggle.

"A revolutionary greeting to all,

"Tatu [Che]

"August 12, 1965" [*Congo*, 55-56.]

This document shows Che's ability to assess his comrades' behavior and the course to be followed to carry out the mission entrusted to them successfully and with dignity. His respect for human dignity and his belief that men's virtues can, in the end, triumph over their weaknesses led him, while remaining firm, to be extremely careful in his treatment of those who wanted to leave the struggle and increased his hope that some might change their attitude, since he didn't consider them traitors or deserters.

The message was sent to the various fronts at which the Cubans were located. That same day, they left to lay the planned ambush. Tom, the political commissar, reported that they reached the Myala River at 1700 hours on Sunday, August 15 and spent the night there. The next day, they continued their march, to a stream around three kilometers from the road. A halt was called at mid-morning, and Azi and Singida were appointed to reconnoiter the site of the ambush. The positions were taken at around 1700 hours. The night passed as usual.

On that same date, as had been planned during the period he spent waiting for Kabila or Masengo to come, Che went up to the upper base, where he organized his tour of the fronts. That day, he received a note from Dreke about a reconnaissance in the Kabimba area and about

Major Calixte's strange decision to lay an ambush — but, since he didn't have enough Cubans, to wait for them.

A good ambush

Tom's report also said that they heard voices at 0600 hours on Tuesday, August 17. Two farmers were walking along the road toward where they were in ambush. Suddenly, one of them said to the other, *Tuende!* (Guerrillas!), and they turned around and took off back toward Front de Force. Clearly, some of the men had been careless, and they had been discovered. This made it necessary for them to change their position. They thought they should do it at night, but Mbili ordered the reinforcement of the posts toward Front de Force and for everyone to be very alert.

They didn't change their position, because they heard the sound of engines coming from Albertville at 1000 hours, and a jeep with a trailer, a light tank and an armored truck appeared. Afende and Sultán acted quickly. Afende set the jeep on fire with a bazooka shot; since he had fired at close range, the fragments of the shell wounded him and Alakre slightly. Sultán, with two bazooka shots, set the light tank on fire. The riflemen's fire and hand grenades wiped out the soldiers on the truck. All that remained was to take the booty, but, at that moment, Singida heard some troops who were advancing from Force in a fan-shaped front and were only around 200 meters away. In view of the enemy's mortar and machine-gun fire, the rebels had to withdraw.

Those in the center, commanded by Mbili, held off the guards, covering the withdrawal of Singida and his men; Azi followed him. Once they had crossed the road, the others withdrew. When the men were counted, Alau, of Singida's group, was missing. They waited for a while and then, as he didn't appear, set off for the Myala River. In midafternoon, they sent a patrol to look for the lost man, but it returned without having found him. Several combatants said that they counted seven dead white mercenaries; they thought that there were more of them and that they were U.S. citizens. They commented that few Rwandans left their positions.

The next day — August 18 — Mbili suggested to Captain Zakarías that they lay another ambush. Zakarías refused, because food was running short. Mbili replied that that wasn't so, and then the Rwandan said that, since they were brothers, if the Cubans stayed, they would, too.

Che leaves for the front

Before that, early on the morning of Wednesday, August 18, after an exhausting march along the plain that separated him from his first goal,

Che arrived at Front de Force at 2200 hours with Tamuine and Danuuse (his aides) and Tano, Chungo, Dufo and Aga, all combatants. Thus, as he put it, he broke through his restraints.

CHE: I felt a little like an escaped criminal, but I was determined not to return to the base for a long time. [*Congo*, 56.]

Che had tremendous revolutionary discipline and respect for the leaders of the movement in the Congo, and these virtues didn't clash with his decision to visit the fronts and try to carry out actions on the spot to prepare the members of the guerrilla army to carry out the long struggle for liberation.

The Rwandans gave him a cordial welcome, but, when it was time to sleep, the biting cold forced the visitors to huddle around a campfire and sleep on some hides. Although they managed to rest, they were awakened by crab lice, which Che called "one of the fiends that infest clothing." On the morning of August 19, after some hot tea and a cigar, Che listened to the complaints of the Cubans there. They complained of the Rwandans' behavior, and especially about Captain Zakarías and his methods of punishment.

When the temperature rose and the mist cleared, Che could see that the camp was next to a woods that began on the other side of a ravine, on a hill with large natural pastures, though there wasn't any grass then, since it was the dry season.

Alau — whom they had given up for lost after the ambush — returned that night. He said that he had followed some Rwandans and lost his way. He told them about the results of the action, which Che considered satisfactory.

On the morning of Friday, August 20, Dreke, Nanne and Paulu arrived. They had been sent to look for Che. After Mbili and Zakarías had insisted that one of the usual assemblies should be held, the Rwandans decided to go with the Cubans and lay another ambush several kilometers away. They had spent the previous day hunting an elephant for food.

On that day, Che and Dreke, using the latest information, were able to ascertain the general composition of the guerrillas' Eastern Front in the Congo. The two were aware that more weapons had been distributed than they knew of, but the number was never exact.

Suffice it to say that, on the Uvira, Fizi, Baraka, Lulimba-Kabambare and Kasongo Fronts, there were more than 2,000 rifles, several cannon, mortars, bazookas and antiaircraft guns. Between Lulimba and Force, there were some groups on which they didn't have any information. In the Kalonga-Kibuye, Makundi and Kabimba regions and in the one in which Calixte, the Rwandan Mundandi and a major called Faunne (with whom it had never been possible to make contact) operated, it was thought that there were around 750 rifles and several cannon, mortars and antiaircraft guns. In addition, the rebels and the reserves had similar weapons beside the Lake, though the exact number hadn't been determined.

Thus, even though the Cubans could get only those approximate figures — and were sure that, in fact, there were many more weapons — they felt that there were more than enough weapons to carry out a successful war. However, the disorganization that the Congolese leaders had created made it impossible to wage one.

The mathematics classes that Che gave were renewed that afternoon and evening.

At 0600 hours on Saturday, August 21, the rebels captured two traders who were heading for Front de Force on bicycles to sell meat and *pombe*. The merchandise was seized but paid for, and Mbili ordered that the alcoholic beverage be poured on the ground, to avoid another scene of drunkenness. Three hours later, another civilian appeared and saw the rebels, but they couldn't catch him, as he ran faster than they did. Aware that the enemy would be told of their presence, they decided to withdraw to Che's camp.

From there, Nanne, Tano, Chungu, Duala, Kigulo and Akike were sent to the Makungo area; among other things, they were to reconnoiter the bridge that had been burned.

At mid-morning, Che, Dreke, Tamusine, Danjuse and Apulu climbed a hill to see the town of Front de Force, or Bendera, and its electric power station in the distance, and decided the following: "On examining it in person, I realized graphically how mistaken we had been in making a frontal attack on it. For us, for our force, it was a veritable bastion."

On August 21, 1965, the Cuban troops of Column Two arrived at Punta Negra, the Congo (Brazzaville). Osmany Cienfuegos and Jorge Serguera, the recently accredited Cuban Ambassador, welcomed them. Two days later, they were in the capital.

Another 50 military men had flown in in small groups, as Agramonte and his comrades had done, to make up a battalion of 250 men under the command of Major Rolando Kindelán.

RAÚL CASTRO: The column that went to the Congo as the Patrice Lumumba Battalion had many tasks. First of all, it was the reserve for Che's column, which it would join whenever necessary.

It was also to help the progressive government of the Congo, which was threatened with aggression by the Leopoldville (now Kinshasa) regime. Therefore, the battalion was ready to fight alongside the Congolese Army against foreign aggression from the other side of the Congo River and was also there to train several battalions of militia.

No less important was the task of working with a group of adviser-combatants on the [Angolan] MPLA's 2nd Guerrilla Front in Cabinda — training columns of Angolan combatants, equipping them and helping them set out toward the 1st Front, north of Luanda, in Angola.

Comrades Risquet and Kindelán were in charge of those tasks.[23]

Nothing important happened on Sunday, August 22. As always when he had any free time, Che read, and other Cubans did the same. On Monday, August 23, they received materials sent from the base. In the afternoon, a message from Nanne arrived, stating that the bridge destroyed by fire had been rebuilt. At night, a message came from Mbili saying that he would arrive the next day.

Early on the morning of Tuesday, August 24, Che, Dreke and four other Cubans went to meet their comrades. As Che reported, "I climbed the steep mountains in high spirits, with greater morale." They heard more details about the ambush — they had already heard over the radio that seven mercenaries had been killed, all Belgians — and Che regretted that no documents had been seized, for prisoners had told them that those mercenaries would be in charge of drawing up special plans for Front de Force and, probably, a future offensive. He knew about the small trailer that the jeep had been pulling, but it had been impossible to find out what it contained. Che believed that "some big fish had fallen there, and that documentation would have been of inestimable use to us." Mbili told him that, before withdrawing, they had tried to demolish one of the posts carrying the electric power lines but had failed because the bazooka missed.

Impossible to do intelligence work

CHE: Then I met Captain Zakarías. Even though those first meetings weren't very cordial, his attitude gradually changed. The two traders who had been taken prisoner were brought in. They were related to each other, and I suggested that one remain as a hostage and the other be sent to work with us to make contact in Albertville, but Zakarías refused, saying that they could be spies. They were sent to the Lake base, from which they tried to escape. Their guards killed at least one of them in a horrifying way.

I sent a new note to Masengo, in which I insisted on the need to follow a consistent, clever policy with the farmers so as to avoid difficulties such as those of the ambush. I proposed beginning

---

[23] Raúl Castro, June 11, 1985.

intelligence work with prisoners and also suggested a plan for supplying the front by encouraging cooperation among the farmers and giving them some of what was brought in from the Lake, where the merchandise was received, since that route wasn't yet open. Moreover, I insisted on the need for having a single command at the front; that dispersal of independent forces wasn't acceptable, especially in view of the trend toward anarchy and the rivalries between the various groups, that even went as far as violence.

I was convinced that, in spite of their latest advances, we couldn't expect much more of the Rwandans and that we should place more emphasis on training the Congolese — who, after all, were the ones who should liberate the Congo. Therefore, it was decided to leave Comrade Mafu with them, in charge of 12 men, so as not to hurt anybody's feelings, and to move the rest of the troops to the Calixte Front for the time being. I was to go there, too. Before leaving, it was decided to send Tom to make a political inspection at the Lake. After that, he was to go to Kabimba to see exactly what the situation was, since I had some reservations about how Comrade Ali was treating the Congolese.

Before Tom left, a meeting of Party members was held, in which we once more analyzed all the problems and decided to choose some of the members to help in his tasks. Ishirini and Singida were chosen unanimously for the group that would go with me, and Alasiri was chosen for the small group that would stay with Mafu. All three are magnificent fellows. In the meeting, however, I criticized Comrade Singida for some violent expressions he had used with the Congolese. In a meeting of the Staff, I also criticized Azi and Azima for their incorrect treatment of the Rwandans. [*Congo*, 58-59.]

Finally, late in the afternoon and early in the evening, Che gave some classes by the light of pressure lamps.

At 0530 hours on the chilly morning of Wednesday, August 25, while it was still dark, Asmari and Ajili were sent to the Lake base to relieve the men who were giving military training to the Congolese. Two hours later, Singida, Abdala, Alakre, Tiza, Rabaine, Sultán, Ahiri, Anane, Bahasa, Marembo, Amba, Akike, Sitini-Natatu and Alau left for the Makungo Front. Soon afterwards, Angalia, Dufu, Jukumu and Chepua went out to look for yucca, and Anga, Changa, Chen and Ñyenyea went out hunting. That same morning, the two civilian prisoners — whose fate we already know — were sent to Kibamba. Baati arrived before midday with a message for Che from Changa, the Cuban "admiral" of the Lake. There were letters from Dar es Salaam and other things, including a letter from the Ambassador, dated August 19, 1965.

Intrigues and worse

Che received the following letter:

"Tatu [Che]:

"This trip was planned in line with your order.[1] It changed because of a cable from Havana saying a messenger was being sent here; the messenger is here, preparing and ensuring the Lake crossing, and will be with you soon.

"Two things. A group of men is going there to organize a training base where Mozambican comrades and comrades from other movements in the area can be taught. At first, this group was requested by the Tanzanian Government for the training of Mozambicans and for carrying out an operation of which I'm sure Osmany has informed you. Because of certain conditions, the plans fell through, and the group was asked to go to Tabora to take charge of the base for training Congolese. But now, in accordance with Soumialot, they have planned for the base to be away from town, so as not to have to take personnel from one place and send them somewhere else, and also to use it for training personnel from Mozambique and other liberation movements in the area.

"Another matter concerns various groups of Congolese who have visited me in recent days and who know you in one way or another. Under the pretext that Kabila doesn't want to go there, they are trying to act on their own. They have ambition for command and, basing themselves on you and our men, they want to create their own group. I told them how dangerous it would be to do this, for it would tend to split the movement, and said they should talk first with Kabila and you before doing anything. I said that our commitments were set up in that way.

"Kabila visited me and explained the situation. He said that he had thrown those comrades out and had talked with representatives of the Tanzanian Government so that anyone who appeared saying he was a combatant should be sent there. He has also explained the situation in the embassies which those comrades have visited.

"In closing, he promised he would go there.

"A big hug,

"Pablo"

[1] This refers to the order to travel from Dar es Salaam every fortnight, which was never followed. [The note is Che's.]

CHE: I answered Pablo, saying that I didn't have any confidence in Kabila but that all the others who were there were worse, not even being intelligent. I said that, in any case, he should tie himself to

[Kabila] and assure him that he would work honestly to consolidate unity under his command, that he shouldn't be concerned about that. I expressed my reservations about the decision to send the instructors to establish a base here, because the men from other movements would be exposed to such a destructive atmosphere of indiscipline, disorganization and complete demoralization that it would be very upsetting for anyone who was entering into the tasks of liberation for the first time. I said I hoped that that initiative hadn't been his idea, because it was politically dangerous. [*Congo*, 60-62.]

A meeting with the Rwandans

At 1900 hours, Che met with several Rwandans — Zakarías, the Organizing Secretary of the Party, the head of the youth organization and others — who had asked to see him.

CHE: We talked about general topics related to the war, how to carry it out, how to train the men, practical problems of that kind. At the end, the Organizing Secretary asked me to make a critical analysis of the Rwandans' work so far, and I pointed out what I considered two weak aspects:

First: their fatalistic attitude toward food. The Rwandans depended on the farmers' bringing them cattle; the most they would do was send some soldiers to look for them. (At our suggestion, they had begun to eat monkeys, which were delicious if you were very hungry and just edible if you weren't. Except in the last few days, they hadn't even gone to look for yucca, which was to be found on the plains.) I explained the need to form a people's army that was self-supporting and was in constant touch with the people; it couldn't be parasitic, but should be a mirror in which the farmers would see themselves reflected.

Second: their excessive distrust of the Congolese. I urged them to unite with them, reasoning that the outcome of the struggle in Rwanda depended on the struggle in the Congo, since it involved a greater confrontation with imperialism.

They responded by accepting the first criticism and giving some examples of how they had begun to correct that weakness, but they didn't mention the second, so it appeared that they didn't accept my observations or, in any case, weren't ready to change their attitude. [*Congo*, 59-60.]

At 0630 hours on Thursday, August 26, 1965, Che, 10 Cubans and two Rwandans (Yerones and Pierre) set out for Calixte's camp on the Makungo Front. Dreke stayed at Front de Force with the other Cubans

Che Guevara in disguise before leaving Cuba.

KAR-13, April 19, 1965

SANITIZED

47

To   :   The Secretary
Through: S/S
From   :   INR - Thomas L. Hughes *Thomas L. Hughes*

Subject :   Che Guevara's African Venture

1964

From December 17, 1964 to March 14, 1965, Che Guevara toured Africa, visiting Algeria, Mali, Congo (Brazzaville), Guinea, Ghana, Dahomey, Tanzania, and the United Arab Republic. The paper discusses his trip in the context of Cuba's growing interest in the dark continent. An appendix containing a brief chronology of Guevara's trip is attached.

1965

ABSTRACT

Che Guevara's recent three-month tour of eight African states was part of a strategy designed to ensure Cuba an important role in the African Revolution. Cuba hopes its African role will help revitalize its position as a leading participant in the world revolution -- a role considerably diminished by the continuing failure of Cuban subversion in Latin America.

The Castro regime also hopes that its African friends can provide some leverage for use against the great powers. Castro would like Africa's political support (including its UN votes) against US military and economic policies towards Cuba. He may also hope that, by increasing Cuba's value as an instrument of revolution in Africa, he can help ensure continuance of economic aid from the communist countries as well as tolerance of his sometimes maverick and independent activities. Guevara candidly admitted that Cuba's chances of expanding trade with Africa were slight, because both areas produce largely competing raw materials.

BUNDY-SM
BATOR
BOWMAN
McCRUDE
COOPER
MANNED
JESSUP
JOHNSON
KEENY
KLIEN
HECKER
MOODY
REEDY
SANDERS
SAYRE
THOMSON

SANITIZED
E.O. 12356, Sec. 3.4
NIJ 87-34
By ___ NARA Date 11-28-89

SPECIAL REPORT

CUBAN TRAINING AND SUPPORT FOR AFRICAN NATIONALISTS

CENTRAL INTELLIGENCE AGENCY
OFFICE OF CURRENT INTELLIGENCE

First page of the CIA's special report on Cuban training and support for African nationalists.

Stopping along the road from Dar es Salaam to Kigoma, in Tanzania. Left to right: José María Martínez Tamayo (Papi in Cuba, Mbili in the Congo), the twins Pablo B. (Sita) and Pedro O. (Saba) Ortiz, Ernesto Che Guevara (Tatu), Eduardo Torres (Coque in Cuba, Nanne in the Congo), Martín Chibás (Ishirini), Salvador Escudero (Arobaine), Víctor Dreke (Moja), a representative of the Tanzanian police who accompanied them, Newris Vernier (an embassy official), Godefrei Tchamlesso (Tremendo Punto, of the Congo), and Julián Morejón (Tiza).

At the base camp in the Congo. Left to right: Godefrei Tchamlesso (of the Congo), Sammy Kent (of Kenya), Che (Tatu) and Kiwe (of the Congo).

Che Guevara in the Congo with a small boy and his older brother.

At the base camp in the Congo. Left to right: Víctor Dreke (Moja), Dr. Rafael Zerquera (Kumi) and Che (Tatu).

Combatants on the Front de Force. Left to right: Ramón Armas (Azima), Manuel Savigne Medina (Singida), José María Martínez Tamayo (Mbili), Aldo Margolles (Uta), Víctor Dreke (Moja), Esmérido Parada Zamora (Azmari), Martín Chibás (Ishirini), Catalino Olachea (Mafu), Carlos Coello (Tuma), Mariano García (Arobo) and Domingo Oliva (Kimbi). Squatting, Dr. Adrián Zanzaligc Laforet (Kasulo, of Haiti), Jerome (of Rwanda) and Justo Rumbaut (Mauro, the communications expert).

Che (Tatu) explaining the area where they will operate. On his right, Santiago Terry Rodríguez. On his left, Carlos Coello (Tuma) and José María Martínez Tamayo (Mbili).

Left to right: Dr. Adrián Zanzaligc Laforet (Kasulo, of Haiti), Argelio Zamora Torriente (Asmari) and Dr. José Raúl Candevat (Chumi).

Right to left: Che (Tatu), José María Martínez Tamayo (Mbili) and Rogelio Oliva.

At the Lulimba base. Left to right: Che (Tatu), Noelio Revé (Kigulo), Rodobaldo Gundín (Hukumu, one of the youngest of the Cuban internationalists), Rogelio Oliva, Manuel Savigne Medina (Singida), Víctor Manuel Ballester (Telathini), Santiago Terry Rodríguez (Ali) and (back to the camera) José María Martínez Tamayo (Mbili).

Che Guevara reading newspaper at Cuban camp in the Congo.

Machado Ventura and Ulises Estrada with a group of
Congolese farmers.

Left to right: Vicente Yant (Andika), Roberto Sánchez Bartelemy (Lawton in Cuba,
Changa in the Congo) and Santiago Terry Rodríguez (Ali).

Che on the boat as the Cubans begin to leave the Congo.

Cubans during the return journey. Some of the Cubans sent to support the Cuban internationalists' departure from the Congo appear in the photo.

Che speaking for the last time, on the returning boat.

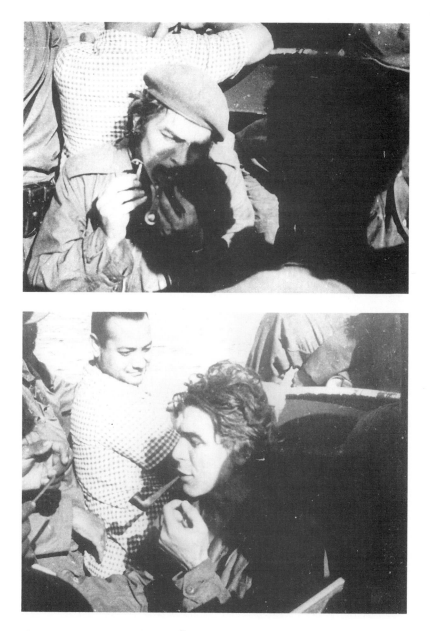

Che shaving and José Luis Torres (Amia) cutting his hair.

Clean-shaven and with a new haircut, Che chats with those around him.

During the return journey.

At the Dar es Salaam airport. Left to right: Israel Reyes Zayas (Azi), Rafael Hernández (Tom), Noelio Revé (Kigulo) and Argelio Zamora Torriente (Almari).

Some of the Cuban internationalists at the Dar es Salaam airport, prior to returning to Cuba.

ADVERTENCIA PRELIMINAR

Esta es la historia de una ~~derrota~~, fracaso, ~~está minuciosamente relatada~~, Desciende al detalle anecdótico como

corresponde a episodios de la guerra, pero/matizada de observaciones y de espí-

ritu critico ya que estimo que ,si alguna importancia puede tener el relato es permitir

mitir extraer una serie de experiencias que sirvan para otros Movimientos Revo

lucionarios. La victoria es una gran fuente de experiencias positivas pero tam

bien lo es la derrota, y mas aún, en mi opinión, cuando, como en este caso, los

actuantes e informantes son extranjeros que fueron a ~~ser~~ arriesgar sus vidas en un terri

torio desconocido, ~~que habla otra~~ de lengua distinta y al cual los unía solamente los lazos

del internacionalismo proletario, inaugurando un método no practicado en

~~las guerras de liberación modernas.~~

~~Por ella se encontrará en este relato una mezcla de episodios de tipo~~

~~anecdótico y de observaciones críticas.~~ Cierra la narración un epilogo que ---

plantea los interrogantes de la lucha en Africa y, en general, de la lucha de li

beración nacional contra la forma neo-colonial del imperialismo que consti tu

ye su modalidad (mas temible) de presentación, d los enmascaramientos y suti

lezas que conlleva y la larga experiencia que . . . tir . . . los lotación tiene

las potencias imperialistas

~~sobre todo, el imperialismo norteamericano.~~

Estas notas seran publicadas transcurrido bastante tiempo desde su --

dictado y, tal vez, el autor no pueda ya hacerse responsable de lo que aqui está

dicho; ~~de todas maneras~~, el tiempo habrá limado muchas ~~asperezas~~ aristas y, si tiene al

guna importancia su aparición, los editores podran hacer las correcciones que -

se crean necesarias, mediante las pertinentes llamadas, a fin de aclarar los a-

contecimientos o las opiniones a la luz del tiempo decantado.

Mas correctamente, esta es la historia de una descomposición. Cuando -

~~nosotros llegué-se al~~ arribamos a territorio congolés, la revolución estaba en un periodo -

de deceso, (luego, ~~comenzaron a sucederse~~ sucedieron episodios que entrañarían por su regre

sión definitiva, por lo menos en este momento y en este escenario del ~~nuevo~~ inmenso cam

po de lucha. Lo que ~~me~~ interesará ~~narrar fundamentalmente~~, no es la historia que a el largo puede aqui

~~trama~~ de la descomposición de la revolución congolesa, cuyas causas y caracte--

risticas ~~no nos atañen directamente~~ son demasiado profundas para abocarlas todas desde un punto de observ , sino mas bien el proceso de descomposición

de nuestra moral combativa, ya que la experiencia inaugurada aqui por nos otros no debe des-

perdiciarse y la iniciativa del ejercito proletario-internacional no debe morir

frente al primer fracaso. Es preciso analizar a fondo los problemas que se plan

tean y resolverlos; Un buen instructor en el campo de batalla hace mas por la -

revolución que el instruir una cantidad considerable de novatos en ambiente de

paz; pero las caracteristicas de ese instructor, catalizador en la formación de

A page from Che's manuscript on the guerrilla struggle in the Congo.

waiting for Captain Zakarías, who had promised to go with 10 of his men to fight alongside the Congolese. An unconfirmed report arrived stating that a Congolese captain and several soldiers had gone over to the enemy. After two and a half hours of skirting the mountain, they reached the camp, which was not as cold.

CHE: It is a perfect place for defense, since the mountainside is very steep, without any vegetation, so it is very easy to prevent access with rifle fire. [*Congo*, 61.]

The camp consisted of several straw huts, each housing from four to ten people. Some of the empty huts were assigned to the visitors. Che reported that they were more comfortable than those at Front de Force but had just as many crab lice.

CHE: Lambert had asked Calixte to go to Lulimba, and he was about to leave. He welcomed me with apparent joy, saying he was glad to have us there, but that he didn't like our being with the Rwandans. I explained that we had been following orders to train that group but that we wanted to work with them. The conversation was friendly, even though there wasn't the direct communication that existed with the Rwandans, because Calixte didn't speak even a word of French, and my Swahili was always very imperfect, so I had to use Cuban translators who didn't understand all the nuances. It was very difficult to make complex explanations. [*Congo*, 61.]

The hamlets of Makungo, Nyangi, Katenga and Front de Force could be seen on the nearby plains. Che told the Congolese leader that they should stay closer to the enemy and harass it constantly so the troops would get accustomed to gunfire. The idea was accepted, and a small guerrilla force was chosen, led by Azi, to operate four kilometers from Makungo.

On the morning of Friday, August 27, planes flew over the Front de Force camp, and antiaircraft guns shot at them.

Cuba and the Soviet Union

OSCAR FERNANDEZ PADILLA: On August 27, 1965, once the men and matériel had been gathered, we left Havana for Moscow, where our arrival couldn't have been more disconcerting. We didn't have visas for traveling to the Soviet Union, and the Soviet authorities hadn't received any information about our going through there or about the tremendous amount of equipment, weapons, etc. we had with us.

The rumpus with immigration and the very bitter arguments with security went on for hours and hours, until their superiors were ordered to let us go through, though they retained custody of the cargo. We were sent to the airport hotel. We didn't like that, and we protested. They protested, too — perfectly justifiably — because they hadn't been informed of our mission. Finally, everything was settled in the office of Marshal Sakhalov, Deputy Minister of the KGB of the Soviet Union, with a bottle of vodka early in the morning after he and I, who held similar positions and had met before, talked it out.

Party in honor of the visitors

Saturday, August 28 was spent choosing the Congolese who would go with Azi. As Che put it, they had to overcome the reluctance the Congolese felt when going closer to the enemy. The plan of action was to lay ambushes at one of the modern bridges on the road between Kastenga and Lulimba and in the outskirts of the small hamlet of Nyangi.

On Sunday, August 29, the farmers held a party in honor of the visitors. Several of them performed ritual dances dressed as demons and then went to adore their idol, a rock with a reed fence around it.

CHE: The ritual seems complicated, but its essence is very simple; a sacrifice is offered to the god, the rock idol [little icon], and then the animal that has been sacrificed is eaten [after its blood is sprinkled]. Everyone eats and drinks a lot. [*Congo*, 62.]

The inhabitants were so deferential to the Cubans that Che was led to take up his profession again until another doctor could be appointed. He began caring for them while also beginning the combat training.

CHE: We once again began the exhausting task of teaching the basic arts of war to people whose resolve wasn't obvious to us; in fact, we had serious doubts about whether they had any or not. That was our work: sowing seeds, scattering them desperately to one side and the other, trying to have some germinate before the bad times came. [*Congo*, 62.]

Dreke, Zakarías and 10 other Rwandans arrived at Che's camp, in the hamlet of Carula, at midafternoon on Tuesday, August 31. It was the first time the Rwandan officer had visited the Congolese front of Makungo. With that step, Che felt that his long-sought plan for creating a united front was beginning. Che commented about this in his manuscript after his reference to the September 11 ambush. In order to place events as much as possible in their real order, I am including it here, since it refers to this period.

CHE: At the end of August, I made my habitual analysis, the most optimistic of all those I have written...

"My time of inaction has ended, which is a step forward. In general, this month may be noted as very positive; to the Front de Force action, I should add the qualitative change effected in the men. Zakarías's presence with 10 men is a clear indication of this. Now, we need our actions to produce results, and we must stabilize the situation here. My next steps will be to visit Lambert in Lulimba and Kabambare and then convince them of the need to take Lulimba and go on like that. In order to do that, this ambush and the following actions must have results.

"I don't know what Kabila will do, but I will try to make him come to Masengo, to visit the fronts. That will make the men feel differently about him. We must then organize the farmers in the whole area and give the front a single command. If everything turns out well, we will be able to surround Force in two months and try to sabotage the electricity, so that it will lose its strategic importance. Everything looks rosier — today, at least." [*Congo*, 68.]

DREKE: In those places, Che was known as the *muganga*. As he had done in the Sierra Maestra, Che again worked as a doctor, and in the same way he won the people's affection.

Che is annoyed

A Congolese delegation headed by Gaston Soumialot, President of the Supreme Council of the Revolution of the Congo (Leopoldville), arrived in Cuba on the evening of August 31 in response to an invitation extended by the Cuban Government. Its other members were Mutchungo, a member of the Executive Council; Kitunwa Placiddes; Diounga, secretary of the delegation; and Major Sumbu Edward Marcel, the organization's representative in Cuba. President Osvaldo Dorticós and Raúl Roa, Cuban Minister of Foreign Affairs, welcomed them. The Congolese had a full program of visits and talks with the Cuban leaders.

Everything indicates that Che — who, by then, was very familiar with the main defects of the new President — hadn't been informed about the invitation. At least, he made no mention of it in his writings. Dreke told me that they found out about that visit to Cuba after the delegation had returned from the trip — which, of course, annoyed Che.

RIVALTA: I knew of a trip that Soumialot and a delegation made to Cuba, but I didn't have anything to do with the invitation. I suppose he received it from our Embassy in Cairo. Che had warned me that I shouldn't give any monetary assistance to their movement without his authorization, and I passed the warning on to Cuba.

6

September 1965

Laying a new ambush

On the morning of Wednesday, September 1, 1965, Azi, six other Cubans and 10 Rwandans left to take up a position on the road from Nyangi and keep the enemy from leaving that place. Che wrote that around 40 Congolese, 10 Rwandans and 30 Cubans took part in the main ambush — what he considered "a troop more than large enough to destroy any enemy that might come along the road." The *Campaign Diary* kept by Dreke's group says that 82 men reached the place at 1540 hours. Dreke, Zakarías and two other Cubans reconnoitered before situating the men, who were distributed as follows: the Cuban chief with some of the troop at the center, Singida at his left and Azima with the same number of combatants at the right. Mbili stayed at the command post, waiting for Che. The *Campaign Diary* also says that five more Cubans joined Azi.

CHE: The newly arrived group of 10 Cubans were, at the beginning, to have been instructors at a base where they would teach not only Congolese but also Africans from other movements. In view of the conditions and the impossibility of getting a stable group of students in these skills, I decided to have them join directly in the fighting, which they did in this action. The reinforcement wasn't very great, because, with a few exceptions, the comrades had more training in orthodox warfare than experience in the guerrilla struggle.

I accompanied the combatants. After crossing the Kimbi [Kimvit] River — which, in the rainy season, has a considerable, quite powerful current but was easy to cross now, with the water only coming up to our waists — we settled in the area that had been chosen.

The tactic was simple. There was a small group around five or six kilometers away, toward Katenga, that was to destroy a plank bridge after the trucks had crossed it and fallen into the ambush, to keep them from fleeing and to prevent reinforcements from coming up. [That group consisted of four Cubans and eight Congolese.] In addition, because antitank mines couldn't be used directly, for lack of detonators (which never arrived), one [mine] was placed on a small wooden bridge two or three meters wide in the middle of the ambush. We had devised an artifact using a grenade fuse that, when pulled by a string, exploded five or six seconds later. It wasn't very reliable, because it depended on the skill of the man pulling the string to make the explosion coincide with the trucks as they drove past, so it was left as an extreme measure, if everything else failed. [*Congo*, 63-4.]

What follows was crossed out in the original, but I think it completes the idea he had of the action.

CHE: The center of the ambush was the strongest and the part that should bear the brunt of the fighting. There were enough men on both sides to halt part of the convoy if it were very large and to keep the trapped men from fleeing. A bazooka shot was to begin the firing. [The command post was located around 500 meters away, next to a small pool of stagnant, dirty water.] [We can consider the men who had just been incorporated as the members of a fifth group. — W.G.] [*Congo*, 63.]

Egypt and Cuba

Padilla and his companions arrived in Cairo on September 1. An Egyptian Security agent was waiting for them and took charge of the cargo. Soviet Security had told the Egyptians to expect them and had also told the Tanzanians that the group would go on to their capital. Naturally, both the Soviets and the Egyptians knew about the Cuban mission in the Congo, though — at least, at that time — they didn't know Che was there.

CAIRO, September 3 (PL). — The Conference of the peoples of Asia, Africa and Latin America will be held in Havana next January 3-10.

The Preparatory Committee meeting in Cairo made the decision. In a call issued at the end of its two days of discussions, the Preparatory Committee also announced the agenda of the Conference, which will be held in the Cuban capital on the seventh anniversary of the triumph of the Cuban Revolution.

The Cuban Government offered to host the Conference in an effort to unite all revolutionaries in the three continents. The Cuban National Committee for the Conference would be headed by Osmany Cienfuegos, Chairman of the International Relations Commission of the Central Committee of the Communist Party of Cuba, who was closely linked to the preparations for and development of the internationalist expedition in the Congo. Clearly, the Cubans hoped that the Conference would help make Che's African dream a reality. The Congolese delegation visiting Cuba began a tour of several provinces on the afternoon of September 3.

Terror sows confusion

On September 2, 3 and 4, the guerrillas remained constantly alert, but the enemy didn't appear at the main ambush. The *Campaign Diary* reported that the only activity was that planes could be heard overhead. It also seems that Che inspected the positions every day, and Azi's men in ambush fired on nine enemy soldiers who came walking down the road on Saturday, September 4. They didn't find out if they caused them any casualties or not, because the enemy began to fire mortar shells at them from Nyangi, which wasn't very far away, and they had to withdraw. However, Che didn't mention this in his manuscript.

CHE: It rained several times, which made our stay more unpleasant. On the first and second days there weren't any worse problems; the men spent them waiting, both tense and bored. The hours seemed interminable, but, at the same time, any noise that broke the silence seemed to be the sound of a motor and immediately made them alert. I was a few hundred meters from the front line, but, even so, I imagined hearing things every so often. [*Congo*, 64.]

Che went on to refer to what took place on Sunday, September 5, saying that the Congolese, who were impatient, wanted to lift the ambush. They claimed that the military vehicles went by twice a month and that, certainly, a caravan had gone by the day before the ambush was laid. They proposed going away, waiting a few days and then coming back. In spite of the shortage of food, the dirty water — they added disinfectant, but it still caused a lot of diarrhea — and their complete inactivity, the combatants didn't move from their positions. On Monday,

September 6, Che wrote the following:

CHE: On the fifth day [shortly before midday], something happened that, although funny, once more showed the weaknesses from which we suffer. While I was placidly lying in my hammock in the command post, I heard a sound like stampeding elephants. It was the six or seven Congolese in charge of the food, who were all jabbering, "*Askari Tshombe, Askari Tshombe*" (Tshombe's soldiers). They had seen them around 20 or 30 meters from our position. I barely had time to put on my equipment, leaving my hammock and knapsack to their fate, when one of the Cubans who was with me also saw the *Askari Tshombe*. The situation became complicated, since we couldn't depend on the Congolese, and I had only four Cubans with me. Moreover, one of them — Singida — was sick. Quickly, I sent Singida to tell Moja [Dreke] to send me reinforcements and to take the Congolese with him, for, in those conditions, they were more of a hindrance than a help. I walked a few meters toward the river to get out of the area the enemy could see, and I found the footprints of those who were withdrawing, intending to go back along the same road after making contact with the guards. A few moments later, word came that, on seeing more clearly, they weren't enemy soldiers at all; they were farmers from the area who, on finding us, had also fled; that was when one of our men saw them clearly, far away.

We were commenting about these things when a scout Moja had sent to find out what was going on arrived behind us, heard our conversation and went running off to say that the guards were already at the command post and had seized it. Everybody panicked: the ambushers began the ambush. Moja, who was in direct command of the action, immediately lifted the ambush and holed up nearby while giving orders that I be found — reports had it that I had gone toward the Kimbi [Kimvit] River.

Two hours later, we were still going around in circles, and some of the Congolese had taken advantage of the opportunity to head back to camp and never returned. We had suffered several losses of this kind, the result of the confusion. To the childish reactions of the Congolese, who ran away like spoiled children, were added the mistakes that some of our comrades made as a result of lack of experience in the struggle.

We decided to move the ambush a few hundred meters, since the farmers had seen us and we didn't know what group they belonged to, and I had to withdraw and return to the camp, because I was told that Comrade Aragonés was on the way there. [*Congo*, 64-65.]

The *Campaign Diary* contained a more or less similar account, except that it said that two farmers were captured near the command post. There was a false alarm on the afternoon of Tuesday, September 7, and it seems that, once more, the men's nerves made them imagine they heard the noise of approaching motors.

Tanzania — liaison and communications equipment arrive

PADILLA: I flew from Cairo to Dar es Salaam on September 7. After our ambassador briefed me, I decided the following: 1) I would send Oliva (whose pseudonym was David) to Kigoma to get information about where Che was. By then, Che had already left the base they had created, and the command post was deeper in Congolese territory. If nobody in Kigoma knew where he was, Oliva was to cross the Lake and get that information. 2) I would get the means of communication ready and transfer them and their operators to Kigoma, preparing to move them to the area where the guerrillas were. At the same time, I would decide where to install the field of antennas and communications cabin in Dar es Salaam so as to maintain communication between that place, the base in Kibamba and Havana. 3) I would investigate the Embassy personnel's real "need to know" concerning the operation. 4) I would assess the access to the logistical support for the guerrillas, which was controlled by the Tanzanian Government at the Tabora military base, in the middle of the country. 5) Finally, I would establish relations with the representatives of the Lumumba National Movement in Dar es Salaam.

I also agreed that my pseudonym for the guerrillas and internal contacts would be Rafael and that I would use "Raimundo" for communication with Havana. Since my arrival, I had maintained very close relations with the Egyptian and Soviet Ambassadors, because of the incident I've already described.

The next-to-the-last reinforcements

CHE: The much-heralded messengers arrived just about then [September 8]. They were [Emilio] Aragonés, [Oscar] Fernández Mell and [Aldo] Margolles, who were coming to stay at the front. [Plus Víctor Chué Colá and six other Cubans, who formed the sixth — and last — group in the internationalist detachment.] When I learned which comrades were coming, I was afraid they might be bringing a message urging me to return to Cuba or to leave the struggle, because I couldn't conceive of the Organizing Secretary of the Party leaving his post to come to the Congo, especially in a situation such as this, where there was nothing definite, and only negative things to report. [*Congo*, 72.]

Che had sent for Oscar Fernández Mell, among the recent arrivals, to strengthen the command cadres. Aragonés and Margolles had asked Fidel to let them join the struggle, and Fidel had agreed. The white Cubans would serve as doctors, for it wasn't sure if they could stay.

ALDO MARGOLLES (UTA): I had spent several days trying to find a boat to buy in Dar es Salaam that would take the Cubans across the Lake as quickly as possible, because the boats that were there were very slow. Rivalta put me up, and Ulises Estrada helped in my work. I went to Kigoma to coordinate things with Lawton.

   While the boat we'd found was being taken to Kigoma, a hole was knocked in it, so we couldn't use it after all and had to cross the Lake in the boat Lawton had, which was in bad condition.

OSCAR FERNANDEZ MELL (SIKI): When Aragonés and I reached Dar es Salaam, we met up with Chué and some other comrades, all blacks, who had also arrived by plane. They were to have gone to Mozambique, but, as that fell through, they were sent to the Congo and went with us. We made the crossing without any trouble.

MARGOLLES: I think we entered the Congo on September 1. We saw Kumi and Terry in Kibamba. The next morning, we began to climb. It was quite a slope. We stayed at the base for a couple of days and spent another two or three trying to find Che, who came to meet us. A few days later, Siki [Oscar Fernández Mell], Karín and I were sent to the ambush where Dreke was.

CHE: We had a position that allowed us to do practically anything we wanted in our camp. The problem arose when we tried to organize things in the Congolese camp.

   Because of his size, Aragonés was given the Swahili name "Tembo" (Elephant). Fernandez Mell's name, based on his character, was "Siki" (Vinegar). The others were also given names. [*Congo*, 72.]

He also mentioned the incorporation of José Palacio (Karín) to replace Rafael Bustamante (Tom) as the political commissar. Margolles was called "Uta" (Arrow), and Chué, "Siwa."

As of that date, 120 Cubans had, by Che's count, entered the Congo. Four of them had been killed in the battle of Front de Force, and two had gone back to Cuba. Changa was in charge of the Lake crossings, and four of the others were doctors and serving as such, so there were 109 Cuban combatants. One group of reinforcements was still to come.

CHE: It was a large enough force with which to attempt something, but, as has been seen, *because of various circumstances that I couldn't or didn't know how to avoid, it was spread over a large area* [emphasis by W.G.], and, when it came time for action, I could never count on more than 30 or 40 men. Add to this the fact that practically every-body had had malaria at least once, and several men more than once, and you will see that it wasn't a force that could determine the result of a campaign. It might have constituted the nucleus of an army with new characteristics if the Congolese comrades had been different. [*Congo*, 72-73.]

The situation gets worse

Two other things were of even greater concern to Che.

CHE: A few days later, the situation clouded over again. Ali had had some serious altercations with the chiefs of his area and was now at the Lake, and without saying so, reluctant to go back, postponing his return trip. Action in the recently abandoned Front de Force area was down to almost nothing. We had sent to Kigoma asking for a pair of oxygen and acetylene tanks, to try to sabotage the electric wires by means of torches, but a thousand difficulties arose in transporting them because of their weight and the people's lack of willingness. In addition, they didn't want to do anything if the Cuban Staff weren't there. There were also no results from the scouting to find an emplacement from which to fire on the water-collecting tube of the hydroelectric plant. And here, after the first moment of euphoria, the soldiers got tired of an active life and demanded that they be allowed to go back to the sweet merry-making of their upper base.

The situation was worst in terms of the relations that Masengo and Kabila had with the chiefs of the Fizi area and the relations the revolution had with the Tanzanian Government. Kabila and Masengo arrived at Kibamba, but this was immediately followed by news that the Tanzanian authorities refused to turn over a series of weapons that we had requested, including the longed-for fuses for antitank mines. They demanded Kabila's immediate presence. It is clear to me that this was true, because Changa, our "Admiral," was the man sent to get the weapons, and he was told that they wouldn't hand over anything and that Kabila would have to go himself to talk about this with the [Tanzanian] government. The only time that Kabila had made a serious attempt to cross the Lake — at least, nothing to the contrary could be proved — he was forced to go back to discuss who knows what problem...

At almost the same time, Masengo sent me a letter that shows the insecurity of the leadership of the Congolese revolution. It was written in Kibamba and dated September 6.

"Comrade Dr. Tatu [Che]
"Makungu [sic]
"Comrade Doctor,
"After some days away, I send you greetings.

"I have followed your advice regarding military matters. That is, Comrade Lieutenant Colonel Lambert will coordinate the activities on the Lulimba-Makungo and Kalonga-Kibuye fronts.

"Comrade Kabila and I were ready to pay you a visit, but, unfortunately, the circumstances don't allow us to do that right now. Five days after our arrival in Kibamba, Comrade Kabila received an urgent call from President Nyerere of Tanzania. The political situation in the country isn't very serious, and we hope that, with our efforts, we can overcome some difficulties. Today, we proceeded to arrest some members of the counterrevolutionary band, and the people haven't made any protest. This means that they understand their defects. The head of the band is the traitor Gbenye, who, after having received many millions, sent these agents all over for the purpose of burying the revolution and then negotiating with the men from Leopoldville.

"The imperialists have promised Gbenye that they will let him form a government if he manages to bury the revolution and include all of the agents of imperialism in his future government, in order to maintain neocolonialism in the Congo.

"During the meeting of all the Heads of State of eastern Africa (Tanzania, Uganda and Kenya), Gbenye declared that we ourselves should solve our problems with Leopoldville, promising them that, after the reconciliation with Leopoldville, we would enter a federation with the eastern African countries. This is why Comrade Kabila has just been called to Dar es Salaam. It may be to put pressure on us. They have even refused to let one of us go to Dar es Salaam with Comrade Kabila.

"In spite of all this, we will never agree to that reconciliation.

"I must also tell you that the Cuban Captain Ali and I are leaving for Uvira today. After my return, I will also go to Kabimba, and I hope to find your reply concerning these matters — especially your good advice on the problem set forth above — when I get back.

"We believe that the top African leaders don't want the complete liberation of the Congo, fearing that, when the Congo is completely free, with true revolutionaries leading it, all Africa will be in danger of following its example.

"In any case, the situation isn't serious yet; we are almost sure that we can survive this period.

"I hope that, based on what I have just written, you will be able to give us some suggestions on how to solve some problems of this kind." [The copy of this document is not signed, and it is followed by a comment. — W.G.] [*Congo*, 68-71.]

CHE: The letter contains several interesting things: Gbenye's action and his connection with the imperialists, which hasn't been proved to the extent described by Masengo; his promises to the African leaders, of which we have no proof, either; and the pressure that Dar es Salaam was bringing to bear on Kabila, which was the case. The fact that he was drawing closer to the Cubans at that time should be pointed out; it should have taken place earlier, in an easier situation for us, because the enemy Army's offensive was about to begin. I answered him immediately, as follows:

"Dear Comrade,

"I have just spoken with Comrade Bemba Charles, your envoy. He will be able to tell you how he sees the situation, but I will give you a brief review.

"I believe that, so far, we have demonstrated the real possibility of remaining on the plains. Following the actions on the Mundandi front, we have just laid an ambush in which seven or eight enemy soldiers were killed and six weapons were captured. We have laid ambushes on the two roads — the one from Nyangi to Lulimba and the one between Force and Lulimba.

"I think that we should keep working in this area and try to expel Tshombe's followers who are close to Lulimba, so as to have an open route to the Lake. I know about the problems in Baraka and Fizi, but it would be very important for us to have a direct road for supplies.

"As regards the problems you have just told me about: first of all, you can be sure that we will support you with the Tanzanian Government and also in your needs, as much as we can. I would like to talk with you, but I understand your difficulties in getting out of the General Staff. In a few more days, I will be free to go and talk with you. Then I would like to visit other regions on this same front. I ask you not to keep me at the Lake; my job is what I am doing now.

"Like you, I am a long-term optimist, but more attention must be given to the political and military organization. We have advanced, but not enough. We can advance more by fighting more. Combat is the soldier's best school. Moreover, our greatest source for obtaining weapons is the enemy Army; if we aren't allowed to use the Lake, we have the field of battle.

"I salute your determination, even though your role will be more difficult. Your real position, in my opinion, should be chief of Frente. I also call your attention to the fact that the Rwandan comrades have fought very well alongside us, and they have already done so with the Congolese comrades, too. Captain Zakarías is courageous, in spite of some defects which can be corrected in time.

"The political policy toward the farmers must be insisted on. Without the support of the people, we cannot be really successful. I hope to be able to talk with you more extensively on this matter.

"With revolutionary greetings,

"Tatu [Che]"

I maintained an optimistic tone, which lasted for some time. No matter what, we had caused the enemy some losses and we felt that we had possibilities of continuing to wage a war of attrition that would force the enemy to abandon some positions as too costly to maintain. [*Congo*, 71-72.]

Regardless of the evaluation Che made both before and after receiving Masengo's letter, he was aware that the letter, more than a report on the situation, was a desperate attempt to seek aid from him, his men and his government, to counter the maneuver which Gbenye might carry out. Masengo's attitude during his trip with Ali proved this.

In his reply, Che expressed his great desire that the struggle should be taken to a more favorable terrain, until it could find its true course and the movement's leaders would understand that wars were won on the field of battle and with the support of the farmers.

CHE: Several members of the rival group of Fizi, who had been engaging in destructive propaganda in the area, had been seized and were being held at the Lake base. Masengo didn't have an appropriate prison in which to keep them and he decided to send them to Uvira for safe-keeping. He decided to take them himself and to take advantage of the trip to make an inspection of the area. They left by boat. This is Ali's version of what happened; it gives a true idea of the turn events took. [*Congo*, 69.]

Ali's extensive report, dated September 8, says that they left at night on August 16. It records the coldness with which they were received in Kasina and Mubembe, where there were expressions of hostility and demands that they hand over the prisoners. It was impossible for them to continue their trip to Uvira. Clearly, Masengo's authority was shattered, which showed once more that neither the guerrillas nor the settlers had any respect for their leaders.

Che felt that the report contained some exaggerations, but he understood that the Cuban captain's description of the situation and of the Congolese leaders was unbiased.

Everything was normal on September 9 and 10, except for the fact that planes were flying overhead and a shot went off at Azi's position.

A new ambush

DREKE: The waiting lasted 11 days; everyone suffered from a lack of food, eating yucca and bananas that were found nearby. The Congolese said several times that they wanted to leave. I told them that we Cubans wouldn't withdraw before the enemy appeared. It seems that our position made them stay there. With great difficulty, Che remained at the command post. I was in the middle, with Zakarías; Kahama was on my left; and Ishirini, on my right.

The *Campaign Diary* contained the following:

Saturday, September 11, 1965
At 1045 hours, we heard a car, and the men in the ambush got ready. A Rwandan from the group in the middle opened fire with the bazooka, hitting the vehicle when it was around five meters from where he fired the shot. The others in the middle — Moja [Dreke], Nanne, Paulu, Captain Zakarías, Pierre, Yerome and Ishirine — immediately opened fire with everything they had. We then became aware that another truck filled with guards was coming and was around 100 meters away. They opened fire on the ambush from the left flank, where there were four Cubans, including Kahama. He had come to report to Moja that due to the shooting it was impossible to take any of the guards prisoner, because all the Congolese had run away and left the Cubans. They had seized six weapons — one Springfield, two FALs and three Belgian rifles — cartridge shells, papers, photos, documents, candy and some enormous boxes in the truck that they couldn't get open to see what was inside. He said that the guards were trying to isolate us on the road.

A withdrawal was ordered, since only a few Cubans and some Rwandans remained — a small group from the initial ambush. They reached the Kimvit River and crossed it, while being fired upon by the advancing guards. On the other side of the river, they went to some little huts, where they found Uta, Siki and Karín, who were coming to reinforce the ambush, and Comrade Siwa and Jukumo, who opened fire on the guards.

The men got ready to lay another ambush for the guards on the bridge that Marembo had to later destroy, since the guards from the second truck had to return with their dead through that same place to get to Katenga. The truck that had been destroyed blocked the way so they couldn't go on to Lulimba. They heard some planes heading toward Lulimba.

Some of the men went to Carula to report to Che. At 1400 hours, Wasiri, Anga and Abdala went to see if they could see Azima on the Nyangi-Lulimba road. Siwa left for the Kimvit River.

In the withdrawal from the ambush, they didn't find Comrades Zulemán and Yolivo at the meeting place, and they didn't know where they were. Moja went out with Karín, Jukumo, Akike and Paulu at 1600 hours to see what the situation was at Azi's ambush, but there was nothing new.

The enemy firing could still be heard, growing ever more intensive. They counted around nine enemy soldiers killed in this last ambush.

Mbili, Pombo and Ansali went out with a Congolese to the hanging bridge to see the site of the ambush. When they reached the bridge, which had to be destroyed, they saw the tracks of the guards, 21 of whom managed to return in the second truck [sic], putting boards across for it. The [first] truck caught in the ambush had been destroyed, and they decided to set it on fire. Comrade Ansalia was [seriously] burned. They arrived at Carula at 2000 hours, Mbili staying behind at some small huts. Milton arrived at 2200 hours; he had been at the river crossing. Today, we heard strafing by the planes at the Force front. It should be pointed out that the [second truck] got away because there were only three Cubans on the bridge with 10 Congolese. The Congolese took off running when they heard that the guards were advancing and shooting, deploying along the road. In short, all of them withdrew and the same thing happened in the other ambush which was ordered to be laid later on.

CHE: The second vehicle wasn't destroyed by the men with the bazooka because it jammed, and the occupants — there were more of them than in the first truck — dug themselves in and put our left wing to flight. Most of the men in that wing were Congolese, but there were Cubans who also retreated, frightened by the others' flight. Instead of completely wiping out the two trucks, we were pursued at one point and had to retreat. As always happened in those cases, there was a complete rout. The Congolese quickly crossed the Kimbi [Kimvit], not stopping until they reached headquarters. We were once more reduced to little more than the group of Cubans, though this time the Rwandans, with greater experience in fighting, had remained. One of them had even used his bazooka against the truck and another, who was in our troop, proudly showed off the boots he had taken from a dead soldier, since his had fallen apart. They had also helped to pick up weapons.

This action showed how far we still had to go to organize forces that would take part in these small battles, even if they didn't do anything more, and how much was lacking in the training of some Cubans, who were bewildered by conditions so different from those in their Army — such as those of a guerrilla war — and didn't succeed in acting with coordination and initiative.

Moreover, the way in which the [enemy] soldiers defended themselves showed that they were trained and were advancing, because they did this after the first vehicle had been destroyed. All of them were Africans, but we could see that — contrary to what the Congolese themselves thought, for they attributed the root of their troubles to the white mercenaries, saying that the Africans were afraid of them — the enemy that faced us could hardly be dismissed.

Before the fighting broke out, the lieutenant who headed Calixte's group had told me that his troops refused to fight alongside the Rwandans, because the latter fired shots while running away and could kill their own comrades. I didn't doubt this at all, because I had experienced this, too. However, I was much more leery of the Congolese, and my opinion was fully justified, since it could be said that none of them fired at all, and they fled upon hearing the first shot. I was very worried about this. The same thing had happened with the Rwandans, but, by this third attempt, a small group of them had displayed some eagerness. The attempts to join the two groups seemed doomed to failure. We had been able to ward off the previous crisis and convince Calixte's people to fight alongside Mundandi's men, but then a dispute arose over the weapons. I insisted that they be given to the Congolese, as a gesture, but the Rwandans felt that they hadn't done anything, and the weapons belonged to them. There was a near outbreak of violence which I managed to control by talking with Captain Zakarías. They grudgingly turned in the rifles, without any friendly gesture. The Rwandans went back to their front; they didn't want to remain there. This happened the day after I gave Masengo my opinion about Zakarías and the unity of struggle.

The result of the battle was satisfactory in the sense that we didn't have any wounded. Hours later, while reconnoitering with Mbili, Comrade Ansalia had torched the truck that the enemy had abandoned and was seriously burned when the gasoline caught fire...

I still felt that things might work out. I gave instructions that new ambushes be set on the road, while I prepared to go to Lulimba with some men to convince Lambert of the need for action. Among the truck's papers, as I have already said, we had found a payroll, which indicated that there were 53 men at Lulimba. I thought it was an ideal opportunity to attack that point with Lambert's greater forces and open the road to Kasongo. If the ambushes between Katenga and Lulimba worked, they would give us a few days' break in which we could surround the latter, assembling all of the forces that were scattered through that large area.

In line with our principles, we began a program of social action. The Indian doctor, who had come from the base, gave health care to the farmers from the area and a system of rounds through the mountain villages was set up. I handed out vegetable seeds which I had received from the Lake and we shared the crops that were grown. We achieved a different, communicative atmosphere. Like farmers all over the world, these were receptive to all human interest in them and were grateful; they had a great spirit of cooperation. It was sad to see how those same men who showed genuine trust in us and interest in working were transformed when they joined the Army of Liberation, becoming undisciplined, lazy soldiers without any spirit of struggle. Instead of being factors promoting the development of revolutionary awareness, the military groups were a dumping ground where everything rotted, because of the disorganization and lack of leadership that I have lamented so often in the course of these notes. [*Congo*, 65-67.]

The Rwandans part company with the Cubans

Enemy activity began the day after the ambush, when, very early in the morning of Sunday, September 12, 1965, the planes returned — apparently scouting, as they didn't attack — a clear indication of what could be the enemy advance. According to the entry for that day in the *Campaign Diary*, Captain Zakarías and his men went off to the Front de Force area. However, Pierre and Yerome, Rwandans who had very good relations with the Cubans, didn't go.

Early on Monday, September 13, an inspection was ordered of the bridge which was supposed to have been sabotaged. It was found that the damage done to it was insignificant. In the afternoon, reports arrived from Jukungo that the enemy soldiers had come up to the Kimvit River. They had arrived shooting, so Dreke and some other comrades went off to investigate what had happened. Mortar and FAL rifle shots were heard, which made them think that soldiers had been met on the Katenga-Lulimba road. Later on, several fighters who had been on another scouting expedition arrived. Yolivo and Zuleimán, who had been lost since the ambush on September 11, also showed up. The explanation they gave Che about their retreat didn't satisfy him, so he ordered their weapons taken away for a few days.

At the end of the afternoon, Che sent instructions to the Cubans at the Makungo front. He received a report from Mbili saying that Pombo's ambush couldn't be set, because the soldiers were already on the bridge they had to cross. Other reports said that Ali and other Cubans were in Kabimba. All that happened that day led to the order that the knapsacks be taken to a reserve command post.

Tuesday, September 14, was cloudy and rainy. Even so, Che decided to take six Cubans and eight Congolese and go to the Lulimba front. Prior to this, he had ordered a scouting party to explore the chosen route. The steady rain held them back, for they frequently had to take shelter in thatched-roof huts. As Che noted, there were many that had been abandoned long before they began the operations which violently disturbed the region. At mid-morning, they heard the sound of heavy fighting with aerial support.

Planes prevent the ambush

According to the *Campaign Diary*, four planes strafed the ambush area and launched rockets at around 0930 hours. They later withdrew, after the Cubans had abandoned their position. Still later, two trucks went by heading toward Katenga, since the bridge had been repaired. They were too far away to be attacked. According to Mbili's report, that happened the day before, but he added that a truck followed by three tanks appeared on September 14, travelling from Katenga toward Lulimba. He thought more were coming. They attacked the first two with bazookas while they were crossing the bridge and the explosions halted them. However, they had to withdraw immediately because of the quick intervention of planes which strafed and bombed them, though without causing any losses.

CHE: The soldiers had penetrated our defenses, suffering some losses in light tanks and probably in men. As a result, they had reinforced Lulimba. From that point, they also moved up troops to help their comrades in the breach, which makes me think that there were never just 53 men, as the payroll we captured indicated, but rather many more. At one time, I thought that the fight was for Lulimba, but, in fact, the key points were reinforced to begin an offensive. Later, because of the great preparatory work at Front de Force and Nyangi, we suspected as much, but we didn't have any information. We lacked any significant intelligence about the enemy camp. At midday, I met up with Azima, who was returning from scouting. He had come by the road from a hamlet we called Lulimba_and hadn't met any soldiers. That road ran parallel to the positions that the rebels occupied in the mountains until it ran into the highway from Front de Force and headed straight for the hills. It climbed them where they were lowest, making feasible the ascent.

Azima told me that he had continued scouting along the highway for a kilometer beyond the point where the road ran into it, up to the Kimbi [Kimvit] River, without finding any traces that people had been there. Moreover, his group had gone to scout the place called La Misión, an old abandoned Protestant church. While going along that road in no man's land, they were spotted by observers on the hills who were six kilometers away. They were fired at some 17 times, using mortars and other weapons that they couldn't identify. The shells were fired with great precision, but it would have been a Herculean task to hit six men advancing along a road, using shells with parabolic trajectories. The result was a monstrous waste of shells, shot against suspicious-looking men in an area that should be full of advance posts. [*Congo*, 74-75.]

Che decided not to go on and spent the night in one of the abandoned huts, but first sent a message to the Staff at Lubondja. He stated that they would detour to Lulimba and gave their route, to avoid any other confusion which might prove disastrous.

On Wednesday, September 15, on the road, they met up with the patrol that had been sent out to meet them, thanks to his warning. Later on, they reached the roadblock at Lulimba, in the mountains. Planes were overflying the Nyangi area, and Mbili reported that afternoon that the bridge had been destroyed once again; this time, they hid the rails and threw the planks into the river. The men laying the ambush at the hanging bridge moved to another ambush, at the Katernga bridge, and reported that there were fewer than 50 soldiers in Lulimba.

In the course of their march, they found several hamlets on the sides of the mountains. By talking with the farmers, Che learned that the enemy didn't go into that area. They asked for a doctor, and he promised that one would go through there every fortnight. He sent a message asking Siki, the doctor, to follow the same route he had taken and see to the farmers' health needs.

From Lieutenant Colonel Lambert's roadblock, a small group of straw huts with tin roofs, infested with crab lice but lacking all vegetation and hiding places, was observed along the road. To repulse any air attack, it had two antiaircraft guns. The antiaircraft guns were not well placed, without the required site, so when planes appeared, instead of attacking them, the crews abandoned their positions and quickly sought refuge in a nearby field of sugarcane. In spite of the lack of cover, the camp hadn't been subjected to a serious raid. Its men hadn't dug trenches for riflemen and bazookas, either.

CHE: Trenches were always a headache, because the Congolese had a superstitious fear of them and refused to get into holes they themselves had dug. They didn't make any solid defenses in which to hold out against attacks. [*Congo*, 75.]

Tanzania

Padilla, Colman and Oliva went to Kigoma on September 15 to learn where Che was, because, when he had left his base, they had lost track of him. However, they couldn't get to the Congo, because the boats couldn't cross the Lake.

In Kigoma, they stayed in the government building, where the Cubans had two rooms used for sleeping, eating and storing weapons and their belongings. Padilla could see the countless difficulties that Changa had to overcome to keep open the means of communication with the other side of the Lake. He also noted that the boats our forces had were inadequate and very slow. Moreover, Changa had few resources and that situation made him dependent on the Kigoma authorities, both civilian and military.

In view of that situation, they took on the task of making a list of what was needed for repairing the boats, although the most urgent need was for a good mechanic. Changa also needed someone to assist in solving the many logistical tasks which arose — which, in another context, might be considered small in number but which took on a serious connotation, because of the underdevelopment of Kigoma at that time. It was really no more than a large hamlet, very poor and absolutely lacking in technical supplies.

"I skewered them with my customary criticism"

As announced, the Congolese major arrived on Thursday, September 16, and told Che that Lambert was in Fizi because one of his daughters was sick, even though he had previously gone to the Lake and spent six weeks there without visiting the camp. His substitute stayed at the so-called Staff at Lubondja, 15 kilometers away, after appointing a lower-ranking chief — who, since he wasn't respected by the others, didn't play any role at all. Che knew that the farmers went to Lubondja to get food. He also knew that, since they didn't have the custom of cooking for a group, each one prepared their own food, mainly *bucali* — occasionally, they went out to hunt deer — which turned the camp into a huge multiple kitchen, where, incredibly, even those on sentry duty cooked.

Out of respect for a visitor, they asked him to address some words to the troops.

CHE: [It was a] group of fewer than 100 men, not all of them armed, and

I skewered them with my customary criticism: the armed men weren't soldiers — they were simply that, armed men. Revolutionary soldiers should become such in combat, but there hadn't been any fighting up there. I invited them to go down — Cubans and Congolese in the same conditions, since we had come to share the sufferings of struggle with them. This would be very hard; we couldn't hope for peace in the immediate future, and there wouldn't be any victory without great sacrifices. I also explained that *dawa* wasn't always effective against modern weapons and that death would be a customary companion in the hours of struggle. I said all this in my elementary French, which Charles Bemba translated into Kibembo, the mother tongue of that area. [*Congo*, 76.]

As a result of the harangue, the commander said he was ready to take his troops down, but he couldn't take part in an attack on Lulimba, which was Che's idea, without orders to that effect from his superiors. Che decided to go on with his men toward Fizi, to see if Lambert would want his men to take part in the action. Before leaving, he sent a message to Dreke, telling him what had taken place. He asked to be kept up to date on what happened in that area and that he send two or three men to serve as messengers. They went down along a narrow path between towering peaks, trying to get to Lubondja first.

CHE:. The farmers gave us a very warm welcome on the great Fizi plain, expressed in food. We could feel an atmosphere of peace and security, since the soldiers hadn't gone into the mountains for a long time and the group enjoyed relative well-being, characterized by a more varied diet, with potatoes, onions and some other foods. It was a more stable situation. [*Congo*, 76.]

They left Lubondja for Fizi early on Friday, September 17. After advancing around 10 kilometers, they found a truck taking troops to the place they had left. The man in charge promised them he would take them where they were going on his return, thus saving them over 40 kilometers of their march.

Like dogs and cats

CHE: I noted several characteristics of the region. First of all, great numbers of armed men wandered through the little towns we saw; in each of them, there was a chief who was in his house or the house of a friend and was clean, well fed, and well supplied with alcohol. Second, the soldiers seemed to have great freedom and were more than content with that situation, going around with their weapons on their shoulders; there were no signs of discipline, eagerness to fight or organization. Third, Lambert's and Moulane's men kept their distance from each other, looking at each other like dogs and cats. They immediately identified Charles, the inspector from Masengo, and surrounded him with a glacial chill.

Fizi is a small town but, even so, the largest one I saw in the Congo. It has two very different sectors: a small sector with houses of rubblework, some of them very modern, and the African sector, with the usual huts, a lot of poverty, no water and no hygiene at all. This sector had the most inhabitants, with many refugees from other areas who had converged at that point. The more modern sector belonged to the officials and the troops.

Fizi lay at the top of the hill that rose from the Lake, 37 kilometers from Baraka, on a plain with little vegetation. Its only defense was a single antiaircraft gun manned by a Greek mercenary who had been taken prisoner in a battle in the Lulimba area. Its inhabitants were very pleased with that precarious defense. General Moulane received me very coldly, because he knew why I had come. Due to the tension between Lambert and himself, he felt it a good opportunity to express his displeasure. My situation was a little strange; I had been given accommodations by General Moulane, a courteous and cold host, at the request of an exuberant Lambert, full of amiability. I was the field of battle for an internal power struggle. The result was that I had two dinners: one with the General and the other with Lambert. They treated each other with mutual respect and Lambert stood at perfect attention before the General.

We had a brief meeting in which I reported to them in general terms about the work we had done throughout the front and of my intention to talk with Comrade Lambert, to see if something could be done in the Lulimba area. The General listened to me in silence and then gave orders in Swahili (he didn't speak French) to one of his aides. Then the aide began to speak of the great actions that had been carried out in Muenga, a city around 200 kilometers to the north, which they had just seized. The spoils were a flag and a shotgun that had been taken from a Belgian priest. According to them, they hadn't been able to advance farther and seize other towns, for lack of arms and ammunition; they had taken two prisoners, but — his exact words — "You know, there isn't very much discipline and they killed them before getting here." The patriots had lost three men. Now they wanted to reinforce Muenga with heavy weapons and had sent a request to the Lake, asking for them and munitions. Then they would begin an offensive toward Bukavu in this area, which had around 300 weapons. I didn't want to ask many questions, because my lack of confidence might become obvious. I let them enlarge on explanations, even though it didn't seem very logical that 300 men, after taking the position in a tremendous battle, wouldn't have more trophies than a flag and the shotgun taken from the village priest.

At night, the General's aide and a colonel from the Kasongo area described the characteristics of all their vast territorial possessions. They said Uvira was a sector in their area that had Colonel Bidalila as its chief — and Bidalila didn't obey their direct orders. The colonel of Kasongo, however, was a faithful subordinate of the General's. Both complained of a lack of weapons. The colonel from Kasongo had been waiting there a long time, but his equipment hadn't arrived. I asked him why he hadn't gone to Kibamba, and he replied that he could wait for what he had requested to get to Baraka; his men would transport the weapons from there and begin the offensive.

Both General Moulane and the Colonel from Kasongo were veterans who had begun the struggle with Patrice Lumumba. They didn't say so explicitly; the aide took it upon himself to explain that they had been initiated in the struggle and were true revolutionaries, while Masengo and Kabila had joined later and now wanted to capitalize on everything. He began a direct attack on those comrades, accusing them of sabotaging his actions. According to my informant, since Kabila and Masengo were from Nor-Katanga, they sent matériel there, keeping this area, which was loyal to Soumialot, in short supply. The same thing happened with Kasongo. Moreover, they didn't respect the hierarchy of command; there was a general there, but Lieutenant Colonel Lambert, who was Chief of Operations of the brigade, had complete independence and worked things out with Kabila and Masengo, obtaining a lot of weapons and ammunition that didn't reach the final destination, thus weakening discipline and keeping the revolution from advancing.

Both the people at Kasongo and those at Fizi asked me for Cubans. I explained that I was trying to concentrate my limited forces and didn't want to spread them too thin along the vast front and that one or two Cubans wouldn't change the situation. I invited them to go to the Lake, where our comrades could teach them how to handle the machine guns and where there were instructors for using cannon and mortars. Thus, they could have their own men trained in using those weapons, without having to depend on a mercenary, as in the case of Fizi. This argument left them totally unconvinced.

The General invited me to go to Baraka and Mbele, his hometown. I accepted diplomatically, but I had to go back that same day, as we had to return to the Lulimba area. Before I left, they took me on a tour of Fizi, and I examined a wounded man who had come from

Kasongo. The bullet had gone into the muscle, and the untreated wound was infected and gave off a sickening smell. I recommended that he be sent to Kibamba immediately — the wound had already been left as it was for a fortnight — to be treated by the doctors living there. We could take him to Baraka as the first step of his journey. They thought it more important to put a large escort in the truck and leave the wounded man in Fizi; I never heard of him again, but I imagine he had a very bad time.

The important thing now was to organize the "show." General Moulane put on his battle dress, consisting of a motorcycle helmet with a leopard skin on top, which gave him a quite ridiculous air, leading Tumaini to call him "The Cosmonaut." Marching very slowly and halting every four steps, we reached Baraka, a tiny town on the shore of the Lake, where we once again noted the so often repeated aspects of disorganization.

Baraka showed traces of having once been relatively prosperous. It even had a cotton baler. The war had ruined everything, and the little factory had been bombed. Mbele was around 30 kilometers to the north, on the shore of the Lake. A very bad road led there, running parallel to the coast. At around every 1,000 meters, we found what they called a roadblock; with two poles and a piece of string, anybody could improvise a stop sign and demand that travelers show their documents. Due to the shortage of gasoline, the only ones who traveled were functionaries, and the only thing those groups did was spread out their forces instead of concentrating them. There was a change of personnel in Mbele; the soldiers who came in the escort truck would replace others who would go to Fizi for their vacation; a military parade was organized, winding up with a speech by General Moulane. There, the ridiculous attained a Chaplinesque dimension; bored and hungry, I felt I was watching a bad comedy movie while the chiefs shouted, kicked the ground and carried out tremendous about-faces. The poor soldiers came and went, disappeared and appeared again, going through their paces. The head of the detachment was an old sergeant major of the Belgian Army. Each time a troop fell into the hands of one of those sergeant majors, the men learned a complicated liturgy of garrison discipline with local touches and never went farther than that. Nevertheless, this was sufficient for them to be mobilized at whim, putting on a parade every time a fly moved in the area. The worst of it was that the soldiers took to all that silliness more easily than to tactics.

At last each one went to the side and the general took us to his house, amiably urging us to recuperate from the efforts of the day. We returned to Fizi that same night, talking with Lambert so as to leave immediately. In addition to the reigning hostility and the coldness in relations that was noted — which was very different from the attitude the Congolese had toward us — there had been so many signs of disorder, or decay, that it required very serious measures and an enormous cleansing. That's what I told Lambert when I saw him, and he modestly replied that that was what General Moulane was like and that, in his own sector, as I had already seen, such things didn't happen.

We left the next day [Saturday, September 18] by jeep, but the gasoline eventually ran out, and we were left stranded at the side of the road, so we went on by foot.

In the afternoon, we stopped to rest at the house of a friend of Lambert's, who sold *pombe*. The Colonel told us that he was going to hunt and took off. Shortly afterwards, the results of the hunt arrived: a piece of meat that we ate with our customary appetite. Lambert arrived much later, showing signs of having consumed a lot of *pombe* but retaining his integrity. We met up with a group of 15 or 20 of Lambert's recruits who had decided to leave because they hadn't been given weapons. He bawled them out, speaking with terrible emphasis, employing the facility with words that comes from a state of euphoria. They picked up our equipment then and there and went to Lubondja with us; I thought they were going back to the front, but, in fact, they only served as porters, and then the others let them go.

I spoke with Lambert about future plans. He proposed leaving the Staff in Lubondja, but I argued that it was 25 kilometers from the enemy. A troop that, with goodwill, had only 350 men couldn't have its Staff that far away. The equipment could be left there, but we should be with our fighters at the front... He took me to see his powder magazine, which was well hidden around five kilometers from Lubondja. Actually, it was large, in view of the conditions in the Congo. It had a large amount of ammunition and weapons, including some that had been seized from the enemy in earlier actions, in the period when it was weaker: 60-mm mortars and howitzers, Belgian bazookas similar to U.S. models that also had some shells and 50-mm machine guns. The powder magazine was much better supplied than the one at Fizi, which gave some weight to their arguments.

We had planned to go down to the plains immediately; concentrate Lambert's men, those at Kalonga-Kibuye and Calixte's, leaving only a few ambushes to intercept reinforcements; and surround Lulimba in an elastic way, using the troops from Kalonga-Kibuye for the double function of picking up recruits along the way and impeding the entry of reinforcements. I thought that, with this kind of struggle, we could cause substantial losses to the enemy. As a reserve, we had the men from the roadblock on the road from Lulimba to Kabambare, also under Lambert's command. [*Congo*, 77-81.]

The power of *dawa*

CHE: We left with all of these good intentions, but, after the corresponding assembly and *dawa* and before we had left the town of Lubondja, the four "giant owlet moths" and the two B-26s appeared and began a systematic strafing of the town. After 45 minutes of the bombing, two people had been wounded slightly, six houses had been destroyed and some vehicles had been hit by shrapnel. A major explained that the results of the action showed the power of *dawa*: only two, very slight wounds. It seemed to me prudent not to begin a discussion about the efficacy of aviation and the powers of *dawa* in a case such as this, and I left things as they were.

On arriving at the roadblock, the clandestine meetings and assemblies began, after which Lambert explained to me that it was impossible to go down — among other reasons, they had only 67 weapons, and his 350 men had spread out through the nearby villages; he didn't have enough forces to carry out a real attack; he would go out immediately and look for those on vacation and impose the required discipline.

I convinced him to send a group of men to the plains to scout and advance somewhat in the work; I would go with them. In the morning, he left with the first group... to look for more men; we were to meet below.

On arriving at the town that we thought was Lulimba, we didn't find anybody. We kept walking toward the Kimbi [Kimvit] River and, around two kilometers from the hamlet, found all of the men who were in the ambush. The town that we had called Lulimba wasn't Lulimba at all; the real Lulimba was around four kilometers away, on the bank of the Kimbi [Kimvit]. Lambert had received some boasting news from Kalonga-Kibuye reporting that all of the positions at that point had been destroyed and that the soldiers had withdrawn into the jungle. Trusting in this, he ordered his men to advance calmly, and, when they arrived, they almost ran into the soldiers — who, it must be said, were just as unconcerned as his own group. They were engaged in exercises in a camp near the town, and there were a good number of them. A small ambush was laid and we sent out scouts, who estimated the enemy strength at between 150 and 300.

The main thing was to concentrate the greatest possible number of fighters, organize them and begin an attack without many pretensions, so as to draw forces to that point. First, we had to create a base that was a little stronger and wait for Lambert to bring in his famous 350 men. We withdrew to La Misión, which was around four kilometers from Lulimba, to wait for the results of the talks that had to be held with each of the various chiefs of the roadblocks; Lambert was in charge of them. [*Congo*, 81-82.]

On Sunday, September 19, they reached La Misión, where Lambert's men were camped.

CHE: Some of them were off for the weekend, and a total lack of precautions prevailed. From a great distance, we could hear the shouts of men arguing and the din of an amusing episode that resounded in the nave of the church where they were quartered. It was a constant struggle to keep the sentries at their posts. Lambert came and went constantly, giving an impression of great effectiveness in searching for his men, but they didn't appear. We couldn't get over 40 together; whenever we managed to get some more, others went back to the roadblocks or to their villages. Nor could I bring down the machine guns to gradually strengthen the position; I barely managed to bring them close to the first hill that controlled access to the mountain. [*Congo*, 83.]

According to the *Campaign Diary*, four planes flew over the Front de Force highway.

On Monday, September 20, scouting showed that Lulimba had many more than the 53 soldiers shown by the captured payroll and that a larger camp was on the other side of the Kimvit River. Moreover, it was thought that there was still another camp, whose location wasn't known. The scouts observed the soldiers' lack of anxiety when crossing the river to pick yucca in the large areas planted by the farmers.

Che sent Banhir out again to find the supposed camp, but he didn't reach the hill from which he could have seen it, because some soldiers who were out hunting nearly caught him.

CHE: They had so much impunity that they even ventured to the spurs of the mountains. From our position, we could hear their rifle shots in various directions, which made the sentries very nervous. When the men at the ambush heard the hunters' shots nearby on the first day, total confusion ensued. [*Congo*, 83.]

Thanks to a message from Dreke, Che knew of the actions in the region between Katenga and Lulimba, in which several losses were inflicted on the enemy, but not as many as expected. The message also reported that only the Cubans took part in the ambushes, since the Congolese never stayed longer than two or three days before going back to their camp in the mountains, having "completely lost their initial, minuscule enthusiasm."

Shrapnel, bombs and propaganda

Very early on the morning of Tuesday, September 21, four T-28s appeared and flew on toward Front de Force, bombing and heavily strafing the region. Shortly afterwards, two B-26s flew by toward Lulimba, and four other planes and a helicopter appeared at mid-morning.

CHE: The planes had bombed the farmers' hamlets of Canja and Kanyanga [and also fired at other places], dropping leaflets with a very blurry photo of some dead people and an explanatory caption saying that that was the result of the Cimbas raids. Below, there was an appeal to the people in Swahili and French, advising them not to get themselves killed or suffer simply to enrich the Chinese and Cubans, who were going to steal all the gold. And, mixed with stupidities of this kind, there were some things that were true, such as the fact that they didn't have any salt or clothes, which they couldn't hunt for or sew, and that their families were threatened with hunger — something that the farmers felt was imminent. At the bottom, there was a safe conduct pass signed by Mobutu. By presenting it, the men could return to their normal lives; Tshombe's Army would guarantee that they wouldn't be killed and that they would be free.

It was the same method Batista used in our war. It undermined some weak individuals, though it did very little damage in Cuba. I was afraid that there was greater weakness here. Naturally, with the same stupidity as Batista, they dropped the pamphlets after bombing and sowing terror; it seems that that is standard operating procedure for repressive armies. [*Congo*, 84.]

While Che was doing reconnaissance for laying an ambush, he was informed that the Congolese had abandoned their posts on hearing shots — apparently those of hunters — near La Misión. This led to a rapid withdrawal, to find the timid fugitives who were seeking refuge in the mountains. These incidents reduced the number of "rebels," until there were only between 20 and 25 of them.

Lambert returned from his search for "fighters" on the Kabambare road on Wednesday, September 22. He brought only 60 of the 120 he had thought he would find, but those 60 were willing to "fight."

CHE: By that time, I didn't believe Lambert very much, because of his frequent acts of irresponsibility. I calculated, as a first approximation, that there were 60 men. I told him what had happened and about the fighters we had left; we couldn't attack with so few men. According to the latest dispatches, Lulimba was greatly reinforced, so I proposed that three small ambushes be laid for the simple purpose of irritating the enemy: two in the yucca fields, where they weren't at all suspicious, and one on the highway. I would move my post to a small river, the Kiliwe, which was to the left of the roadblock, to try to organize my men. In fact, I was trying to separate myself from Lambert and attempting to organize a mixed force, a dream I never managed to realize, because I never had enough Congolese for the nucleus it required. Lambert said he was going to discuss the new tactic with his men and would reply later, but no such reply ever reached me, both because of his own character and because things got out of hand. [*Congo*, 84-85.]

The entry in the *Campaign Diary* for that day said, "Bombing and strafing at 1530 hours, which we deduced was close to [Front de] Force. The attackers withdrew at 1605 hours."

New instructions
On the morning of Thursday, September 23, Che sent Dreke instructions:

CHE: 1) Singida: Stay in the huts at the stream with three or four men; one of them should go out to scout.

2) Azima: Go to Azi's ambush with four Cubans and a bazooka with instructions to maintain several lines of resistance, using the greatest possible number of Congolese.

3) Mbili: Stay in charge of the echelon of two ambushes in Katenga with 10 Cubans; at least two should be good bazooka men, stepping up the resistance along the way.

4) Mbili and Azima: Keep in contact with the messenger. Don't let anybody else there, except for a Congolese sentry.

5) Singida: Be in charge of supplies.

6) Tell Major Calixte everything and say that Lambert agrees to it.

7) The rest of the men should march to the stream with the broken bridge as quickly as possible, sending me news so we will see each other there.

8) Other groups will have to be organized: one to lay ambushes similar to Mbili's in Kalonga-Kibunja, another to head the attack on the soldiers on that flank and a third to help on that side of the stream. We will agree on their leaders.

9) Tell Doma to send the arsenal that's at Lulimba to the front as quickly as possible.

10) I should send somebody to bring news, food and other necessary things.

11) Take the radio and get new batteries.

12) Send somebody to tell Zakarías that I spoke with Lambert, and he doesn't know anything about the prisoners; there shouldn't be any problems.

13) Almari has to supply us.

14) You and Tembo can make any changes in these instructions that you believe necessary and communicate them to me later.

15) The doctor has to make some time to go through the hamlets where Siki went.

16) I need some personal things: *The Iliad* and *The Odyssey*, a Swahili notebook, the French book and notebook, paper, envelopes, the blue first aid case and some more medicine (Siki can choose it), a change of clothes, salt and lard. [*Campaign Diary*, 42-43.]

The last reinforcements

On Friday, September 24, four Cubans reached Dreke's camp. They included two doctors, one of whom — Kasulo — was of Haitian origin and, as Che noted, was extremely useful, more for his mastery of French than for his knowledge of his profession. The third was Lieutenant Mario Armas (Rebocate), Azima's brother, who was an expert in communications. On Saturday, September 25, Che left for his meeting with the commanding officer at La Misión, taking the recent arrivals and some other men with him, and, on the afternoon of September 26, they met with him at a small river five kilometers from Lulimba. They could hear planes in the direction of Katenga and Fizi-Baraka, and the rebels thought that they might be covering reinforcements heading for Lulimba. That day, a worrisome thing happened which Che described below.

CHE: On one of his anarchic excursions from one side to the other, Lambert met up with an enemy soldier who was out hunting and killed him. That caused new worries for me; evidently, Tshombe's followers must have heard the burst and have known that the dead man had only a Springfield; however, they hadn't buried him or left the place where he fell. I told Lambert that he should bury the body so as not to leave any traces and maintain uncertainty over the soldier's fate, but I encountered nothing but difficulties, because nobody wanted to do it; they were all terrified of the dead. I had to wage a hard struggle to convince them of the necessity of hiding the body; I don't know if they did it or not, but, that afternoon, they said they had buried him in a hidden spot.

It wasn't advisable to stay there any longer, because it wasn't safe. The sentries left like a shot at the slightest sign of danger and sometimes didn't warn anybody, heading straight for the mountains. I proposed that we pull a kilometer back, and Lambert accepted this in principle but then didn't do as we had agreed. [*Congo*, 86.]

Che felt that he shouldn't abandon Lambert, so he agreed with him that he would leave Dreke with 10 of his men. For his part, the Congolese would select a similar number of volunteers to be given military training. According to Che, the agreement was half kept, for the men were neither selected nor volunteered and weren't good for anything.

CHE: Counting the men who would go with Moja [Dreke] to help Lambert, there were 35 of us: a very tiny troop. The others of the group of 120 men were spread out at the Lake, at the upper base, at Front de Force and on Calixte's front. Every time we advanced, our troop grew smaller, and we couldn't concentrate it. I didn't dare leave any point without any Cubans, because, if I did, it would immediately regress to its previous state. [*Congo*, 86.]

The problem of communications

Che ordered the radio technician who had just arrived to install the equipment at the upper base so communications could be maintained with Dar es Salaam and Kigoma. He had come with instructions to remain in the Tanzanian capital. He asked to be allowed to look for more equipment with a greater range that would allow him to link up with Cuba. Che felt that, "The war couldn't be directed from the Congo, as was my intention, if we had to depend on Dar es Salaam for everything." They saw that some Chinese short-wave radios weren't being used, because the men who owned them didn't know how to operate them and because they were very far apart. The worst thing was the argument about radio ownership, as they did with everything that was sent to them; nobody could convince them to give them up.

However, they tried to create a communications group in order to train Congolese operators. Che told him that he would go back through the Fizi area to examine the long-wave equipment, which hadn't been damaged by the air attacks, to try to install a guerrilla radio station in that region. He sent a letter to Masengo with the comrades who were leaving, saying that it should be under a central control so as to avoid individuals using it for their own self-promotion. He referred to the enormous lies about battles which had been published in their newspaper, which Kiwe headed; the newspaper also was of low quality, but Che didn't go into that in his letter.

CHE: They were terrible. Anyone who manufactured reports in the Batista era could have learned from Comrade Kiwe's feverish imagination. Later, he explained that it was due to his reporters. [*Congo*, 86.]

In line with Che's plans of not abandoning Lambert and of avoiding worse problems, Dreke and 11 other Cubans set out on the morning of Monday, September 27. Che had ordered several groups out scouting, some to learn where the enemy was and others to find a place for setting up a provisional camp. He had decided to abandon the huts at the side of the path, since planes flew by frequently; he also wanted to reorganize his personnel at the new camp.

The offensive with mercenaries
On that same date, according to what appeared in the press, Belgian mercenaries and the government troops began landing at Baraka to carry out an offensive against the guerrillas and especially to wipe out the Cuban positions.

In the afternoon, planes attacked the La Misión area, and the guerrillas responded with antiaircraft fire. Heavy shooting could be heard coming from the direction of the Katenga-Lulimba highway. Dreke and the others deduced that the enemy was concentrating its troops at that point. Planes attacked the positions at La Misión once again on the morning of Tuesday, September 28, and soldiers advanced to Lulimba. Dreke reported to Che on what happened that day, and it should be noted that it seems they didn't know about the enemy's landing at Baraka:

"September 28
"Tatu [Che]:
"The soldiers began to advance from Lulimba toward La Misión at around 1030 hours today, along the highway and on foot, in a surrounding maneuver, firing with mortars and bombing from planes. I was at the antiaircraft gun with the colonel and some of our comrades. I gave the order for the gun to shoot, to keep the soldiers from surrounding the comrades at La Misión. The Congolese in our containing ambushes didn't shoot, and they haven't appeared yet. Comrades Tiza and Chali, who were at La Misión cooking, managed to withdraw to where I was. Comrades Bachir and Rabanini had left at 0400 hours on a scouting patrol, and I don't know what their

situation is; I think they may have gone back to where you are.[1] Almost all of the Congolese have been lost. The idea I have is to shoot at the soldiers from this position, using our men, since, when the planes began to fire, the Congolese pulled the antiaircraft guns out of position and, when I told them to put them back, threw them on the ground. I've put a Cuban on the machine gun and I sent another comrade of ours to the big gun. The gun is two hills behind us; I had told the colonel to bring the gun up to this position yesterday, but it hasn't been done yet. Comrade Compagni,[2] who was with Comrade Tiza at La Misión, withdrew with the Congolese, and I don't know what his situation is. Therefore, right now, there are eight of us. If we don't manage to stop the soldiers, we will go higher up, because the hill is very barren. Moreover, we have heard shots toward Fizi, which is a little strange.

"The comrade colonel assures me that they are our men, but I am not completely convinced by that assurance. The soldiers halted at La Misión and are there now.

"Moja [Dreke]"

[1] That is what happened. They were the two comrades I referred to.
[2] A Rwandan soldier. [Both notes are by Che.] [*Congo,* 87.]

CHE: The plane activity didn't center on the abandoned houses; the planes strafed the area of Lambert's roadblock. We were worried by the attack when two of Moja's men arrived, saying they had been sent out to do scouting but had run into enemy troops that were deployed and advancing; they had managed to hide but not cross to La Misión. [*Congo,* 86-87.]

From Front de Force, Mbili reported the destruction of one of the two light tanks that attacked, but said that they couldn't keep the enemy from getting through. Later, planes caught them in the open, though there were no losses.

CHE: The end of the report was pathetic. Several Cubans were sick, and only three Congolese remained in the ambush; those three withdrew to their base. Once again, the soldiers broke through the ambush, this time with relative ease, for the fighters were badly demoralized. [*Congo,* 87.]

Shooting at La Misión
In his manuscript, Che recorded all the other happenings in the La Misión area that Dreke reported to him.

"September 29, 1965

"Che:

"Yesterday, I talked with the colonel, asking him to bring down the gun and the mortar and fire on the concentration of soldiers who are this side of Lulimba and have seized La Misión. Lambert went out to get the gun and mortar accompanied by Nanne, to keep him from returning. I also proposed that, after shelling the concentration, we should withdraw to another hill, so the planes wouldn't inflict losses on us today. Yesterday, the planes flew very low, and the soldiers showed them where to bomb by shelling us with mortars. At around 1700 hours, yesterday, Comrade Nanne returned with two mortars and a gun, and we prepared the emplacements. The colonel didn't come back with Nanne, but returned later, at around 1800 hours, totally drunk, bringing some men from the camp and saying that, after we fired the guns and mortars, we should go down to La Misión with the men he had brought, since the soldiers would withdraw when fired upon. I told him that was very dangerous, because the enemy surely had laid ambushes, and to do what he said would be equivalent to getting surrounded by the soldiers, and, with the confusion that would be created among our own men, they would kill each other. He disagreed, saying that that was what had to be done and that he had spoken with you and that you had agreed on attacking Lulimba. I told him I was taking the responsibility for having our men stay. He also said that the soldiers were going to keep the blankets they had seized at La Misión and that that wasn't right.[3] After the attack, he was going to go to China. We fired with the guns and mortars and went back to his camp, along with him and all of his soldiers."

[3] The day before, the withdrawal had been so precipitate that the belongings of those who were absent, such as the lieutenant colonel [Lambert] and Moja [Dreke], were left behind. [*Congo*, 87-89.]

The matter couldn't be taken up again at night, because the Colonel was still drunk. An ambush was left to keep the enemy from advancing from La Misión, where it had camped. Later, Dreke set forth his idea:

"At night, shoot at La Misión, wait for a few days to do some scouting there, since it is possible that the soldiers may withdraw and not be seen. I am in charge of our men — except for the comrade at the gun. I told the colonel today to take his men out of the houses early, because of the planes, and he did so; I'm thinking about building some shelters. My relations with Lambert haven't suffered; the whole problem was he had drunk too much *pombe*. We can make contact here in the camp, since, even though we're going to another position, we will always leave somebody here.

"I await further instructions from you.

"Moja [Dreke]"

The mercenaries take Baraka

That took place in the afternoon and evening of the previous day. On the morning of September 29, thanks to Paulu's and Amia's scouting, Dreke knew that there weren't any soldiers at La Misión, but they had been there. Planes continued to fly over the area, and the sound of mortar shelling could be heard. On the radio, Che learned of the landing of September 27.

CHE: ...a report from Mobutu's Staff, according to which a troop of 400 [the figure is unclear; it may be 2,400] men, headed by Lieutenant Colonel Hoare, is attacking in the Fizi-Baraka area, trying to destroy the last rebel redoubt, and Baraka had fallen to his troops. [*Congo*, 87.]

For his part, the mercenary officer named by Che was also writing his account of the events:

The enemy forces in Baraka were a surprise to me... These enemies were completely different from those we had confronted up to now. They were well equipped, acted in line with precise tactics and moved on the basis of specific orders. They were clearly led by well-trained officers. We intercepted radio messages in Spanish... and it seemed clear to me that the defense of Baraka was organized by Cubans. At dawn and dusk, as regular as clockwork, they carried out precise attacks, which were distinguished by a lack of the noise and shouts which usually accompany rebel activity. [Michael Hoare: *Mercenario nel'Congo*, 309-10.]

To enhance his own standing, Hoare described a resistance that didn't exist, because there weren't any Cubans there. After listening to the news, Che sent a message to Dreke. On September 30, when Dreke conveyed it to the Congolese chief, the Congolese didn't believe it and said it was nothing but foolishness.

CHE: For his part, Lambert announced that Baraka had been attacked but said the attack had been repulsed... with 20 white and countless black enemy dead. As may be seen, the Congolese themselves didn't bother to count the number of blacks killed; the important ones were the whites...

The Lieutenant Colonel's irresponsibility was deplorable. The news they had given me about Baraka was false; that post had been taken almost without fighting, so our situation was becoming ever more difficult, and the plan for an army with an arsenal of weapons, men and ammunition was falling through our fingers. [*Congo*, 87-88.]

The Cubans have to do everything

CHE: The analysis for the previous month was full of optimism; this one [for September] can't be so optimistic, even though some progress has been made. It is clear that we won't be able to surround Force within a month. Moreover, we can't put a date to it now. The mercenaries have gone on an offensive. It is true that our communications are weak, but it is almost impossible to make this group fight under present conditions, and the Cubans have to do everything alone. However, Masengo named his friend Lambert (who isn't good for anything but is respected by the others and respects me) coordinator of the front, and he wrote me a conciliatory[4] letter asking me to reply about some specific problems. My struggle should center on the creation of a perfectly armed, well-equipped, independent column that can be both a shock force and a model. If this is achieved, it will have changed the panorama considerably. Until this is done, it will be impossible to organize a revolutionary army, for the low quality of the chiefs prevents it.

In summary, this was a month in which some progress was made, but there is less optimism. Such things are to be expected.

[4] My diary contains the word "conciliatory," but it wasn't the right one, as there were never any harsh words between Masengo and me. [*Congo*, 88-89.]

On that day, September 30, planes continued reconnaissance in the Fizi-Baraka area. Dreke reported to Che that he was going to Fizi at Lambert's suggestion to find out what had happened.

7

October 1965

The situation was the same on October 1, so Che thought about moving, since this place wouldn't be a good one in case of an enemy offensive. He was worried by the food problem, because the number of deer brought in by the hunters was declining, so hunting was becoming more dangerous. It was carried out in no-man's-land, and both the rebels and the enemy could hear the shots — even though, as Che put it, the enemy "maintained a suspicious, almost defensive attitude."

Siki left for La Misión in the morning, to care for the population and help Dreke in his work. Aware of the need to be able to depend on the farmers, Che did everything possible to win them over.

The *kapitas* and the presidents

CHE: I had a meeting with the president of one of the nearby hamlets. Each tiny hamlet has a *kapita*, or minor chief, and each larger one or a group of hamlets has a president. Our man spoke French and was quite clever. In a long conversation, I set forth our requirements. We needed some porters to go to the Lake and bring back canned goods and other supplies; the farmers should provide us with yucca and some vegetables and leaf tobacco. We would give them a part of the foodstuffs or other objects brought from the Lake, pay for the food they supplied us with, provide them with free medical care and medicine (as much as possible) and give them vegetable seeds. We would share the crop.

The president took note of all these things and held an assembly with his comrades. Two or three days later, very ceremoniously, he brought me a typed, signed reply covered with a multitude of seals, in which he said that he would look for men to send to the Lake and that they would guarantee our food and try to find tobacco, but that they couldn't accept payment, because it was a norm of the revolution that the farmers should feed the army and maintain it. [*Congo*, 90.]

At the same time that pleasant reply arrived, bad news came in from Front de Force. Mbili reported that the enemy had again broken through their defenses, even though the guerrillas had destroyed another armored car.

CHE: ...That time, by means of an ingenious device: the mine was buried in the road. Its detonator was the fuse of a grenade, held in place by a string which, when pulled by the pressure of a vehicle, released the safety, so the mine went off six seconds later; a light tank, at least, was blown to bits by that rudimentary artifact. [*Congo*, 90.]

Another piece of bad news was the explosion of a powder magazine in Lubondja, in which a large number of weapons of various calibers were lost. Nobody knew the cause of the explosion, but the Cubans blamed it on negligence.

Dispersal is harmful
Che noted that Mujumba, who had been the Revolutionary Council's representative in Dar es Salaam, joined them on October 1, with the task of carrying out sabotage along the Albertville railroad lines in the Makungo area. He asked for six Cubans to help him.

CHE: My reaction was violent. I explained that I was waging a practically nonstop struggle to centralize our forces, trying to created a powerful mixed army, and that I had to struggle constantly against the dispersal of forces of this kind (for the first time with them, I said the Cubans were "becoming Congolized": they were being contaminated with the prevailing spirit). Dispersal did more harm than the good that might be achieved, and we should discuss that very seriously, because I believed that, if the revolution continued along the same path it was on, its future was very dim. The discussion and, above all, descriptions of things that had happened impressed him greatly. He told me that he was willing to stay there with me, that he would look for 20 farmers to be trained and that he would make an inspection of the Mukumdi area and then return. He asked me if I would accept recruits who were farmers without any military training. I said I would prefer them, in that new people who hadn't had any contact with the habits of the bivouac would be a thousand times better than those soldiers already corrupted with life at camp. [*Congo*, 91.]

A communications technician and some assistants arrived in Dar es Salaam from Havana to install the antennas and communications equipment in the Ambassador's residence. Meanwhile, Sandino and Braulio, who had been chosen to strengthen the rear guard, had also arrived. This facilitated preparations for going to the Congo and making contact with Che.

New agreements

At last, Masengo and his entourage visited Che on October 2. It was late, so they did no more than exchange greetings, eat and go to sleep. They would talk the next morning.

CHE: The discussion was very clear, and I straightforwardly set forth the problems we were confronting and the decision he should make to create a powerful, disciplined army, if we weren't to be reduced to scattered groups in the mountains. We agreed that we would create a front in this area under Lambert's command but that, in addition, I would have a column that would be independent of Lambert, since the consequences of his irresponsibility were too much for me. [*Congo*, 91-92.]

The "new agreements" included one on the founding of an "academy for fighting." Che demanded that all of his students be farmers, but Masengo and Mujumba said that they should be trained along with soldiers from all the fronts, which didn't please Che. Another idea concerned the creation of a more centralized Staff, which would make it possible to direct operations on all the fronts. Che was enthusiastic about this and said he would make Siki adviser to the Staff and put Tembo in charge of political work, with Dr. Kasulo, the Haitian French translator, working with them.

Masengo asked him to write Rivalta, requesting that he approach the Tanzanian Government officials to get them to solve the existing difficulties, which grew more numerous every day. In summary, he asked for more military cadres, and, even though Che agreed, he warned them that they would have to be selected very carefully, since it would be a special school in which the quality of the individual cadres would be important and mere numbers couldn't compensate for deficiencies. Only his desire for that nation to make its revolution led him to believe that, this time, the Congolese leader might keep his word.

The ministries of health

Che harbored new hopes that the army of liberation would arise from the ruins, but that night an accident that he described as tragi-comic cast a dark shadow over his dream.

CHE: One of the guys dropped a lit match, and those straw huts, which were extremely dry, since the rainy season was just beginning, flared up like torches. Some things were lost, but the thing that most annoyed me was the danger this put the men in, since some grenades remained inside and kept exploding. Above all, we gave Masengo and those with him the impression that we were disorganized and careless.

In the midst of all the noise of bullets and grenades going off, accompanied by explosions of larger caliber, [José Ramón] Machadito, our Minister of Public Health, arrived with some letters and a message from Fidel. His colleague, Mutchungo, Minister of Public Health of Soumialot's Revolutionary Government, was with him. They were lost and had been guided to the camp by the light and the sound of explosions. [*Congo*, 92.]

The meeting with his old comrade in struggle, who was both a doctor and a guerrilla and who had reached the rank of major, lessened his anger. Siki also came, bringing a slew of complaints. But one of them, besides being surprising, had its funny side: it was that, even though they might be attacked by planes at any moment, when it came time to sleep, those in charge of the antiaircraft guns took them down and hauled them off, since they hadn't managed to make a good emplacement with sleeping quarters in a shelter. Moreover, the chief said he couldn't sleep anywhere but in his own house, and nobody could take over the guns from them, because they felt they were theirs. But waking them up and getting them to set up the guns again was a torment. After that night's fire was put out, they all went to sleep.

Taking it silently

That same day, October 3, the names of the members of the first Central Committee of the Communist Party of Cuba were announced in Cuba. Immediately after this, Fidel read the farewell letter that Ernesto Che Guevara had left him. Two decades later, Fidel explained his reasons for making that document public at the time:

> [Che's] stay in Africa was temporary, awaiting creation of conditions
> for traveling to South America. During this whole period the
> situation became highly awkward for us as Che had already said
> good-bye. He had written the letter before he left, and he left quietly
> of course — you might even say clandestinely. We kept the letter
> quiet and this gave rise to many rumors as well as some genuine
> slanders. Some said that Che had been made to disappear, others that
> Che was dead, or that there were differences — all sorts of stories.
> We took that flood of rumors and intrigues silently, so as not to
> endanger the mission he wanted to accomplish and the personnel he
> intended to take to his final destination — South America.[24]

Because of its importance, I am including Che's farewell letter written in
Havana in 1965, just prior to his departure to the Congo:

> "Fidel,
> "At this moment I remember many things — when I met you in
> María Antonia's house, when you proposed I come along, all the
> tensions involved in the preparations. One day they came by and
> asked who should be notified in case of death, and the real possibility
> of that fact struck us all. Later we knew that it was true, that in a
> revolution one wins or dies (if it is a real one). Many comrades fell
> along the way to victory.
> "Today everything has a less dramatic tone, because we are more
> mature. But the event repeats itself. I feel that I have fulfilled the part
> of my duty that tied me to the Cuban revolution in its territory, and I
> say goodbye to you, to the comrades, to your people, who now are
> mine.
> "I formally resign my positions in the leadership of the Party, my
> post as minister, my rank of commander, and my Cuban citizenship.
> Nothing legal binds me to Cuba. The only ties are of another nature
> — those that cannot be broken as can appointments to a post.
> "Recalling my past life, I believe I have worked with sufficient
> honesty and dedication to consolidate the revolutionary triumph. My
> only serious failing was not having had more confidence in you from
> the first moments in the Sierra Maestra, and not having understood
> quickly enough your qualities as a leader and a revolutionary.
> "I have lived magnificent days, and at your side I felt the pride of
> belonging to our people in the brilliant yet sad days of the Caribbean
> crisis. Seldom has a statesman been more brilliant than you in those

---

[24] Gianni Minà, *An Encounter with Fidel*, 224.

days. I am also proud of having followed you without hesitation, identified with your way of thinking and of seeing and appraising dangers and principles.

"Other nations of the world call for my modest efforts. I can do that which is denied you because of your responsibility at the head of Cuba, and the time has come for us to part.

"I want it known that I do so with a mixture of joy and sorrow. I leave here the purest of my hopes as a builder and the dearest of my loved ones. And I leave a people who received me as a son. That wounds a part of my spirit. I carry to new battlefronts the faith that you taught me, the revolutionary spirit of my people, the feeling of fulfilling the most sacred of duties: to fight against imperialism wherever it may be. This comforts and heals the deepest wounds.

"I state once more that I free Cuba from any responsibility, except that which stems from its example. If my final hour finds me under other skies, my last thought will be of this people and especially of you. I am thankful for your teaching, your example, and I will try to be faithful up to the final consequences of my acts.

"I have always been identified with the foreign policy of our revolution, and I continue to be. Wherever I am, I will feel the responsibility of being a Cuban revolutionary, and I shall behave as such. I am not ashamed that I leave nothing material to my children and my wife; I am happy it is that way. I ask nothing for them, as the state will provide them with enough to live on and have an education.

"I would have a lot of things to say to you and to our people, but I feel they are unnecessary. Words cannot express what I would want them to, and I don't think it's worthwhile to keep scribbling pages.

"Hasta la victoria siempre! Patria o muerte!
"I embrace you with all my revolutionary fervor.
"Che"[25]

JOSE RAMON MACHADO: Our meeting and everything else were just as Che described them, but he forgot that he was the one who told me about the creation of our Central Committee and that I was a member of it. He had heard the news on the radio. He also knew that Fidel had read his farewell letter, and he wasn't very pleased, because of his excessive modesty. [Moja [Dreke], Siki [Fernández Mell] and Tembo [Emilio Aragonés] were also members of the Central Committee.]

---

[25] Ernesto Che Guevara, *Che Guevara Reader*, 353.

The wave of lies

Monday, October 4 was cold and rainy. After coffee, calm once more, Che took Machado aside.

CHE: I knew of the long talks Soumialot and his colleagues have had with Fidel. The people of the Revolutionary Council hadn't presented things honestly — partly, I imagine, because this is always the case with such things, and partly because they had no idea of what was happening inside the country. They had been outside the country for a long time, and, as the wave of lies rose from the soldiers, constantly being exaggerated as it made its way up, I imagine that, because of their goodwill, they couldn't imagine what was really happening.

The fact is that they painted an idyllic picture, with active military groups on all fronts, forces in the jungle and constant battle — a picture that was a far cry from what we could see. Moreover, they had managed to get a substantial amount of money for making a series of trips throughout Africa, explaining the characteristics of their Revolutionary Council, exposing Gbenye and his clique, etc. They also asked for support for a number of groundless, ill-advised military actions, and there was talk of asking other friendly countries to contribute heavy weapons, 5,000 rifles, torpedo boats for the Lake and of preparing utterly fantastic plans of attack and penetration. They had gotten Cuba to promise to send 50 doctors, and [José Ramon] Machadito had come to scout out conditions.

Earlier, from Tembo, I had gotten the impression that the people in Cuba thought my attitude was very pessimistic. This was reinforced by a personal message from Fidel in which he urged me not to lose hope, asked me to remember the first stage of the [Cuban guerrilla] struggle and reminded me that obstacles always arose. He reiterated that the men were good. I wrote Fidel a long letter... setting out my points of view. [*Congo*, 92-93.]

That afternoon, Che asked Masengo to ask the heads of the front to come so he could talk with them the next day. On Tuesday, October 5, Dreke left to meet Che in Kilomwe and reported on his travels through Fizi.

CHE: Moja [Dreke] arrived from Lubondja, where he had gone to make an inspection after the powder magazine had blown up, and he brought news that Baraka had been lost — in his opinion, without a struggle. The big gun had been lost, as had the mortars, whose crews — who I think in that case were the new Bulgarian instructors[3] — had thrown them aside...

[3] I am following the custom established in the Congo of identifying students by the nationality of the country in which they were

trained. [*Congo*, 95 and 99.]

Plowing in the sea

According to the *Campaign Diary*, the meeting with the Congolese chiefs was held at 1500 hours.

CHE: With all this background, I held a meeting with the chiefs who had been called in for it — and who appeared at last. Up until then, we hadn't achieved any cohesive action by Calixte or Ila Jean, the commander at Kalonga-Kibuye. I don't know whether to blame that on them or on Lambert, whose bizarre work style made it impossible to achieve anything organic. Masengo himself, Comrade Mujumba, the Minister of Public Health, commanders Ila Jean and Calixte, Lieutenant Colonel Lambert, other commanders of Lambert's front and the usual political commissars and onlookers were present. Zakarías had been sent for but hadn't replied, so the Rwandans weren't represented. My address went more or less as follows:

First, I introduced those who were there, the Minister of Public Health of Cuba, who had come to make an analysis of health needs; Siki; Tembo, Organizing Secretary of the Party, who had given up his post to come here to fight; and Comrades Moja and Mbili, who had a long history of struggle. I explained more or less the same things as Masengo, but I added an analysis of the behavior of each chief. Lambert was, doubtless, a dynamic comrade, but he did everything himself, not assigning responsibility; he hadn't created an army; his men did some things when he went ahead of them, but if he wasn't there they didn't advance. I gave the example of the dead soldier. Lambert was on the front line because his comrades had demanded that he go and stay there. In contrast, Calixte had never appeared on the front line. Both attitudes were bad; the chief shouldn't remain so close to the front line that he couldn't see what was going on all along his front and make decisions as a whole, but neither should he be so far away that he lost all contact with it. I said that the claim of the chief of Kalonga-Kibuye that he had set a roadblock wasn't true, because there had never been even one clash with the Army, and there was no reason to keep 150 men in those conditions. Then I made an analysis of the acts of indiscipline, of the atrocities that had been committed and of the parasitic characteristics of the army. That was like a broken record, and although they withstood it with resignation, none of them was happy about it. [*Congo*, 95-96.]

Che's deeply-rooted habit of saying what he felt didn't allow him to remain silent, even though he would have to pay a political price for it.

It became very clear that it would be very difficult to achieve anything positive from that meeting. As Che himself said later, "There are sacrifices that a revolutionary leader must make at a given time."

As a result of the meeting with the chiefs, some modifications were made in the composition of the academy, which then had 150 soldiers sent by the chiefs from the three fronts — Lambert, Ila Jean and Calixte — plus 60 more sent by Mujumba and some farmers who had been recruited in the area.

CHE: Making some observations about the meeting, Comrade Tembo told me that, in his opinion, it hadn't provided any practical solutions for the problems of the Congo; I had spoken of all the negative aspects but not of the possibilities of guerrilla warfare. It was a fair criticism. [*Congo*, 96.]

Harsh analysis

Che later met with the Cubans, because he had heard rumors of mounting despair. According to Che, some of them said that they were only in the Congo because Fidel didn't know of the real situation.

CHE: I told them that the situation was difficult, the Army of Liberation was collapsing and we had to struggle to save it from utter destruction. Our work would be very hard and thankless, and I couldn't ask them to trust in victory. As for myself, I thought that matters could be fixed, but with a lot of work and many partial failures. Nor could I demand that they trust in my leadership capacity, but as a revolutionary I could demand that they respect me for my honesty.

Fidel was aware of the basic issues, and none of the things which had happened had been hidden; I hadn't come to win laurels for myself in the Congo, and I wasn't going to sacrifice anybody for my own honor. While it was true that I hadn't passed on to Havana the view that all was lost, it was because, honestly, I didn't believe that. I had reported on the state of mind of the men, their vacillations, their doubts and weaknesses. I told them that there had been days in the Sierra Maestra when I had felt utter despair over the lack of faith of the new recruits — who, after swearing by all the saints their firm determination to fight, would take off the next day. That was in Cuba, with the degree of development we had and the strength of the Revolution. What could we expect in the Congo? The Congolese soldiers were here, among the masses, and we had to discover them, one by one; that was our main task.

The need for this explanation shows the ferment that was weakening the new troops' morale. It was hard to get the guys to work;

comrades with a lot of discipline carried out the letter of their instructions but did nothing on their own; they had to be told several times, and there had to be strict controls over everything. Moreover, I had to resort to my proverbial critical sessions, which weren't very gentle, to get some tasks done. The romantic stage in which I could threaten the undisciplined with sending them back to Cuba had passed a long time before; if I had done that now, I would have been left with half the men, if that many. [*Congo*, 96-97.]

Replying to Fidel: "I'm sure that most of them are good"
CHE: "The Congo
"October 5, 1965
"Dear Fidel:
"I received your letter, which caused contradictory feelings in me, since, on behalf of proletarian internationalism, we are making mistakes that may be very costly. Moreover, I am worried that, whether because of my lack of seriousness when writing or because you don't understand me completely, it may be thought that I am suffering from the terrible disease of unwarranted pessimism.

"When your Greek present[1] arrived, he told me that one of my letters had caused the sensation of a condemned gladiator and that, on conveying your optimistic message to me, the Minister[2] confirmed the opinion you had. You may converse at length with the bearer, and he will give you his first-hand impressions, since he has toured a good part of the front. Therefore, I am not including any anecdotes. I will simply tell you that here, according to some, I have lost my fame for being objective, instead remaining optimistic about the real situation — without any foundation. I can assure you that, if it weren't for me, this beautiful dream would have disintegrated in the midst of general catastrophe.

"In my earlier letters, I asked you not to send me a lot of people, but to send me cadres. I told you that weapons aren't needed here, except for some special ones. To the contrary, there are more than enough armed men; what we need is soldiers. I warned you very specifically not to give money except by doling it out after many petitions. None of these things have been taken into account, and fanciful plans have been made that place us in danger of falling into international discredit and may leave me in a very difficult situation.

"To explain:
"Soumialot and his comrades have sold you a huge streetcar. It would be tiresome to list the large number of lies they have told; rather, I will explain the present situation with the attached map. There are two areas where it can be said that there is something of an

organized revolution, the one in which we are and a part of Kasai Province, where Mulele — the great unknown — can be found. In the rest of the country, there are only disconnected groups surviving in the jungle; they have lost everything without fighting, just as they lost Stanleyville without fighting. This isn't the most serious thing; rather, it is the spirit that prevails among the groups of that area, which is the only one with outside contact. The arguments between Kabila and Soumialot are ever more serious and are used as a pretext for continuing to hand over cities without fighting. I know Kabila well enough not to have any illusions about him; I can't say the same about Soumialot, but I know some things about him — such as the string of lies he has foisted off on you; the fact that he hasn't deigned to come into these God-forsaken lands; his frequent drunken sprees in Dar es Salaam, where he stays in the best hotels; and the kind of allies he has here against the other group[4]. Just recently, a group from Tshombe's Army landed near Baraka, where a major general who supports Soumialot had at least 1,000 armed men, and seized that strategically important point almost without firing a shot. Now, they are arguing about who was to blame: those who didn't fight or those at the Lake who didn't send them enough ammunition. The fact is, they fled shamefully, abandoning a 75-caliber recoilless gun and two 82-caliber mortars. The crews of those weapons have disappeared, and now they are asking me for Cubans to rescue them where they are (which I'm not really very clear about) and fight alongside them. Fizi is 36 kilometers away, and they aren't doing anything to defend it — they don't even want to dig trenches across the only access road, in the mountains. This gives you a faint idea of the situation. *With regard to the need to carefully select the men and not send me quantity, you assure me with the emissary that those here are good — I am sure that most of them are good; if not, they would have cracked long ago.* [Emphasis by W.G.] This isn't the point. They have to have a really tempered spirit to be able to stand the things that are happening here. I don't need good men; here, I need supermen...

"My 200 are still here; believe me: more men would be harmful unless we decide, once and for all, to fight on our own. In that case, I will need a division, and we will have to see how many the enemy will throw against us. Perhaps this last point is exaggerated, and a battalion will do to return to the frontiers we had when we arrived here and to threaten Albertville, but, in that case, the numbers don't matter. We alone can't liberate a country that doesn't want to fight. A spirit of struggle must be created, and soldiers must be found with Diogenes's lamp and the patience of Job — a task that becomes more difficult as they find more idiots to do things for them...

"The boats deserve a separate paragraph. For some time, I have been asking for two engine technicians, to keep the landing stage at Kigoma from turning into a cemetery. Three Soviet packet boats came a little over a month ago; two of them are already out of service, and the third, in which the emissary crossed, takes in water on all sides. The three Italian boats will go the same way as the others unless they have Cuban crews. For this and the matter of the armed vessels, we need Tanzania's approval, which won't be very easy to get. These countries aren't Cuba and won't risk everything even on a strong hand (and our hand is very weak). I have asked the emissary to find out from the friendly government how much assistance it is ready to give. Make it known that almost everything that came in the ship has been seized in Tanzania, and the emissary should talk about this, too.

"The money is the thing that hurts me the most, because of the many times I have warned about this. At the peak of my daring as a spendthrift, after a lot of begging, I had promised to supply one front, the most important one, on the condition that I would direct the fighting and create a special mixed column under my direct command, following the strategy I had taken part in drawing up. For that, racking my soul, I calculated $5,000 a month. Now I find that a sum 20 times as large is being given to the idlers, and in one lump sum, so they can live well in all the capitals of the African world, not considering that they are put up at the expense of the main progressive countries, which often pay their travel expenses. Not one cent will reach a miserable front where the farmers are suffering from all imaginable miseries, including the rapacity of their own defenders, nor will any money reach the poor devils who have dropped anchor in the Sudan (whisky and women aren't included in the list of expenditures covered by the friendly governments, and that mounts up, if you want good quality).

"Lastly, with 50 doctors, the liberated part of the Congo will have the enviable proportion of one doctor for every 1,000 inhabitants, a ratio surpassed only by the USSR, the United States and two or three of the other most advanced countries in the world, not considering that, here, they aren't distributed in line with political preferences and there isn't any health organization at all. Rather than that large-scale gesture, it would be better to send a group of revolutionary doctors and add to them, in line with my request, some experienced nurses of the same kind.

"Since the attached map gives a synthesis of the military situation, I will limit myself to some recommendations, which I beg you keep in mind objectively: Forget about all of the leaders of phantom groups, and train up to 100 cadres for me, not all of whom should be black. Choose the best from Osmany [Cienfuegos]'s list, plus other outstanding combatants. As for weapons, the new bazooka, electric caps with their power source, a little R-4 and nothing else for now; forget about the rifles, because if they aren't electronic, they don't solve anything. Our mortars should be in Tanzania, and, with them, we will have more than a new crew to spare for now. Forget about Burundi and try very tactfully to solve the problem of the boats (don't forget that Tanzania is an independent country, and we must treat them honestly, apart from my peccadillo). As soon as possible, send the mechanics and someone with navigation knowledge for crossing the Lake with relative safety; I have already spoken about this, and Tanzania agrees. Don't repeat the mistake of spending money like that, because they come to me when they feel in a bind, and they won't pay any attention to me if they have money. Trust a little to my views, and don't judge by appearances. Shake up those in charge of providing reliable information, who aren't capable of getting to the bottom of these tangles and who present utopian images that have nothing to do with reality.

"I've tried to be explicit and objective, brief and truthful. Do you believe me?

"Hugs,

[The signature appears to have been crossed out in the original.]

"¹ Tembo.

"² Machado.

"³* I am following the custom established in the Congo of identifying students by the nationality of the country in which they were trained.

"⁴ A source in the other group told me about the drunken sprees; they appear not to be true." [*Congo,* 93-95 and 99.]

Machado informed Che about the high-level reception given to the Congolese delegation and, of course, about the talks that had been held. The highest-ranking leaders of the Cuban Revolution met with the delegation in the places it visited. The Congolese leaders appeared on

---

* The number for the footnote doesn't appear in the text. However, a note 3 is placed on page 95 of the original which Che corrected, three paragraphs after the end of the letter to Fidel. From its content, it agrees with another part of the text, but this note was put together with the ones that do pertain to the letter. In his own handwriting, Che wrote that all of them referred to page 99 of his original. This jump in the order of the notes in the text probably confused Che when he checked Colman Ferrer's typing. The author cites Che's text — and his note — on an earlier page of this book. (Editor's note.)

television, and their speeches were harangues to the struggle to the death to achieve victory and install socialism in the Congo; they even adopted the watchword of "Homeland or Death." However, we learned later what they achieved on the basis of presenting a triumphant image of the struggle when the facts were otherwise, mainly because of their lack of willingness to fight and the incapacity of their leaders — mainly Mr. Soumialot and his followers.

Tembo also wrote a letter to Fidel, in which he described the situation as it was at that time, mainly through anecdotes. It seems that Machado returned to Cuba with this background information and his own view of reality in the Congo.

Keep the enemy from continuing to advance

Che and Masengo once again discussed the situation of Baraka, and Che agreed to have Siki and several other Cubans go to Fizi and prepare the defense, to keep it from being seized by the enemy, since taking that hamlet was absolutely necessary for his advance. They would also make a study of a possible attack on Baraka. Che demanded that only Cubans be in command — something that was absolutely necessary at that time. Following the failure of the attempt to attack Lulimba, the Cuban internationalists were commenting that, if they were left alone and died uselessly again, many of them would ask to leave the struggle, because things couldn't go on that way.

With regard to the attack on Baraka, Che thought that even though the enemy's beachhead was surrounded by mountains, which made an attack easy, it wasn't a good idea to carry out the action without knowing what troops were there.

CHE: I almost begged Masengo to use his authority to get the people at Fizi to think and to write to Kabila once more to tell him he had to come to the Congo. He couldn't go around criticizing Soumialot and his team while, at the same time, presenting the spectacle of continually saying he was going to arrive but continuing his sprees and orgies in Kigoma and Dar es Salaam. I had vacillated a lot about saying such delicate things, but I believed it was my duty to say them to Masengo, so he would directly convey them to Kabila. It wasn't my intention to become a governess or tutor, but a revolutionary chief has to make sacrifices at a given moment.

Masengo promised to write to Kabila; I don't know if he did so or not. He went to the Fizi area with Siki, while Mujumba left for the Mukundi area, promising to send me 60 farmers in seven days, a promise he never kept. I don't know why, as he never showed any more signs of life. [*Congo*, 98.]

The *Campaign Diary* indicates that this took place on Thursday, October 7.

Tanzania — The liaison looking for Che

PADILLA: From Dar es Salaam, I told Changa that I would be in Kigoma on October 14 to cross the Lake. The communications group would go with me to install the equipment there and at the Cuban base in the Congo. We had a heavy load: in addition to the transmission equipment, we had to take in generators, fuel and batteries.

Buying the plants and, above all, that large number of batteries in Dar es Salaam could be an unequivocal signal for any of the enemy information services that were observing the level of sales — a level unheard of in such a short time before. At that time, there were only three places in the city for acquiring the articles we needed. The owners of those stores were Indians. At first, we tried to spread our purchases, so as not to arouse suspicion; later on, we realized that they talked among themselves, at least about our purchases.

In the midst of the preparations, Rivalta made me accompany him to the reception the Chinese Embassy gave on October 2 to mark the anniversary of the triumph of their Revolution. There, we met Soumialot. I had already seen him in Dar es Salaam a few days earlier, after his trip to Cuba. On that occasion, I had proposed, among other things, that we should both visit the front, and he had accepted, saying that he intended to meet with Che and that he had indicated that when he was in Havana.

After the customary hugs and greetings with me and with Colman, who was with me, I asked him if he had any idea of when we could visit the front. He replied that everything was ready and that he would leave for Kigoma for that purpose on October 7. The fact that he hadn't told me earlier surprised me, since we had agreed to go together. Nevertheless, I took him at his word and said that I would make the arrangements for the trip, including buying the train tickets for his entourage — which amounted to eight people at the time, and to which one more was later added.

In the course of the conversation, as in the earlier one, Soumialot stated with apparent conviction that he should be there in the territory where his men, as he put it, were fighting shoulder to shoulder with the help of their Cuban brothers. Soon, Abdulrahane Babu and some others joined us. Babu was a minister in the Tanzanian Government, a leader from Zanzibar who at that time was considered one of the main ideologues of the progressive elements in the country. Later, he was in conflict with President Nyerere and was implicated in the death of Karume, President of Zanzibar at the time.

Babu's presence didn't keep Soumialot from continuing to speak of the good impressions he'd had during his trip to Cuba. When it became possible, I took him aside to confirm what we had already agreed on and to leave the reception, because our agreement changed my plans, and I needed the remaining days to make the necessary adjustments. From then on, I was in almost daily contact with Soumialot and his group until we boarded the train on October 7. In addition to the communications group, Oliva and Colman went with me.

I placed Soumialot in my compartment so I could talk with him in greater detail during the long trip and learn all about his ideas and plans. Our conversation lasted less than three hours. During that time, he showed me the Makarov pistol which he said Raúl Castro, Minister of the [Cuban] Revolutionary Armed Forces, had given to him. I invited him to sit with me at table so we could continue talking, but he said he should eat with his entourage. He spent the rest of the time that way, in the dining car, in animated talk with his friends and drinking beer.

When we arrived at Tabora, a city in the middle of the country, where we had to change trains, something unexpected happened. My guest bought a ticket for the first-class car, thus separating himself from me, saying that he didn't want to run the risk of his belongings being stolen. We were 12 hours from Kigoma. When we arrived there, Laurent Kabila, supposed to be the number-three man in the hierarchy of the Higher Council (Pierre Mulele was the number-two man), was waiting for him. We said good-bye and agreed to meet in the afternoon.

Kabila also lived in the government building in Kigoma, in quarters next to those that we Cubans occupied. I used to meet him frequently — practically daily — in Dar es Salaam, for one reason or another. We had reached the point where we spoke frankly to each other, so I went to his apartment. When he saw me, he invited me to sit down, poured a drink and said, "I know why you've come. If you have anything else to do, don't waste your time; he won't cross the Lake." I was shocked but didn't show it; I got up abruptly, pushing back my chair, and replied, "I have his word that he will go." Kabila smiled and patiently began to explain that Soumialot wasn't the right man for that struggle; that he knew him very well; that the situation in his country was very difficult; that the latest news that had reached Kigoma was bad; and that, because of that, Soumialot would surely refuse to cross the Lake.

I asked Kabila if he would go with us in case Soumialot, as he said, finally refused. He replied that he couldn't just then, because he had been in Kigoma for several days waiting for some matériel and food that the Tanzanian Government had said it would deliver there, and he had to guarantee its rapid shipment to Congolese territory. Kabila took the occasion to repeat his complaints about the Tanzanians' failure to keep agreements in that regard.

It was true that some of the weapons and food that the Soviet, Chinese, Bulgarian and Cuban Governments had sent for the guerrillas was at the Tabora military base, but no matter how hard he tried to achieve its delivery, he couldn't get anywhere. Neither the two of them nor we, who were constantly besieging the Tanzanian leaders Lucinde and Cambona about the need for the supplies, would achieve anything. The Tanzanian leadership had put Lucinde, who was Minister of the Interior, in charge of giving us the material support and facilities we needed. Oscar Cambona, who was Minister of Foreign Relations and worked closely with President Nyerere, openly showed his support for the Cubans.

Cambona later clashed with Nyerere and went over to the camp of his adversaries and conspired at the service of the CIA. He lived in Kenya and Great Britain. The supplies crisis continued, and the Tanzanian Government didn't take any measures to solve it. Later on, all of us understood why.

My talk with Kabila had increased my doubts about whether or not Soumialot would accompany me to where Che was. His unexpected behavior during the train journey had already made me wonder. The way things were, I decided not to wait until evening (the time for crossing the Lake) but went to talk with him. I found him in his hotel room in the afternoon.

He was talking with a group of people. I waited discreetly for Kabila to tell him I wanted to talk with him. I told Soumialot that everything was ready for our departure that evening and asked if he wanted me to pick him up or if he would go to the boat on his own. Before replying, Soumialot asked Kabila to come over, to learn what I had said.

They spoke for a long time in their mother tongue, after which Soumialot told me that they were faced with a serious situation with the Tanzanian Government, which wasn't handing over any of the materials that had come, and for that reason he would have to remain in Kigoma to see to the shipping of the materials, if they were released.

I told the two of them about everything that had been done in that regard and about the agreement [which the Tanzanians never kept] of allowing one of us to go to Tabora to inspect the weapons deposited there and list their priorities. Soumialot returned to his attack on the Tanzanian leaders for their reiterated failure to keep their side of agreements in handing over the materials.

Then I said that the best thing at that time was for both of them to enter the territory where their followers were. After a judicious time, if the materials hadn't been handed over, they would have more authority for returning to Tanzania and demanding them. Soumialot said he didn't believe anything the Tanzanians said, he thought they didn't want to continue to support his movement, and he would return to Dar es Salaam to clear up the situation.

Once again, I insisted on the need for the two — or at least one — of them to be in their country. Kabila replied that they had thought about this, but that would have to be in the future. Kabila's attitude now, backing up Soumialot's position of not going to the Congo on the pretext of the weapons stored at Tabora, showed a two-faced behavior that I couldn't understand at the time. I kept insisting that it was necessary for both of them to go. It brought only a reply that made it impossible to keep up the pressure: "Tell Che that we will go when all the material has been handed over." Weeks later, I learned that Soumialot had gone to Cairo. Most of the people who had accompanied him to Kigoma had gone to Ghana, and Kabila was in Dar es Salaam again, as usual.

The Congo: Lambert's bragging

It seems that, after Masengo left the Congo, a letter from Lambert arrived in which he told Che there were rumors that Fizi was already in the hands of the enemy and at the same time asked him for permission to recapture Baraka — or, if not Baraka, Fizi, if it was true that the soldiers had seized it.

CHE: I didn't have the authorization to give that kind of permission, but, in my opinion, there were many weak aspects on his front, the enemy was about to attack, and it was absolutely necessary for him to be there. However, it was impossible to think that, with 25 or 50 men, he could recapture what had been lost by hundreds. He had the courtesy to send me a reply while he left for Fizi with his 25 men. [*Congo*, 98.]

From the account in the *Campaign Diary*, it seems that when Masengo learned of the irresponsibility suggested by Lambert, which was simply a false alarm, he had ordered him to remain in camp and prepare the defense. However, he left for Fizi with 30 men the next day. Before leaving, he asked a Cuban to advise him, but the Cuban refused, saying firmly that what he had to do was stay at the front with his men.

CHE: Masengo didn't have the presence to make him stay to defend the last point that kept apart the Lulimba forces and those that had landed at Baraka — the mountain roadblock. [*Congo*, 102-03.]

Because of Lambert's new act of irresponsibility, Che made the following assessment:

CHE: The possibilities of bothering the enemy in the Lulimba area were practically zero; the soldiers at the main roadblock had stopped going down to the plains. A contact group was sent to the roadblock on the Kabimbare road to cross the Kimbi [Kimvit] and scout on the other side to find out where the soldiers were, and the report was that everything was at the same general level. The lieutenant who commanded the roadblock said that he couldn't keep his men in position (there were only 25 left), they didn't obey him, they did what they wanted and they would desert if he took them into action. He said that it was a theoretical roadblock, and the group should be discounted as a fighting force. [*Congo*, 98-99.]

From what can be seen, Lambert didn't send 50 men to the training academy, either.

CHE: I kept trying, by all means, to get Congolese to join our small army and give them rudimentary military training, so as to try, with that nucleus, to save the most important thing: the soul and presence of the revolution. But the Cubans, who were supposed to infuse them with the divine breath of inspiration, found their own spirits steadily sinking. [*Congo*, 100.]

The few men they had managed to recruit subsequently deserted, giving a series of pretexts — the most common one was that they had to leave because of *dawa*. In that situation, Che felt impotent because of lack of direct communication; he ordered all the new recruits to meet so he could address them: "Since you came, two or three days ago, you have behaved badly; first, more than half of you have left, and those of you who have stayed refuse to work."

He paused at that point so the translator could repeat what he had said, and then renewed his criticism: "What do you think? That the revolution has to give you everything?" His tone became angrier; rather than annoyed, he was furious.

"You're acting like women, not men! Perhaps we should give you skirts and baskets, so you can carry yucca, the way the women do. It's better to have an army of women than to have one of individuals like you." Another pause, so the translator could speak. Both Che and the men with him thought those harsh words would offend the men at whom they were directed, but the young men, with "disconcerting naïveté," began to howl with laughter. Naturally, that was the end of it.

Later, Che, who had come to the conclusion that *dawa* and its demands might well be the most constant enemy, ordered one of his helpers, "to look for the closest *muganga*."

A very clever *muganga*

They soon returned with a *muganga*, who was described as of the second rank but whom Che thought well of. He agreed to remain at the camp and to take charge of the situation. But Che, who knew that if the ambushes had to be maintained for many days, the Congolese would abandon them, told the *muganga*, "I need you to accompany the group that is going to set the ambush. You know, this may take several days, and, if so, the *dawa* loses its power."

The witch doctor looked at him seriously and, in a tone that tried to embody the height of wisdom, replied, "Don't worry about that. I'll make a reinforced *dawa* for those men, one that will last 15 days."

Clearly, the *muganga* was intelligent, and Che could do nothing but accept what he said, so the men went out with a reinforced *dawa* — which, together with their speed and the chance they might catch the enemy on the road, had excellent results.

In line with what Che had told Masengo about the need to begin practical training in the Kalonga-Kibuye area, Mbili was sent to that region with Ishirini (as his second-in-command) and 18 other men.

CHE: This comrade [Ishirini] was an enlisted man in Cuba, but because of his qualities I had decided to try him out in tasks of responsibility, training chiefs so we would have them as needed if we enlarged our army to make it an operational group with enough Congolese soldiers. [*Congo*, 101.]

It was decided that the men shouldn't stay in the ambushes for more than 20 days at a stretch, since the climate was hard on them — especially the Cubans, who also began to get gastroenteritis.

In his diary, Che wrote, "Until the rigors of being on the road overcame the scientific spirit, the statistics in my case were over 30 bowel movements in 24 hours. Only the wilderness knows how many more there were."

The enemy keeps advancing

Soon after Mbili had left to cross the Kimvit and begin action on October

10, two notes arrived within a few hours of each other: a short, pathetic one from Siki and one from Masengo. Che copied the former in his manuscript:

"Moja [Dreke]:
"The soldiers are advancing on Fizi, and there's nothing to stop or even delay them. We're going from Fizi to Lubondja. I will try to destroy the bridges. Tell Che my trip was a failure.
"Siki [Oscar Fernández Mell]
"October 10, 1965"

CHE: Masengo's note brought the news that Fizi had fallen and gave instructions for the Kalonga-Kibuye group to be placed under my orders. [*Congo*, 101.]

Even so, Che pointed out one positive thing: as a result of his work with the farmers, they brought food and medicine from the Lake. Keeping their promise, the men gave the porters some of the sugar and salt, and the Cubans — all except Che, who drank his tea and coffee without sugar — had the pleasure of drinking sweet tea. Reference was also made to correspondence from Ali, who said that the Congolese in the ambush were even worse than usual but that, at the end of the "operation," which lasted a week, many of them were promoted "in reward for their valiant action."

PADILLA: I left on the night of October 9 and reached Kibamba early the next morning. After stretching our legs a little and organizing the group, we set out to climb that interminable mountain on whose peak the Cuban base was located. The assent itself was difficult, but it was even more so for our group because we were carrying the heavy communications equipment on litters. I was amazed to see the Congolese carry the no less heavy and troublesome batteries on their heads. Naturally, not all of the batteries reached their destination. We slept at the base, where we met Machadito and Ulises on their way back.

On Monday, October 11, the men were ordered to occupy the defenses toward Lubondja to contain an enemy attempt to advance from Fizi. Planes went out scouting and went back in that direction. On that day, Padilla and the others went on looking for Che.

Trying to contain the offensive
Siki arrived on October 12, in the afternoon.

CHE: He came at a forced march, in view of the situation, and told us of the vicissitudes of his trip. The many mouths through which his conversation with General Moulane passed (Siki didn't speak French or Swahili, and the General didn't speak French) were too numerous to guarantee a correct translation, but, in short, Siki presented my ultimatum and the immediate need to dig trenches. The existing defense was a "roadblock" consisting of three men, one with a bazooka and a helper and the last with a submachine gun, plus the good old piece of string across the road to keep everybody from going past. They hadn't dug any trenches or even done any scouting.

After Siki spoke, General Moulane took the floor and launched a diatribe against Comrade Masengo, blaming him for everything, since he hadn't sent him weapons and ammunition and hadn't sent him Cubans to do the fighting. He said that, under those conditions, he wasn't going to defend Fizi. He said he wasn't a dead man, so there wasn't any reason to go around digging holes (fortunately, he was still alive), and that all the responsibility should be Masengo's. Masengo didn't even react; I don't know whether for lack of character or because he was in enemy territory, since that area could be described as such. In any case, he took it all in silence. They didn't sleep that night in Fizi.

Some of the comrades felt that the general couldn't be so stupid, that he was in cahoots with the mercenaries. That's something that isn't clear to me... I think that the delay may explain that attitude, but, in practice, he played into the enemy's hands.

The fact is that the internal squabbling reached the extremes reported. Baraka and Fizi are 37 kilometers apart, connected by a hilly road which offers many possibilities for laying ambushes. There is even a river, which constitutes a barrier that it is quite difficult for vehicles to cross. Its bridge was already half down, and the only thing they had to do was destroy it completely to achieve good possibilities for defense. It would at least have slowed the advance. But they did none of that. [*Congo*, 102.]

The enemy seizes Lubondja

MARGOLLES: Moja, some other fighters and I went to look for somewhere to move to and build a powder magazine. During our scouting, we heard heavy shooting toward Lubondja. Planes were also overflying it. Later, we learned that the enemy had taken the hamlet without any resistance by the rebels, who had abandoned their positions and abandoned the heavy weapons in the jungle. Che was immediately informed of this. Orders were given to take the supplies to a thatched-roof hut around two or three kilometers away, but this was very hard to do, because most of the Congolese didn't want to carry the boxes of shells.

They managed to get them to carry only one box of munitions. When the men returned, they said they were very tired and went to sleep. Masengo explained the importance of ferrying the things, but nobody paid him any attention, so he decided to go to sleep, too.

Mbili and his men arrived a 1030 hours to lay an ambush, because in his reply to Mbili's message, Che told him to change the instructions he had given him before. Later, the two Cubans who operated the Lubondja antiaircraft gun arrived, explaining that the Congolese who had been with them had abandoned their posts and the weapons.

Early on the morning of Wednesday, October 13, the Cubans began to wake the Congolese so they could all transfer the supplies, but they found many of them had gone to Che's camp. They had to throw water on those who were still sleeping. That's how they moved most of the shells. Since the enemy might continue to advance at dawn, the men were ordered to hold their first position, but when two Cubans went to reinforce them, they found that they had abandoned the weapons and they had to hide them so they wouldn't fall into the hands of the enemy.

Bahasa's gun

The Cubans and some Congolese they managed to assemble occupied that position. The planes appeared before dawn, and the lights of vehicles could be seen far away. When the sun came up, an air attack began, and the Congolese mortar crews abandoned their weapons and deserted. On seeing the soldiers advancing, Dreke ordered Bahasa to fire. The planes intensified their fire and forced the fighters on the hill to abandon it, because the strafing was concentrated there. After several cannon shots, they withdrew to the little house that had been chosen some days earlier as a reserve camp.

All of the reports that Dreke received from the defensive points said that the Congolese had left the Cubans alone. Aware that, with the few men he had, he couldn't stop the enemy, he decided to draw back and avoid possible encirclement. He sent a message to Che. In the withdrawal, Bahasa left the gun hidden and said that the Congolese who had been with him had abandoned it, but Dreke ordered him to look for it and assigned other rebels to look for the mortar, since nobody knew where it had been thrown. The only weapon they managed to take with them was the antiaircraft gun.

Mbili and his men arrived in mid-afternoon and withdrew under enemy fire. However, they found the gun and brought it with them. When they took a tally, six men were missing: four of Mbili's and two who were sick and had gone to Che's camp without authorization. Once again, the problem arose of trying to save as much of the supplies as possible, because the Congolese who showed up refused to do it. Meanwhile, the enemy torched all the huts in its path and captured the powder magazine, which contained a large amount of ammunition that the Congolese refused to carry. Three of the lost men returned during the night.

Che's concern increased after he received the message and whenever larger numbers of those who had abandoned the defense and the two sick Cubans arrived. The loss of supplies had irritated him, and he ordered all of those who arrived without having been ordered in to be disarmed.

Kasavubu removes Tshombe — beginning of a maneuver

On October 13, in Leopoldville, President Kasavubu declared the end of Tshombe's "temporary mandate." He charged Evaristo Kimba, also from Katanga, with creating a "Government of National Reconciliation." Curiously, no mention of what happened in the Congolese capital that day appeared in Che's account or in the *Campaign Diary*.

On Thursday, October 14, the rest of the Cubans and Congolese — those who with great difficulty had saved several boxes of ammunition — were at Che's camp. They included Masengo, to whom Che said — obviously quite exasperated at the time — that he couldn't take the responsibility for defending the camp from a double attack with the men he had. Che believed that the withdrawal had turned into flight.

CHE: Our men's attitude was worse than bad; they left weapons that were under their responsibility, such as mortars, in the hands of the Congolese, and they were lost. They didn't show any fighting spirit. Like the Congolese, they thought only about saving their own skins, and the retreat was so disorganized that we lost one man and still don't know how, because his comrades didn't know if he got lost, was wounded or was killed by the enemy soldiers... I gave strict orders, and all of the Congolese who showed up... were immediately disarmed. The next day, I had considerable booty, as if we'd had a very fruitful ambush: the 75-mm cannon with a large amount of ammunition, an antiaircraft gun... supplies, grenades and 100 rifles. Comrade Bahasa, who had been in charge of the cannon, had remained alone at his position and, when the soldiers advanced, had withdrawn, leaving it when he heard an alarmist report from another Cuban. The mercenaries weren't advancing quickly, and Moja gave timely orders, saving the gun. He severely criticized that comrade, who was a member of the Party, and several others. [*Congo*, 103-04.]

Positive things

With Masengo's consent, the next day they disarmed all those who had fled and demoted the chiefs. The idea was to create a new force with those who hadn't fled — Che hoping that there would be few of them. "I arranged beforehand that it would be only those who demonstrated their seriousness and fighting spirit," Che noted. Dreke and Mbili also went out with several Cubans and Congolese, looking for the rest of the weapons and the other things that had been lost. Later, Che called a meeting of the Congolese. Once more, his language was tough. He explained that a new army would be created and that, therefore, those who wanted to leave could do so, but without weapons.

CHE: Addressing all of the men there, I asked those who wanted to stay to raise their hands; nobody did so. Since I had spoken with two or three of the Congolese men, asking them to stay, and they had agreed, this seemed strange to me. Then I looked at one of those I had chosen and asked those who wanted to stay to take one step forward; two of them took a step forward and then immediately the entire column did the same; all of them joined. I wasn't convinced of their willingness and asked that they think it over well and discuss it among themselves before we would decide. Around 15 men withdrew from that new parliament, but we obtained some positive things; a major decided to remain as a soldier, since I didn't accept any of the previous ranks, and there were more volunteers than I had foreseen. [*Congo*, 104.]

That same day, it was decided that Masengo, advised by Siki and Tembo, should go to the Lake base. Kasulo went along as translator.

Dreke and the other men who had gone to look for the weapons that had been jettisoned returned on October 16. They hadn't found Aurino, and Che believed that he might be dead or a prisoner. The air attacks had continued in various places.

That same day, in Dar es Salaam, Soumialot disproved rumors that he had been killed in Fizi. He also announced that he was going to Ghana to attend the Organization of African Unity's Summit Conference, to be held in its capital on October 21.

Creating the new organization

On Sunday, October 17, the guerrillas spent part of the time creating the new organization, which Che wanted to go into operation immediately.

CHE: We divided our forces into two companies, headed by Ziwa and Azima as second-in-commands, since they would go into combat under the orders of Mbili and Moja, respectively, when they had completed a minimum training period. Their basic composition was 15 Cubans and around 15 Congolese; some more were added to meet the need. Each company had a company leader and three platoon leaders, all Cubans, and each platoon had three Cuban squad leaders. Each squad consisted of five men. Each company, therefore, had three platoons, and each platoon had three squads; there were nine squad leaders in all, three platoon leaders, one company leader and a small auxiliary squad, all Cubans. [*Congo*, 105.]

Since the measures to be taken included moving the camp, that was done early on the morning of Monday, October 18. The new site was only an hour's walk away, in the spur of the mountain, on a small elevation with better conditions — though not perfect, because it was close to the plains. Water came from a small spring created by a swamp, which caused gastric upsets. Another disadvantage was the lack of visibility. As a solution, they put Ziwa's company on it, so as to keep an observation post that could see the road. Azima's company was placed so as to cover the left flank. Orders were given to construct a powder magazine on the top of the elevation, so the 150 boxes of ammunition of different calibers that had been saved at Lubondja would be well protected. Moreover, a platoon was assigned to defend the stores in case of attack.

That same day, Padilla, Colman and Oliva arrived at the camp. They reported that Machado and Ulises still hadn't crossed the Lake to Kigoma.

CHE: We had a discussion in which we agreed on fundamental matters. The chief of transmissions should be at the operations site; in addition, there should be a radio transmitter capable of communicating with Havana. A weekly ration of food should be sent to the base of the new army, which was to be given the best supplies possible. A comrade from Dar es Salaam would go to Kigoma to replace Changa, who didn't speak Swahili and was having difficulties; Changa would come to this side and be in charge of the boats. [*Congo*, 104-05.]

Change of position
CHE: As for supplies, I changed my earlier position, which hadn't proved feasible. I had come with the idea of creating an exemplary nucleus; going through all difficulties shoulder to shoulder with the Congolese; and showing them, with our spirit of sacrifice, what a revolutionary soldier should be. However, the result was that our men were starving and had no clothes, while the Congolese had

plenty of shoes and other clothing that reached them by another means. The only thing I had achieved was to increase the Cubans' discontent. It had been resolved that a nucleus of a better army supplied with equipment and better food than the rest of the Congolese troops should be formed; it would be directly under my command, a practical school turned into the nucleus of an army. To achieve this, it was absolutely necessary that basic supplies be sent to us regularly from Kigoma and that their transfer from the Lake to the front be organized with the farmers, since it was very hard to get the Congolese soldiers to work, and if we did that task ourselves, we wouldn't have any fighters. [*Congo*, 105.]

They heard bursts of fire near the road that day, October 18, probably because soldiers were moving along it. The tactic of shooting along both sides of the route to avoid possible ambushes was an old one.

PADILLA: The previous night, we stayed in a hamlet where we met up with Siki, Tembo and some other Cubans. Che had ordered them to go to the base so that, together with Masengo, who was with them, they could reorganize the Staff of the front. At dawn, we continued our march, and at night we got to where Che was, a tiny place around two square meters in size. He had his hammock and a few belongings there. He offered me cold, unsweetened tea. I reported to him in as much detail as possible about the work that had been done, which things I had given the highest priority to, which were still pending, how many comrades worked with me, what they did and the contacts that had been established both in the capital and in Kigoma.

I told him that our people complained that the Congolese fled at the sound of the first shot. He replied that at first many had run in the Sierra Maestra, too.

I dropped that subject so he would give me his opinion about a more general one: the political situation in the Congo at that time. Along the way, we had heard over the radio of Tshombe's removal. It seemed to me to be the first step in a large-scale political maneuver, part of which could be the military offensive unleashed against the eastern front (the front where Mulele was holding out, even though weakened and with fewer men) in order to hit it hard and discourage the vacillating elements of the armed opposition, attract the weakest of those who appeared to be revolutionaries and effect a change in the situation by means of political negotiations that would destroy an armed solution.

Che replied that all he saw in this was a clash of interests within the ruling group.

I commented that I had heard that Fizi, Baraka and Lubondja had been abandoned without the Congolese firing a shot, which produced quite generalized demoralization. Moreover, neither Soumialot nor Kabila had wanted to come to the front to help raise their men's morale.

He replied that the catastrophe had one good result for us, which was that, from then on, we could begin to create a revolutionary army. It would take at least five years, he concluded.

Some tactical mistakes

PADILLA: Finally, I told him that I didn't understand his order that food shouldn't be sent for our men. He replied, "I've made some tactical mistakes. That's one." I saw the possibility of taking the initiative at that moment and proposed that we take on the task of providing our men with food, shoes and other clothes, since they were hungry, barefoot and in rags. I didn't leave it at that but argued as follows: If we can't depend on the Congolese for supplies and communications and can't trust anybody else for those purposes, why don't we set up an underground network of supplies and communications that could have one point at the Lake, with small, fast boats, and a logistics base where we can receive from Cuba what's needed for those five years? Perhaps the revolutionaries in Zanzibar can help in this. He didn't reject the idea, but neither did he agree to it that night.

He told me that I should inform the Tanzanian Government of his presence in the Congo and insist that we be given access to the weapons that were at Tabora. The Government should be told that he and his men would withdraw from the Congo unless those who had asked for Cuban cooperation asked him to stay. My head nodded with exhaustion, and he told me to go to sleep, saying, "We'll continue talking tomorrow."

The next day (October 19), we got down to details on the need for supplying all kinds of things, and he gave me his instructions for a number of practical matters, which were as follows:

1. Communications: The equipment for direct communication with Cuba should be in Congolese territory, not Tanzanian. He told me to see the Chinese in Dar es Salaam, to obtain some portable equipment they had.

2. Boats: Get two rapid vessels for carrying our things independently of the Congolese. Establish an independent loading base. Insist that personnel be sent from Cuba for these operations.

3. Kigoma: Send David there, provisionally, until the man requested from Cuba arrives. Changa will go to the Congo.

4. Supplies: Siki will draw up a weekly list for 200 men.

5. Reserves: Gather reserves of essential things within the operational territory in the Congo.

6. Ask the Tanzanian Government for access to the weapons stored in Tabora and send those most urgently needed.

7. Inform Cuba of the need for personnel to operate the vessels.

I wrote down each of these things and warned that the only approval obtained for my proposals was a partial one as regards the boats, apart from the request for supplies and food, and the reply regarding the boats didn't specify whether or not the point on the Tanzanian shore of the Lake should be clandestine (as I had requested).

Then I asked him if he didn't agree to my suggestion of the night before. He thought about it and replied, "First, we have to find out what the Tanzanians really think. We must get the Tanzanian Government to state how far it will go along with us in this effort. You should tell the Tanzanian Government about my presence here, saying that Kabila had said he would tell it himself and that I've been waiting for him to do so. Since time has passed and he hasn't done so, we're doing this ourselves."

Continue the struggle up to the last minute

That same day, October 19, Tchamlesso (Tremendo Punto) joined them, to serve as a kind of high-level commissar. Charles, who had been with Che before, came with him. He would do the same work, but this time in the fighting units; he knew Kibembe, which most of the new men also spoke.

CHE: I considered Tremendo Punto's presence to be very important, because I was looking for cadres who could be developed. Our Ambassador in Tanzania reported that the government of that country was exerting very strong pressure to come to an arrangement with Gbenye. I didn't know what might happen, but I was ready to continue the struggle up to the last minute. It was good for me to have somebody at my side who would raise the flag if an agreement were reached with those people. [*Congo*, 106.]

On October 20, more farmers appeared, seeking to join in the struggle, and the third company was formed with them.

CHE: I thought about continuing until we had four companies and stopping there to make an analysis of the situation, for I didn't want to increase the number of men before making a rigorous selection in combat. Responding to Comrade Masengo's call, the farmers of the area came in to sign up. I read the regulations to all of them myself; Charles had translated them in energetic terms. [*Congo*, 106.]

Padilla and his companions left for Dar es Salaam that same day.

The final offensive is announced

CHE: Paradoxically, the political situation couldn't be better, since Tshombe had fallen and Kimba was trying fruitlessly to form a government. We had an ideal situation for continuing to act and take advantage of the disorder in Leopoldville; but the enemy troops, far from the events in their capital, efficiently led and without any serious opposition, were still in the field. [*Congo*, 104.]

It seems that the message from Machado, who hadn't yet been able to leave the Congo, arrived that day, October 21. He reported that he had tried to convince the colleagues who had asked to leave to stay until March of the following year. They hadn't agreed, but he had decided to leave them behind, anyway.

MACHADO: I told the doctors that they would have to stay for at least six months before their replacements would arrive. If no replacements came, they would have to stay as long as necessary, because they had taken on the mission voluntarily. I couldn't believe they would leave their comrades without doctors in such a situation.

CHE: The procedure was a little expeditious, but it couldn't be denied that it was effective in achieving what we sought, and I agreed with him entirely. [*Congo*, 106.]

The same message stated that the rebels were very worried about the frequent patrols made by the enemy vessels, which sometimes halted a few miles from the coast of Kasima and at other times came quite close. That place was just a few hours from Kibamba. It also reported the death of a commander and several soldiers who fell into an ambush when the officer insisted on making an incursion into Baraka.

Willing to risk their lives

CHE: That day, the men were ordered to look for the deserters who had sought refuge in the hamlets and, moreover, were living off the people by means of extortion. Charles took on that task, and the captured men were disarmed and demobilized. Our neighbors were very happy about the measure. Work on the construction of several installations and on a study plan was also begun, with the double purpose of giving the Congolese soldiers and the internationalists a little instruction and filling in their time. To get both tasks started, two meetings were held: one of the Staff and another of the Party. The first meeting established the method of military teaching, set down the characteristics of the companies and decided on the next actions to be taken and on what methods should be used to achieve internal discipline and integration with the Congolese. The officers' spirits weren't very high; they exhibited great skepticism toward the tasks, even though they carried them out acceptably well. Work began on building houses, latrines and a hospital and on cleaning the well and digging trenches for defense in the more vulnerable areas. However, everything went very slowly, because the rain was now more intense, and I didn't have enough determination to make the men move the powder magazine. I waited for the construction on the higher area to be completed — a weakness of mine that proved fatal. Moreover, relying on the false security of being several kilometers from the enemy, who didn't frequent those sites, we didn't post pickets at a distance, which was the usual measure, but had men out only at posts that were quite nearby.

In the Party meeting, I once more insisted that they should support me in creating a disciplined, exemplary army. I asked those who were there if any of them thought there was a possibility that we would be victorious. Moja, Mbili, Fizi and Morogoro — the two doctors who had just arrived — were the only ones who raised their hands. It made me think that this was the product of either real confidence or of a greater affinity with me — in short, a demonstration of loyalty. I warned that sometimes I would have to ask them to make such great sacrifices that they might lose their lives, and I asked if they were willing to make them; this time, all of them raised their hands.

I went on to analyze the weaknesses of several Party members, making criticisms that were accepted. When I came to the case of Bahasa, the comrade who had left the gun, he didn't agree. Bahasa had demonstrated tremendous qualities, among them an unquench-able enthusiasm that served as an example for his comrades, both Cubans and Congolese — but he had had a moment of weakness, and the proof was that the gun had been retrieved after he had abandoned it. I kept insisting on this until, at last, with an air of reproach, Bahasa replied, "OK, so I'm guilty." Of course, that wasn't what I wanted; what I sought was an analysis of our weaknesses, so I asked several other comrades for their opinion, and they acknow-ledged the weakness I had attributed to him.

I ended the meeting, convinced that very few men shared my dream of creating an army that would lead the Congolese fighters to victory, but I was reasonably sure that the men were willing to risk their lives, even though they believed it would be for nothing.

The main thing was to achieve unity between the Congolese and Cubans — a difficult task. We had made communal cooking fires to avoid the anarchy of individual cooking. The Congolese didn't like our food (the cooks were Cubans because, when they weren't, all the food disappeared) and protested constantly; there was a lot of tension. [*Congo*, 107-08.]

The OAU meeting

As Head of State of the Congo, Kasavubu attended the OAU meeting in Accra, the capital of Ghana. The meeting called for the departure of the mercenaries and of the foreign forces that supported the guerrillas.

CHE: Ila Jean, the Kalonga-Kibuye commander, came to join us and brought 70 men with him, but I already had too many men and couldn't accept them. I sent him back to his area, assuring him that a group of Cubans would go to lay an ambush on the Lulimba-Katenga road, on which we might still carry out some effective actions. I took away a mortar, a broken-down machine gun that had some parts missing and a Soviet model bazooka that didn't have any shells. He wanted to take the weapons back with him, but I ordered him to leave them with me because I thought they would be safer there.

Before they left, at Ila Jean's request, I spoke to his men, warning them that we should work together and criticizing their way of treating the farmers, as if they had forgotten their own origins. That address of mine and another to our troops, in which I warned that anybody who deserted would be shot, didn't go down well with the Congolese. Desertions with rifles occurred continually, and the only way to prevent it was by taking very drastic measures and, at the same time, making it easier for those who wanted to leave without taking their rifles with them to do so.

We continued to scout through the neighboring areas, looking for scattered weapons, and we had found a machine gun which also had some parts missing. By taking parts from both this one and the one from Kalonga-Kibuye, we managed to have one operational machine gun. Responding to my warning and to the offer that I had made them at the same time, fighters began to be demobilized. [*Congo*, 108.]

Early on Friday, October 22, they heard mortar shots coming from the direction of Lubondja, and Che and the others thought it was an enemy advance. They took some immediate measures, and Che sent Masengo a letter which he himself said he considered hasty.

CHE: In it, I asked him to send for some men from the Lake base to reinforce that position so I wouldn't have to go into defensive combat now. In passing, I gave him some advice (so as not to break the habit), such as to send men to Fizi and Uvira to find out how our troops were positioned. [*Congo*, 108.]

However, it was reported from that same area that the powder magazine had been evacuated in two parts; one was hidden by the Cubans, and the other, by the Congolese. Cubans and bazookas were requested but weren't sent, so as not to keep breaking up the troop. It was learned that the farmers from the Kibamba area were leaving their homes to hide in the wilderness.

Tanzania — An unenforceable decision

At about that time, Padilla, Colman and the others who had gone with them were in Kigoma, where they bought provisions to send to the Cuban camp. As Padilla said, they violated all the norms of discretion, if any had been created to conceal the existence of Cuba's contingent in the Congo. Everything seems to indicate that from the start, discretion was dependent on luck and on the merchants from whom they made their purchases — who, it seems, had no interests other than to sell their goods; they were of Hindu origin and went to the extreme of giving the Cubans several thousand dollars' worth of credit. Padilla, Colman and the others met Kabila there.

PADILLA: Kabila showed me a map of the Congo and began to explain a plan that he said he proposed to apply immediately. According to his idea, all of the coastal region would be abandoned, and the guerrillas would be deployed in the central-southern part of the country. He said that the present demoralization in the Congolese ranks was due to the fact that the people living in the area where they operated weren't combative.

I objected to the topographical conditions of that region and proposed that, rather than give any orders to his comrades in the interior, he should go there to explain everything to Che — or at least let him know — because it was of basic importance that our forces should be informed of any change of that kind in the theater of operations. I asked of his efforts to convince the Tanzanian Government to hand over the arms and other resources it was holding, and he told me he was still waiting for a reply but kept on insisting. I informed Che of all the details of the conversation with Kabila.

Brazzaville

First a synthesis and then a more detailed report of events were sent from Dar es Salaam to Havana as a matter of the greatest urgency. In line with Che's idea of having a fund of Congolese (Brazzaville) currency, Padilla told me he sent Ulises with $20,000 to Brazzaville. He had to go via Paris, since there weren't any direct flights from Tanzania. Before leaving Paris, he was to see if Ulises could exchange the money there or in Brussels.

Nothing could be done in Brazzaville with currency of the Congo (Leopoldville). The currency exchange was effected in Brazzaville, but not at as good a rate as had been expected. Ulisis met with Risquet, Kindelán and Serguera and reported on everything he had seen in the part of the Congo where the guerrilla front and the Cubans were located.

JORGE RISQUET: What Ulises said worried me greatly. I told him what my column had done: it was working on training four battalions of Congolese militia; a group of combat instructors was taking part in the Angolan guerrilla force in Cabinda; and we had begun training an MPLA column that would go to the First Front of Angola, north of Luanda. In addition, the battalion was alert to counter any attack by the mercenary Leopoldville regime. It was training a group of Lumumba's followers headed by Mukuidi, so it could join Mulele's front.

In fact, that was the only exchange of information between the two columns, which were in the Congo River Basin at the same time only for three months (from August 21 to November 21).

The Congo — Rain and disaster

The guerrillas' situation on Saturday, October 23 was normal, which made it possible to continue with the building and study plans — except that they were interrupted by heavy rain every day, which held back all their activities and upset their routine.

CHE: It was October 24 — which, among other things, marked six months since our arrival in the Congo. It kept on raining heavily, and straw houses get wet when the rain is steady. Some of the Congolese asked for permission to go and get some sheets of tin that had been left at the old camp, and I agreed. About an hour later, we heard rifle fire and then cannon fire. The Congolese had been caught off guard and had run into the army, which was advancing in an offensive action. The soldiers had attacked them but, fortunately, fired from a considerable distance, and all of them escaped. Pandemonium broke out in the camp; the Congolese disappeared, and we couldn't organize the defense. They had gone to the *muganga*'s house to get *dawa*; after that, they began to take up their positions. I began to organize the defense with Ziwa's company, which should occupy the first line, and I prepared to give the soldiers a hot welcome. Suddenly, several comrades told me that contingents of enemy soldiers were coming closer through the mountains. I couldn't see them, and I asked how many there were. They replied that there were a lot. How many? A lot; there was no way of knowing exactly how many, but there were a lot. We were in a difficult situation, because they could cut off our retreat, and we couldn't defend ourselves well if the enemy held the hill. I sent out a platoon under Rebocate. [*Congo*, 108-09.]

MARIO ARMAS (REBOCATE): Che ordered me, "Rebocate, take your platoon and clash with the soldiers as far uphill as possible. Try to halt them there." My platoon consisted of around seven Cubans and 15 Congolese. We went up at a forced march, taking security measures. What a hill! We got up to one terrace and didn't find anybody. We did reconnaissance and couldn't find any trace of the soldiers, though there were clear signs that the farmers had fled.

We stayed up there for over an hour. When I was going to send a message, I saw the soldiers in the camp and the planes shooting. We didn't fire at them, because I thought that Che would withdraw along the same route we had used in climbing the hill. Then I arranged our defense in case the soldiers tried to ascend. At night, we withdrew.

CHE: My dilemma was as follows: if we stayed, we could be surrounded; if we withdrew, we would lose the powder magazine and all of the equipment we had salvaged, including two 60-mm mortars and a radio plant. We didn't have time to take anything with us. I preferred to face the enemy, hoping to hold out until nightfall, when we could withdraw. We were in that state of tension, waiting, when enemy soldiers appeared, and I fired on them, but our fire lasted barely a minute. Immediately, a comrade came running back; he seemed to have a serious wound, but it was just the bazooka's recoil. He said that the soldiers were at the front line, which had been overwhelmed. I had to give a hurried order to fall back. A machine gun whose Congolese crew had fled was abandoned by the Cuban gunner, who didn't make any attempt to recover it. I sent men to warn those at the other end to protect themselves and withdraw hurriedly, saying that we would do the same at one flank, and we went to the road, leaving countless things behind: books, papers, food and even the two monkeys I had as pets.

One group, which didn't receive the order to withdraw, stayed and faced the enemy, causing it several light casualties. Bahasa and Comrade Maganga had fallen back, saving the gun. After delivering it to the Congolese, for them to put it in a safe place, they remained fighting alongside Ziwa, Azima and some other comrades whose names I don't remember — who saved our honor that day. On finally falling back, they used the bazooka to try to blow up the powder magazine, but without result. [*Congo*, 109.]

RAMON ARMAS (AZIMA): When we were caught off guard by the enemy, around four or five of us Cubans stayed to shoot it out with the mercenaries, protecting the others as they fell back. Two or three of the Congolese stayed. Bahasa and Maganga saved the gun and then went back to continue fighting. It was raining hard, and that helped us hold the Belgians off until we began to withdraw — under a hail of bullets — so we wouldn't be surrounded.

Suddenly, I saw that Bahasa had fallen to the ground, shot, and wasn't moving. He was simply unlucky. It could have been any of us. We all carried him; he was awfully heavy, but we didn't abandon him. We crossed a stream and climbed the side of the hill.

CHE: As I've said, we fell back along one side, eluding any encirclement that the soldiers might have been laying from above. I was terribly depressed; I felt responsible for that disaster because of a lack of foresight. The group of men who followed me was quite large, but I ordered some to go ahead to open the way if any enemy soldiers were there trying to encircle us. I ordered them to wait for me on the side of the hill, but they kept on walking, and I didn't rejoin the Cubans until several days later. The Congolese began deserting immediately. Resting on the side of the hill where they should have been waiting, I reflected bitterly that there were just 13 of us — one more than Fidel had had at one point, but I wasn't Fidel. Moja, Mbili, Karín, Uta, Pombo, Tumaine, Danhusi, Moustafá, Duala, Sitini, Marembo and Tremendo Punto were with me, and I didn't know what had happened to the rest of the men.

When night fell and the soldiers who had dominated our position stopped shooting, we reached an abandoned farmers' hamlet. With the philosophy that everything that was there would be lost to the enemy the next day, we took some fat hens, which were very good. We kept walking to put a little more distance between us and the enemy, since we were only two or three kilometers from the camp — we had made a tremendous detour along a bad road. A kilometer or one and a half kilometers farther along, there was another hamlet, where we found some farmers. We took some more chickens and were going to pay for them, but they said that we were in defeat and were brothers in misfortune, so we shouldn't pay.

I wanted some of them to serve us as guides, but they were terribly frightened. They told us that there was another hamlet a short distance away where the doctors and somebody else were. I sent a man to go there, and, after a while, Fizi, the doctor; Kimbi, the nurse; and two other comrades arrived. They had gone out early that morning to visit the hamlets and had halted there when they heard the sound of battle. Soon a large number of Congolese had gone by, fleeing. They included one who was wounded and who paused to be treated before continuing on his way. Everybody was heading toward Lubichaco. They had heard of the slightly wounded man they treated, that there may have been another Congolese who was also slightly wounded and that Bahasa had been seriously wounded. Azima sent word, explaining where they were, and, after sleeping for a while to recover our strength, we left at 0400 hours [on Monday, October 25], guided by a farmer who overcame his fear. At 0600 hours, we reached the hamlet where Bahasa was, wounded; there was a large group of men, both Cubans and Congolese.

The extent of the disaster and its causes were soon ascertained. The men I had sent to try to stop the soldiers who were coming to encircle us on the side of the hill hadn't met them. Even later, they hadn't fired at the enemy entering the camp, because they thought we would be climbing the hill in front of them if we had fallen back (which we didn't do, because of the news that the enemy was in the mountains). Ziwa's statement, later confirmed, that those "soldiers" had been farmers who took to the hills when they saw the real enemy troops coming and that the enemy never left the plains made my anguish more bitter. We had lost the opportunity of laying a good ambush and wiping out a large number of enemy soldiers, and we had failed because of that misinformation which had disrupted the defense and because of the unjustifiable collapse of one of the wings. At the time of the withdrawal, Comrade Bahasa had been shot and carried on the men's shoulders... to that tiny hamlet.

I sent men up on the sides of the hill, because we were still in a hollow, while Bahasa was treated. The bullet had fractured and gone right through the humerus, hit a rib and ended up in his lung. His wound reminded me of that of a comrade I had treated years before in Cuba, who had died a few hours later; Bahasa was stronger, and his powerful bones had slowed the bullet — which, it seemed, hadn't reached the mediastinum — but he was in great pain. A splint was put on his leg — it was the best thing that could be done — and we began an exhausting climb through the very steep hills, which the rain had made very slippery, with a very heavy weight carried by exhausted men and without the Congolese comrades' helping to carry him, as they should have.

It took us six hours to carry Bahasa; those were terrible hours. The men couldn't carry the wounded man on their shoulders for more than 10 to 15 minutes at a time, and it became more and more difficult to get new men to carry him, because, as I have explained, the Congolese wouldn't do it, and there were relatively few of us. At one time, it seemed that soldiers were coming up to cut us off on one of the sides of the hill, and we had to leave comrades to defend the wounded man's withdrawal; in fact, they were fleeing farmers. From our vantage point, we could see the countless bonfires that were lit, because the soldiers set fire to all of the farmers' houses. Walking along the path that linked the hamlets, they burned each one to the ground as soon as they reached it. Rising columns of smoke marked their advance, and we could see the farmers fleeing to the mountains.

At last we reached a tiny hamlet that was full of refugees and where there was practically nothing to eat. All of them silently blamed the men who had come to defend their safety. They had made them believe that they would be victorious and had then withdrawn without defending their homes and crops. All that silent hatred was expressed in one disconsolate and heartbreaking phrase: "And now, what will we eat?" All of their plots and animals were down below; they had fled with what they could, carrying their children, as always, and hadn't been able to bring food for more than one or two days. Other farmers told me how the soldiers had suddenly appeared and seized their women; saying that they would have been able to defend themselves with a rifle but had had to flee with their spears.

Bahasa seemed to be much better; he could talk and said the pain was a little less, but he was restless. He had eaten some chicken soup. Reassured by his state, I took his picture; his large, protruding eyes expressed an anxiety I couldn't foresee.

Early on the morning of October 26, the nurse came and told me that Bahasa had had a crisis, torn off his bandages and died, apparently of acute hemothorax. Later that morning, we carried out the sad but solemn ritual of digging a grave and burying Comrade Bahasa. He was the sixth man we had lost and the first for whom we could honor his body. That body was a mute accusation — as was his conduct from the moment of being wounded — of my lack of foresight and stupidity.

Calling together the small troop of defeated men, I gave the funeral oration, almost a solliloquy loaded with reproaches against myself. I acknowledged the mistakes I had made and said — it was very true — that, of all the men who had been killed in the Congo, Bahasa's death was the most painful for me, because he was the comrade I had reprimanded seriously for his weakness. He had responded as a true communist, but I hadn't fulfilled my responsibilities and was to blame for his death. I said that I would do everything I could to make up for my mistakes by working hard and by having more enthusiasm than ever. I explained that the situation had become worse and that, if we didn't achieve integration with the Congolese, we couldn't create our army. I asked the Cubans to think seriously, that now it wasn't just proletarian internationalism that would have to give us strength in the struggle, because keeping the base going would give us a point of contact with outside; if that were lost, we would be incommunicado for who knows how long in the inner regions of the Congo. We would have to struggle to keep that route open. [*Congo*, 109-12.]

Tremendo Punto also gave some heartfelt words, speaking on behalf of the Congolese.

CHE: I later talked to the Congolese, explaining the seriousness of the situation and also saying that our defeat stemmed from having been afraid to demand special work of them. I said that there should be more trust between us, and a more united army should be created that would allow us to react more quickly in all situations; I appealed to their revolutionary feeling. As soon as the sad ceremony was over, we went to Nabikumo, a rather large hamlet on the banks of the stream of the same name, in a fertile, pleasant valley. The Congolese broke into two groups: a small one, led by Tremendo Punto, wanted to go closer to the base; the other, consisting of most of the men in the region and led by Charles, wanted to stay there, closer to the soldiers, defending the area. [*Congo*, 112.]

The choice of campsite wasn't very good, though they could put up a good defense there and defeat the enemy, as Che later said, if they hadn't made some mistakes. Considering that they were surrounded and knowing that it would be a long time before night fell, giving the guerrillas a better chance to escape, I think it would have been more appropriate to fall back. Even though that kind of withdrawal is always painful, many brilliant warriors have had to do precisely that.

I don't think Che was to blame for Bahasa's death. I agree that his reprimant was too harsh, but a military leader who doesn't act firmly in response to his subordiates' mistakes is doomed to failure. He might be considered to blame if he had sent him on a suicide mission or ordered him not to abandon his position under any circumstances. Bahasa was wounded, as might have happened to any of the other Cubans who were with him, who, as Che said, "saved our honor that day." That was his duty.

Continuing determination to struggle

CHE: I decided to stay; to continue withdrawing was to add new defeats to those we had already suffered and further demoralize the men, who had already lost a lot. The Cubans wanted to go to the base, because the Lake had gone sour on them. They felt closer to the possibility of escape, but we stayed there, taking up again the task of forming two companies with those who were left. We brought in the Congolese we could find and called in all of the Cubans who, in our flight, had been dispersed. [*Congo*, 112.]

The enemy's plan had been implemented without any strong resistence by the rebels, even though they didn't know exactly where the Cubans' campsite was. The mercenary Michael Hoare described the situation as follows in his book: " ...attack Lubondja [which had already been taken], the key to the fortress of Lulimba, and, finally, attack the Lulimba garrison. If we had achieved that, the enemy would have been enclosed in a semicircle, with its diameter running along the coast. The center of the encirclement was Yungu, a tiny port nestled at the foot of some steep crags on which it was thought the rebels' general headquarters and training camps, which were run by Cuban advisers, were located."[26]

It seems that Che sent a note to Siki at the Lake that day, October 26. The following paragraphs come from that note.

CHE: The men are terribly discouraged, and everybody wants to go to the Lake. Many of them will probably show up there; if so, send them to me immediately with plenty of supplies. Only those who are really sick should stay. In principle, I decided to stay here at Nabikumo, 10 hours from the Lake (upper base), one and a half days from Kasima and two hours from a weak roadblock near Lubondja. If I were to go toward the Lake, it would be a terrible political defeat, because all the comrades trusted me and would consider themselves abandoned. Once reorganized, we will be able to provide effective help. The classes in shooting with a Soviet Mauser, for which we have bullets here, will begin this afternoon. We don't have any ammunition for the .30 (SKSs) and don't have enough for the FALs. If available, send us 5,000 rounds for the SKSs and 3,000 for the FALs. If you don't have any ammunition for them, please let me know; this

---

[26] Michael Hoare, *Mercenario nel'Congo*, 308-9.

lack of news is maddening.

Rumors are coming in that three boats arrived with ammunition, that Kabila has crossed the Lake to Kabimba and that there are 40 Cubans there. Try to keep as few of them as possible and send the rest to me. After learning about the (objective) situation there, I'll be able to make a decision. [*Congo*, 116.]

Later, he clarified that the information about Kabila and the Cubans was provided by a Congolese messenger and that it wasn't Kabimba, but Kibamba.

The farmers' loyalty and the chiefs' revenge

The campaign diary noted that it was Wednesday, October 27 when Che sent to look for the Cubans, but it says that they went to the Lake base. According to the reports of Siki and Tembo, treason was brewing, and the Rwandans who were there intended to steal the boats and leave the Congo. It also says that work on the construction of a tiny hospital in the jungle two or three kilometers from the hamlet began with the help of the Congolese.

CHE: My first concern was to struggle to obtain the farmers' loyalty. I had to do it because of the adverse forces with which we were faced. The situation was made more difficult by our army's continued retreats and defeats, the mistreatment or abandonment suffered by the inhabitants of the region and now the malevolent interpretations with which the various chiefs took revenge. I called a meeting with the *kapita* of the place; notables from other, neighboring hamlets; and the farmers who lived there and spoke with them with the assistance of the invaluable Charles. I explained the present situation, why we had come to the Congo and the danger confronting the revolution because we were fighting among ourselves and not tending to the struggle against the enemy. The *kapita* was receptive and willing to cooperate. He told everybody who would listen to him that it was an infamy that we were compared to the Belgians (a comparison that had already been made) — first of all, because he had never seen a Belgian in the area, much less seen a white man eating *bucali* out of bowls with his enlisted men, getting the same amount as the others. The farmers' opinions were comforting, but we had to do something more than personal recruitment. There were so many hamlets scattered throughout the area that, if I had had to spend a few days in each one eating *bucali* from a pot to earn its confidence, success would be problematical.

I asked that they supply us with yucca and some other foodstuffs and also that they help us build a hospital nearby but off the path the soldiers might take if they advanced. I also asked that they lend us their tools for digging trenches and providing better defenses for the position and that a small body of scouts be formed so we could know more about the enemy. They immediately agreed, and a quite large and comfortable hospital was ready in a short time. It was on a hill, but protected from planes, and we dug a series of holes in which to keep supplies so we wouldn't again lose them to the enemy, as had been happening recently.

A lamentable episode contributed to the speed and enthusiasm with which the farmers responded to the call. At the Lubondja road-block, a group of Congolese decided to use grenades to make booby traps. They did this but didn't warn their comrades; another group of Congolese passed by there and fell into the trap meant for the enemy. Three of them suffered slight wounds, and one was wounded seriously, with a perforation of the abdomen. They brought him to the hospital, claiming that he had been hit by a mortar thrown by the advancing enemy. The slight wounds were quickly treated, but the man with the serious wound had to have a delicate operation in which bits of the intestine were removed under very difficult conditions, in the open air, with the constant danger that planes might pass close by, since they were overflying the area. In spite of everything, the operation was carried out successfully, adding to the laurels of Comrade Morogoro, the surgeon, which enabled us to insist that the hospital — a quiet place where such tasks could be carried out in safety — be completed rapidly.

That same night, another man came in with two wounds. What had happened? On hearing the explosion the whole group had fled, but there was one who remained. Perhaps he couldn't move because of the seriousness of his condition, or it may be that he was paralyzed from fright. As night was falling, seeing that the soldiers weren't advancing, some of the Congolese decided to go back and look for their weapons (which they had jettisoned when they ran away). That was when they found this wounded comrade. They took him to the hospital that night. We didn't have a lamp or adequate light; with only two lanterns, we had to do an operation that was even more complicated than the other one; moreover, the patient was in terrible physical condition, and we didn't have the right medicine. At dawn, in spite of all our efforts, when the perforations had already been treated, the patient died. All this, plus the treatment we gave a woman who had been in singular combat with a buffalo (which succumbed to its wounds), did much to raise us in the farmers' esteem, and we managed to form a nucleus that could withstand the evil influence of the chiefs. [*Congo*, 114-15.]

Not entirely to blame

CHE: From the military point of view, I made my first mistake when I chose our campsite without making a more thorough investigation and without having organized a firmer defense. The pickets weren't far enough away to enter into combat several kilometers from our position. I didn't manage to get the men to do a little more work or make a little bigger effort to build our powder magazine at the higher level, which would have given us more flexibility in action. In addition, the mortar and some other weapons which were lost in combat might have been installed there. However, the reports that soldiers were surrounding us on the hill upset all our plans and turned our defense from a coordinated action into a group of men distributed every which way. Moreover, our wing, where there were a lot of Cubans, had crumbled almost without fighting. This time, I couldn't put the blame on the Congolese running away; we Cubans were there, and we had fallen back. When the soldiers were already coming over the small hill that protected us, I wanted to take an automatic and go to fight there; then I reasoned that this would mean risking everything on a single strike, and I chose to withdraw. The fact was that they weren't on the hill at all; that had been the result of nervousness at the time the information came in, just as nervousness had made men see soldiers where there were farmers and large numbers of them where there couldn't have been more than 15 men. [*Congo*, 112.]

It should also be pointed out that there weren't any scouts in the rear guard, who might have prevented confusion. Moreover, there is another element that is absolutely necessary so as not to be caught unawares by the enemy: intelligence work, which could detect where the enemy was concentrated and where it was headed. No intelligence work was ever done, in spite of Che's reiterated requests for it. The defenders' abandonment of one of their flanks almost immediately after the first shots rang out and their failure to learn in time that the people behind them were farmers rather than soldiers also contributed to the disaster. In that situation, from the military point of view, it was correct to withdraw, and it was also correct to decide not to risk everything on a single strike. The question arises, however: what responsibility should be borne by the Cuban officers and the Congolese who were in the camp? They, too, were partly to blame.

CHE: From the military point of view, we had lost the powder mag-

azine, around 150 boxes of ammunition for the howitzers, cannon —
which was now practically useless — mortars and machine guns. We
had lost an 82-mm mortar, a machine gun, two 60-mm mortars and
two machine guns that had some parts missing and were in storage.
Also a Soviet bazooka without any shells, a Chinese transmitter that
it had taken us a long time to get and a lot of smaller pieces of equipment. The bazookas that the Congolese had were lost along with the
gunners, and so were the shells. Above all, we lost the beginnings of
organization that we had managed to give our men.

The attitude of the Congolese hadn't been as bad as at other times.
It is true that all of them disappeared at first, but that was to get
dawa. After that, they came back, and quite a few of them behaved
well. We would have been able to begin to select fighters from
among them if we hadn't been confronted with such a difficult
situation — because of the defeat — that it made them desert after
having behaved so well. [*Congo*, 112-13.]

It was not only defeat that made them desert, because there were
frequent desertions even after the Cubans arrived. Many deserted
because most of their superiors set them a bad example, mistreated them
and deceived them, and they observed and suffered from all that.

Slander, the weapon of cowards

CHE: From the political point of view, all the credit that we had gained
from our fraternal, understanding and fair attitude toward the
farmers was wiped out by the dire fact that all of their houses had
been burned and they had been forced to leave the area where they
had managed to eke out a living and go to live in the mountains,
where they had practically no food and were constantly threatened
with the possibility that the enemy soldiers would advance and
occupy that area, too.

The local chiefs delighted in taking revenge. All of them —
Calixte, Ila Jean, Lambert, Lambert's majors, a commissar named
Bendera [Foston] and perhaps some presidents — began to spread
rumors that the Cubans were puppets and that they talked a lot but
withdrew and went away when it came time to fight, and the farmers
had to pay the consequences. They had wanted to stay in the
mountains, defending the key points; now everything had been lost
because of the mountebanks.

That was the kind of propaganda the chiefs spread among their
soldiers and among the farmers. Unfortunately, they had some
objective facts on which to base their malice. I had to struggle very
hard to regain the confidence of those men who, though barely

knowing me, had given me and our men much more confidence than they had given the commissars and chiefs, from whose high-handedness they had suffered so long. [*Congo*, 113.]

But the malice continued, based on the explosion of the grenade, which the chiefs had heard rumors about, as Che noted. They blamed the Cubans for it, saying that they had placed it there so the Congolese would fall into the trap. The main target of the attacks was Che, and the main mud-slingers included the chiefs mentioned by Che: Major Huseini and Lambert's men. They even went so far as to accuse the Cubans of cowardice, of having provoked the enemy and then run away. The men at the mixed roadblock at Lubondja jeered at those who were with the Cubans, because the Cubans made them work, while they of the road-block lived in houses and did sentry duty only once in a while. They also refused to say where the powder magazine was.

Major Huseini told his men that the Cubans ate everything and stole their weapons and that Che scolded him as if he were a child.

CHE: The saddest thing was that they had asked us to be there. Despicable as they were, however, the attacks had some extenuating factors: the really tough treatment I had given the chiefs, their ignorance, their superstition, their inferiority complexes, the wounds I had inflicted on their susceptibility and the fact that it was a white man who was reprimanding them, as in the bad times — all of this may have really stuck in their throats. [*Congo*, 115.]

It seems that there was something behind the Congolese chiefs' behavior that went beyond what Che said: their lack of desire to continue the struggle and to live alongside the Cubans, who urged them to fight.

The following note from Mafu, who had remained with the Rwandans at Front de Force, which Che received on October 27, shows that this was true on all the fronts. Che included it in his manuscript.

"This is to tell you about the existing situation. I have asked the captain and the major to cut the line, but they have told me that they have neither bullets nor food. All the canned goods have been used up.

"After receiving your message, they said the same thing.[1] The day the captain came, he told me that the Cubans had laid an ambush for the Congolese, defeated and disarmed them and brought the rifles here. The major had been called to attend a meeting there, and he told me that the situation was very bad and that he couldn't go, because the Congolese would kill him.[2] However, they hold two meetings every day, with lots of applause and shouting. I thought it was because they wanted to fight, but I have learned that the meetings were about how to leave the Congo. At first, they had said it would be next week, but then, in another meeting, they agreed to send scouts to the Lake to see where the boats were and seize them. That's why they have sent out a captain and 10 enlisted men. Moreover, they have sent the commissar with another group to Kigoma on another mission for the same purpose.

"The eight Congolese who were in a meeting were beaten, and only three of them are left.

"The man who told me about this hasn't said if they've talked about what to do with us if they leave. He said that, if they catch him talking about this with me, they will shoot him. If I find out anything more exact, I will let you know."

¹ This refers to a message urging them to carry out acts of sabotage as soon as possible.

² That was the meeting Masengo presided over, to which I have already referred. [The notes are Che's.] [*Congo*, 115-16 and 126.]

After reading the message, Che decided that its author and his men should go to reinforce the Lake base and ordered Azi and the other Cubans to set out for his camp. Because of these developments, Che tried to regroup his fighters and sent others to look for the weapons that were still scattered. They managed to recover Bahasa's gun, mortars, machine guns and several rifles, which reduced the number of weapons that were thought lost.

Because of its content, the following letter must have reached Che on October 27.

"Comrade Tatu [Che]:

"…We hope that, by the time you receive this letter, you will have forgiven us for our apparent negligence as regards the reports and shipments of material…

"We don't know how you could have been so naive as to believe that Kabila had come with four boats. He remains imperturbable in Kigoma… The only Cuban who has arrived is Changa, who has made two trips in three or four days after delaying 19 in coming. He told us he wanted to keep on making trips because he's afraid that we would be sent off and that communication by the Lake would be lost. This idea is new, since he had already agreed to come, and is due to the situation that he senses both in Kigoma and here at the Lake.

"The messenger told us that there was a letter for Masengo, but, in fact, it didn't come. We think that it's useless to take up anything with him, because right now Masengo is completely defeated and doesn't feel like doing anything, nor does he have the authority to order anyone around, as he himself told us yesterday. Masengo told us that if he were to come, not even Kabila has the authority to solve anything, that everybody is blaming the disaster on the two of them. Masengo's attitude during our conversation made us sorry for him. He told us that nobody had the authority even to arrest those who had sent letters to the fighters urging them to lay down their weapons. He attributes all this to tribal differences and things like that. He insisted a lot on our helping him to find hiding places for the weapons and ammunition, to keep them safe until the struggle may be renewed in the future. This, together with what we have already told you about his preparing to go to Kigoma (something that he didn't want to tell us but which he had told Njenje), will give you an idea of his state.

"As for the situation at the Lake, at the base and on Ali and Tom's [Kasima's] front, we went into that in our last report. The only change is that things are getting steadily worse (but that's normal here).

"As for controls over the things that leave here, of which you spoke in your letter, we send you a detailed list of everything in each report... There aren't any weapons, because, even though Njenje has control of everything down below, that control arrived too late, and there isn't anything (he controls nothing). There are 15 FALs in the reserve here at the base, but we aren't sending them, because we don't know what you want to do.

"We think that the reports already sent will give you a more complete idea of the general situation, objectively stated, and that it will help you in making a decision, as you say in your letter...

"As for bullets, we are sending 2,000 rounds for the FALs and three boxes for the 7.62s; we don't have any for the AKs.

"We think that the enemy knows about everything that is happening here, and also where you are. Masengo also thinks this, since there are a lot of men, including high-ranking officers, who have gone over to the enemy, and many whose whereabouts aren't known.

"Another thing that Masengo told us (and we agree with him on this) is that he expected the base and the Lake to be attacked at any moment. The surprise attack they made on you confirms this in our view.

"Siki thinks that the position you have chosen is very bad and that we may be isolated at any time...

"Remember that there is almost nobody left here and that we

have two comrades at the mortars toward the Lake and two in an observation post toward Ganya and that we are having to set up a post here to protect the storehouse (the 'Congos' are 'tifi tifi'). They have already ruined half a sack of dry beans and a sack of salt on the way from the boat to the base.

"Embraces from

"Siki, Tembo" [*Congo*, 116-18.]

The situation at the Lake and at the base

Immediately after this, Che mentioned another letter from the Lake, dated October 26, seemingly written shortly after the last one. Everything indicates that he received it before dawn on Thursday, October 28. He included the following paragraphs from it in his manuscript:

"Siki's meeting with Masengo resulted in the following agreements. Njenje was named chief of the Lake camp, with all of the authority inherent in the post, and was put in charge of defense. He is authorized to take all the measures he deems pertinent to ensure that his orders are carried out, and the only chiefs above him are Masengo and Siki. Njenje and Kumi were also made responsible... for the things that come to the Lake by our independent channel. I attach a sketch of the defenses, with the placement of all the fortifications and heavy weapons. As you will see, the defense is well organized in line with the means we have, which include two lines of trenches. Siki (and I feel the same) trusts only in the weapons manned by Cubans, since there is the same problem with the others as exists everywhere else. *Hapana masasi, hapana chakula, hapana travaille*; and there's always the question of where the retreat will be. All this is in the framework of Masengo's manifest lack of authority. In addition to this, the Lake has turned into the refuge of all the fugitives, with a resultant relaxation of discipline. The Staff organization was brought up in the meeting with Masengo. I presented my proposal, and it was decided to use the military part I suggested with their adaptations for the civilian part. Justice and finances — to be considered as military issues — were added to my proposal. As I have already reported, they are thinking of naming you Chief of Operations.

"I already have control of supplies and of the other things, as Masengo had agreed with you. How long this luck will last is something else again. I think problems will soon arise, since they are already asking for supplies, though they don't ask for anything with which to work and fight, and there has been some friction, both at the Lake and at the base. I'm standing firm with the slogan, 'Everything for the front,' and anybody who wants supplies has to go to the front. I have also suggested solutions, such as that of assigning a third of the personnel to go to the nearby hamlets to look for food. Even so, they prefer to stay in their houses, hungry, without doing anything to solve the problem. For sure, they don't have anything to eat.

"The situation on Ali's front; Kabimba
"The men at Katala are a little closer to Kibamba, because the soldiers seized Kabimba, burned it and withdrew. The major from there didn't allow Ali to confront them or advise him. Moreover, he is set on staying at the Lake, disregarding the possibility that the soldiers may take the hills. Siki sent orders to Ali that the Cubans should take the hills on their own, to prevent being encircled or caught off guard. Ali's situation with the major is a little ticklish, because the major told him that the best thing the Cubans could do was go to the base (what he actually said was that they should rest). A Congolese political commissar took Ali aside and told him that the chief had called the troops together and had told them that it would be best if the Cubans left. Siki told Masengo all about this, and he said he would talk with the major of Kabimba and solve that situation."
[*Congo*, 118.]

VIDEAUX: As long as we Cubans stayed at Kabimba, the Belgians never took it. This information that was sent to Siki was mistaken.

In the first paragraph, they say that Masengo lacked authority; if so, how could they expect him to solve the situation? At one time, they walked three days to lay an ambush on the Albertville road; they caught some civilians and held them. The civilians said that an enemy supply truck was about to come by, but the "Congos" insisted on leaving anyway, without waiting for it. This shows you the morale on that front. I sent them some supplies. There were a total of 11 Cubans on that front.

The report Che had received continued:

"The situation at Kasima
"As I had already told you, the soldiers seized Kasima. They advanced as far as Kaela by sea, burned it and fell back. At least one antiaircraft gun was lost (it had been put out of commission and hidden by a Cuban whom the Congos left alone; he said that he had to withdraw under fire by planes). I will tell you about these things exactly as I was told about them. Fifty Congos were sent to the front with a major, to place themselves under the orders of the Cubans and form a roadblock. Later on, a commander who had been in Cuba

arrived with seven others, saying he was going to Baraka. Tom, the political commissar, explained the situation to him, trying to dissuade him, but he was stubborn and went on, falling into an ambush. He and three others were killed (that was on October 21). Asmari asked Siki to go there with 10 Congos and medicine for emergency treatment. Right now, there are three ambushes between here and Kaela. Of course, with all the difficulties involved in ambushes with Congos, who run away, you have to pressure and threaten them, and still they run away. Tom says the only reason he hasn't begun to shoot them is he would have to shoot them all. There are a total of six Cubans on that front.

"Communications

"We have communication with Kigoma three times a day using the R 805 band: at 0800, 1430 and 1900 hours. We are also trying to establish communication with Dar es Salaam... Kabila is using the Kigoma service with the base, so we are better off now. There are possibilities for installing a shortwave on a boat so we can communicate during the crossing (if you authorize this). We're reorganizing telephone communication...

"After we had finished the general report on the situation, Njenje called from the Lake to say that Masengo was preparing to go to Kigoma. Shortly after that, there was a second call from down there to tell us that Masengo and all the big shots had had a meeting. Njenje and Kumi attended. In the meeting, Masengo said that he was going to Kigoma, because he was the only leader who was in the Congo. The big shots protested, and Masengo agreed to stay. However, we have been told that he is continuing his preparations for departure.

"A third call told us that they were continuing to meet. Masengo said that Kasavubu had sent him a message offering him a ministry. The message also said that a ship was waiting for him off Kibamba and that all he had to do was take a boat and board it. Masengo says that he replied that his brother Mitudidi had died in the struggle and that he, too, was willing to die.

"Njenje and Kumi are on the alert, with instructions to report [on] whatever may happen. Masengo is referring all problems presented to him to the Cubans, saying that they are the ones who will solve them. This even includes Ali's problem with the major from Kabimba, which had been submitted to him for a solution; he says Tembo must solve it.

"Siki and I are going to go down tomorrow to talk with Masengo as if we didn't know anything about these extremes, to see what he says. Meanwhile, we are on the alert.

"We have informed Padilla about all these things by radio in code so he will be on the alert, since we suppose that if people have been talking with Masengo, they will also be working on Soumaliot and Kabila. In the first contact he made with us from Dar es Salaam, Padilla asked us for a report on the latest happenings and the situation at the Lake. And — something that seemed a little strange at the time but which now seems understandable — that we should give him our opinion of Kabila."

Forestalling betrayal

CHE: As may be seen, the last part of the report was very alarming. According to it, Masengo was about to leave the struggle. I wrote the following in response:

"Tembo and Siki:

"First, I will answer your letter point by point and then tell you about the situation here and other things.

"The international situation isn't very bad, whether or not Kabila and Masengo become traitors. Soumialot's statements are good, and we have a beachhead there. I talked with Tremendo Punto, asking him to take command if Masengo leaves and to organize the resistance resolutely. As for Kabila's plans, there won't be any problem as long as he conveys them by radio; if there's anything wrong with them, we will censor them and see what happens. We shouldn't leave the base for now, no matter what. Ask Dar es Salaam for the results of the meeting with the Tanzanian Government.

"About the Lake and the base, the sketch of the defenses indicates that they are very vulnerable to a flank attack. The machine guns should have a land field of fire, defending the flanks, and [you should] dig trenches there, too. The heavy weapons should be manned by staunch Cubans — which isn't the same as saying "Cubans" without any qualifying adjectives — since I've had painful experiences in this regard here. Scouting should be done and defenses prepared on the sides of the hill that give access to the base. Take as firm a stand as you can on the use of supplies.

"As regards Ali, send him a note saying he should join the defense; with them and Mafu's men, we have enough people concentrated there, and you can arrange the defense so as to have a reserve. Don't forget the bare hill that dominates the base, because it is one of the keys to the defense (where the mortars and the antiaircraft guns are).

"Regarding Kasima, I told you about the scouting I ordered done. I think that if the soldiers don't hurry, we will be able to give them a shock there while I reorganize my team a little.

"As for communications: that is great news, but it seems excessive to me to communicate three times a day with the other side and twice a day with Dar es Salaam. Soon you won't have anything to say, the gasoline will be used up and codes can always be broken. This is without considering that planes can locate the base. Apart from the technical conditions, I recommend that you analyze the possibility of having normal daily communication with Kigoma at a set time once a day for extraordinary news and once every two or three days with Dar es Salaam. That will allow us to save gasoline. They should be at night, and the radio should be protected against an air attack. I think your idea of the shortwave is a good one, with simple codes that are changed frequently."

On receiving the above-mentioned report on Masengo's attitude, I talked with Tremendo Punto, as stated in my letter. He was floored. He said that he wasn't the man to take on the leadership, that he didn't have the personality for it and was nervous. He was willing to give his life in carrying out his duty, almost like a Christian martyr, with resignation, but he couldn't save the situation; his brother Mujumba could do that. I decided to write to Mujumba, but I couldn't say what I wanted in the letter, because of the danger that it might fall into enemy hands. I begged him to come, to talk about very important things. Two messengers took the letter, and I never learned if it reached its destination, because I never got a reply or heard anything more of the messengers. [*Congo*, 120.]

On October 28, Che — wearing an olive-green beret and smoking his usual pipe — went over to where Dreke was resting. Even though he'd had a fever and a headache since the night before, he got up, but Che asked him to sit down. As Dreke recalled it, their conversation was as follows:

"How do you feel?"

"Better, Major."

"Then, can we talk?"

"As you wish."

"Look, Moja [Dreke], I want to know what the matter is, because you seem worried. Is it about the latest developments?"

"Major, it may be that my fever makes it seem that I'm worried... But it's true that you may be right..."

"Can you tell me why?"

"Look, Major, it seems to me that the propaganda that all those people are making against us may lead to something serious..."

"I think so, too. The situation is more serious than it seems..." Che paused for a moment to pull on his pipe. "The attitude taken by the Congolese and Rwandans may lead them to betray us. From what I've learned, Masengo has all his things packed, ready to go. He has also said that Kasavubu has offered him a ministry..."

"How did Masengo learn that?"

"The men at the Lake told me that he said he'd received a message from Kasavubu... They also told me that the defenders at Baraka, Fizi and Lubondja refused to fight, and that's why the enemy didn't meet any resistance... All this — more than the slander by the military chiefs — leads me to think that treachery is in the wind.

"What do you plan to do?"

"We must regroup, to confront any act of provocation... Our situation is far from easy, and it's aggravated because several comrades are sick. I think we should send the sick to Cuba, along with those who can't cope with the conditions in the mountains and those who don't want to keep on fighting. What do you think of this?"

"I think it's a good idea, but I want you to know that I'll stay as long as necessary, as many years as need be, with you," Dreke replied very seriously.

"I'm going to stay with those who want to stay voluntarily."

"Major, I think that, when we tell the men this, the best ones will stay, even if there are only a few of them, and even if they don't have much faith in the struggle in the Congo."

"I know that's so, Moja, and I agree with you that it's better for us to be a small group, because, when we have to leave here, we may have to do so through another area or Brazzaville... What does Mbili think?"

"There won't be any problem about that; he will stay as long as necessary."

"I'll tell you when I'm going to make the list of those who should go. I'll talk with the ones who want to stay. Well, keep resting and take the pills for your fever... I'm going to see about something else."

Everything indicates that Che received a letter from Masengo that same day, October 28, long after talking with Dreke, because, if he had received it earlier, he wouldn't have said what he did about the Congolese leader. The letter made him reflect about what had been written to him from the base.

CHE: I should state that all of the reports about Masengo seem exaggerated; his later conduct, which he maintained at all times with me, makes me think that Siki and Tembo's reports (which weren't firsthand, but passed on information received from other people) were exaggerated by nervousness; distrust; lack of direct, precise communication, because of the language barrier; and other factors. I think this because Masengo wrote me a long letter dated October 27, the day after that of Tembo and Siki, in which he made a review of all the measures that had been taken along the front, the farmers who had been requested and the defense measures that had been adopted. He used the phrase, "No matter what happens, we should always be optimists." Of course, it's only a phrase, but it does indicate a very different mood from the one our comrades attributed to him in their report, one that is much more in accord with his real attitude — unless he was a master of deceit, a thing that seems far from his character. I had decided to disregard the warning of Tembo and Siki when an urgent letter dated October 29 reached me on the night of October 30. I have copied some excerpts from it. [*Congo,* 120-21.]

It should be emphasized that, if the date of the letter isn't mistaken, the entry in the *Campaign Diary* must be, because the entry on page 61 states that Che was reading *Capital* to several comrades on the afternoon of Thursday, October 28 when a rebel arrived, saying that there was a sick Cuban around five kilometers away who had brought letters from the Lake. Che immediately sent out to find the letters and, while he was waiting, kept on with his reading. The men at the Lake had sent a letter to Che, which got to him at midnight, so it would be a day before Che had written. Because I don't have the original of the letter, I can't say that the mistake was that of Che; however, the comrades who kept the *Campaign Diary* did so with care in regard to times and dates. I doubt they could have been mistaken, so I will continue with their entries for the chronology. Here are excerpts from the letter which Che copied on page 121 of his manuscript.

"Urgent
"Luluaburg base
"October 29, 1965
"1830 hours

"Tatu [Che]:
"We are sending you this urgent message because seven planes have been strafing and dropping some large objects which seem to be tanks of gasoline near Kabimba and the Jungo [Ñyunga] area toward the Lake ever since 1200 hours. Since this is the usual procedure prior to an advance or landing, we are warning you before it may be too late. The strafing forced the comrades who manned the machine guns to withdraw, and one of them hasn't appeared. Njenje is going to investigate and will let us know immediately...

   "As we have told you in all of our prior reports, we don't trust the 'Congos' who are defending the Lake any farther than we can throw them, and we have ever more doubts about them, because demoralization is steadily increasing. The total number of Cubans at the Lake and at the base, many of whom are sick, isn't enough for a serious defense of our single vital base of communications with the outside.

"In earlier reports, we tried to give you as objective a picture as possible of the reigning demoralization, so we don't think it necessary to insist on this, but you should know that it is truly alarming. Every scoundrel who was ever on the fronts has taken refuge at the Lake, joining the scoundrels who have been here all the time. There are many prisoners, even though, as we explained to you yesterday, there is an even larger number of criminals and traitors whom no authority is able to catch. Every day, Masengo (he hasn't left yet) asks Kabila for frequent reports on the faithfulness of certain officers. Another frequent accusation [sic] [incitement] is that the officers keep asking the 'revolutionaries' to lay down their weapons and spreading rumors that Soumialot is a great friend of Kasavubu's...

"As we told you in our last report, we don't like the position where you are; we know that there are paths from the Lake that the soldiers can take and leave us isolated. We think that the best solution would be to lay a roadblock where you are and to move the bulk of the Cuban troops here.

"We think that we're keeping you up to date on both the international situation and the one here. We almost sound like gossipy old ladies. We beg you to do the same with us, since we're always eager to get news (and so there will be three of us gossipy old ladies).

"Siki and Tembo, Ltd."

The entry on page 61 of the *Campaign Diary* was as follows:

After reading the report, Moja asked Tatu [Che] if he wanted to go to the base to talk with Siki and Tembo in more detail and see the situation, but he said he didn't, that they would all go to the base the next day and leave Mbili at the Ganya roadblock to prevent the soldiers, if they learned of our withdrawal, from advancing. He added that Comrade Rebocate would stay there in the hamlet for Comrade Uta, who was sick. Singida and some others [would also stay], to keep the farmers from thinking they weren't supported. At the same time, he asked Moja if he felt well enough for the trip, and Moja said he was OK and would go with him. Before leaving, Che met with the people living in the area.

CHE: I talked with the farmers, and they understood my decision perfectly, feeling safe with those who remained and with the doctors who would also stay at the hospital with the wounded Congolese and some of our men who were sick. We said good-bye very amicably. [*Congo,* 121.]

Moroccan revolutionary leader Madhi Ben Barka, a member of the Preparatory Presidium of the Afro-Asian-Latin-American Solidarity Council, was kidnapped in Paris on October 28. The blow was aimed at sabotaging the preparatory work for the Tricontinental Conference to be held in Cuba in January 1966. Neither Che nor the *Campaign Diary* kept by Dreke's group mentioned his disappearance, however.

Mundandi wants to leave the Congo

Che, Dreke and a group of Cubans and several Congolese left for the base at 1400 hours on Friday, October 29. After walking for over two hours, they heard planes bombing and strafing in the Nganja area. The victims were around 20 or 30 cows. Naturally, that day they gorged on the meat and carried away as much as they could. While they were enjoying that special menu, the Rwandan Mundandi appeared.

CHE: I had a serious talk with him. I told him that his attempt to flee at that time was crazy, that the fate of Rwanda was linked to that of the Congo and that he wouldn't have anywhere to continue the struggle — so, was he thinking of abandoning it? He admitted that it was crazy; some people had suggested it to him, but he had dissuaded them and was on his way to talk about sabotaging the electric power line at [Front] de Force, drawing the enemy's attention to that point. [*Congo,* 122.]

They were caught in a heavy downpour that forced them to spend the night in the hamlet and set out again the morning of the next day, Saturday, October 30. Dreke left first with some of the men. Another downpour soaked them before they reached the base camp.

When Dreke arrived at the camp, he met with Siki and Tembo and told them everything Che had said to him and his future plans. Then Siki and Tembo did the same, adding that Ali had laid an ambush in the Kasima area on Wednesday, October 27, causing several enemy casualties and seizing weapons and documents that outlined a planned offensive. The enemy documents noted how many Cubans there were on each front. Evidently, the enemy intelligence network was working well, whereas the rebels didn't have any. Che and the rest of the men arrived that night.

Bitter arguments

CHE: When I arrived at the base, I found a defeatist atmosphere and a climate of outright hostility toward the Congolese, which led to some bitter arguments with the comrades. They had made a long list of all the chiefs who had fled to Kigoma, a list that wasn't entirely correct but which clearly reflected the reality of the chiefs' cowardice, disdain for fighting and treason. However, it included some names that shouldn't have been on it, because their owners stood firm to the last. The two notes I'm transcribing give an idea of the prevailing spirit. One is a letter from Tembo to a comrade; although I neither have nor have read the letter to which Tembo was replying, it shows how his friend must feel.

"Base
"Thursday, October 28, 1965
"1300 hours
"...Your letter reflects the mood that is the product of the latest events and the picture of desolation and moral bankruptcy of the 'Congolese revolution.' It worries me. I would like to give you my frank opinion and ask you once more to trust me, even though I can't guarantee that your trust will survive another disappointment.

"I know that you are no coward. To the contrary, I think you are a revolutionary who does his duty, no matter what the circumstances. Therefore, I won't appeal to your steadfastness, because I know that it would be useless and ridiculous to do so, but I do want to remind you of the old saying that 'Caesar's wife must not only be but also appear to be honest.' Don't let anybody think that your opinions about the situation or about the specific measures that are taken in view of that situation mean that you are defeated and lack the spirit for struggle. You should remain ready to fight, and your attitude, which should be manifest, should serve as an example and motivate the other comrades in the difficult circumstances we are going through.

"There may be some things you don't understand, and measures that are taken which seem wrong to you, but that shouldn't lead you to conclude Che and the other leaders aren't aware of the real situation, which can be seen clearly. Don't forget that difficult times call for extreme measures to protect morale and stave off debacle...

"I trust Che more than ever before, and you should, too.

"I absolutely deny that he may be mistaken, but even if he should be, our duty, after presenting our views, is to carry out his instructions, no matter what. I am not joking when I say that it's a thousand times better to die fighting — even though we may believe it's in a useless cause — than to be party to the spectacle of a defeat brought about by not wanting to fight. Cuban revolutionaries may be killed, but they can never be frightened.

"I hope... I'm sure that you will carry out your revolutionary duty as a soldier, as a Cuban and as a man, setting an example both as an individual and as a leader.

"We will overcome."

This other letter was addressed to Tembo:

"Comrade:

" ...There is complete disillusionment here. I found out that most of the Cubans who came with Che will ask you for a meeting and say they want to leave. Seventeen here plus seven in the group that came feel the same. Emilio, that attitude is almost generalized among the comrades. I am trying to convince them that this is the time to be more steadfast than ever, but there is great discontent, great distrust and an enormous desire to leave the Congo. This is based on the attitude they have observed on the part of the Congos — who, according to them, believe the fight is over. The comrades say that the situation has reached this extreme because of Che and say that he shows little desire to find a way out.

"This is what I wanted to tell you so your help may be more effective.

"Heavy"

As can be seen from this last letter, the troops were falling apart; there had even been a case of several Party members who asked for a Party meeting so they could raise the question of withdrawing. I was extremely harsh in my replies, letting them see that I wouldn't accept any kind of demand or meeting of that kind and that I would consider even allowing those proposals to circulate to be an act of cowardice and betrayal. I still had some authority, with which I maintained some cohesion among the Cubans. [*Congo,* 122-23.]

Leaving the Congo

DREKE: I can't deny that the last things that happened further discouraged the new comrades, but there weren't so many of them. Some of them, to justify their position, claimed that others felt the same way — even though they didn't — and said that, although they didn't agree with how the Congolese acted, they were willing to follow Che's orders.

A few Party members talked about asking Che to analyze the situation and return to Cuba, because the Congolese didn't do what they should, didn't want to fight and acted as if the only thing they wanted to do was get the hell out of there. Therefore, they felt that we, too, should leave. But most of the Party members didn't agree. It seems that Che found out and got furious. The meeting wasn't held, and, even though those who were discouraged remained discouraged, they stayed there until the very end. Moreover, most if not all of them suggested leaving the Congo but joining another guerrilla group that was more willing to fight. They made the same suggestion soon after we left there.

VIDEAUX: There was a lot of discouragement because of how the Congolese acted — especially the chiefs — because, when the vanguard sets an example, the people follow it, and when it doesn't, the people don't follow it; that's what happened there. Many of the Cubans felt that it was a fraud, and that's why they wanted to leave the Congo but continue fighting in another country, such as Vietnam or in Latin America.

MARGOLLES: It's true that there was a suggestion of not continuing to fight in the Congo. There was a lot of talk to the effect that the struggle was pointless and wouldn't get anywhere. The men asked why we didn't go somewhere in Latin America, why we didn't open another guerrilla front... I never heard anything about going to Vietnam.

ZERQUERA: Everybody talked with me... When the topic of our staying there came up, all of us were disgusted. The doctors told me that they were going to ask Che to send them to Vietnam or Peru. They had already carried out internationalist missions of the same kind in other countries. Their reason for wanting to leave wasn't because they were cowards but rather because they had seen that most of the Congolese weren't interested in fighting for their cause. However, most of us said that we wouldn't leave Che, no matter how long he stayed in the Congo. I believed that he had a superior mind; besides, Fidel supported him, and I told myself they knew what they were doing.

CHE: Much more serious things were happening among the Congolese. I received a letter dated in that period and signed by Makambila Jerome, "Provincial Deputy and People's Representative to the National Liberation Council," in which he accused Masengo of murdering women and, after making a long presentation of the case, invited me to meet with him in Fizi to analyze the situation in that area. At a time when our line of communication abroad was in greater danger than ever and we had a central communications point and a Staff to defend, that man sent scads of letters (I received several from him) about holding a meeting. This paragraph gives an idea of the limbo into which the revolution was sailing:

"Allow me to list, below, the aspirations, desires and suggestions of all the people in this region of Fizi:

"1. The people demand that the military power of our revolution be entrusted to the friendly forces that have come to help us and that they remain in control until the country has been stabilized.

"2. The people ask for intense support from friendly countries, this support to consist of

"A. Military operations, personnel, weapons, equipment, money, etc.

"B. Technical assistance, engineers, technicians in different branches, doctors, etc. Social assistance, teachers, merchants, industrial workers, etc."

The initiative of giving all the military power to the Cubans was simply an attempt at sedition, with them trying to use us and was rooted in the tribal differences between those people and Kabila and Masengo's group — unless it was the work of the enemy. [*Congo*, 123-24.]

Ali's new battles

CHE: The only news that broke with that absurd and gloomy picture was a report from Ali, in which he said he'd had two battles and had inflicted several casualties on the enemy Army. All this was in spite of the fact that Ali was continually at odds with the military chief of the region and that he'd had to carry out the attacks on the Army practically alone, except for the group of Cuban comrades. In one of those attacks, they seized some documents containing the enemy's plans and several maps, a radio, two mortars, a bazooka, four FALs or super-FALs, ammunition and supplies. It had been a good attack, a hard defeat for the enemy, but it didn't change the situation. [*Congo*, 124.]

The papers that had been seized included a secret document entitled ORDER OPS No. 2. SOUTHERN OPS. It contained two maps: one, a No. 1 of Bendera, at a scale of 1:200,000, and the other of Katenga, at a scale of 1:100,000. It went on to describe the enemy forces — that is, the rebels — on various fronts and then their own forces at some points. No date was given for the attack.

CHE: The intention was to occupy the entire shore of the Lake and destroy our installations near Kigoma. It could be seen that, in spite of some details, they had a very precise idea of our weapons, of the men we had and also of how many Cubans were here. That is, the enemy's intelligence service functioned perfectly, or nearly perfectly, while we didn't know what was going on in its ranks.

The picture that came to me from the base was far from pleasing. We knew what the enemy wanted, but we didn't need to seize those documents to know that, because it was clear, and the panorama of discouragement was terrible. [*Congo*, 124-25.]

Preparing the defense

After the unpleasant argument to which Che referred, he decided that Dreke (Moja) and Oscar Fernández Mell (Siki) should be in charge of preparing the defense of the base. He also talked with Masengo by phone. Masengo sounded resolute, saying he had planned an attack on Kasima, and Che told him they would discuss it the next day, as he would go down to see him.

Che spent the morning of Sunday, October 31 touring the base with the other Cuban officers and showing where the lines of trenches should be dug. He wanted to make it an impregnable fortress if possible, or at least make it strong enough to inflict heavy losses on the enemy if they were to take it. He ordered that pits be dug and that the equipment be hidden in them. He also inspected the radio, noting its organization and the technicians' readiness to work.

CHE: The comrades' complete dedication to their work and the effectiveness with which they did it contrasted sharply with the climate of abandonment and lack of willpower that prevailed among our men. It is a fact that sending men who were skilled and loved their work and who — it's only fair to say this — separated from the daily struggle with the Congolese soldiers, produced magnificent results. In spite of the proviso noted, I would say that, if all of the cadres had been of the same quality, [not only] our performance but also the final results would have been different. [*Congo*, 127.]

RUMBAUT: Since communications were secret, almost nobody visited us. We had very little contact with the Congolese. We lived apart from the others, which helped us to keep everything in good condition. We were very demanding in terms of discipline.

FLORENTINO: After we had been there for 15 or 20 days, Che came back; that was the first time I had seen him in person. I had never had the opportunity to meet him in Cuba. He greeted us affectionately and asked us to show him where the radio was. It was underground, with only the electric plant — and, naturally, the antenna — aboveground. He liked the installation, and I remember that he said, "This is the best thing I've found on my return." I remembered his words, and many years after his death I read in a magazine that he had been largely responsible for the establishment of Radio Rebelde in the Sierra Maestra, so I imagine that's why he said it.

RUMBAUT: We were on the air four times a day. First at 0700 hours, with Kigoma, to learn when the boats were coming and everything else related to the Lake crossing; then at 1100 hours, also with Kigoma; at 1500 hours with Dar es Salaam; and finally at 1800 hours, again with Kigoma. Before the communications group arrived, communication was by means of comrades who served as messengers; they traveled by road or railroad from Dar es Salaam to Kigoma and crossed the Lake with Changa. Then they would go into Congolese territory to look for Che. Replies went back along the same route, and went from Dar es Salaam to Cuba by diplomatic pouch. It's easy to see how long letters took, using that method. When we arrived, that problem was solved. Information was sent directly to Cuba by means of the powerful equipment installed in the Embassy.

I had my 18th birthday in the Congo. I was impressed by Che's exacting character and affability with the comrades. He considered himself as just one more fighter, although everybody knew he was the chief. If there was food enough for everybody, he ate; if there wasn't, nobody did.

FLORENTINO: At that time, many of us didn't understand why the men had split into two groups. Many comrades said that they had gone there determined to help and to give their lives if necessary, but it had to be for somebody who really deserved it, and that was a mess. When I found out that Che had divided the group, I didn't understand, but I did see clearly that we had to bolster the Congolese groups with Cubans.

There was one comrade who told a Congolese that if Fidel had had the weapons they had, Batista wouldn't have lasted so long.

If they close the Lake...

RUMBAUT: One night, Che heard a broadcast in French that said the Government knew there was a group of foreigners with the guerrillas and that all of their supplies were entering through Lake Tanganyika. It said that if the foreigners kept on attacking the Army, they would blockade the Lake so they wouldn't get any more provisions. He called the Cubans and told us about the news.

FLORENTINO: One comrade — I don't remember who — told him, "If they close the Lake to us, we'll go down to the plains and obtain the food and everything else we need." That pleased Che; he said he hadn't expected any other response from us.

At close to midday, Che went down to meet with Masengo to analyze plans and wait for Changa — who, according to a cable from Dar es Salaam, would be coming with a messenger. Almari's note said that there had been a clash with the enemy at the Kakoma roadblock, on the road between Kasima and the Kibamba base, where two Cubans were. When the rebels opened fire and the enemy replied, both groups fled in great confusion, the Government soldiers leaving some abandoned ammunition.

Che and Masengo couldn't agree about the attack on Kasima, because the Cuban scouts said there weren't any soldiers there, and the Congolese said the opposite, so the plan was put aside until new scouting would ascertain the true situation. Mundandi said that he would carry out Che's instructions to better defend the base as well as carry out several actions that would draw forces from that region. In exchange, he asked for shoes and other clothing, food and Cuban technicians to carry out acts of sabotage and man the gun. Che said he would send him six men.

Che decided to wait for the incoming message at the Lake, using the time to talk with the military leaders of the various fronts who were there, pointing out their mistakes and criticizing their behavior — which has already been described — and suggesting how they could do better.

A month of disasters without extenuating circumstances

CHE: Another month — October — has just ended. In my diary, I wrote the following: "A month of disasters without any extenuating circumstances. To the shameful fall of Baraka, Fizi, Lubondja and Lambert's front was added the surprise they gave me in Kilonwe and the loss of two comrades — Awirino, who has disappeared, and Bahasa, who is dead. All this would be nothing if it weren't accompanied by the utter discouragement of the Congolese. Nearly all the chiefs have fled, and Masengo seems to be about to weigh anchor. The Cubans aren't much better, from Tembo and Siki down to the enlisted men. Everybody blames the Congolese for their own mistakes. However, in our battle, the serious weaknesses of the Cuban fighters are added to my own mistakes. Moreover, it has been very difficult to achieve friendly treatment between the Congolese and the Cubans and to get the Cubans to stop acting like bossy big brothers with special rights when it came to supplies and carrying loads. In summary, the next month may be definitive, and we will have to throw everything we have into it."

My observation concerning the relations between Congolese and Cubans was due to the fact that, since all of the cooks were Cubans, they looked out for their comrades when serving the food, and there was a tendency to give the Congolese the heaviest loads to carry. We haven't established completely fraternal treatment, and people always feel bad when others acting superior come along and give advice. [*Congo*, 121-22.]

8

November 1965

On the morning of November 1, 1965, the darkness of the night was broken by the traces of illuminating projectiles crisscrossing over Lake Tanganyika, the unmistakable sign of a battle. Che and his comrades were worried and remained so until Changa and his boat reached the shore. What had happened was that he had been seen by an enemy patrol while still a few miles from the Congolese side, and, when told to halt, had responded with gunfire. Two Cubans were wounded, one in the hand and the other, Changa himself, in the face by the recoil of a bazooka.

Tanzania

PABLO RIVALTA: At the end of October, President Nyerere asked me to see him. First he showed me a list of petitions that the Congolese had addressed to him, most of them about personal problems. He told me how they lived in Dar es Salaam and Kigoma, in drunkenness, with women, going from one party to another and making frequent trips to Cairo. Then he told me about the new situation that had arisen and said that they were asking the Cubans to leave. Che's name was never mentioned, either then or later. I think that, if he didn't know Che was there, he guessed he was. But neither Kawawa nor Lucinde talked to me about him.

The Congo

In the Congo, news of the following reached Che from Dar es Salaam.

> "Comrade Tatu [Che]:
> "This morning, Pablo [Rivalta] was called to the Government and told that, in view of the resolutions of the meeting of African states concerning nonintervention in the internal affairs of other countries, both the Tanzanian and other governments which had been helping the Congolese Liberation Movement would have to change the nature of that assistance. We were requested to withdraw what we had there, as our contribution to that policy. They acknowledged that we had given more than many African countries and that the Congolese Liberation Movement wouldn't be told anything about this until we had withdrawn, when the President himself would inform them of the decision made by the African states. A report on this has been sent to Havana. We await your opinion.
> "Greetings,
> "Rafael"

CHE: That was the coup de grace for a dying revolution. Because of the nature of the information, I didn't say anything to the Congolese comrades, waiting to see what would happen in the next few days, but in conversations I hinted at what might be a new Tanzanian policy, using developments such as the freezing of supplies in Kigoma. [Mainly weapons and ammunition.] [*Congo*, 128.]

The Tanzanian Government's policy couldn't be described as anything other than "a coup de grace for a dying revolution," as Che put it. It had pledged Cuba it would guarantee the passage of all assistance that Cuba sent to the Congolese guerrillas — such as it was doing with the weapons and other war matériel contributed by China, the Soviet Union and Bulgaria. As Che put it, Tanzania couldn't risk everything even on a strong hand. He was aware of the situation that country was facing when he wrote, "I understand Tanzania's current difficulties, but I don't agree with its statements." His not agreeing wouldn't change the situation. Nyerere didn't have enough strength to oppose the Accra resolution; he hadn't been placed in power by an armed struggle with the support of the majority of the people, as had happened in Cuba. Tanzania would have been in serious danger if Nyerere hadn't acted as he did. Moreover, his country was a member of the Commonwealth. The Tanzanian President was forced to accept the resolution.

However, why didn't the Tanzanians turn over the weapons and other matériel sent by Cuba, China, Bulgaria and the Soviet Union which arrived in Tanzania during September? They had done so before. The answer may be found in the fact that Foreign Minister Oscar Cambona was one of President Nyerere's most trusted colleagues. Padilla told me that he had been an enemy agent for quite some time, as was confirmed much later. That traitor may have held back deliveries of the weapons and urged the Nyerere to suspend the assistance to the guerrillas, using the danger of possible conspiracies financed and abetted by the Government of the Congo as a pretext.

We will support any decision

CHE: Rafael's telegram from Dar es Salaam was received on November 4. The emissary also brought a letter from Fidel, whose main points were as follows:

1. We should do everything except the absurd.

2. If Che thinks that our presence is becoming unjustifiable and useless, we should think about withdrawing.

3. If you consider that you should stay, we will try to send as many human and material resources as you deem necessary.

4. I am concerned that, mistakenly, you may be afraid that the attitude you take may be considered defeatist or pessimistic.

5. If you decide to leave, Che may maintain the present status quo, coming back here or remaining somewhere else.

6. We will support any decision.

7. Avoid total annihilation. [*Congo*, 128.]

These points sum up the reply to the letter Che had written Fidel on October 5. Che was probably more than pleased with it, since it clearly expressed the confidence placed in him for deciding what he considered best. However, the message that he had just received worried him greatly.

On November 2, 3 and 4, the daily chaos increased, as did Che's concern over the message. Work on the fortifications continued, and Che suggested that they operate with a smaller, more flexible Staff. Masengo opposed this, because an organization had already been created and was awaiting Kabila's approval.

CHE: It was a matter of introducing my operational plan of the Staff, which seemed like that of the Soviet Army on the eve of the taking of Berlin, but there was nothing to do but give in. I asked that he make me responsible for the men's training, so as to continue the attempt at a practical academy. Instead, he made me Chief of Operations — theoretically, second in command of the army, in charge of organizing the artillery — in addition to Chief of Instruction. The command was very relative, but I threw myself into doing everything humanly possible to halt the collapse. [*Congo*, 131.]

Enemy vessels could be seen crossing back and forth in front of the camp. Mail from Dar es Salaam arrived on November 4 saying that Comrades Dreke, Fernández Mell and Tembo had been elected members of the Central Committee of the Communist Party of Cuba. Che informed them of this from Kibamba by telephone. He also told them that he would go up to the upper base that afternoon. They also learned that Fidel had read the farewell letter that Che had left him. The following message from Havana arrived on Friday, November 5:

"To: Tatu [Che]
"From: Rafael
"Message received on November 4. No matter what the new situation may be, Tshombe's white mercenaries will stay in the country attacking the Congolese and committing all kinds of villainy and crimes. In that case, it would be treason to withdraw our support from the Congolese revolutionaries unless they ask it or decide to leave the struggle." [*Congo*, 128-29.]

The above was Fidel's reply to the report sent him from Dar es Salaam on the new position of the Tanzanian Government. Che replied through Rafael.

CHE: "…In recent days, the soldiers have begun to advance on all sides, giving the impression of preparing the final attack on our base. However, no attack has occurred yet, and our defenses are quite strong, at least in weapons, although we need some kinds of ammunition and can't trust the Congolese recruits.

"We have a quadrilateral in the mountains marked by the following points, which are held by the enemy, near our forces (perhaps you can find it on some map): Baraka, Fizi, Lubondja, Force Bendera and Kabimba. Ali put up resistance against the enemy three times on the Kabimba front. The second time, he captured the general order of the offensive, which called for taking our base and combing 25 kilometers around it. Four PTs (Hermes Luckas) are patrolling the Lake to keep supplies from reaching us. The enemy's aviation consists of 8 T-28s, 2 B-26s, a DC-3 for reconnaissance and service and a helicopter for liaison. That tiny air fleet inspires terror in the Congolese comrades.

"From the military point of view, the situation is difficult because our force is a collection of armed men without the least discipline and with little if any eagerness to fight, but the conditions of the terrain are unbeatable for defense.

"Today, I was named Chief of Operations of the area, with full authority in training the men and command over our artillery (a battery of 82-mm mortars, three 75-mm recoilless cannon and 10 12.7-mm antiaircraft guns). The Congolese chiefs' spirit has improved with the succession of [enemy] defeats, and they have become convinced that they should take things seriously.[2] I prepared them for what Tanzania has done, as if it were a supposition of mine based on the Accra conference and the Government's strange silence concerning the weapons it is holding and not handing over. Some people here say they are willing to risk everything to keep the revolution going at all costs. However, I don't know what Kabila — who has announced that he's coming — will think."

[2] Unfounded optimism on my part. [*Congo*, 129-30 and 134.]

CHE: I have received Fidel's latest cables. One seems to be in response to the letters I sent, and the other, to the latest news of Tanzania. As for my letter, I think it was exaggerated again; I tried to be objective, but it wasn't entirely pessimistic. There was one moment when there was talk here of the massive flight of all the Congolese chiefs. I had decided, in that case, to remain with around 20 chosen men (the goat doesn't give enough milk for more), send the rest to the other side and keep fighting until either this developed or the possibilities for struggle were exhausted — and, in that case, go to another front by land or make use of my "sacred" right to asylum on the neighboring coast. As for the latest news of Tanzania, my reaction was just like that of Fidel: we can't leave. Even more, no Cuban should leave under the proposed conditions. Somebody should speak seriously with the Tanzanian leaders to make things clear. [*Congo*, 130.]

Che hadn't decided to withdraw from the Congo, especially in view of the message received from Fidel on November 4. Che considered that no country has the right to demand that internationalists leave; only the leaders of the liberation movement who requested the help can do that. However, the Ghana resolutions were opportune for some of them, since they hadn't known how to ask the Cubans to leave or to justify their own abandonment of the struggle — which took place in the following days, when several Congolese guerrilla chiefs started to act strangely, motivated by who knows what, and began to turn a cold shoulder to the Cubans.

Cuba doesn't go back on its promises
CHE: "These are my proposals: that a high-level Cuban delegation — or

Tembo, from here, or a combination of the two — visit Tanzania. They should say more or less the following: Cuba offered help subject to Tanzania's approval; it accepted, and the help was given. It was without any time limit and with no strings attached. We understand Tanzania's current difficulties, but we don't agree with its statements. Cuba doesn't go back on its promises, nor can it accept a shameful flight, leaving its brothers to the mercy of the mercenaries. We would abandon the struggle only if, for well-founded causes or forces majeures, the Congolese should ask us to do so, but we will struggle to keep that from happening. The Tanzanian Government's attention should be drawn to the agreement; it's like the Munich Agreement in that it gives neocolonialism a free hand. There can be no backing up or appeasement of imperialism; the only language it understands is that of force. If the present government in the Congo is preserved, Tanzania will be in great danger, surrounded by countries hostile to it, to a greater or lesser degree. The revolution here could subsist without Tanzania, but at the cost of great sacrifices; we won't be to blame if it is destroyed through lack of assistance, etc., etc.

"You might demand that the Tanzanian Government maintain telegraphic communication, allow food to be sent to us at least once or twice a week, allow us to bring in two speedboats, send us as many of the weapons it is holding as it can in one shipment, and give us permission to send and receive letters once every fortnight. [According to Che's notes and to what Padilla and Rivalta told me, the commission for talking with the Tanzanian Government was never created, and Che's suggestion was never made. — W.G.]

"I'm including a reference to the boat because the situation is desperate: the little Soviet boats are very slow, and the others have speedboats. We have to shoot our way through, and, the last time, Changa was injured and a boy wounded in the hand. Two boats should go together, because they often break down en route, and one could tow the other. Tanzania certainly won't accept this kind of solution (of daily battles), which is why we must have the boats on our side and take them out to get things, returning the same night. One of the boats should be so easy to carry that we can take it up steep mountains if we should lose our toehold on the Lake shore for a while. Emphasis should be placed on our present capacity to have a point in Tanzania that is known to very few people where we can arrive at night and leave before dawn and where, with good boats, we would engage in a smuggling operation, which is normal on these coasts. We can be aboveboard, however. This is our method, and we need tranquillity to dedicate ourselves to the important things. Moreover, I recommend that the final text about communications that is drawn up be placed in the hands of the Soviets and Chinese, to prevent any discrediting maneuver.

"Don't fear for us; we will reflect honor on Cuba and won't be wiped out, but I will always disassociate myself from some who have got weak knees after our position is clarified. Big hugs from all of us to all of you.

"Tatu [Che]

"P.S. I think you should talk with Karume and explore the possibility of having an air base, either in Zanzibar with a stopover in Tanzania or in Zanzibar with no stopovers. The type of plane should depend on what you can get. One offer that may be acceptable to Tanzania is that of having doctors in the Kigoma hospital, which would allow them to move around with some freedom. They should speak English, be efficient in their profession and be good revolutionaries, or at least come close to this prototype.

"Tatu [Che]" [*Congo*, 130-31.]

A hair-raising incident

Mafu returned on November 5 with the 10 Cubans who had been with Mundandi at Front de Force and reported that the same disorder and lack of combativity prevailed there. He also reported an incident that Che described as hair-raising.

CHE: One night, two Congolese emissaries from Calixte's base, which was nearby, arrived at the camp. Our comrades invited them to stay and sleep there, since it was already late, but they said Mundandi had invited them to spend the night in his hut, and they were on their way there. They didn't show up the next day. When our men asked Mundandi about them, he said he had thrown them out because they had deceived him; they had told him they were political commissars, whereas they were nothing but enlisted men. Soon afterwards, two Rwandans started wearing blue jackets like those worn by the comrades, which were the only ones of their kind ever seen in the camp. They also wore helmets, which the Rwandans didn't have. Soon after that, Calixte sent word asking where his men were, as they hadn't returned to the base. All that makes us assume that Mundandi's people had murdered them. We don't know exactly why — whether to rob them or because discrepancies between the two groups may have reached those extremes. I conveyed my suspicion to Masengo, but because of the haste of the unfortunate events, no measures were taken. [*Congo*, 131.]

Che ordered that Azima's company, which had been dismantled at the time of the attack on October 24, be completed. He regretted the lack of weapons and the arbitrary distribution that had been made of those in the last shipment. Then he inspected the fortifications and sent Dreke to Kibamba to see how things were going. Ali had come from Kabimba and was there.

The same picture

First thing on Saturday, November 6, Che inspected the fortifications again and ordered Mafu to take his men and occupy the defense at Kisosi. On their return, the men who had gone out to scout at Kasima told him that there weren't any soldiers there. Then he chose six Cubans to sabotage the electric power line between Front de Force and Albertville. Mundandi sent some of his soldiers and a 75-mm gun for the defense of the Lake, as he had promised Che. Che warned the comrades not to become separated until they went into action and to be very cautious with the Rwandans.

A report from Mbili, at the Lubondja front, reiterated that the Congolese were stepping up the pressure and were very demoralized. The most serious thing he said was that some of the Cubans were conspiring to request that they be taken out of the fighting. Another letter, from Karín, the political commissar, said that he had written to Tembo to warn him of the situation and that he was willing to do everything in his power to do his duty. He enclosed a list of those of Mbili's men whom he knew wanted to stop fighting in the Congo. He thought there were some more, but these were the ones he was sure of.

CHE: Defending the political commissar against the imputations implied that I would consider it an act of cowardice to allow manifestations of defeatism, since Karín was helping him a lot in a difficult and thankless task. [*Congo*, 132.]

Dreke and Ali — both veterans of the guerrilla struggle in Cuba — returned that afternoon. Dreke said that everything was just the same. Ali expressed his disagreement with the chiefs of the area, who had the same attitude as the others. He was so mad about people who didn't want to fight that his stutter got worse. For his part, Che felt that even though Ali was fully justified in getting mad, his lack of tact made him lose his patience with those comrades sooner than he might have. Years later, Ali remembered that conversation with Che:

"L-l-look, Ma-ma-ma-major. I d-d-don't w-w-want to g-g-go on with those p-p-p-people... Le-le-let me s-s-stay w-w-with you."

On hearing this, Che yelled, "If you don't go back there, I'll send you back to Cuba!"

Without stopping to think, Ali pointed at his chief and said, "Y-y-yes, b-b-b-but w-w-with you."

Dreke told me that that reply totally disarmed Che, who had to smile. He was well aware that Ali was one of the men he could count on, even though he wasn't very convinced about that struggle.

Trying to find a solution, Che talked with Masengo and Tremendo Punto, and they decided that Tremendo Punto and Ali should go back to Kabimba to see what the situation was and decide if it was necessary to replace the Cuban adviser with another one or to withdraw all the troops from that area. Later, Che send a message to Mbili authorizing him to move away from the troops who were at the Lubondja roadblock.

News came from Kigoma that Vice-President Kawawa was there and that, in a conversation with Kabila, he had promised to help him, taking an interest in the needs of the front and assuring him that the Lake would be opened. Che noted, "If what Kabila says is true, Tanzania's attitude is even more incorrect."

Quackery and malice

On November 7, Dreke, Uta and Saba left to inspect the Kisosi defenses and once again see if there were any soldiers in Kasima, because the Cuban and Congolese reports were contradictory. They took a radio with which to communicate with the base. In Kibamba, Masengo was to send an officer with them for the verification. A note from Mbili said that scouts found that there weren't any soldiers at Lubondja. What they did find were enemy proclamations calling on the guerrillas to abandon the struggle. Mbili added that there was almost no movement of vehicles at Lambert's old roadblock and on the road to Fizi.

He also reported that Lambert went to visit them, and they had to listen resignedly to accounts of his imaginary battles. He said he had 900 men surrounding Baraka and Fizi and asked for mortars, cannon and antiaircraft guns. Of all these, only antiaircraft guns were available, and they sent them back to the base as soon as possible to keep Lambert from taking them. Even so, Che thought that they would have to keep an eye on his activities in the future, as he considered that Lambert and his men wouldn't give up on the weapons so easily.

The worst thing of all was that Lambert said the Cubans had behaved badly in a battle (that had never been fought). He also criticized Che for having gone back to the base. He said that the enemy had offered money and work to those who turned themselves in but that he had said he would stand firm in the struggle. Finally, he ordered a major to call together all of his armed men.

CHE: That was a direct attack on me. Even though he maintained a firm attitude and was willing to continue the struggle, he went around sowing division. [*Congo*, 133.]

It seems that, hoping that Lambert would behave differently, Che wanted to believe that he would continue the struggle. (Lambert's behavior could hardly be considered "a firm attitude" showing that he was "willing to continue the struggle.") Only a man with so much faith in his fellow mortals could believe that.

To prevent worse problems, he ordered Mbili to return to the base but to leave a group of Cubans to continue the classes at the training camp, that was far from the primitive roadblock.

Nothing of importance was reported on November 8 and 9. Work continued on building and improving the fortifications. Dreke reported on November 8 that Masengo hadn't yet assigned an officer to accompany him and told his chief that, if he didn't do it soon, they would go without him. The most important thing — if it had been believable — would have been the news that Kabila would arrive that day.

Planes were observed throughout the region starting early on Wednesday, November 10. Later on, the information came that the enemy had begun its advance toward the guerrilla fronts at Front de Force. Enemy troops were advancing in three directions, guided by farmers from the area. The two comrades who brought the news had been with Mundandi, who had decided to withdraw without putting up any resistance. Che told the two, however, that they should go back, because it was more necessary than ever to support the Rwandans, and they did so the next day. It was important for the guerrillas to maintain control of that area, because, in addition to giving access to the base, that was where they kept their cattle. If it fell into enemy hands, the enemy would close off communication with the Lake.

Immediately, all possible measures were taken so that, when the soldiers appeared, they would be able to repulse them. Training in armaments — about which the trainees still didn't know enough — was stepped up starting at dawn. The crews for the 75-mm cannon, three mortars and two antiaircraft guns were given priority.

When Changa reported that he wouldn't be coming because he didn't have any food to bring, angry cables were sent to Kigoma and Dar es Salaam. That day, November 10, Che sent two messages, one to Havana and the other to Kigoma and the Cuban Embassy. The first read, "Enemy pressure increasing, attempt to blockade the Lake continues. Urge substantial amounts of Congolese money, foreseeing isolation. Offensive maintained and advancing. Must move rapidly. Preparing to defend the base."

The second said, "If forced to withdraw due to offensive and lose contact with you, don't fail to call us daily at 1230 and 1700 hours until contact is reestablished." [*Congo*, 134.]

Reverberations of the letter

Che received a letter from Masengo on November 12:

"Comrade:

"In accord with our phone conversation of yesterday, I don't see any problems with Comrade Moja [Dreke]'s proposal. That is, his proposal is a good one.[1]

"However, I still insist on presenting my own proposal, which consists of the following:

"First: Make some crews for heavy weapons available to me. I will tell you how many later.

"Second: Lend me 50 FAL rifles, which I will give to men I trust, as follows: 20 rifles for the 20 fighters at Rwandasi who don't have weapons, 10 rifles for the Kibamba register, 20 rifles for the Kavumwe roadblock and 20 rifles for the 20 fighters whom you think it wise to bring down from the base.

"My main purpose is to launch an attack on Kasima, in spite of present difficulties. I am ready to assume that responsibility.

"In the present circumstances, I think that the Cuban comrades should be concerned mainly with the defense of the coastal base and Nganja. I think that you will agree with me on all of the above."

CHE: This letter had reverberations. Leaving aside the arithmetical mistake of asking for 50 rifles in order to distribute 70, it was based on calculations made by the Congolese's ideas of our reserve of FAL rifles which contradicted our statements to Masengo himself. We had had 15 rifles, which we had distributed to the Congolese comrades. At that moment, there were only one or two in reserve. I had distributed them with many doubts, because those weapons had belonged to comrades who had taken on the responsibility of manning heavy weapons and who would be left without any weapons if we lost the heavy ones or if we had to withdraw, leaving them in a safe place. Not believing me, he insisted on the number 50 or 70 and, after saying that he was assuming responsibility for the attack, recommended that we concern ourselves with the defense of the Lake and Nganja. That was a few days after he had named me Chief of Operations of the area with broad powers, which implied that I should handle the defense of the whole front. Lack of confidence remained.

In addition to the letter's discrepancies, there were some other causes of friction: the order to place antipersonnel mines on some access roads against my express request to delay that action until it could be coordinated, so as to avoid accidents to our scouts; and Masengo's refusal to have Ali concentrate his men at Kibamba to defend the southern flank of the base in case of attack.

[1] To defend the base along the north. [*Congo,* 135 and 140.]

A theoretical Chief of Operations

First thing on Thursday, November 11, Che went to the Kibamba base to talk with Masengo.

CHE: I talked with the Chief of Staff once more. I didn't tell him about the Tanzanian Government's semiofficial attitude this time, either. I stressed the need to continue a strategy that would make it possible for us to be independent at the Lake, and said that my post as Chief of Operations was entirely theoretical. There was talk of attacking Kasima, and responsibility for that attack was being taken — an act within the powers of the Chief of Staff (even though I didn't think it was the right time to do that, especially since we didn't have exact knowledge about the enemy's positions because of the very poor quality of the Congolese and Cuban reconnaissance) — but I couldn't allow myself to be relegated to the defense of a single sector. As could be easily understood, the defense should be a single harmonious whole, with a reserve to be sent to the points of greatest danger, due to the speed of events. Lastly, I had recommended several times that weapons and ammunition shouldn't be handed over to phantom groups which did nothing but lose them. I said that most of the reports about large-scale actions at Fizi and other places were outright lies.

Comrade Masengo complained about my attitude toward Kasima, since tension had arisen over the attempt to have the Congolese forces fall back. That was true, for I had ordered Moja to concentrate all of the Cubans at Kisosi, keeping them as a reserve force, and he interpreted that the Congolese should go, too. They refused to obey and, in the struggle, took off with some parts of a mortar, which was left incomplete in the hands of the Cuban operator.

Masengo promised to call Salumu to talk with Moja and that Moja would direct the projected attack, using a simple plan: advance on one of the points, with ambushes at others where reinforcements might be sent or where the enemy might try to flee. He wanted to have as few casualties as possible if there should be a precipitate withdrawal or rout. He also agreed to allow Ali to come and said he wouldn't hand out any more ammunition without a precise idea of how much was really needed.

In the course of the conversation, I gave him Mundandi's letter. Furiously, he said that he himself would go and disarm him the next day, because he knew what the Rwandan comrades were like. I immediately wrote to Mbili, telling him to get things ready, to ask him for the heavy weapons he had and to tell them that I guaranteed they could cross the Lake to Kigoma if they handed in all of their weapons. I thought I could influence Masengo and get him to facilitate their transit, wanting to prevent any useless bloodshed at such a tense time. Nothing happened, because Masengo couldn't go. He promised to send a political commissar, but in the end nobody went to disarm Mundandi. [*Congo*, 135-36.]

An unpleasant conversation

CHE: We also had a talk about Kabila in which Masengo assured me that he would come in the next few days. My reply was categorical: Kabila won't cross the Lake, and he won't do it because he has seen that this is ending, and he doesn't have any interest in doing so in these conditions.

The conversation on this sensitive point was unpleasant, because three comrades were present, but I was straightforward in my opinion of the commander in chief's arrival.

The corrosive action of the people at Fizi continued, as if we were in an electoral period in a country at peace. Two or three more messages came, one of them notifying me that I should attend a meeting on November 15 and send an acknowledgment of receipt. I replied, explaining that I thought the meeting a waste of time and that I couldn't attend, since I had to defend the base at all costs. Further, I said that I considered those things to be an insurrection against the revolutionary power; my government hadn't sent me to take part in that kind of activity. Things reached the extreme that, in one of the letters accusing Masengo of being a murderer, they promised not to do him any harm while he was in Fizi — the members of the army promising the Chief of Staff they wouldn't harm him! That was what things were like. [*Congo*, 136.]

A message also came from Kigoma announcing that Kabila hadn't crossed the Lake because his boat hadn't been repaired. He also sent a note to Kiwe, in which he told him to get ready to accompany him to the Tricontinental Conference, that would be held in Havana in January 1966. "Well, how about that!" Che remarked.

Imposing views

The weapons training classes began again at dawn on Thursday, November 11, as did work on the fortifications. The men returned to Nganja, with Rafael Hernández, the political commissar, leading them. It was learned that Dreke had finally gone to Kisosi with just the two Cubans. That morning, Masengo arrived in order to meet with Che.

CHE: I had another talk with Comrade Masengo. I didn't tell him about the Tanzanian Government's decisions this time, either. Rather, we talked mainly about the attack on Kasima. Once more, I imposed my view to the effect that they should do more reconnaissance before making that decision. I shrank from the attack because I was afraid there would be a rout and morale would plummet. Earlier, I wanted to guarantee that I would have some heavy weapons for sustaining intense fire on the enemy and keeping the enemy from counter-attacking. [*Congo*, 133.]

Reports arrived that night on the tour of Kisosi by Dreke and the others. Planes had strafed them and the Congolese who were there had left them. It was also reported that 13 boats had come menacingly close to the coast, but nothing had happened.

A childish proposal

At around that same time, Che was given more proof that the Congolese leaders didn't have their feet on the ground. This time, it involved the correspondence of Mutchungo, Minister of Public Health. Che cited a letter in which the Minister accused the Cubans of stealing some heavy weapons. Naturally, Che sent him an extremely irate reply, which led the doctor to visit his colleague, demanding an explanation.

CHE: I had to give him a long explanation of what Lambert's attitude had been in all that business. A second [accusation] referred to a farmers' meeting near there, at Jungo. I was informed of the results of the meeting, since I hadn't attended. I hadn't received any announcement of it, nor was there any reason why I should go to those farmers' meetings, which weren't part of my work. The list of petitions became so absurd that it had to have caused a reaction by Comrade Mutchungo. By way of a small sample, point three said,

"Request of Friends:

"Every friendly country should send us 12,000 volunteers. This means revolutionary countries. Tshombe is fighting against us with the help of foreigners."

Supposing they asked 24,000 to 36,000 men from two or three friendly countries — which could be considered a children's game, since this was a meeting of farmers with a minimum level of development who were desperate about the situation — it should have caused some reaction by Comrade Mutchungo. He was Minister of Public Health and a high-ranking representative of the Higher Council of the Revolution.

After showing him how childish the proposal was, I asked if he knew about the corrosive attitude of the comrades from Fizi. He replied that he had heard something, but what he knew was that 300 men were coming from Fizi to reinforce and save Kibamba. In view of those statements, I couldn't continue to discuss similar topics. Touching on the personal, he complained about Masengo's attitude, saying that he had a wife and six children and that they refused to be evacuated, creating a very difficult situation. I spoke with Masengo about that, and it was decided that all of the fighters' wives and children would be evacuated to Kigoma at the first opportunity. [*Congo*, 136-37.]

See if action is possible

The same bustling about continued at the upper base on Friday, November 12, and Che ordered Mbili to go to the roadblock near Lubondja, in Nganja. He sent a message to Dreke, telling him to send for the two Cubans and assign them to the defense of Kisosi.

Masengo left for Kisosi that day to talk things over with Dreke, to see if it would be possible to attack Kasima. He would sleep at the Lake. At midday on Saturday, November 13 he got in contact with Dreke. A scouting party related to the attack found that soldiers were already at Front de Force, ready to advance toward Nganja. In view of that, the most important thing was to defend the base.

Even so, Masengo insisted on attacking Kasima, claiming that he had enough men to do so. When Masengo left, Dreke ordered that Che be told of the results of the talk. However, to avoid more friction, Che sent Salmari to talk with Dreke on Sunday, November 14 to see if the action was possible or not and to tell him to go to Kibamba the next day to meet again with Masengo.

A secret base

CHE: Changa crossed the Lake early on the morning of November 14, this time without incident, bringing plenty of food and a message from Rafael in which he explained that the situation remained the same as regards the attitude of the Tanzanian Government, which was waiting for my reply. It hadn't tried to hurry things or changed its mind. Rafael asked if I thought it correct to begin working to establish a secret base, because of the attitude of the Tanzanian authorities. I immediately replied that yes, it should be done. [*Congo*, 137.]

The *Campaign Diary* kept by Dreke's group states that Che was at the upper base that day and that he went down to the lower base on November 15. One of the two made a mistake regarding the date, but the important thing was what he did, not when he did it.

CHE: That day, even though he didn't know about Tanzania's explicit decision, Masengo sent the following telegram, which illustrates both the general situation and his own state of mind:

"Kabila:
"Military situation very serious. Mundandi front invaded by the enemy. Enemy advancing on Nganja toward base... Enemy infiltrations along many paths toward base. Food shortage. Urgent you send dry beans, rice, salt. Insist immediate shipment weapons and ammunition for 30s and Mausers, submachine guns, mortars, cannon shells, antitank bazookas and mine fuses. Possible enemy offensive encirclement by Mukundi favorable. Our forces risk general annihilation unless immediately supplied. Request energetic intervention directed Tanzanian authorities. We consider Congolese Revolution strangled by negligence of African countries. Consider this last call.
    "Send financial assistance to counter hunger.
    "Masengo" [*Congo*, 137.]

CHE: Except for the optimistic statement about the possibility of an offensive in Mundandi, about which he lacked data, Masengo's telegram summed up the situation. Some of my telegrams sounded almost panicky, partly to make the comrades open their eyes and partly as a result of the situation. In response to a question by our official who was in Kigoma regarding a request of Kabila's to go to Dar es Salaam, I replied, "Absolutely necessary they [the boats] come today. Hungry and surrounded. Kabila can go."
    The S.O.S.s circulated as far as their pathos would take them. The impediment that Changa brought included 40 Congolese who had been studying in the Soviet Union. As a first measure, they asked for 15 days of vacation, complaining, among other things, because they didn't have anywhere to leave their suitcases and there weren't any weapons for them. It would seem funny if it weren't so sad to see the willingness of those young men in whom the revolution had placed its trust.

Masengo placed them under my orders, and the only satisfaction I got out of it was to make the regulations very clear to them, since we could speak in French. Not an atom of revolutionary spirit was to be found in them. I had the chiefs go up to the upper base and stated things very frankly, telling them they would be tested in shooting, and those who passed the test would go straight to the front. They wouldn't be forced to take the test, but if they didn't want to take it they should withdraw immediately, because I didn't want to waste my time (there wasn't any time to waste). Their leader, who was quite reasonable, accepted the conditions, and they went up to the base in the following days to reinforce the defense — or, rather, to take the weapons of some who had fled, because they didn't bring any weapons with them. [*Congo*, 137-38.]

On November 14, Parliament rejected the government formed by Kimba, but the Head of State charged him to form yet another cabinet, to be presented to the legislative body.

Nobody was at the controls

On Monday, November 15, Che was waiting for Dreke, to exchange views on the events of the past few days. Even though the following is undated, it may be assumed that Che was referring to what was going on at that time.

CHE: Mbili sent the latest information. The scouts saw soldiers near the Jungu road, so he sent some comrades to lay mines at the entrance to the road. That mine field endangered our men, because Mbili was scouting along one side of the road, and I had sent out scouts on the other side in the same direction; it was mere luck that one of them didn't go off under our men's feet. Nobody was at the controls, and each bit of the machinery moved under its own steam.

Four roads led from the Nganja-Kañanga area to the Lake, and we didn't know which one or more of them the enemy forces would take. They were even more familiar than we were with the terrain; they had better guides, the farmers from the area who lived among them and supplied them with food. This time, the soldiers had learned some lessons from the anti-guerrilla struggle, and it seems that they treated the farmers well, whereas we paid for the errors of our previous attitude with their present unfaithfulness.

Following his custom of sending me all the groups of men who turned up, Masengo gave me seven "suicides," whose destructive impulses were aimed at sinking a cargo ship that ran between Albertville and Kigoma. I told them that it was relatively easy to do, since the ships didn't go in convoy. We could sink one at any time, but I thought it was the worst possible time to do it now, when our relations with Tanzania were so chilly, for that country might use the action as a pretext for clamping new restrictions on us. However, I had another job for them: to go behind the enemy lines with some Cubans, carry out some actions there and seize weapons; however, they would have to be under strict discipline. They replied that they would think it over, and I never heard from them again.

Changa had some problems in crossing the Lake; there were ever more boats on patrol, and his Congolese crew wasn't willing to confront the dangers of the crossing. An annoying situation arose as a result of the order to evacuate the women and children. There were some rather large ones among them — 20 to 25 years old — who pushed others out of their way. The boat tried to leave two or three times. Situations of this kind occurred night after night, causing friction with our men, who were in charge of the boat's safety, and further discouraging them.

A message from Kabila arrived:

"Masengo, I'm sending your message to the Tanzanians. I'm leaving for Tabora today and will return immediately with weapons and ammunition. I'm sending you all the rest of the Congolese money. The authorities here are plotting with the imperialists to suffocate our struggle.

"There's no money.

"Kabila"

Kabila announced that he was going to Tabora, but he had told us that he was going to Dar es Salaam, which is what he did. He went to argue with the authorities, but at the time of the disaster he was in Dar es Salaam, not Kigoma. [*Congo,* 138-39.]

To support the Cubans' departure

ULISES: When we were back in Havana after having passed on what Che had told us and what we had seen there, Ramiro [Valdés] sent for me, and we talked about our trip. Some cables had just arrived from Dar es Salaam saying that the situation had gotten worse. Ramiro told me that Fidel was up-to-date on everything and that, if the circumstances made it necessary, the Cubans would have to leave the Congo.

At that time, another column of 100 men, under the command of Major Sergio del Valle, was ready to leave for the Congo to reinforce Che, but because of our report and the latest information received, their departure was suspended. We began working on bringing back those who were there.

MANUEL ALVAREZ (MANOLIN): I was sent to Tanzania to see to it that everything that was sent to the Congo and left for Kigoma would arrive without any hitches. That was at the end of October or in early November 1965, but I stayed too long in Dar es Salaam waiting for Kabila, whom I was supposed to take to the Congo. I waited for several days, but he didn't appear.

Then reports came in about the danger Che and the other Cubans were in, and Padilla sent me to Kigoma to help get them out. Colman and Oliva went with me. When we got there, we coordinated everything with Lawton, whom everybody called Changa. Luis M. Mustelier (Positivo), Víctor Mendiola, Avelino Azcuy, Froilán Macías, Andrés Rodríguez D., Rafael Moreno and Alfonso Enseñat Díaz (Guanabo) went with me. Sandrino (Marcelo) and Braulio Rodríguez joined us, too.

On Tuesday, November 16, Che was back at the upper base.

CHE: Our defensive positions at that time were as follows:

Mbili, with a group of Rwandans under his orders, controlled the road that goes from Nganja straight to the Lake, and Azima and the Congolese defended the other that went to the base.

Moja [Dreke] was in charge of the defense of the Lake from Kasima, and Ali, in Kabimba. We had what I considered a reasonable hope for facing the enemy when a note arrived from Comrade Mundandi which went as follows:

"Comrade Tatu [Che]:

"With regard to the situation, which is very serious, I must inform you that I cannot hold the position and ensure the defense. The people have already betrayed us and have given cows to the enemy soldiers. They are working with the enemy, which has better guides and more information than we have about our position. I beg you to understand me. I have decided to fall back. I'm not abandoning the Cuban comrades; it's just that I must carry out my responsibility to the Rwandan people. I can't expose all the forces of the Rwandan comrades to the danger of being wiped out; if I did so, I wouldn't be a good revolutionary commander, and a revolutionary — especially one who is a Marxist — who should analyze the situation and fight only when it serves the long-range objectives. It would be my fault if all the comrades were killed. I have tried to help this revolution, in order to be able to carry out another in our country. If the Congolese

don't fight, I prefer to die on our own soil, that of the Rwandan people. If we die on the way there, that will be all right, too.
   "With revolutionary greetings,
   "Mundandi"

Comrade Mundandi was preparing to leave the struggle once and for all, and this worried me, because his forces were along the flank from which, reasonably, we should expect the enemy attack to come (in the Nganja area). With his desertion, that's where we would be weakest. Just when I had thought that our defense area was ready, a new crack appeared. [*Congo,* 134.]

In view of the situation, Che sent for Ali and the other Cubans.

VIDEAUX: Tatu [Che] sent Tremendo Punto and Amía to get me. It wasn't easy to leave, because the people looked on us Cubans as their security that the Belgians wouldn't come. With the messengers, there were around 12 of us who had to go back. We left in two rowboats. When we got to the base, we saw Dreke; I had over 30 letters from my family.

The following note, dated November 16, which Che included in his account, increased his concerns:

   "Comrade Siki:
   "The following lines are to explain that I now have only 14 Congolese and nine Cubans; it's very difficult to fall back, and our position has no cover at all. There's no withdrawal to hide from the planes. The Congolese have said they want to leave and aren't going to fight. They say I'm holding them here against their will. Ever since the soldiers began to advance, they have wanted to leave. I'm explaining this to you because the situation is hard; pardon the expression, but I think I have lost my balls. I'm having to force men to fight, and I don't think this is logical. I really believe it isn't right to force them. I don't have great experience, but this looks very bad. There isn't any food; there's a crisis with the meat, and there's nothing to give them to eat. In addition, it rains every day; it starts to fall in the morning, and there's no protection. Forgive me for any spelling mistakes.
   "Azima"

CHE: I considered this letter to be very serious, and I ordered Siki to investigate. His opinion was that it was a case of Comrade Azima talking off the top of his head, something he tended to do. Because of my doubts, I asked Kisua, Ali's second-in-command, to go up (he and his men had already arrived from Kibamba), to take charge of the defense if he considered Azima to be very weak. [*Congo,* 139.]

VIDEAUX: While I was reading the letters, Che ordered me to come see him. Since I assumed he was going to send me on a mission and thought I shouldn't travel with the letters on me, I burned them.

CHE: Tremendo Punto arrived at the same time as Ali, with whom he had traveled, and he gave me a letter in which he explained that the tense situation in Kabimba was due to Ali's character and recounted some encounters he'd had. He said that he had done everything possible to create unity, that his relations with the other Cubans were friendly, but that Ali and the major didn't agree. After that, he reiterated those statements, adding anecdotes. Ali reacted violently to Tremendo Punto's lack of discretion. He said that Tremendo Punto had insisted on going to the Lake during the day, which Ali didn't approve of. A plane had appeared on the horizon just after he had left the shore. In a flash, Comrade Tremendo Punto had thrown himself into the water, so hard that he tipped the canoe over. But the most serious thing was that Ali didn't know how to swim and nearly drowned. His resentment against Tremendo Punto, expressed in the frequent pauses in the narration caused by his stuttering, plus his indignation, was very funny in those tragic moments. [*Congo,* 139.]

The enemy: signs of advance

CHE: Mbili sent me the latest information explaining the measures he had taken at the Jungo railway junction and announcing that there were signs of the enemy's advance, and neither the Congolese nor the Rwandans were in their positions. There were eight Cubans in each of the two wings in which the defense was divided, and they couldn't count on many defenders. Majors Calixte and Husani stayed in the rear guard in spite of being urged to accompany their men. Mbili didn't trust anybody except the Cubans, and not even all of them, for defending that point. They figured that there were around 40 enemy soldiers facing them and thought that enemy reinforcements had arrived.

That was the situation on November 16, when several telegrams were sent. One of them, signed by me, read as follows:

"Rafael, we urgently need SKS bullets and shells for the 75-mm gun and for the Chinese bazooka. If possible, send 200 rifles with ammunition. The first is extremely important; the men at Kigoma are blockaded. If you can't give me these things, say so frankly. Insist on clear speaking. Changa can't leave here. There are enemy ships. We need things to move quickly."

Masengo sent this message:

"Impossible carry out offensive. Therefore, plan for evading enemy encirclement impossible. Insist on seriousness of situation. Urgently request information possibility supplies weapons and ammunition.

"Masengo"

The situation was steadily becoming more complicated, and nothing favorable could be observed anywhere. We simply had to wait to see what the enemy's forces were and how determined it was to carry things through to the end. [*Congo*, 139-40.]

On a new tour of inspection that Siki made of Mbili's and Azima's positions, he reported on Wednesday, November 17 that the places chosen for turning back the enemy attack were good and facilitated a withdrawal in stages. It should be kept in mind that, because of the Congolese's lack of willingness to fight, it was impossible to maintain a defense to the death. However, he reported that the Rwandans were saying that they would fight side by side with Mbili, but only if combined with the Congolese.

RAMON: Siki told me what Che thought about my note. You know I don't know how to express myself very well, but you know me, because we were together in the [Cuban] war, and you know I'm not a coward. That's why I sent a note to Che swearing I would defend that place as if it were a little bit of Cuba.

MARGOLLES: The catchcry was that we had to defend it as if it were a little bit of Cuba. The motivation for dying 10,000 kilometers from Cuba was saying you were defending a little bit of Cuba.

Run like hell

CHE: Tremendo Punto arrived that afternoon with a comrade whose name, unfortunately, I don't remember and didn't write down. He seemed intelligent and wanted to do something, only he didn't have any experience. We talked about many things, but the main thing was this statement of mine: we're faced with a situation of utter collapse. We can take one of two positions: undertake a flexible defense, giving up territory bit by bit, withdrawing from one point to another, or we can make a rigid defense, fighting to the limit of our forces. What we can't do is stand around with our arms crossed waiting for the soldiers to advance to a new place and let them drive us out without putting up a fight; that would cause more men to desert. That tactic (or lack of tactics) would lead us to lose everything and leave us utterly disorganized. Tremendo Punto's friend asked to speak and said that, if there were two possibilities, he would immediately choose the rigid defense. The Cubans who were with me looked as if they would like to kill or even eat him alive; I was embarrassed. The place and the circumstances suggested a rigid defense, but a rigid defense with whom? The Congolese and the Rwandans had left. Could I demand of the Cubans that they die in their trenches to defend that little bit of nothing? And, more important, if I did, would it be productive? In fact, I had set forth the possibility of a rigid defense as an educational alternative; the only thing that could be done was to draw a line. [*Congo*, 142.]

At last, the Rwandans left

The Congolese and Rwandans' willingness to fight, which Siki had reported on the day before, immediately evaporated, according to two notes that Mbili sent Che on Thursday, November 18, when Che was at the Lake base. He had arrived there that morning to speak with Masengo. The first note reached him at 0900 hours, and the second, two hours later.

"Tatu [Che]:
"The Congolese who stayed have refused to dig trenches, and their chief says he wants to attack the soldiers — which, he says, is better than digging trenches. I sent Charles to talk with him, explaining that it was better to dig trenches. Charles and the chief of the Congolese had a big argument and came to blows, and the chief grabbed a rifle to kill Charles. We took it away from him. The chief accused Charles of being on the Cubans' side; he said that the Cubans were bad, that Charles was the same and that, when the soldiers came, they would withdraw and we would shoot ourselves. This was because one of the chiefs who is here was the one who told me in the ambush[1] that we Cubans were bad; I think that he has kept on saying that here. The Congolese have an attitude of outright hostility, manifested in doing nothing."

"Important, 1115 hours.
"Tatu [Che]: All of the Rwandans have left. I was told at 1000 hours. I sent Akika out to see and, sure enough, they had gone. Yesterday, we agreed on a plan, and today, without saying anything to me, they left. I think they're headed back to their country, as they had said they would do some days ago.
    "When the news arrived, Mundandi's aide was with me, and I told him about it. He was astounded. He left and hasn't come back.

"From what I can see, they took their weapons and didn't say anything to me. Yesterday, they had said they would reinforce me with 10 men and a mounted machine gun, since the Congos had gone and nobody had come. I sent somebody to ask for Calixte, but nobody has seen him and nobody knows where he is.

"They may have betrayed us. I propose that we go a little farther back, as we had planned; split into two groups; take up new positions; and mine the road. We urgently need reinforcements. I'm taking precautionary measures in case they have betrayed us. Tell the comrade who brings your reply to come by the new road. Homeland or death.

"Note: ...The Congos here already know about it and are leaving."
[1] During the days of the Katenga ambushes, that chief had used the same arguments to incite the men to rebel. [The note is Che's.] *[Congo, 141 and 148.]*

They requested weapons

DREKE: At that moment, when the Rwandans and some of the Congolese abandoned us, all of the Cubans who had asked to go back to Cuba requested weapons, which were given to them. That was proof that they weren't cowards. Rather, it was the course of events and the bad behavior of most of the Congolese chiefs that had led them to become disillusioned about the struggle.

In view of that situation, Che ordered Dreke, Ali, Ishirine and Nanne to go to Ñyungu, a little farther south, to study the terrain. He was considering a possible move to there since the enemy had taken Kasima, aggravating the situation. Parachutes were being dropped, apparently with food, weapons and ammunition. This worried Che, and he said that they should leave for Ñyungu by boat that night.

Shortly before they were to leave, it was learned that the enemy was advancing from Nganja toward Ñyungu. It was decided to suspend their departure, for they might become isolated. To reinforce the defense, Che ordered the young men who had come from the Soviet Union to occupy the front trenches, but they demanded that everybody go, which caused an angry rebuke by Che: "Either go to the front trench or leave." He said that quite a few were willing to go to the front line.

Later, Che met with Masengo in the presence of Mojungo and Kent (of Kenya) and inducted Charles Bemba and some others in the Liberation Army.

CHE: I deliberated about the possibilities of struggle, ruling out rigid defense, because, really, there were very few people — just our men — and I couldn't rely only on that. I also ruled out a withdrawal toward Fizi, because of the conditions prevailing there. I was left with two possible refuges: Uvira — we would have to go along the Lake, a dangerous route, on foot, crossing the enemy lines and going near Fizi in a very long and hard march, to get there — and the south, where there were some towns, such as Bondo, that offered possibilities for reorganizing the defense. It was decided that Ali and Moja [Dreke] make a quick, one-day reconnaissance of Bondo; then I would have to decide. Ali attributed it to a new trick of Tremendo Punto's, since, according to him, it was a bad position. I had a small argument with Ali, who muttered that he'd had enough of going up and down hills without any cooperation from those people; I replied cuttingly that we would organize the evacuation from Bondo and that he could go with the group that was leaving the struggle; he immediately rejoined that he would stay with me to the end — but, so as not to lose the argument, added, "chasing around hills for 20 years." [*Congo*, 142.]

Masengo proposes ending the struggle

CHE: I felt the time had come to tell Comrade Masengo of Tanzania's decision, as I didn't think it correct to keep it a secret any longer. The attitude of the Tanzanian Government wasn't honest. Even though it may be said that it had treated us correctly, there was a revolutionary procedure to be upheld, which it didn't follow. I told Masengo that I had received a cable some days earlier which informed me of the Tanzanian decision, but because of the situation I had tried not to make it public, not even among the Cubans. At that time, I was telling only him about it, so he could come to his own conclusions.

He must have immediately discussed it with his comrades, because Tremendo Punto came to see me that night, telling me that Masengo wanted to talk with me to propose ending the struggle. Since I had talked to him about evacuating to another place and about a series of tasks we had to carry out, he didn't feel happy about telling me this. However, all the commanding comrades were agreed on ending the struggle for now.

I responded that that was a very serious decision; there were men at Fizi and Mukundi, on that front, who were still organized; moreover, there were those at Uvira, and Mulele's front. As for our leaving, the enemy troops would be free to attack those groups. Our flight would contribute to their dispersion; we knew that they weren't strong enough to put up much resistance. I asked him to give me a letter from Masengo stating that decision. Tremendo Punto looked shocked and somewhat hurt, but I insisted. I told him that what we call history is composed of many fragmentary data and that can be twisted. In short, I wanted to have the letter so things could be clarified if our behavior were ever misinterpreted. To buttress my arguments, I reminded him of the latest slanders used against us. He replied that it was a harsh demand and that he didn't know if Masengo would accept it. It was clear to me that if Masengo didn't agree to give me that letter, it would prove he felt he was doing something wrong and we could never be blamed for the withdrawal, and I told him so. [*Congo*, 142-43.]

The enemy breaks through the defenses

CHE: Our conversation was cut short, because Tremendo Punto went to confer with his comrades. At that point, a telephone call came from the upper base; the soldiers had advanced, and Azima had withdrawn without fighting. There were many of them, in three columns. Azima's men were attacked during their withdrawal but didn't suffer any casualties. However, the sentry seemed to have taken refuge from the air attack that had preceded the advance and hadn't seen the soldiers coming. They had little hope that he had managed to get away. His name was Suleimán. The other lookout, a Congolese who was with him, hadn't appeared, either. [*Congo*, 143.]

RAMON: The Congolese had some positions in front of ours. When I saw the mercenaries, I sent a messenger to warn them, but he delayed. We saw that the enemy was getting close, and Tom, the political commissar, went to the forward positions, but nobody was there.

Just imagine, there were hundreds of soldiers deployed against us and advancing, and there were only six of us Cubans! We all agreed we had to fall back.

CHE: I immediately went to inform Masengo about this and proposed to organize an immediate withdrawal, which was accepted. Tremendo Punto spoke out, saying that it had been discussed and that we should withdraw once and for all. The Chief of the Military Police was there and heard the conversation. Within five minutes, the telephone operators had disappeared, all the military police had fled and the base was in chaos.

I proposed to Masengo that he go ahead with his men and that I organize the withdrawal from all points held by the Cubans. This was done, and I gave orders to store all of the equipment, including the transmitter, in the hiding places that had already been prepared. They left that same night. [*Congo*, 143.]

COLMAN: I had close relations with the Congolese, and one of the strongest pretexts they gave me for abandoning the armed struggle was Mobutu's coup. The Congolese guerrillas, who were already demoralized, simply interpreted the end of Tshombe's power as the end of the conflict. For most of them, as I see it, the struggle wasn't against a policy or system but against an individual — in this case, Tshombe — not only because he had assassinated Lumumba but also because of tribal differences, his use of mercenaries and other things.

The withdrawal begins

The following comment about what Che told Masengo and what happened on November 18 appears on page 67 of the *Campaign Diary* kept by Dreke's group:

Tatu [Che] told Moja that he would send the sick men out first — a group of Cuban comrades and a group of "Congos" — toward Kigoma, and that they would be the last ones out. He also said he had asked Masengo for a letter saying that they had been the ones to decide to give up and also that he — Masengo — had decided to dissolve the front for the time being.

Around 15 minutes later, Comrade Siki called... reporting that the enemy had approached our positions on the road from Ganya [Nganja] to the base, where six Cubans were falling back under heavy fire; Azima was leading them.

Mbili had withdrawn from his position, which was bombed. There wasn't any protection from the planes and as everything seemed to indicate [that] the enemy would continue advancing toward the base the next morning, Che decided to talk with Masengo. At the same time, he sent for Mafu, and [they told him] that we would be falling back to the south, toward Ñyungu, before daylight, since we had to cross the road from Ganya and keep the soldiers from cutting off our retreat.

When Che finished talking with Masengo, it was discovered that all the "Congos" at the garrison had gone. Che ordered Moja to stay with Mafu's group and said that the comrades who were at the base would head the same way. Siki would go down with the rest of the men from the base, toward Ñyungu. He would leave after Moja and would wait until Azima had burned the houses at the base, as Siki had ordered. Since communication was broken with Mafu, Alau was sent to warn him. Ali would leave heading a group that included the doctors and the men who were sick. Wasiri, who was sick, and Yenye were taken to Celi by boat.

At the base, Pombo was in charge of burying the radio plant

(transmitter and receiver), some books, boxes of cigars and civilian clothes, and some other things. Azima was to burn everything else.

Azima and Mbili were ordered to fall back in an organized way.

Rebocate and his platoon had been sent to the road from Ganya to Ñyungu, where a roadblock was to be set up to hold back the soldiers' advance. At the same time, it would serve to cover our withdrawal for the base, for that part of the road was mined. [*Campaign Diary*, 67-68.]

VIDEAUX: Che had sent me, with the group of men who had come from Bulgaria, to reinforce Mbili, who was on the outer ring of defenses. Later, we were ordered to fall back to the inner ring.

Before dawn on Friday, November 19, Siki ordered some of the men who were at the upper base to begin evacuating toward Kibamba. Those who remained were to burn the huts and hide the heavy weapons and ammunition, a task which delayed them until 0500 hours, when they left the site for the last time. According to Che, communication was established with Kigoma from the upper base, but the *Campaign Diary* noted the following:

It was impossible to communicate with Kigoma at 0900 hours. Communication was established at 1500 hours but was interrupted. Moreover, Kigoma radio reported ("Everything has been purchased; nobody has arrived"), from which Che thought that something had happened to Changa (the comrade in charge of the boat) on the Lake. He had left for Kigoma the day before, half an hour before the order to fall back was given. Moja suggested that a comrade be sent to the other side to see if anything had happened and take whatever measures were needed, since there wasn't any communication at that time.

Changa... was ferrying women and children on that trip.

Everybody was confident, naturally, that, if Changa heard the news, he would come back as quickly as he could.

All the other Cubans from all of the positions who were falling back toward Ñyungu came together on the way.

The situation collapses

CHE: In the meantime, a series of telegrams had been read over the radio which described the situation on that day, November 18. [The number of the day is illegible in the photocopy of the original, but I deduce it was November 18 because of the mention of Changa's departure, which appears in the *Campaign Diary*. — W.G.]

"Rafael:

"The situation is collapsing, and entire units and farmers are going over to the enemy. None of the Congolese troops can be relied on. Starting today, the main radio's broadcasts may be interrupted. We will maintain communication with Kigoma using the auxiliary radio. Changa here because of mechanical difficulties. Crew and boat in good condition."

However, at last Changa had managed to make the crossing with a tremendous load of women and children, which caused a dispute with the Commissioner of Kigoma, for he said that we were bringing nothing but vagrants and parasites and that we should take them back where they had come from — which, of course, we didn't do.

Rafael sent a telegram that same day in which he said the following:

"Tatu [Che]:

"In second talk with Kawawa I presented the situation energetically and demanded delivery materials. He promised to solve this before leaving for Korea. On the road to Kigoma, I saw a truck with very few things for you. Talked with Cambona yesterday; he promised to get moving and to give me reply today on talk with the President. Spoke directly and definitively making them responsible for consequences. Talked with Soviets and Chinese informing them of evasive situation re delivery of material they have sent. Propose speak with Ambassadors UAR, Ghana and Mali telling them Accra resolution responsible for Tanzanian refusal to deliver materials to nationalists fighting white mercenaries, that responsibility for annihilation will fall on African leaders and Tanzanian Government. In coordination with me, Kabila is meeting with government figures and making same statements; also with Chinese and Soviets, ditto."

I sent this reply:

"Rafael:

"Want to know results of Cuba's latest report on Commission to discuss issues with Tanzanian Government. Re matters to discuss with Ghana, Mali, UAR Governments, handle this in question form. What the resolution really says and if it was to leave us in our present condition. I think your efforts will be too late. That will take around a month, and we can't hold out that long. Planning to evacuate this place and get most of the Cubans evacuated as second stage. Small group will remain as symbol of Cuba's prestige. Inform Cuba." [*Congo*, 143-44.]

Here is more proof of Che's determination not to give up his dream of creating a Congolese Liberation Army that would serve as an inspiration and starting point for the creation of others in Africa. Fernández Mell (Siki) told me that, in order to make that dream a reality, Che considered going to look for Mulele.

They wouldn't leave him alone

CHE: I intended to send home the men who were sick, the weak and the weak-kneed ones and remain with a small group to continue the struggle. Therefore, I held a small tea at which the comrade combatants could discuss the idea. The results were discouraging, as hardly anybody wanted to keep on struggling. [*Congo*, 144.]

DREKE: After Che talked with me, he talked with several other comrades. Most of them replied that they thought the best thing to do would be to return to Cuba, because if nobody wanted to fight alongside those of us who had come to help them, why should we fight? But almost all of the men in that majority also said that if Che stayed there, they wouldn't leave him alone.

In 1965, most of our revolutionary people weren't very clear yet about the real meaning of internationalism — even though hundreds of Cubans had demonstrated their internationalism in the Spanish Civil War between 1936 and 1939. National boundaries had been erased from Che's mind a long time before.

It was clear to Che that this cause was worth dying for. Those who didn't think that way erroneously compared the Congo with Cuba and the other Latin American countries.

Years later, however, those comrades and hundreds of thousands other Cubans fought in Africa to help various sister peoples. In the specific case of the men who went with Che to the Congo, most of them had a low educational level and averaged a little under 20 years old.

Saving what they could, the rest going up in smoke

CHE: One of the problems that was raised concerning the evacuation was that Mafu had sent two of his men scouting at Kasima, and they hadn't returned. It was decided that another comrade should go out to look for them, and all should come back as quickly as possible. They were to hide the heavy weapons that we couldn't carry. Some comrades, such as Mbili and his group, would have to make a very long march if we wanted to leave the lower base early in the morning. In line with the characteristics of the enemy attacks, I calculated that we would have a day's rest before trying other maneuvers. That would allow us to leave relatively easily, but we should take measures to avoid contact and save most of the things.

Our three nurses, together with Njenje, who was in charge of the base, left by boat for a tiny town called Mukungo, where I was planning to organize the resistance. They took with them some of the heavy weapons from Azi's team. The Congolese were heading for the Fizi area. At first, I intended to head them off, but on thinking it over, I ordered that anybody who wanted to leave should be allowed to do so because at the time of the evacuation — if we had to evacuate — we wouldn't be able to take everybody with us.

Early in the morning [on Saturday, November 20], I burned the house that had been my home for nearly seven months. There were a lot of papers, many documents which could be forgotten, and it was better to wipe them out once and for all. Soon afterwards, after the sun was up, the powder magazines began to burn. Neither Masengo nor I had ordered this; to the contrary, we had tried to convince the Congolese of the importance of moving the material at least into the nearby woods, if not to the new base. None of that was done, and somebody tossed a match; thus, we lost a lot of weapons and ammunition. From the first hill on the way to Jungo — while waiting for the stragglers to catch up — I watched the burning and exploding stores going up in smoke. There were a lot of these stragglers, and they came with what seemed to be centuries of accumulated exhaustion and an alarming lack of vitality. They dropped parts of the heavy weapons, seeking to lighten their loads, not caring what the weapon might mean in a battle. There were practically no Congolese left in the groups, and the Cubans carried everything. I insisted on the need to take care of those weapons, which would be of vital importance to us if we had to withstand a last attack, and the men staggered about dragging their feet and stopping frequently, carrying a cannon and a machine gun, having left two others along the way. [*Congo*, 144-5.]

Communications with Kigoma fail

RUMBAUT: When the order to return to Cuba came, we went down at around 0100 hours. The soles of my boots were worn smooth, and I kept slipping and falling on my butt. Florentino wanted to help me, but he was just as weighed down as I was, and I told him, "Go on down and leave me." At around 1000 hours, a comrade came and told me that Che had said to hurry.

CHE: I was waiting for the communications team. We were supposed to try to make contact at 0600 hours, and I saw Tuma, the head of the team, coming down the opposite hill from the upper base toward the Lake. It was enough to drive you to despair: the comrades took three hours to get down a hill that should have taken them 10 minutes. Then they had to rest before going on. I ordered them to leave everything that was superfluous and try to walk faster. Among the superfluous things they left, the telegraph operator forgot the key, and we had to send somebody back to look for it. [*Congo*, 145.]

FLORENTINO: After I came back with the key, Che asked when we would be able to communicate and was told we would be ready at 1000 hours. That's when we set up the equipment.

CHE: I talked seriously with the operators, making them see how important they were for communication and urging them to make a special effort. We tried to make our customary 1000 hours broadcast and failed. Then we went on at the slow pace that the three comrades imposed; totally unused to walking, their spirits were all that sustained them. [*Congo*, 145.]

RUMBAUT: After failing to communicate, we went on walking, which was really terrible for us. At a little after 1400 hours, we stopped to rest and eat something. Che looked at his watch and said we should keep on walking. We asked if we could wait another hour to see if Kigoma would reply, and he agreed.

DREKE: Since we couldn't establish communication with Changa, it was decided to send a message through the Lake, so they asked for two volunteers. One of them was Uta.

MARGOLLES: I was supposed to paddle, and the other Cuban — whose name I've forgotten — and I were to make the crossing in a little canoe in which you had to kneel to paddle. I asked for authorization to return whether or not we made contact with Changa, and it was given. Since communications were established, we didn't have to make the crossing, as they authorized Changa to leave.

The best thing is to get out as soon as possible

CHE: We hadn't made much progress; a normal hiker could cover the distance between Kibamba, where our base was, and Jungo in three or four hours. At 1500 hours, when we should have our second contact with Kigoma, we were still relatively far from the gathering point.

We managed to send the following message:

"Changa:

"We lost the base and are using the emergency equipment. Urgent you reply if you can come tonight."

Then, a second message:

"Changa:

"The enemy isn't at the shore yet. Our position is Jungo, around 10 kilometers south of Kibamba. Masengo decided to leave the struggle, and the best thing for us is to get out as soon as possible…"

We got to Jungo in time to sleep. Everything was in disorder; no food had been prepared. We had a roll call, and four men were missing: the lookout who had been lost when the soldiers advanced, the two who had gone to Kasima scouting and a fourth who had come in one of the groups from the upper base and had inexplicably disappeared without anybody knowing anything about it.

A comrade had been sent back looking for the Kasima men, but he had returned without finding them. Not wanting to be left behind, he had made a superficial look and then returned. A calculation of the hours spent in that task showed this, but I didn't say anything to him, because it wouldn't have done any good. I organized a group under Rebocate's command to take the path that came from Nganja through the mountains and thus control the two points where the soldiers might appear: the heights and the Lake. While the men were heading there, we heard an explosion on the top of the hill. Since the terrain was mined, we thought it was the guards advancing. We didn't have time to organize a good defense. We took some heights, structuring a reduced defense, and went on walking toward Sele, a town very near Jungo. [*Congo,* 145-46.]

The enemy didn't enter the base

FLORENTINO: The next day, at 0700 hours, when we were trying to communicate, we heard an explosion far off. We all got ready for action, and Che sent out scouts to investigate. He told me, "If we have to run, you run with me." I stayed with him. The scouts came back in around an hour and reported that it had been some elephants that had stepped on a mine. We started on our way again and didn't communicate at 1100 hours. However, we did at 1500 hours. Once again, we resumed walking until we got to the place where Changa's boats were supposed to pick us up.

VIDEAUX: Some other comrades and I came to the conclusion that the mercenaries didn't want to face Cubans — not because they were afraid they would be defeated, but because they knew there were bound to be a lot of casualties. They knew we were ready to fight to the end.

CHE: The attempts to communicate at 0600 and 1000 hours on November 20 were also unsuccessful. The telegraph operators walked so slowly that we didn't reach Sele until midday, when the distance we had covered shouldn't have taken more than an hour. Most of the men were there, and we had something to ease our hunger. Banhir, the man who had been left behind on the way, showed up that the evening. He had fallen and sprained his ankle. He had asked a comrade to get somebody to take his knapsack and waited there. The other man either didn't do as he'd been asked or got the message wrong. In the morning, the man was still there waiting where he'd had the accident, entirely alone. He stayed at the base until 0900 hours on November 20, when he left, thinking he had already lost contact with us. The soldiers hadn't entered the base; all the paths were empty and all the houses abandoned.

At 1430 hours, we established communication with Kigoma; our message said, "Changa: Fewer than 200 men to evacuate. Each day it will be more difficult. We're at Sele, 10 to 15 kilometers south of Kibamba."

And the long-awaited message arrived: "Tatu [Che]: Crossing tonight. The Commissioner didn't let us leave yesterday."

Everybody was euphoric. I talked with Masengo, proposing that we leave from that same point at night. Since there were a good number of Congolese, a Staff meeting was held in which it was resolved that Jean Paulis and his men would stay in the Congo and that the various chiefs and we would be evacuated. The Congolese unit would stay there. I didn't tell them that we intended to withdraw; rather, using various pretexts, I sent them to the nearby town. One of the small boats we still had for going between various points on the Lake arrived and took a large number of the Congolese, but those who were in our unit sensed something and wanted to stay. I ordered that a selection be made of those who had best conducted themselves so far, so they would be taken along with the Cubans; Masengo authorized me to do as I liked. [*Congo*, 146.]

DREKE: We received information that the enemy had made an air landing in the area we had to go through. Che ordered scouts out to see if it were true. Roberto Hernández and Luis Calzada went with several Congolese.

We told them several places where they might find us, but we didn't see them again. Trying to avoid running into the enemy, the scouts left the path, went into the jungle and became lost.

The conditions didn't exist

CHE: The situation was decisive. Two of the men I had sent on a mission would be abandoned for carrying it out correctly and exhaustively if they didn't come back within a few hours. As soon as we had gone, the weight of all the slanders and misrepresentations, both inside and outside the Congo, would fall on us. My troop was a heterogeneous conglomerate. I had found from my investigations that I had 20 men who would follow me, although reluctantly. And then, what would I do? All of the chiefs were withdrawing, and the farmers exhibited ever increasing hostility toward us. But the idea of pulling out completely — leaving defenseless farmers and armed but helpless (because of their limited ability to fight) men behind, defeated and feeling that they had been betrayed — hurt me deeply.

I didn't consider staying in the Congo — for one or the five years with which I had threatened my men — to be a sacrifice. It was part of an idea of struggle that was totally clear in my head. I could reasonably count on having six, seven or eight men accompany me without hesitation; the rest would do so out of a sense of duty — some out of a personal duty toward me and others out of a moral duty to the Revolution — and I would sacrifice men who couldn't fight with enthusiasm. Not long ago, right there, I had felt this. I broke into a conversation in which the men were asking me jokingly about some of the Congolese leaders; my reply was violent. I told them they should ask themselves first what our attitude had been, if we could say truthfully that it had been the most correct, for I didn't think it had been. There was an embarrassing, hostile silence.

In fact, the idea of remaining there stayed with me until the end of the night, and it may be that I never made a decision but was simply one more fugitive. [*Congo*, 146-47.]

Dreke said that Che was so annoyed that they preferred not to reply. They decided to do it later, but it wasn't possible because after the withdrawal from the Congo they never saw him again.

FIDEL: He followed the approach of teaching Zairians [Congolese] how to fight... The idea was not to fight the war in place of the Zairians but rather to help them, to teach them how to fight.

But that movement was just beginning. It didn't have sufficient strength or unity. In the end the revolutionary leaders of the former Belgian colony decided to halt the struggle, and our personnel were withdrawn. That decision was quite correct. It had become clear that conditions did not exist at the time for developing the struggle.[27]

The November 20 entry in the *Campaign Diary* kept by Dreke's group contained the following:

---

[27] Gianni Miná, *An Encounter with Fidel*, 223-4.

A group of Cubans slept at Ñyunga [Che spelled it Jungo]. Early in the morning, they left for Celi [Che spelled it Sele], their departure point, where the sick and others had previously been sent. Ali was in charge of them. There was no communication with Kigoma at 0900 hours. Che, Mbili, Almari, Nanne, Danhisi and Tamuine sat on the shore of the Lake talking about the comrades who were lost.

MANOLIN: Lawton said that if they didn't let us leave, we would leave anyway, using our weapons if necessary. If they tried to stop us during the crossing, we would shoot our way through, as he had done a few days earlier.

We didn't have any problems leaving, but we took up combat positions with the rifles and bazookas while crossing the Lake. Lawton kept saying that we couldn't abandon Che and his men, that the enemy would have to kill us all to keep us from taking them out of the Congo.

Waiting for Changa

The *Campaign Diary* continued as follows:

Since we didn't manage to establish communication, we kept on going toward Celi. This group arrived at 1200 hours. Comrade Masengo was already there. We organized the defense where we were and were told to wait to see if communication with Kigoma could be established. A message came in saying that the equipment had something wrong with it but that they had received the previous day's message that they should come to pick us up at Ñyungo. However, the Commissioner of Kigoma hadn't given them permission to leave. After that, we knew that Comrade Changa (boat) would come to pick us up. The men started taking the things they most needed out of their knapsacks, which they would have to leave behind. Comrade Che also ordered that a big gun be mounted in one of the boats and that a 12.7-mm antiaircraft gun be mounted in the other.

Somebody was sent out to look for Comrades Yenye, Wasiri and Amia, who were somewhere nearby, on the same shore of the Lake. Tiza and a group of Cuban comrades were sent to the Celi beach, which was some distance away from the Ñyungu beach, to wait for Changa (boat) in case he wasn't familiar with the area and got lost, to show him where we were. Meanwhile, the Congolese with the best conduct were selected, to be taken out with us. The various chiefs of the groups made the selection, choosing a total of eight Congolese, plus the members of Masengo's group. [*Campaign Diary*, 68-69.]

Che's account of what happened at around dawn on Sunday, November 21, 1965, is as follows:

The last hours in the Congo

CHE: I felt bad about what the Congolese comrades might think about our evacuation. Our withdrawal was simply flight, and worse, we were accomplices in an act of deceit in which some of the men were left behind. But who was I now? It seemed to me that after my farewell letter to Fidel, the comrades had begun to look on me as someone of other latitudes, as something apart from Cuba's specific problems, and I wasn't motivated to demand the final sacrifice of having all of us remain. Thus, I spent the last hours alone and perplexed. Finally, at 0200 hours, the boats with the Cuban crews arrived... There were too many of us for the boats, and it was getting late. I said that we had to leave by 0300 hours at the latest; it would be light by 0530 hours, and we would be in the middle of the Lake. [*Congo*, 147.]

Was Che being too harsh on himself, calling their departure a flight? It is true that some of them had to leave first, and the enemy might attack the camp and kill those who were still there, since, when the Cubans and the best Congolese combatants had left, the others had no defense. But Che forgot several things: first, no Cubans were included in the initial evacuation; second, the enemy wasn't very close by; third, not all of them could fit in the boats; and, fourth, the evacuation continued on November 22, as reported in the *Campaign Diary*.

His question "Who was I?" once again brought out his extreme lack of pretentiousness. Che's total dedication to the Cuban Revolution gave him a place among the great figures in our history. Because of his merits, Cuba cherished him as a son. He had time to learn of the impact of his farewell letter on the Cuban people. Che never drew away from Cuba's specific problems, and he never stopped being exemplary, admired and much loved, as Cuban as the most Cuban of us all. I have spoken with many of those who were with him at that unpleasant and dangerous time, and all of them thought that, if anybody should get out of there alive, it should be Che.

A dangerous and bitter return

CHE: The evacuation was organized. The sick got in, then all of Masengo's Staff — around 40 people he had chosen — and all the Cubans. Then began a painful, mournful spectacle without glory. Men begging to be taken along had to be turned back. There wasn't any greatness about that withdrawal, not a gesture of rebelliousness.

The machine guns were ready, and I had men ready to repel any attack they might want to launch against us from the shore, but none of that occurred — only laments while the chief of the fugitives swore as the mooring lines were loosed. [*Congo*, 147.]

On Sunday, November 21, the *Campaign Diary* included the following:

We heard some speedboat motors at 0100 hours and thought they were enemy boats, so we didn't signal. They went toward Ñyungu and came back at 0200 hours, so we knew it was Comrade Changa (boat). Comrade Tiza and the other comrades who were there waiting returned with him. The order of getting into the boats was established, though the Congolese pushed and shoved, wanting to get in every which way. This delayed the departure. Masengo's group, with his Chief of Staff, were the first to board, and, when the pushing and shoving started, Che had to say that if everybody wasn't on board by 0300 hours, the boats wouldn't leave.

We left Celi for Kigoma at 0300 hours. Before that, the machine guns and a big gun had been mounted in the boats, as follows: an antiaircraft gun in the prow of the first boat, in which Che, Siki and Tembo traveled, and another antiaircraft gun in the prow and a 75-mm gun in the stern of the second boat. We could hear and see an enemy boat far away, but it didn't change course.

CHE: I would like to put down the names of those comrades whom I always felt I could rely upon, because of their personal qualities, their faith in the revolution and their determination to do their duty, no matter what. Some of them weakened at the end, but let's forget about those final moments, since the weakening was of their faith, not their determination to make whatever sacrifices might be required. I am sure that there were more comrades of the same quality, but I wasn't in close touch with them and so can't bear witness to that. This is an incomplete, personal list that is greatly influenced by subjective factors. I hope that those who aren't on it will forgive me and think that they are as good: Moja, Mbili, Pombo, Azi, Mafu, Tunaini, Ishirini, Tiza, Alau, Aziri, Agane, Hukumu, Ami, Amia, Singida, Alaziri, Semori, Anene, Angalla, Bodalo, the doctors Kumi, Fizi, Morogoro and Kasulo, and the ineffable Admiral Changa, lord and master of the Lake. Siki and Tembo deserve special mention; I disagreed frequently — sometimes violently — with them in my assessment of the situation, but they always gave me their complete devotion. And a final mention for Ali, a courageous soldier and bad politician. [*Congo*, 147-48.]

Che continued:

CHE: We crossed the Lake without any problems, although the boats went slowly. We reached Kigoma in daylight, the cargo boat that went between Albertville and Kigoma arriving at the same time.

It seemed as if a fastening had broken, and the exaltation of the Cubans and Congolese spilled out of the tiny boats like boiling liquid, wounding but not contaminating me. During those last hours in the Congo, I had felt alone, more alone than ever — more so than in Cuba or in any other place I had been in my extensive wanderings. I might say, "Never before have I felt as alone as I feel today." [*Congo*, 148.]

The *Campaign Diary* describes the next stage of the withdrawal:

At 0700 hours, near the Kigoma shore, Che ordered the two vessels to be brought to a halt near each other and addressed all the comrades.

Che's words
"Comrades:
"Because of reasons which you know, the time has come for us to part. I won't land with you, for we must avoid any kind of provocation. This struggle that we have waged has been a great experience. In spite of all the difficulties we've had, I hope that if some day Fidel proposes another mission of this kind, some of you will volunteer. I also hope that, if you get home by December 24, you will pause while eating the roast pork that some of you have missed so much and think of this humble nation and of the comrades we have left in the Congo. You are only a revolutionary when you are willing to leave all your comforts to go to another country to fight. I hope we meet again in Cuba or some other part of the world." [Dreke wrote down his words.]

MARGOLLES: Che shaved before arriving in Kigoma, and José Luis Torres gave him a haircut. I took several photos of the process.

The struggle wasn't what you thought it would be
FLORENTINO: Before saying good-bye, he told us more or less the following: "I know how you feel, because this struggle wasn't what you thought it would be. I know you're annoyed, but you will go back to our free homeland and spend the end of the year happily, together with your families. You know what my situation is, that the enemy is looking for me in many places, so I have to take measures not to be discovered."

He also told us, "I'm sure that, when Fidel says that it's necessary to carry out another mission, many of you will step forward."

DREKE: Mbili, Pombo, Tuma and one of the telegraph operators accompanied him. "I'll see you later, Moja," was the last I heard from Che, when he finished his farewell address. It was terrible; we all cried or at least felt lumps in our throats. It was a mixture of joy and sadness. I didn't see Che again.

We landed in Kigoma at 0830 hours. Comrades Colman, Oliva and some others from the Embassy in Tanzania were waiting for us. Ambassador Pablo wasn't there. Later on, we went into a reception room after leaving all the weapons in the boats; the Tanzanian police collected them. The Congolese were in the room, too. We slept on the floor, because there weren't any beds. [*Campaign Diary*, 70.]

COLMAN: Everybody was in one place, and I went back to the house where Che was. I don't remember who came with him.

He took a bath, changed clothes and ate something. Then I got instructions by radio from Dar es Salaam that I should go there with him and whichever comrades Che chose. We left at a little after 2:00 or 3:00 that afternoon, in the van with the canvas top.

My plan was, first of all, to cross the river on the ferry, because it stopped working at 7:00 p.m., which meant we had to go as fast as possible. The road was bad, sandy and muddy.

We left immediately and got to the ferry in time. When we reached Dodoma, I phoned Dar es Salaam, since I had instructions to keep the Ambassador and Padilla informed of where we were. I also called from Morogoro. They told me that when we reached the capital a car would be waiting for us at the first traffic circle. They asked what time we would arrive, and I said it would probably be around midnight. When we got to the place they had told me about, Padilla and another comrade were waiting for us, but Che stayed with me until we got to a house that belonged to the director of prisons or something like that, near the Dar es Salaam airport. That's where Che and the other comrades stayed.

I went to see Che the next day in Dar es Salaam to do some errands for him, buy him some things. After three or four days, he went to live in a room on the second floor of our Embassy, where he stayed until he left the country. I was told to work with him as long as he needed me. Access to that floor was limited. Only Rivalta, Padilla and the telegraph operator Delfín — who took him his food — were allowed to go up there. We had two rooms: an air-conditioned office and his room. He didn't like working in the office.

The Cubans who had been in Kigoma were all in Dar es Salaam on November 29, except for six volunteers who had stayed in Kigoma to rescue their compatriots who were still in the Congo. They stayed at La Feria, where their living conditions improved considerably.

DREKE: During the crossing, Che told me we had to rescue the comrades who had remained in the Congo. When I asked for volunteers, the vast majority offered to go on the mission.

9

December 1965 – February 1966

Che's Epilogue

What will Che's destiny be?

COLMAN: The Cubans left for Cuba before December 24. They all traveled together, except for those who had stayed in Kigoma to rescue those who were still in the Congo. After they left, I started working with Che. Even though it was December, it was hot; it's always hot there. He worked in his BVDs, because his room wasn't air-conditioned, and the sun burned down on it all day long. The Embassy was in the Hupanga neighborhood, near the coast, but it didn't have a view of the sea. All we could see was houses. Che smoked cigars or a pipe, drank unsweetened tea and ate what was brought to him.

As soon as the Cubans had left, he began work on his book. He had spent the days before that reading, putting his papers in order and making notes. He also burned some papers. In his room, he taped the text he took from the diary he had kept throughout the campaign in the Congo and then gave it to me to type in the office.

When I finished, I gave it back to him for corrections and changes. We worked from 8:30 in the morning until midnight or 1:00 a.m., depending on when he decided to stop.

Rivalta, Padilla, Fernández Mell [Siki] and I saw the old year out with Che. We gathered in his room at midnight to greet the new year, 1966. Aleida arrived at a later time. I think she spent a week there. I also remember when Fisín arrived; Che still hadn't finished the book and the evaluations he made of the comrades who had been with him in the Congo.

Che used to play a lot of chess, study mathematics and read. Once, when I was tired, he asked me what was wrong and said, "Look, when you're tired, the best thing to do is play chess." I replied, "Listen, Major, I can't do that. When I'm tired, I *can't* play chess." He also discussed politics and African problems.

Che's book ends with an Epilogue in which he appeared more relaxed. In it, his analyses were more consistent with what happened in the Congo, which he insists on describing as a "failure."

Epilogue

CHE: All that's left to do, as a kind of epilogue, is to draw some conclusions that encompass the scene of the struggle, the behavior of the various factors and my opinion about the future of the Congolese revolution...

[Geographic information about the region where the guerrilla unit operated followed on pages 149-50 of the manuscript.]

The human aspect of the revolutionary forces' side can be divided for analysis into three groups: farmers, leaders and soldiers.

The farmers were grouped in different tribes, of which there is a large variety in the area. If you look at the enemy army's report of its general plan of attack, you will see that, in each case, it specifies the tribe to which the men of the region belong — an important piece of information for political work. The relations between them are usually friendly, but they are never fully fraternal, and there are serious rivalries between some of the tribal groups. That phenomenon could also be observed between the Rwandans and the Congolese tribes, but it was also clearly seen between the tribes belonging to the ethnic area of Nor-Katanga, who occupied the southern part of our guerrilla territory, and the tribes belonging to the ethnic area of Kivu Province, who occupied the northern part of our territory. Their most outstanding representatives were Kabila (of the first group) and Soumialot (of the other).

The farmers posed one of the most difficult and gripping problems of a people's war. A basic characteristic of all wars of liberation of this kind is hunger for land: the terrible poverty of the farmers exploited by large landowners, feudal lords, and in some cases, capitalist companies. There weren't any of this last phenomenon in the Congo, or at least where we were, and it is probable that there weren't any in most of the country, which has only around 14 million inhabitants in over 2 million square kilometers of land — that is, the population density is very low. The land is quite fertile. On the eastern front, you don't notice this hunger for land; nobody has put up fences, and, in the cultivated areas, custom guarantees that the crop belongs to the cultivator. Property isn't defended against intruders; small defenses are put up only around the vegetable gardens, to protect them against goats and other destructive animals. In all the areas we visited, there was practically no concept of land ownership, and the vast extents of the Congo River Basin offer anyone who is willing to work the opportunity to take possession of land without any great prerequisites. I understand that feudalism is much more developed in the northern part, in the Kudavu area, and there are veritable feudal lords and serfs, but in the mountain area where we lived the farmers were completely independent, and that phenomenon didn't exist.

How can the degree of development of those tribes be described? That would require a much more profound study than the one I had the opportunity to make, with much more information, dividing them into subregions — because, clearly, each corresponds to special historical and social conditions that make its development differ from that of others. I think that the nomadic groups still have characteristics of primitive communism; at the same time, there are traces of slavery, which are especially obvious in the treatment of women, though I couldn't note this with regard to men. Women are treated as merchandise, objects to be bought and sold. In that area, their individual possession isn't restricted by any laws or conventions; each man's economic means determine how many he can have. Once purchased, a woman becomes the absolute property of the owner, or husband — who, generally, doesn't work or works very little in household chores and the cultivation of the land. He only engages in some tasks such as hunting, but also accompanied by women, who take an active part in the hunt. Women work the land, transport the crops, cook the meals and take care of the children; they are veritable domesticated animals. As I have already noted, there isn't any feudalism in the mountainous areas, where there isn't any land ownership. Capitalism is superficial, barely affecting the panorama, seen only in small traders installed on the periphery who, copying the Americans, become what I might call a showcase, bringing in some articles for the farmers. For example, aluminum pots are quickly replacing earthenware ones, factory-produced spears are replacing homemade ones or those forged in the area; some modern dresses and cloths are used by the farmers, and radios can be seen in the homes of the families that are better off. The farmers acquire these products by bartering the products of the earth or of hunting.

In the past, they used to work as laborers or, simply, through intermediaries, taking gold out of the rivers that come down from the mountains to the Congo River Basin. You can see the trenches dug for that purpose, but the workings have been abandoned. Some crops, such as cotton, are given capitalist treatment in terms of using modern machines — cotton gins and balers. There are no textile plants in the area — they are in Albertville — so there aren't any industrial workers (except at the Londo Central, whose status I don't know). I didn't see any signs of wage labor; the farmers gave their produce to the Army and spent the rest of the time hunting, fishing or working in agriculture. Surpluses are sold for cash. Congolese currency, which is the medium of exchange, is accepted, but it hasn't penetrated far below the surface of the relations of production.

Imperialism gave only sporadic signs of life in the area; its primary interest in the Congo is in the large reserves of strategic minerals in Katanga, where there is an industrial proletariat; the diamond deposits in Katanga and Kasai; and the tin deposits near but not in our region. Agricultural crops include cotton, peanuts, and, to some extent, palm trees (for the extraction of oil). Primitive relations prevail in the harvesting and barter.

What could the Liberation Army offer those farmers? That was the question that always bothered me. We couldn't talk about an agrarian reform and property, because the land was there, and everybody could see it. We couldn't talk about credits for purchasing equipment, because the farmers got enough to eat from the labor they performed with primitive tools, and the physical conditions of the region weren't appropriate for machinery. It would have been necessary to stimulate a demand for articles produced by large-scale industry which, evidently, the farmers would be willing to accept and pay for, and it would bring the need for a more developed exchange of goods — but in the conditions in which the struggle developed, I couldn't conceive of that.

We could have spoken a lot about exploitation, but how did it work? It was more like mistreatment. It could be shown that in the areas occupied by the enemy Army more women were raped, and more men, women and children were murdered. The farmers were forced to provide the Army with food and to perform other services. The main thing was the denial of respect for individual human beings, which even included their physical elimination, since that Army, like any other modern body, had its organized logistics, foreseeing a lack of supplies and the hostility of the people living in the area.

But what to offer? Protection: in the course of this account, we have seen that very little was given. Education, which could be a vehicle: none was offered. Medical services: only that provided by the few Cubans, with little medicine, a quite primitive system of administration and no health organization. I think that a more thorough investigation and deeper thought is required about this problem of revolutionary tactics posed by the lack of relations of production that make farmers hungry for land. The farmers are the only social stratum in that area; there isn't any industrial proletariat, and the petite bourgeoisie of intermediary traders isn't very developed.

What kind of leaders has the revolution had? For purposes of study, they can be divided into those at the national and local levels. Kabila and Masengo were those at the national level whom I got to know. Unquestionably, Kabila is the only one who combines a clear brain, a capacity for developed reasoning and the personality of a leader. His presence is imposing and can inspire loyalty — or, at least, submission. He is skillful in his direct contacts with the people (though he doesn't have many). In short, he is a leader who can mobilize the masses. Masengo has very little character. He doesn't know anything about the art of war and lacks organizing ability, being completely overwhelmed by events. He had one distinguishing characteristic — his tremendous loyalty to Kabila — and showed a desire to continue the struggle longer than had been foreseen, even though this went counter to the opinions of a large number of his closest followers. It would be unfair to ask more of him; he did as much as he could.

None of the leaders of the different sections of the Staff or the so-called chiefs of the brigades can be said to have the qualities of a national leader. The only one who may develop in the future is Comrade Mujumba, who is still in the Congo; I don't know in what situation. He is young, serious, apparently intelligent and determined, as far as I have observed, but nothing much can be said about him.

Of the national leaders of the Congo, Mulele is the great unknown, almost a ghost: he has never been seen in meetings; he hasn't left his area since the struggle began. Many things indicate that he is a better quality figure, but his representatives — or those who say they are his representatives — display all the negative characteristics of their peers, the members of the various commissions and sectors of the Liberation Movement, who go around the world swindling the revolution. [In fact, Mulele's only official representative to the Eastern Front was Mitudidi — of whom Che had a good impression — Secretary of Finances of the African Solidarity Party, of which Mulele was General Secretary. I don't know what other representatives Che was referring to. As for Mulele, he kept fighting for a long time, until he was forced to go abroad. On September 29, 1968, he agreed to go back to his homeland, intending to continue the revolutionary struggle and trusting in the solemn word of Marien N'Goabi and Mobutu, the heads of state of the two Congos, that there would be no reprisals. Mulele paid with his life for his naïveté in trusting Mobutu. Welcomed with a banquet on his arrival, he was horribly assassinated three days later. — W.G.]

One of those who have attained some prestige in recent times is General Olenga, whose story I have included as narrated by somebody else in this account and who has demonstrated, whether truly or not, his inability to make any sacrifices. For months that are turning into years, he has lived off the myth of the revolution as a general in exile. Others frequently act the same as political leaders, but Olenga is a general who directs his operations by telepathy from Cairo or some other capital of that kind. [He has maintained the same farce, but I don't know what he is doing now. — W.G.]

Soumialot is another. I regard him as being useful as a middle-level leader of the revolution. Well controlled and guided, he could have done some good work. As Chairman of the Higher Council of the Revolution, his great task is to travel, live well, give dramatic press conferences and do nothing else. He lacks all organizing ability. His struggles with Kabila did more than anything else to contribute to the temporary failure of the insurrection. [He accepted the Government's offer and a farm so he could live well; Tchamlesso told me he thought he had died. — W.G.]

Ghenye's not worth mentioning; he's simply an agent of the counterrevolution.

There may be some young men who have the qualities of leaders with a true revolutionary spirit, but I haven't met them, or they haven't yet demonstrated those qualities.

There are two kinds of local chiefs: those of military groups and the farmers' leaders. The military chiefs have been appointed through the most arbitrary methods and have had no training of any kind — theoretical, intellectual, military or organizational.

Their only merit is that they have some influence over the tribes of the regions in which they live, but they can be removed with a stroke of the pen without causing the revolution any loss.

The local farmers' chiefs are the *kapitas* and presidents, who were appointed by [Patrice] Lumumba's old administration or by its successors and were to be the beginning of a civilian power. However, faced with the reality of the tribes, the easy way out was taken, and the traditional tribal chiefs were made presidents and *kapitas*. They are nothing more than tribal leaders in disguise. Some are good, some bad; some are more progressive, others less so; and some have more awareness of the meaning of the revolution, and others less — but none of them has achieved even a middling level of political development. Each controls a group of farmers and is in charge of providing food for troops in transit and bearers for transporting things. Each is in charge of supplying a troop that is settled nearby, helping in the construction of housing, etc. They were useful intermediaries for solving that kind of problem, but they do no political work at all.

Each troop had its political commissar, a title copied from the socialist versions of a liberation or people's army. Anyone who has read about the work of the commissars in all wars of liberation or who learned from accounts of the heroism and spirit of sacrifice of those comrades wouldn't have recognized them in the Congo. The Congolese political commissars were elected from among men who had had some education — almost always, they knew French. Their families belonged to the urban petite bourgeoisie, and they carried out a kind of work similar to that of sporadic spokesmen. At a given moment, the troop would be called together and the commissar would give them a pep talk about specific problems, after which the other men would get into the discussion. Neither the political commissars nor the chiefs — with a few honorable exceptions — took a direct part in the fighting; rather, they took very good care of their own skins.

[Che went on to criticize the recruiting methods and behavior of the political commissars and soldiers, which has already been described throughout this book. — W.G.] They are saturated with fetishistic concepts about death and the enemy and have no organized political education — and, therefore, no revolutionary awareness, no ideas about the future and no horizons other than those traditionally included as the territory of their tribes...

Even with the full support of the chiefs, it would have been an enormous task to make such individuals into revolutionary soldiers;

in view of the worthlessness of the higher command and the obstruction of the local chiefs, it became the most thankless of all my tasks, and I failed utterly in my effort. [*Congo*, 149-54.]

Che did not mention that the support of the chiefs in that thankless task was in name only and that neither he nor his comrades ever managed to have a real command. The Epilogue continues:

CHE: Many of the political commissars and some special weapons instructors were [Congolese] students who had come from some socialist country, where they had studied for six months. The largest groups came from Bulgaria, the Soviet Union and China. You couldn't work wonders with those men. The earlier selection had been very bad, and it was a lottery whether or not you would find among them any real revolutionaries or even any who had been tempered by struggle. They had a very high opinion of themselves, a very highly developed concept of the personal obligation to take care of cadres (themselves) and the idea — which was clearly expressed in their actions and demands — that the revolution owed them a lot because they had spent that time studying abroad and that this debt should somehow be paid now that they were coming to make the sacrifice of joining their comrades. They hardly ever took part in the fighting, asking to be instructors, for which all but a few were not qualified. They created parallel political organizations which they said were Marxist-Leninist but which tended to exacerbate the divisions. I think that most of those ills were due to the lack of a good prior selection. A good education will do a tremendous job in developing an individual's awakening consciousness, but the only thing that was developed in these domesticated and opportunistic revolutionaries during their months in the socialist countries was the ambition to get a leadership position based on their colossal knowledge — and, on the front, a yearning for the good old days when they had been abroad.

The question arises: What is left after the defeat? From the military point of view, the situation isn't so terrible. The small hamlets which our army controlled had fallen, but the troops around them remain intact. They have less ammunition and fewer weapons, but in general, are largely unhurt. The enemy soldiers don't occupy anything more than the territory where they happen to be — that is a great truth. From the political point of view, scattered groups remain alone, in a continuous process of decomposition. In the future, a guerrilla army may arise from the nuclei that remain. Right now, there are forces in the Fizi-Baraka area that don't control any specific hamlet or territory. In Uvira, they control the Baraka-Bukavu highway — quite a long stretch of it — where they are still more or less organized. In Mukundi, Comrade Mujumba is based with what may be the germ of an organization with a political sense of the struggle. Some troops also remain in Kabimba who have quite good weapons, and nuclei should be hanging on in the woods in Kabambere and Kasongo, even though we haven't had any contact with them for a long time.

It is important to point out that those groups have very little to do with one another. In practice, they don't obey orders from higher levels, and their horizons don't go beyond their own areas. Therefore, they constitute the remains of the old army rather than the germs of a new one. There may be between 4,000 and 5,000 weapons in the area, which were distributed without rhyme or reason to individual farmers and which it won't be easy to recover; some heavy weapons were saved, but I don't know how many. If a single chief with the required characteristics should appear at one place, the Eastern Front would soon have the same territorial conquests it had achieved up to the moment of the defeat. Recently, Bojira, Foreign Minister of the Higher Council of the Revolution, who stayed in Uvira, has arisen as a competitor of Soumialot and Kabila, but I don't have any specific opinion about him; events will show if he is really a leader with the capacity required by the Congo.

What characteristics does the enemy have? First of all, in explanation, it should be said that the old Congolese Army was a legacy of the Belgian colonial era. It was badly trained, had no leadership cadres and lacked a spirit of struggle. It was wiped out by the revolutionary wave and became demoralized that cities were taken without a fight (it seems to be absolutely true that the Simbas used the telephone to announce their intention of reaching a city, and the government troops withdrew). Later, it was placed in the hands of U.S. and Belgian instructors and was turned into an armed body with the characteristics of a regular army, capable of fighting without assistance, even though, in the last stage of the struggle, it was helped by white mercenaries. It is a trained force, has trained cadres and discipline. The white mercenaries fight efficiently — at least, while they aren't hit — and the blacks fight at their side. The enemy army doesn't have any impressive weapons at present. Its most effective weapon has been the P.T. boats, which have hindered traffic on the Lake. Its planes, to which I have referred, are old and not very effective, and its infantry weapons only began to be modernized at the last minute.

In general, the Liberation Army had better infantry weapons than Tshombe's Army. It is inconceivable but true: it was one of the reasons why the patriots didn't take the trouble to take the weapons of the dead and maintained a state of absolute indifference toward that source of supply.

The enemy's tactics were the usual ones in this kind of war: air protection for columns attacking population centers; air patrols of the highways; and, at the last moment, when the demoralization of our army became obvious, direct attacks on the mountain redoubts by columns which advanced on our positions and took them — without a fight. It is an army that needs to be hit to reduce its morale — a thing which, in view of the geographic conditions, could be carried out very easily, proceeding with correct tactics.

I should make an analysis of our group: most of them were blacks. That could have led to greater camaraderie and a greater sense of unity with the Congolese, but it didn't work out that way. It couldn't be seen that being black or white had much influence on our relations; the Congolese recognized the personal characteristics of each man.[1] My comrades had a very limited cultural base and relatively low political development, too. As always happens in these cases, they came full of optimism and goodwill, thinking they would make a triumphal passage through the Congo. Before beginning the struggle, some of them met and commented that Tatu [Che] was too far removed from the realities of war; that because of a timid evaluation of the balance of forces, he couldn't keep them from carrying out an intensive action. They felt that we were going to go in at one side and come out on the other, having liberated the country — and that, then, we could all go back to Havana.

I always warned that the war could go on for three or even five years, but nobody believed me. All of them were inclined to dream about a triumphal passage, a farewell with long speeches and great honors, medals and Havana. The reality of the situation was quite a blow: food was in short supply, and there were many days when the only thing we had to eat was yucca without salt or *bucali*, which is the same thing; and there wasn't enough medicine — or, at times, shoes and other clothes. We also lacked that sense of common identity which I dreamed would come about between our troop of experienced men, with an army's discipline, and the Congolese. This sense of common identity was never achieved.

We never had the required integration, and it can't be blamed on skin color, because some of our men were so black that they couldn't be distinguished from the Congolese comrades. However, I heard one of those very black Cubans say, "Send me two of those blacks"

— meaning two Congolese.[28]

Our men were foreigners, superior beings, and they made this felt with too much assiduity. The Congolese, who were extremely sensitive because they remembered the insults from which they had suffered at the hands of the colonialists, noted certain scornful gestures in the Cubans' treatment of them and felt deeply wounded. I couldn't manage to have the food distributed absolutely fairly, although it had to be recognized that, most of the time, it was carried by the Cubans. Every time an opportunity arose, an insensitive effort was made to press a Congolese into carrying it. It's a little difficult to explain this contradiction, because it involved subjective interpretations and subtleties, but one example may throw some light on this: I couldn't get the Cubans to call the Congolese "Congolese"; they were always "the Congos," a form that seems simpler and more intimate but which implied a large dose of venom. Language was another barrier; it was hard for a troop such as ours, submerged in the mass of Congolese, to work without knowing their language. Some of [the Cubans] who lived alongside the Congolese right from the beginning learned to speak very quickly and functioned quite well in basic Swahili, but there weren't many of them, and we always ran the risk of misinterpretations which could sour our relations or lead us to make mistakes.

I have tried to describe the process of our troop's breakdown as it happened; it was gradual and didn't increase steadily. Rather, explosive material accumulated and went off at times of defeat. The critical moments were the Front de Force failure; the various desertions of the Congolese in the Katenga ambushes, where the men suffered greatly from sickness; my personal disaster with the escort transferring the wounded, which was carried out with little cooperation from the Congolese; and the final desertion of our allies. Each of these events aggravated the lack of morale and disillusionment of our troop.

At the end, they had been contaminated with the spirit of the Lake and wanted to go back to Cuba. They dreamed of going home and, in

---

[28] Che crossed out note 1 that is shown in the text. With regard to that note, it seems that a mistake was made in copying it, because, even though note 1 on page 156 of the original copy was written in by hand and crossed out on page 160 because it isn't related to this, the following appears on the next page without any number: "[1] Here, I'm not able to begin an attempt to demonstrate this goal and show how it isn't opposed to the description of the era as the transition to socialism. This would lead us along troublesome lateral paths and would require an abundance of data and arguments. I leave it as a supposition that it is our practice." He didn't write anything for note 2 on page 158 of the original.

general, showed themselves incapable of risking their lives so the group could be saved or the revolution advanced. All of them wanted to get to the other side, to salvation. Discipline was so badly damaged that really grotesque episodes occurred that warranted the application of very severe punishments to some of the combatants.

If I were to make what I might call an impartial analysis, we would find that there was considerable — very considerable — justification for the Cubans' demoralization and that many comrades maintained their discipline and sense of responsibility to the end, even though they lacked spirit. I have placed emphasis on our weaknesses because I think that the most important aspect of our experience is the analysis of the collapse. This occurred under the action of a series of interrelated adverse factors. The problem lies in the fact that the difficulties with which we were faced are going to be difficult to do away with in beginning the next step in the struggle in Africa, for they are characteristic of countries with a very low degree of development. One of our comrades said in an offensive tone that all of the conditions contrary to revolution could be found in the Congo. That caricature has a grain of truth, if you view it through the lens of a mature, crystallized revolution. But the basic characteristics of the Congo were very similar to those of the farmers of the Sierra Maestra mountains in the early stages of the [Cuban] Revolution.

What qualities must a Party member have that will enable them to rise above the violent traumas of an adverse reality they will have to face? I think that the candidates should first go through a very rigorous selection process, plus a process of prior disillusionment. As I have already observed, nobody believed me when I said the revolution might take from three to five years to emerge victorious. When the facts bore this out, they experienced a terrible inner collapse, the collapse of a dream. The revolutionary Party members who are going to go through a similar experience should begin without any dreams, starting from the premise that everything that makes up their lives and keen desires is already lost. Furthermore, only those who have far greater revolutionary fortitude than normal — even in a revolutionary country — gained from practical experience in struggle and with great political development and solid discipline, should be selected. The process of incorporation should be gradual, starting with a small but tempered group, removing from the field of battle anyone who doesn't meet the requirements. A cadre policy should be implemented. In this way, the number of groups can be increased without weakening the nucleus, and new cadres from the sending country can even be created in the insurrectional area of the recipient country. We shouldn't be only teachers, but should also attend the new revolutionary schools.

Another difficulty we have to which special attention should be given in the future is the support base. It swallowed up relatively large amounts of money, and infinitesimal amounts of food and equipment reached the troops. First condition: the command should be unquestionable and absolute in the zone of operations, with rigorous controls over the support base, apart from the natural controls that will be exercised from the higher centers of the revolution. In addition, those who are to carry out those tasks should be seriously selected long before. You have to see how much a pack of cigarettes means to an individual who is in an ambush without doing anything for 24 hours at a stretch, and you have to see how little the 100 packs that may be smoked in a day mean in an overall budget — compared with the cost of unnecessary things or things that are lost uselessly in the course of the action.

I also had to make the most difficult analysis: that of my own behavior. Going as deeply as I was able in self-critical analysis, I came to the following conclusions: from the point of view of my relations with the revolutionary authorities, I was limited by the somewhat abnormal way in which I entered the Congo and wasn't able to overcome that drawback. I didn't always react the same; for a long time, I maintained an attitude which might be described as excessively complacent, and I sometimes gave vent to extremely cutting and wounding outbursts, perhaps because of an innate characteristic of mine. The farmers were the only ones with whom I maintained correct relations without any pretense, because I'm more accustomed to political language, to explanations that are direct and by means of example, and I think I was successful in that field. I didn't learn Swahili quickly or well enough. The first aspect was attributable, first of all, to my knowledge of French, which enabled me to communicate with the chiefs but separated me from the bases. I lacked the determination to make the required effort. [*Congo*, 157-58.]

Che couldn't have entered the Congo in any other way. In general, when carrying out an internationalist mission of that kind, you should accept the orders of those you have gone to help. Even though his complacency was extreme, he had to accept it, just as we accept his outbursts, which cannot be otherwise in a military leader. As Che wrote, it was "an innate characteristic" of his. As for his relations with the farmers, they remained good in most cases until the enemy appeared, when it hadn't been possible to achieve closer ties. It is true that he should have learned Swahili, but he didn't lack the determination. Nobody who knew him could ever have accused him of that. Simply, he thought that he could solve the most important problems with his use of French.

CHE: As for my relations with my men, I think I made enough sacrifices so nobody could accuse me of personal or physical shortcomings, but my two main weaknesses were supplied in the Congo: tobacco, which was almost always available, and reading materials, which were always abundant. The discomfort of having dilapidated boots or dirty clothes or eating the same pittance as the men and living in the same conditions they had, didn't represent any sacrifice for me. Above all, the fact that I could withdraw to read, escaping from day-to-day problems, tended to place me at a distance from the men, aside from the fact that some aspects of my character make me hard to get to know. I was tough, but I believe not excessively so, nor was I unjust. I used methods that aren't used in a regular army, such as making the men go without dinner; it's the only effective method I know of in a guerrilla war. At first, I wanted to apply moral sanctions, and I failed. I tried to get my men to have the same point of view I had regarding the situation, and I failed; they weren't ready to view with optimism a future that had to be glimpsed through the dark fogs of the present. [*Congo*, 154–8.]

Che hardly seems to have succeeded in "escaping from day-to-day problems" — much less any tendency to draw apart from his men. To the contrary, Che was never out of the daily struggle and was always together with the others, much more than his duty as their leader required. Most of the times he went to his hut to read were at night, stealing time from sleep.

His toughness was in line with the demands of all military organizations. General Máximo Gómez was much tougher in Cuba's war of independence at the end of the last century, for he sentenced wrongdoers to the pillory, with no food during the period of punishment. Moreover, the punishments that Che imposed, both in the Sierra Maestra mountains and in the Congo, were never carried out completely, because there were always some comrades who took food to the one being punished, and Che always looked the other way.

If any mistakes were made with regard to what Che characterized as the failure, it was that he wanted to measure all of his comrades by his own standard.

CHE: But I didn't demand the maximum sacrifice at the decisive moment. I was held back by something in my psyche. For me, it would have been very easy to stay in the Congo; from the point of a combatant's self-esteem, it was what had to be done. However, in terms of my future activity, it wasn't a good idea to stay, so I didn't care one way or the other. When I made my decision, the fact that I knew how easy the decisive sacrifice would be for me was something that weighed against me. I think I should have overcome that self-critical analysis and told a given number of combatants that we should make the final gesture and should have remained.[2] [The text of this note doesn't appear in the original.] [*Congo*, 158.]

Viewing these events from the perspective of history three decades later, Che's fervent desire to have remained in the Congo with 15 or 20 men would not have prevented the collapse of the Lumumbist movement. To the contrary, it would have meant a fruitless sacrifice of the best combatants of the column and its chief.

CHE: Lastly, my farewell letter to Fidel weighed in my personal relations — I could feel this clearly, even though it was a completely subjective matter. It caused the comrades to view me (as had happened many years before, when I began in the Sierra [Maestra]) as a foreigner in contact with Cubans. In the Sierra, it was as somebody who had just arrived, and now, as one who was about to leave. There were certain things that we no longer held in common, certain shared desires which I had tacitly or explicitly renounced and that are the things each man holds most dear: his family, his homeland, his milieu. The letter which caused so many laudatory comments in Cuba and elsewhere drove a wedge between me and the other combatants. [*Congo*, 158-59.]

Dreke later explained that most of the Cubans there didn't learn about the publication of the letter until after they had returned home.

We should also recall Che's testimony on bidding farewell to them before landing at Kigoma. In addition, there was the behavior of those who maintained relations with him from the time he left the Congo until he returned to Cuba; while he was in Cuba preparing to go and fight in Bolivia; and, the strongest objective proof of all, during the campaign in Bolivia until he was murdered. His Bolivian diary and his last records of the fighting contain no references to any sense of separation from the other combatants.

CHE: These psychological considerations may seem strange in the analysis of a struggle being waged on a nearly continental scale. I remain true to my concept of the nucleus. I was the chief of a group of Cubans, a company — nothing more. My function was to be their real leader, leading them to the victory that would promote the development of an authentic people's army — but my specific situation also turned me into a soldier representing a foreign power; an instructor of Cubans and Congolese; a strategist; a big-time political figure in an unknown setting; and a Cato-like, repetitive, tiresome critic in my relations with the leadership of the revolution. With so many strings being pulled, a Gordian knot was formed that I didn't cut. If I had been a better soldier, I would have been able to have a greater influence on the other aspects of my complex relations. I have reported how I reached the extreme of taking care of the cadre (my precious self) in certain moments of the disaster in which I was entangled and how I didn't overcome subjective considerations in the final attempt.

I have learned in the Congo. There are mistakes that I won't make again; others may be repeated, and I may make new ones. I have left with more faith than ever in guerrilla struggle, but we have failed. I bear a great responsibility; I won't forget the defeat or its most valuable teachings. [*Congo*, 159.]

It is true that we should learn from mistakes, but who hasn't made mistakes — over and over again? An old refrain says that humans are the only animal who stubs their toe on the same stone twice. This is especially so if that stone is the struggle for the revolution, so his having done so isn't very important.

Although Che had modified the term "failure" at the beginning of his preface, he kept using that term and even spoke of defeat. Che's Congo Diary provides readers with enough information to appreciate the effort by Che and the Cuban combatants in their attempt to lead those insurgents to victory.

In writing his manuscript, Che kept in mind that useful lessons for the cause of the peoples' liberation could and should be drawn from both positive and negative experiences. This is why the self-critical aspect prevails in his analysis. The important thing, for him, wasn't the human dimension of his actions or those of his comrades in arms.

For Che, internationalism was a duty, the most exalted duty a revolutionary can embrace. The most elementary material privations are something natural for an internationalist combatant, as is the spiritual suffering of being far from your homeland and family. The risk of dying didn't worry him; it was simply something inherent in his chosen path. The only prize for that offering was for the objective to be achieved. On not achieving it, he considered the enormous efforts of all kinds that Cuba had made to help revitalize the Congolese people's insurgency to have been a failure.

In that narrow, momentary, circumstantial sense, that term "failure" may be applicable. But what that heroic episode and the subsequent mission to Bolivia generated turned that first experience of the Cuban internationalists in sub-Saharan Africa into a milestone marking the starting point of Cuba's heroism in that continent. Hundreds of thousands of his compatriots would follow his example and Cuba would win victories against colonialism, the mercenary armies and racism, fighting alongside the African peoples in the next quarter of a century (1965-90).

History has denied the permanent validity of that term, as it has also denied Che's other statement that the fighting morale of Column One, which withdrew and crossed the Lake without any great difficulties, was crumbling. In fact, what had disintegrated was the fighting morale of most of the leadership of the Congolese rebel troops, whose own deficiencies kept them from resisting the fierce attack by an enemy which the United States and its NATO allies had provided with all the resources it needed.

Raúl Castro's words bear out this view:

It wasn't possible to unite the Lumumbist forces and make them a cohesive unit. A time came when the internationalist column was fighting alone on unknown terrain. Faced with such adverse circumstances, the column had to leave that country. It wasn't defeated by the enemy, but the purpose of its mission couldn't be achieved, because of the absence of an organized patriotic movement with which it could cooperate.[29]

CHE: What will be the future of the Congo? Victory, of course, but a distant one.

A people's army must be created, a fighting vanguard that has come from the heart of the farmers. In this case, one with greater ideological development and greater capacity for sacrifice. It should grow up slowly around the tempered nuclei of the first groups, educating a people that must pass like a whirlwind through the various historical stages by engaging in revolutionary struggle. Little by little, that people must be armed, so that the weapons reach men eager to bear them rather than waiting for men to come along, as happened here. May each weapon be a reward for the combatant who bears it, and may they do everything necessary to maintain the people's army as a prerequisite for receiving it; may that be the confirmation of their "state of grace" as a combatant for the people.

To achieve this, the present cadres must be swept away and new leadership cadres created who will appear and be tempered by sacrifice and battle, facing the rigorous selection of death on the

[29] Raúl Castro, November 7, 1985.

battlefield. This requires leaders who see farther and who are selective; self-sacrificing leaders with prestige who, inside the country, direct the impetuous development of revolutionary conditions. That great process of struggle should, at one and the same time, create soldiers, cadres and leaders, because none of them exist now. This should be done around one or a few nuclei, from the bottom up, from the countryside to the towns and then to the cities, without having to defend any ground at first, or perhaps defending some strategic transit areas, sowing the seeds of revolution and setting examples everywhere.

Thus, victory will come. The sooner self-sacrificing, capable leaders arise who can select the self-sacrificing, capable intermediate-level leaders who will control the development of the people's army based on the farmers who are already there, the sooner that victory will come.

When, through the combination of revolutionary practice and theory, the correct methods for linking the farmers and the people's army and creating a single force out of that combination are found, the final stretch leading up to victory will have been reached, and it won't matter how long and hard it may still be. [*Congo*, 159-60.]

Unfortunately, none of his predictions have come about in the Congo in the years since then. However, other African countries have achieved their independence and defeated racism. Like Che, I believe that some day the Congo will have reached the final stretch leading up to victory and that the people of Zaire will, one way or another, free themselves of the present opprobrious regime.

Later, Che went into an evaluation of how assistance should be given to revolutionary movements; he thought that it would have to be conditional, so it would be necessary to really know those asking for it. He said, "When you help someone, a position is taken, and that position is taken on the basis of certain analyses of the loyalty and effectiveness of a revolutionary movement in the struggle against imperialism and for a country's liberation... The assistance should be conditional; if not, we run the risk of its being turned into the opposite of what we want." He then went on to make a strong criticism of the freedom fighters of the African revolutionary movements.

Che's opinions, based on his painful experience in Africa, should be analyzed keeping in mind when they were written and the international situation at that time.

Cuba draws lessons of Congo experience
Taking what happened in the Congo as a basis for their studies, the

Cuban leaders drew up clearer guidelines for their internationalist solidarity with the African peoples. Cuba considered the definition set forth in the Charter of the Organization of African Unity, adopted in the mid-1960s, to be correct. It consisted of respect for the borders drawn by the colonialists, because redrawing them to rebuild ancient kingdoms, empires and other more incipient forms of states on an ethnic basis would imply a fratricidal war between the African peoples, from which only imperialism would benefit.

Cuba strictly abided by that principle, not only by omission — that is, by abstaining from supporting secessionist movements, as was the case of the two Shaba wars (1977 and 1978) unleashed by the Katangan repressive forces — but also with its action defending the territorial integrity of friendly countries that were victims of foreign aggression and requested Cuba's aid. Examples of this were the Cuban contingent that went to Algeria in 1963, when that recently liberated Arab country was threatened with military aggression by the expansionist Moroccan monarchy; and the Congo (Brazzaville), where Cuba's Patricio Lumumba Battalion and the battalions of national militia trained by Cuban instructors, together with the patriotic armed forces of that country, were ready and willing to confront an attack by Mobutu's army led by mercenaries, in the period when that danger existed (1965 and 1966).

Likewise, in 1973, Cuba sent a tank regiment that fought alongside the Syrian forces on the Golan Heights to halt the deep advance of the Israeli aggressors; in 1975, Cuban troops fought alongside the Angolans to repel the South African soldiers and mercenaries who were trying to destroy that country's independence; and, in 1977, Cuban military units fought shoulder to shoulder with the Ethiopians on the desert of Ogaden, against the expansionist Somalians.

It may be said that the assistance in those cases was conditional on a principle: the defense of the territorial integrity of friendly nations confronted with foreign aggression. But what conditioned it was the cardinal principle of struggle, not how the struggle was waged — which is the exclusive prerogative of the government or liberation movement that is supported.

The other conclusion that the Cuban leaders reached was that in Africa we should concentrate our forces — remembering that Cuba, a small country, has limited resources — in supporting peoples that were fighting to free themselves from the yoke of colonialism or from racist oppression and that asked for Cuban assistance. The only condition was the strategic principle of eradicating colonialism and racism. The liberation movements — the African Party for the Independence of Guinea and Cape Verde (PAIGCV), the People's Movement for the Liberation of

Angola (MPLA), the Zimbabwe African National Union (ZANU), the Zimbabwe African People's Union (ZAPU), the South West Africa People's Organization (SWAPO), the African National Congress (ANC), the Communist Party of South Africa and the People's Front for the Liberation of Saguía El Hamra and Río de Oro (POLISARIO Front) — were in charge of the political and tactical leadership of the struggle.

This policy which Cuba outlined in Africa not only corresponded to the objective conditions in that continent but also had the support of the vast majority of the African governments; the OAU, the regional organization; and the Movement of Nonaligned Countries, representing 100 Third World countries.

In other aspects, which may be termed tactical and organizational, the Revolutionary Government of Cuba also assimilated what had happened to Column One and from then on kept it clearly in mind that it was absolutely necessary to make a detailed analysis of the character-istics of the movements which requested assistance.

Another important way in which Cuba helped the African people was by sending thousands of civilian personnel, mainly health workers, to those countries that requested them and by training thousands of young Africans as professionals and technicians in many specialties in Cuba.

Of course, the world situation is very different now from what it was when Che outlined his strategic vision of creating two, three, many Vietnams.

We now live in a world in which the United States, the only superpower, is trying to impose its unipolar hegemony on the rest of the world. The richer countries — the so-called G-7 and other members of the First World — are using the most barefaced, brutal neoliberalism in their efforts to globalize the world economy so as to maximize profits and concentrate in the hands of the big transnationals the wealth they extract from the peoples of the Third World and from the wage workers in their own opulent societies.

There is, however, increasing opposition to this globalizing offensive, in which those who unlawfully retain the power of money, of scientific-technical advances and of the mass media resort to military force whenever they deem it necessary, using the hypocritical pretexts of "humanitarian assistance and respect for human rights."

In this end-of-the-20th-century world, the defense of Cuba's survival as an independent nation and of its socialist regime has become the first internationalist task of the Cuban people. It means saving the source of hope for hundreds of millions of men and women who, from all parts of the world, look to Cuba, ardently desiring its victory as a reply to their own problems and as proof that the peoples' unity, steadfastness and struggle can successfully withstand the onslaught of international imperialism.

Che's conclusion

CHE: Lastly, if anyone were to ask me if there is anyone in the Congo who can be considered to have possibilities as a national leader, I couldn't respond affirmatively — leaving aside Mulele, whom I don't know. It seems to me that Kabila is the only man who has the qualities of a leader of the masses. I believe that if a completely pure revolutionary doesn't have certain leadership qualities, they cannot lead a revolution. And, conversely, if someone has leadership qualities but nothing else, they cannot lead a revolution, either. It is absolutely necessary to have revolutionary seriousness and a guiding ideology and a spirit of self-sacrifice which accompanies your actions. So far, Kabila hasn't demonstrated any of this. He is young, and he may change. I am moved to set down on paper — which won't be made public for many years — my very great doubts about whether or not he will be able to overcome the defects of his milieu. Almost all of the other leaders I have met will be swept aside by history. However, new ones are probably already there inside the country, beginning to write the true history of the liberation of the Congo. [*Congo*, 160.]

10

Che's departure from Africa

Searching for the lost men

The *Campaign Diary* kept by Dreke's group said that Siki, Ishirine, Ahalla, Achali, Alau and Wasiri stayed in Kigoma to rescue the comrades who hadn't left the Congo.

DREKE: Since the lost men were from Martín Chibás's (Ishirini) group, I said he would be in charge of looking for them. Back in Cuba, he told me that Fernández Mell (Siki) went to Dar es Salaam and sent instructions from there, because they had to wait for the enemy's patrols — which were trying to keep the Cubans from returning — to be suspended.

They made the crossing around two months later but couldn't land, because enemy forces on the shore shot at them. Several Congolese told them they knew where our comrades were, but the would-be swindlers asked for money without taking them there. They crossed the Lake again but didn't find the Cubans in the *kimbo* to which they were taken. They made a third attempt, but it was also in vain.

It wasn't until the second week of June that a Congolese took them to where they found two Cubans. They were sick, in a *kimbo*. Chibás told me that the meeting was very emotional. On returning to Kigoma, they sent word to Fernández Mell. They stayed a few days more, hoping to hear news of the third Cuban, but, on hearing nothing, were ordered to leave for Dar es Salaam and then return to Cuba.

The rescued men were Ñyennñyea and Chepua. Aurino didn't appear and was given up for dead. Finally, the *Campaign Diary* listed the internationalists killed in combat:

1. Captain Crisógenes Vinajeras (Anzurune), June 29, 1965
2. Lieutenant Norberto Pío Pichardo (Inne), June 29, 1965
3. Sergeant Víctor M. Ballester (Telathini), June 29, 1965
4. Corporal Wagner Moro Pérez (Kawawa), June 29, 1965
5. Enlisted man Orlando Puente Mayeta (Bahasa), October 26, 1965
6. Enlisted man Francisco C. Torriente A. (Aurino), October 13, 1965
Nothing more was ever heard of this last comrade.[30]

FIDEL: Having now spent about six months in Zaire, Che stayed for a while in Tanzania, assessing the experience he had just lived through. His conduct on the mission was, as always, exemplary to the highest degree. His stay in Africa was temporary, awaiting creation of conditions for traveling to South America...

So after finishing the phase in Zaire he went to Tanzania, marking time...

Once Che's farewell letter had been made public — politically, it had become unavoidable to publish it — Che, with his particular character, felt very awkward about returning to Cuba after having said farewell. But in the end I persuaded him to return, because it was the best move given all the practical matters he wanted to take care of. So he secretly returned to Cuba.[31]

COLMAN: After several days of work, Che would occasionally come to the office to talk. Sometimes it was about an aspect of the book he was writing, but we also talked about everything. With regard to the help that was given to the Congo, Che was always convinced that the action had been correct. He may have felt disillusioned, but he still thought that it had been correct to provide that assistance. He even said there were prospects for struggle if a liberation army had been created. He spoke of some Congolese leaders who, if they changed

---

[30] *Campaign Diary*, 70-1.
[31] Gianni Miná, *An Encounter with Fidel*, 224.

their way of acting, might achieve the goals of the struggle.

Preparing to leave Africa

ULISES ESTRADA: Once more, [Manuel] Piñeiro told me I would have to go back to Tanzania, this time by plane. I would take Fisín with me. Fisín would be in charge of disguising Che again. We met in Cairo. While Fisín did his work, Che continued writing, staying on the second floor of the Embassy with Colman.

LUIS C. GARCIA GUTIERREZ (FISIN): I was told to appear in [Minister of Interior] Ramiro Valdés's office at 1:00 in the afternoon; I thought it was for something else. Osmany Cienfuegos was there, too, and they showed me a photo of Che as he had looked when he left for Africa. They asked me if I knew that person. I looked at the photo and didn't recognize him. Then they told me who he was and said, "Look, this is what we want. You've worked in this field for several years, and we need you to go where he is, because we have to get him out of there."

Then we began to prepare all the conditions, looking for resources, etc. I went alone to Cairo, where I met with Ulises Estrada. Before that, I had gone through Prague and Paris. I knew that I was going to make contact with Ulises in Cairo. In principle, we decided that I would continue my journey, and he would join me in Tanzania, but that wasn't possible, because it was just before Christmas.

I don't remember who met us in Dar es Salaam and took us to where Che was. Ulises and I went in the back door, walked up some stairs and went along a hall to a room. Colman was there. That was the first time I had talked with Major Guevara.

He was shaved and was working at a little table in his BVDs, because the summer there in December is very hot. After a short conversation on general topics, we talked about the reason for my trip. Since I had come from a cold region, I asked for permission to take off some of my clothes. He replied, "You can strip down to what I have on," and we laughed. I explained the idea I had in principle, the things we could do — that is, to create another personality. For example, people are identified by a series of details, not just one.

I decided to change his height. He stood erect, and I wanted him to hunch over. I also decided to change his face, increasing the distance between his nose and chin. This would change his appearance a lot — especially if I made him look foolish. I couldn't change his superciliary arches, which were very prominent, but I decided to remove his widow's peak and make his hair recede at the temples. His widow's peak was very distinctive, and the enemy could identify him from it.

I talked about this with him, and he agreed. While in Paris, I had bought some wax for removing hair and making his hairline recede. He withstood all that stoically. All I did was make his hair recede and take away his widow's peak.

I also made upper and lower prosthetic devices to put on his teeth, to make them larger. I did all that there. I had brought motors, equipment and the materials I needed for the job. I had bought it all in France; the motors were portable ones that hung from the ceiling. I had to work hard, sometimes late into the night, because nobody knew how to help me; it took an effort to finish as quickly as possible.

Throughout that time, I had a chance to talk a lot with Che. We discussed moral and material incentives and the life of armed struggle. My opinions were different from his, perhaps because I had been a communist for a long time.

I remember that he told me he wanted any opinion I might give him to be the product of my own thinking rather than of what I had read.

After I finished with all that work, I thought about dyeing his hair and tried it out on a comrade who worked in the Embassy, but I didn't like it, and he didn't, either. I think it was Rivalto who cut his hair. I made a vest for him which made him hunch over. His shoes had built-in lifts, so they looked like normal shoes; I couldn't put on higher heels, because then it would be obvious that it wasn't his real height. I decided against glasses.

When all that was done, I took him outside the house and to an anteroom in the Embassy where Padilla was. Che knocked on the door, Padilla opened it and Che greeted him and then walked down the hall. Padilla was surprised that somebody he didn't recognize had walked in, so the test was a success.

I finished my work before December 31, and Fernández Mell arrived about then. That was when Che was in the phase of getting his hair cut and having his photo taken. I also made a passport for him — that is, I took out the photo in his old passport and replaced it with the new one. The seal had to be put on, too. I did that there.

RIVALTA: During the days he spent in the Embassy, we talked about basic things and the problems that arose in the Congo. I wanted him to stay there until he returned to Cuba or left definitively for somewhere else.

He kept asking whether or not the comrades who had stayed in the Congo had been rescued. One of the things he asked me before leaving Tanzania was not to abandon them but to do whatever was necessary to find them, living or dead.

Only the people he authorized were allowed to go up to the second floor: Colman, who stayed at his side, working on the book; Padilla; Delfín, the encoder; and I. Oscarito [Fernández Mell], Fisín, Ulises and Aleida also saw him. We played chess several times.

ULISES: After Fisín finished his work, we returned to show Fidel the photos of Che in his new disguise and explain the route he would take on his return to Cuba.

RIVALTA: One of the tests that were run to see if he was well disguised took place when Major Edy Suñol was there, heading a military delegation. Che agreed to sit in my office and have Suñol come in; Suñol didn't recognize him. He only realized who he was much later, when Che purposely began talking with an Argentine accent.

A letter to his daughter
In a letter to his eldest daughter, Che wrote:

February 15
Dear Hildita,

I am writing you now, although you'll receive this letter much later. But I want you to know I am thinking about you and I hope you're having a very happy birthday. You are almost a woman now, and I cannot write to you the way I do to the little ones, telling them silly things or little fibs.

You must know I am still far away and will be gone for quite some time, doing what I can to fight against our enemies. Not that it is a great thing, but I am doing something, and I think you will always be able to be proud of your father, as I am of you.

Remember, there are still many years of struggle ahead, and even when you are a woman, you will have to do your part in the struggle. Meanwhile, you have to prepare yourself, be very revolutionary — which at your age means to learn a lot, as much as possible, and always be ready to support just causes. Also, obey your mother and don't think you know it all too soon. That will come with time.

You should fight to be among the best in school. The best in every sense, and you already know what that means: study and revolutionary attitude. In other words: good conduct, seriousness, love for the revolution, comradeship, etc.

I was not that way at your age, but I lived in a different society, where man was an enemy of man. Now you have the privilege of living in another era and you must be worthy of it.

Don't forget to go by the house to keep an eye on the other kids and advise them to study and behave themselves. Especially Aleidita, who pays a lot of attention to you as her older sister.

All right, old lady. Again I hope you are very happy on your birthday. Give a hug to your mother and to Gina. I give you a great big strong one to last as long as we don't see each other.

Dad[32]

The sleazy cabaret

ULISES: When [Fidel Castro] approved of the plan, I was sent back to Tanzania, to accompany Che. I made that third trip at the end of January or beginning of February 1966. On leaving Dar es Salaam, Che told me, "Well, I'm a guerrilla; you're a conspirator… You're the one who knows about these things, so you're the head of the group." The group consisted of him and me. Then I told him, "No, Major, you're the chief." But he replied, "No, you're the chief, and don't call me 'Major'; you have to call me 'Ramón' and talk to me informally."

In view of that, I had to see myself as the chief.

The flight we had to take had a very irregular schedule; it might arrive two, three or four hours late, and, since he should be in the airport as short a time as possible, he agreed that we should stay in a tiny cabaret at the side of the road and that Colman should go ahead and do the paperwork for the trip. When we heard the plane come in, we were to go to the air terminal.

Oliva and I were with Che. There was a kind of show in the cabaret and several women who asked you to dance.

We were waiting for the plane to come by, but we must have gotten too interested in the show, and nobody heard the plane when it arrived. Suddenly, Colman came in, looking very worried and saying the plane was leaving, as it had arrived around an hour before. We left quickly, and Che and I managed to catch it just a few minutes before takeoff.

COLMAN: Che left Tanzania on the flight that came from Madagascar. I went ahead and made the reservations.

They were supposed to leave at around 9:00 or 10:00 at night [in late February 1966]. We had to be at the airport a few hours before departure. I left first, to see to the luggage. Then the others left and were supposed to wait for me in a bar near the airport. While I was checking the luggage, they told me the flight was two hours late. I went to where Che, Ulises and Oliva were to tell them about the delay, and Che decided we should wait there, because the plane had to pass overhead.

But time went by, and we didn't hear the plane. I went out to the airport again, and the plane had already arrived. I ran back to get the comrades, and, when we got there, the plane was waiting for them, which helped speed the immigration procedures, and they left without any difficulties.

The Tokyo Olympics

ARBEZU: Aleida, Che's wife, went through Cairo in January 1966. I think she was traveling with Padilla. To me, that confirmed that Che was in the Congo. She spent two days waiting for the flight to Tanzania. She stayed at the Embassy residence, since we had information about her trip. I tried to keep other comrades from seeing her, on a need-to-know principle, but it was impossible to avoid. Somebody happened to come in and saw her, though he never told me if he had recognized her or not.

Soon after that, Major Suñol visited me. He was heading a military delegation that was going to Tanzania.

On their return, the members of his delegation accepted an invitation to visit some military units in Cairo, which took around four or five days. Ulises sent a note with him, telling me he would be arriving with a comrade. Suñol forgot to give me the note on his arrival, and it wasn't until the night he was leaving that he said, "Oh, Ulises gave me a note for you," and gave it to me. When I read it, I realized that they would be arriving early the next day.

We had planned to have them stay in an apartment, but there wasn't time to get it ready, so we decided they should stay at the residence. The Ambassador wasn't there, as he had gone back to Cuba to attend the Tricontinental Conference and would be staying there for several days more. Che was coming in a new disguise, but I already knew who he was. The first thing he said to me, jokingly, was, "The last time you were an idiot, because you didn't recognize me."

They came with a false itinerary. From Cairo, they were supposed to go on to another country that wasn't Czechoslovakia, so the next day I had to go out and buy the new tickets and get visas so they could leave on the first flight out of there. Everything worked out OK, and, when I returned in the afternoon, Ulises told me that Che wanted to go to the movies, because he had seen in a newspaper that they were showing a documentary on the Tokyo Olympics. He told me he had said it wasn't a good idea to go to the movies, because it was dangerous, but Che had told him to go to hell, he was going.

Ulises asked me to talk to him, and I did, but Che said, "If you two are chicken, I'll go alone."

At that time, when you went to the movies in Cairo, you went and bought your tickets ahead of time, choosing where you wanted to sit from a seating plan. I bought three seats in a row in the center section and four behind that row as a matter of security. Che and Ulises sat in front, and I sat behind them. I spent all the time looking from one side to the other. If you were to ask me what the movie was, I couldn't tell you, because I didn't see it. When it was over, Che, very happy, told me, "Now I want to go to that place where you once took me to eat."

That was the cafeteria in the Hilton Hotel. We opposed the idea, and he got mad again. And we took him there, because there was something he liked to eat, but I can't remember what it was. In short, we went to those places, and nothing happened. The next day, in the afternoon, they left for Prague. That's what his stay was like that time. He said some things about the Congo — not much — and he asked me a lot of questions about Egypt and the Sudan, where there was a progressive movement at the time. He had made contact with some of the Sudanese leaders during his official visit there. All this is what I remember about the last time I saw Che.

Leaving Africa

On leaving Egypt, Che left Africa behind. He had finished his mission in that beautiful land. In the future, he would begin working for another country. Although Che's account abounds in harsh criticism and self-criticism, all of which is included in this book, he also made some assessments in which he recognized or at least hinted that the epiosde was not completely negative.

CHE: In closing, it should be emphasized that, although I have given a detailed account of various cases of weakness, of isolated men or groups, and have placed emphasis on the general demoralization into which we had sunk — adhering strictly to the truth and in view of the importance it may have for future liberation movements — this doesn't make that effort any less heroic. The heroism of the Cubans who participated is a reflection of the general attitude of the Cuban people and Government. Our country, a lone socialist bastion at the doors of U.S. imperialism, sent its soldiers to fight and die in a foreign land, in a distant continent, and assumed full, public responsibility for its actions. That defiance, that clear stance on the great problem of our era — the struggle without quarter against U.S. imperialism — embodies the heroic significance of our participation in the struggle of the Congo. This is the way to seè the willingness of a people and of its leaders not only to defend themselves but also to attack. When confronted with U.S. imperialism, it isn't enough to be staunch in your defense; you must also attack it at its supporting bases, in the colonial and neocolonial territories which serve as the underpinnings for its world domination. [*Congo*, 2-3.]

The preceding is the final paragraph of Che's preface — which, because of its content, I think should close the sad history of the guerrillas in the Congo.

Finally, although Che and the Cuban internationalists didn't succeed in their mission, I, for one, don't consider that they failed. I leave it to the reader to decide for themselves.

Interviews

List of those interviewed, with the posts they held in the 1965-66 period.

NORMANDO AGRAMONTE: Officer in the Revolutionary Armed Forces.
MANUEL ÁLVAREZ (MANOLÍN): Officer in the Ministry of the Interior.
JOSÉ A. ARBEZÚ: Official in the Cuban Embassy in Cairo.
MARIO ARMAS (REBOCATE): Officer in the Revolutionary Armed Forces.
RAMÓN ARMAS (AZIMA): Officer in the Revolutionary Armed Forces.
JUAN CARRETERO: Officer in the Ministry of the Interior.
ANTONIO CARRILLO: Cuban Ambassador to France.
ROBERTO CHAVECO NÚÑEZ (KASAMBALA): Enlisted soldier in the Revolutionary Armed Forces.
VÍCTOR DREKE (MOJA): Major in the Revolutionary Armed Forces.
ULISES ESTRADA: Officer in the Ministry of the Interior.
TOMÁS ESCANDÓN CARVAJAL (TULIO): Soldier in the Revolutionary Armed Forces.
OSCAR FERNÁNDEZ MELL (SIKI): Major in the Revolutionary Armed Forces.
OSCAR FERNÁNDEZ PADILLA (RAFAEL): Deputy Minister of Interior.
COLMAN FERRER: Official in the Cuban Embassy in Tanzania.
LUIS C. GARCÍA GUTIÉRREZ (FISÍN): Officer in the Ministry of Interior.
ARCADIO B. HERNÁNDEZ BETANCOURT (DOMA): Officer in the Revolutionary Armed Forces.
FREDDY E. ILANGA YATÜ: Congolese guerrilla. Now lives in Cuba.
ANDRÉS JARDINES JARDINES (AU): Enlisted man in the Revolutionary Armed Forces.
FLORENTINO NOGAS: Enlisted soldier in the Revolutionary Armed Forces.
JOSÉ RAMÓN MACHADO VENTURA: Minister of Public Health.
ALDO MARGOLLES (UTA): Deputy Minister of the Interior.
EMILIO MENA (PAULU): Soldier in the Revolutionary Armed Forces.
CATALINO OLACHEA DE LA TORRE (MAFU): Officer in Revolutionary Armed Forces.
ROGELIO OLIVA: Official in the Cuban Embassy in Tanzania.
JORGE RISQUET: Head of Column Two, the Congo (Brazzaville).
PABLO RIVALTA: Cuban Ambassador to Tanzania.
ARNOLD RODRÍGUEZ: Deputy Minister of Foreign Affairs.
JUSTO RUMBAUT: Officer in the Revolutionary Armed Forces.
JORGE SERGUERA: Cuban Ambassador to Algeria.
GODEFREI TCHAMLESSO (TREMENDO PUNTO): Congolese, member of the leadership of the Congolese Liberation Movement.
EZEQUIEL TOLEDO DELGADO (AMIA): Soldier in Cuban Armed Forces.
ERASMO VIDEAUX (KISUA): Officer in the Revolutionary Armed Forces.
RAFAEL ZERQUERA (KUMI): Civilian doctor.

Bibliography

ALCÁZAR, JOSÉ LUIS, *Ñacahuasu, la guerrilla del Che en Bolivia* (Mexico).

ÁLVAREZ BATISTA, GERÓNIMO, *Che: una nueva batalla* (Paris, 1994).

BAYO, ALBERTO, *Mi aporte a la revolución cubana* (Havana, 1960).

BENÍTEZ, JOSÉ ANTONIO, *El Apartheid* (Havana, 1988).

BERRENECHEA ZAMBRANA, RAMIRO, *El Che en la poesía boliviana* (La Paz: Roalva, 1988).

BORREGO DÍAZ, ORLANDO, *El estilo de trabajo del Che* (Havana, 1988).

CALCHI GIAMPAOLO, NOVATI, *Le revoluzioni nell' Africanera* (Milan: Dall'Oglio, 1967).

CHÁVEZ ANTUÑEZ, ARMANDO, *Del pensamiento ético del Che* (Havana: Editora Política, 1983).

CUPULL, ADYS and FROILÁN GONZÁLEZ, *Un hombre bravo* (Havana).

DAVIDSON, BASIL, *Historia de África* (Writers' Union of Angola).

FANON, FRANZ, *Los condenados de la tierra* (Havana, 1965).

FRANCO, JOSÉ LUCIANO, *La diáspora africana en el nuevo mundo* (Havana).

GADEA, HILDA, *Che Guevara, años decisivos* (Mexico City, 1972).

GIANTURCO, CORRADO, *La rivoluzioni congolese* (Milan: Dall'Oglio, 1970).

GRANADO, ALBERTO, *Con el Che por sudamérica* (Havana: Editorial Letras Cubanas, 1986). Typed manuscript, checked and with handwritten corrections by Ernesto Che Guevara. The author has copy of the original.

GUEVARA, ERNESTO CHE, *Obras: 1957-1967.* (Havana, 1970), 2 vols.

— *Pasajes de la guerra revolucionaria: Congo* (unpublished).

— *El Che en la Revolución Cubana* (Havana: Ministry of Sugar), 7 vols.

GUEVARA LYNCH, ERNESTO, *Mi hijo el Che* (Barcelona, 1981).

HOARE, M, *Mercenario nel'Congo* (Milan: Ed. Sugar, 1969).

KOROS, CLAUDIA, *El Che y los argentinos* (Buenos Aires, 1988).

LUMUMBA, PATRICE, *Libertad para el Congo*

MALDONADO VILLAGRAN, DAVID, *Recopilación* (La Paz, 1988).

MARRONES, LUDO, *Pierre Mulele au la seconde vie de Patricio Lumumba.*

MAY, ELMAR, *Che Guevara* (Mexico City: Ed. Extemporáneos, 1975).

MENA, EMILIO, *Campaign Diary* of the column headed by Víctor Dreke (Moja), Unpublished manuscript. The author has copy of the original.

MINA, GIANNI, *An Encounter with Fidel* (Melbourne: Ocean Press, 1991).

PEREDO, INTI, *Mi campaña con el Che* (La Paz, 1970).

PRADO, SALMÓN, GARY, *La guerrilla inmolada*

RODRÍGUEZ HERRERA, MARIANO, *Ellos lucharon con el Che* (Havana).

— *Abriendo sendero* (Havana: Editorial Gente Nueva, 1980).

ROJAS, MARTA and MIRTA RODRÍGUEZ CALDERÓN, *Tania, la guerrillera inolvidable* (Havana: Instituto del Libro, 1970).

ROSALES, JOSÉ NATIVIDAD, *¿Qué hizo el Che en México?* (Mexico, 1973).

SORIA GALVARRO, CARLOS, *El Che en Bolivia, documentos y testimonios* (La Paz: Cedoin, 1994), 3 vols., 2nd edition.

SURÍ QUESADA, EMILIO, *El mejor hombre de la guerrilla* (Havana, 1980).

40 years of the Cuban Revolution
A new series from Ocean Press

FIDEL CASTRO READER
Edited by Mirta Muñiz and Pedro Alvarez Tabío
The voice of one of the 20th century's most controversial political figures —
as well as one of the world's greatest orators — is captured in this new
selection of Castro's key speeches over the past four decades.
ISBN 1-876175-11-7

PSYWAR ON CUBA
The Declassified History of U.S. Anti-Castro Propaganda
Edited by Jon Elliston
Newly declassified CIA and U.S. Government documents are reproduced
here, with extensive commentary providing the history of Washington's 40-
year campaign of psychological warfare and propaganda to destabilize
Cuba and undermine its revolution.
ISBN 1-876175-09-5

CUBAN REVOLUTION READER
A Documentary History
Edited by Julio García Luis
An outstanding anthology documenting the past four decades of Cuban
history. This Reader presents a comprehensive overview of the key
moments in the Cuban Revolution, with most materials published in English
for the first time. An unprecedented documentary history of the Cuban
Revolution in the years 1959-98.
ISBN 1-876175-10-9

JOSE MARTI READER
Writings on the Americas
Edited by Deborah Shnookal and Mirta Muñiz
This Reader presents an outstanding new anthology of the writings, letters
and poetry of José Martí—one of the most brilliant and impassioned Latin
American intellectuals of the 19th century.
ISBN 1-875284-12-5

CUBA AND THE UNITED STATES
A Chronological History
By Jane Franklin
Based on exceptionally wide research, this updated and expanded chron-
ology relates day by day, year by year, the developments involving the two
neighboring countries from the 1959 Cuban revolution through 1995.
ISBN 1-875284-92-3

THE SECRET WAR
CIA covert operations against Cuba, 1959-62
By Fabián Escalante
The secret war that the CIA lost. For the first time, the former head of Cuban State Security speaks out about the confrontation with U.S. spy agencies and details the CIA's operations in 1959-62, the largest-scale covert operation ever launched against another nation.
ISBN 1-875284-86-9

CIA TARGETS FIDEL
The secret assassination report
Only recently declassified and published for the first time, this secret report was prepared for the CIA on its own plots to assassinate Cuba's Fidel Castro. Included is an exclusive commentary by Division General Fabián Escalante, the former head of Cuba's counterintelligence body.
ISBN 1-875284-90-7

ZR RIFLE
The plot to kill Kennedy and Castro
By Claudia Furiati
Thirty years after the death of President Kennedy, Cuba has opened its secret files on the assassination, showing how and why the CIA, along with anti-Castro exiles and the Mafia, planned the conspiracy.
"Adds new pieces to the puzzle and gives us a clearer picture of what really happened." — Oliver Stone
ISBN 1-875284-85-0

IN THE EYE OF THE STORM
Castro, Khrushchev, Kennedy and the Missile Crisis
By Carlos Lechuga
For the first time, Cuba's view of the most serious crisis of the Cold War is told by one of the leading participants.
ISBN 1-875284-87-7

GUANTANAMO
Bay of Discord: The story of the U.S. military base in Cuba
By Roger Ricardo
This book provides a detailed history of the U.S. base on Cuban soil that has remained from the beginning of the century to the present day. It documents how the base has been used for continued violations of Cuban territory and why it remains a sticking point in U.S.–Cuba relations.
ISBN 1-875284-56-7

CHE GUEVARA READER
Writings on Guerrilla Strategy, Politics and Revolution
Edited by David Deutschmann
Three decades after the death of the legendary Latin American figure, this book presents the most comprehensive selection of Guevara's writings ever to be published in English.
ISBN 1-875284-93-1

CHE GUEVARA AND THE FBI
U.S. political police dossier on the Latin American revolutionary
Edited by Michael Ratner and Michael Steven Smith
Thirty years after the death of Che Guevara, a Freedom of Information case has succeeded in obtaining the FBI and CIA files on Che Guevara.
ISBN 1-875284-76-1

CHE — A MEMOIR BY FIDEL CASTRO
Preface by Jesús Montané
Edited by David Deutschmann
For the first time Fidel Castro writes with candor and affection of his relationship with Ernesto Che Guevara, documenting his extraordinary bond with Cuba from the revolution's early days to the final guerrilla expeditions to Africa and Bolivia.
ISBN 1-875284-15-X

MY EARLY YEARS
By Fidel Castro
Introductory essay by Gabriel García Márquez
Edited by Deborah Shnookal and Pedro Alvarez Tabío
Fidel Castro, one of the century's most controversial figures, reflects on his childhood, youth and student activism. In an unprecedented and remarkably candid manner, the Cuban leader describes his family background, his childhood and education at elite Catholic schools, and the religious and moral influences that led to his involvement in politics from a very early age.
ISBN 1-876175-07-9

LATIN AMERICA: From Colonization to Globalization
Noam Chomsky in conversation with Heinz Dieterich
In a series of new interviews by Mexican-based academic Heinz Dieterich, Noam Chomsky addresses some of the major political issues confronting Latin America today.
ISBN 1-876175-13-3

Ocean Press, GPO Box 3279, Melbourne 3001, Australia
● Fax: 61-3-9372 1765 ● E-mail: ocean_press@msn.com.au

Ocean Press, PO Box 834, Hoboken, NJ 07030, USA
● Fax: 1-201-617 0203